Kinship and Marriage in Burma

Books previously published by Melford E. Spiro:

An Atoll Culture (E. G. Burrows, co-author)

Kibbutz: Venture in Utopia

Children of the Kibbutz (with Audrey G. Spiro)

Context and Meaning in Cultural Anthropology (editor)

Burmese Supernaturalism: A Study in the Explanation and Resolution of Suffering

Buddhism and Society: A Great Tradition and Its Burmese Vicissitudes

Kinship and Marriage in Burma

A CULTURAL AND PSYCHODYNAMIC ANALYSIS

Melford E. Spiro

University of California Press BERKELEY · LOS ANGELES · LONDON

University of California Press Berkeley and Los Angeles, California
University of California Press, Ltd. London, England

Copyright © 1977 by The Regents of the University of California

ISBN 0-520-03220-9
Library of Congress Catalog Card Number: 76-7768
Printed in the United States of America

To the fighters for Burmese freedom,
especially Bo Let Ya, Bo Ya Naing, Nai Shwe Kyin,
Saw Kya Doe, U Law Yone, U Zali Maw

Contents

Preface

Conceptual Orientations

This is the third volume in a continuing series in which the Upper Burma village of Yeigyi is the setting for the study of society and culture in Burma. The previous volumes were concerned with the two facets of Burmese religion, the *nat* cult (Spiro 1967) and Buddhism (Spiro 1970). The present volume is concerned with kinship and marriage. A final volume will deal with other facets of social structure, notably politics and social stratification, in relationship to personality.

Although it is my intention that these volumes contribute to a greater understanding of Burmese society and culture (and, hence, of Southeast Asia in general), my primary concern is theoretical rather than ethnographic. The ethnographic research was undertaken in part to explore the extent to which psychodynamic personality theory, in conjunction with functionalist cultural theory, could be fruitfully used as an analytic framework for collecting, organizing, and interpreting ethnographic data. Ethnographic data, as I conceive of them, are the expressions of tradition—traditional ideas and traditional action. Anthropology, as I conceive of it, is the study of the persistence of and change in tradition. Expressed as ideas, tradition comprises a cultural system; expressed as action, it comprises a social system. Both systems are intimately related to each other, and each, in turn, to personality.

"Culture," to begin with the term by which idea systems are denoted, is defined as "a system of traditional ideas, beliefs, and values which, expressed in public symbols, are shared by, acquired from, and guide the action of the members of a social group." If, then, culture (as anthropologists have long believed) is holistic, its elements being organized in some fashion to comprise a "system," then part, at least, of that organization must surely be found "inside the heads" of social actors. That anthropologists can construct cultural wholes may testify to their organizational skills, but it does not as such demonstrate how the culture itself is organized (unless it is conceived as a model inside the heads of anthropologists). If this is the case, then, although culture is "expressed in cultural symbols," the only way to understand the meanings of those symbols is, somehow, to get access to—or at least to make some educated inferences about—the cognitive and motivational systems of social actors.

If culture, by definition, "guide[s] the action of the members of a social group," its relationship to social systems is apparent, for it is their action—or, more specifically, their social action—that comprises a social system. Thus if social action is guided (in part) by culture, to study culture without studying society is like studying anatomy without physiology. For just as the biologist can make sense of anatomical structure only if he understands the physiology of the organism, the anthropologist (so I would contend) can make sense of cultural structure only if he understands social action. For the same reason, the study of action, no less than that of culture, requires attending to the cognitive and motivational systems of actors, for it is these attributes of actors that organize and integrate action.

By having alluded twice already to the cognitive and motivational systems of actors, I hope I have explicitly indicated the signal importance of personality for understanding social and cultural systems. As I define it, "personality" refers to "the configuration of cognitive, motivational, affective, and perceptual systems which characterize individual actors." The importance of personality to these other systems is best expressed by analogy with transformational linguistics. Personality is to culture what deep structure is to surface structure, and it is to social action what competence is to performance.

A personality-oriented ethnography, it will then be noted, is unabashedly "emic"; that is, it is concerned with ethnographic data in terms of what the actors think, feel, believe, desire, and so on. Their action, of course, may have unintended or unrecognized consequences which are crucial (functionally or dysfunctionally) for the understanding of their social and cultural systems, and the student of society or culture ignores them at his peril. But these are the *consequences* of action, not its *instigations*, and functionalist theory, as is well known, has frequently committed the *post hoc ergo propter hoc* fallacy of construing the former as the latter. I stress the emic character of such investigations because a reviewer of a previous volume in this series observed that it might have been saved from interpretive extravagances (as he conceived of them) had I not been obdurately opposed to understanding "how the natives think." This critique is somewhat misplaced, since as I have here emphasized, that is exactly what the primary data of any personality-oriented ethnography consist of. But such an ethnography, it should be added, deals not only with *how* the natives think, but also with *what* they think, and with *why* they think what they think. The latter question is at least as important as the former two, for the "how" and "what" question is explicable only by reference to the "why" question, which means that cognition (of the kind, at least, that is relevant to the anthropologist) cannot be separated from motivation and affect.

Important as it is, however, the emic enterprise (at least for me) is only the beginning, not the end, of anthropological inquiry, and in the volume alluded to above, I stressed this fact by stating that for its scientific goals (in contrast to its humanistic ones), anthropology cannot regard emic description "as an end in itself." The reason should be obvious. If the concepts of emic description are not ultimately converted into the universal concepts and categories of scientific discourse, ethnography would contribute nothing to a comparative science of man, and anthropology would be confined to the writing of unique and incommensurable ethnographies. Indeed, given the staggering problems involved in any translation, a thoroughgoing emic approach would require that the ethnography of each group be written in its own language.

Although in the first instance, at least, a personality-oriented ethnography is an emic study, it differs in at least three respects from that branch of anthropology—variously termed cognitive anthropology, ethnosemantics, or ethnoscience—whose hallmark is its distinctive claim to emic investigation. First, the former approach, unlike the latter, includes motivational and affective as well as cognitive variables, for cognition (from a personality perspective) cannot be understood in isolation from these other psychological processes. Second, the former approach adopts a much broader conception of "cognition" than cognitive anthropology, which is almost exclusively concerned with terminological systems and the ways in which they partition semantic domains. Third, cognitive anthropology, as it is usually conceived, is concerned with the cognitive dimensions of particular cultural (or, more accurately, semantic) domains, as they are segregated from other domains. Personality-oriented studies, committed to the traditional, holistic conception of culture, are concerned rather with exploring cultural concepts not only within, but also across, cultural domains. Thus, if an ideal-typic study of ethnoscience is the componential analysis of a set of domain-bounded terms, that of culture-and-personality (in its cognitive aspect) is the delineation of a cultural ethos.

If, then, culture is conceived as a more-or-less organized whole; if, moreover, it is properly studied as it is expressed in social action, as well as in public symbols; and if, finally, social action sustains important relationships to the personalities of social actors, it would seem to follow that the investigation of culture is best conducted in those settings in which the interaction of these conditions obtain, namely, in natural settings. To be sure, I do not doubt that kin terms are just as easily collected from an informant in an air-conditioned office as in a jungle village, or that a corpus of myths is even more readily obtained from a good ethnographic library than from native myth-tellers. I doubt, however, that a componential analysis of such a list of kin terms in itself provides an adequate understanding of the cognitive bases for kin classification, or that a structural analysis of such a corpus of myths is anything more than an untested hypothesis.

Similarly, I do not doubt that a well-designed laboratory experiment can study human behavior much more rigorously than it can be studied in the field. I doubt, however, that its findings can be generalized to complex social action, or to settings other than those similar to the original experimental conditions. The contrary proposition, so far as I know, remains an untested hypothesis, and ethological studies of infra-human animals, when compared to laboratory studies of the same species, suggest that for non-humans, at least, these doubts have strong empirical foundations.

These comments, I wish to emphasize, do not imply that anthropological field investigations (including those reported in this series) necessarily yield findings of even face validity, and we all know the vexatious problems of reliability that these studies pose. Although at this stage, therefore, we are best advised to follow the counsel of letting a hundred flowers bloom, those anthropologists who are committed to the three assumptions formulated above will place their bets on field investigations as the most promising, if not the royal, road to the study of culture and of social action.

Caveats

Field investigations, at best, are fraught with formidable methodological (not to mention practical) problems, and in addition to the usual caveats regarding their validity and reliability, two others must be pointed out with respect to the present monograph. The first relates to the vagaries of Burmese politics, the second to my professional interests and competence at the time that these investigations were undertaken.

When I began field work in Burma in 1961, the focus of my inquiry was religion, with kinship being of peripheral concern only. Nevertheless, there were a number of reasons why I collected kinship data. First, given the theory of religion that guided my research, it was necessary to investigate other social and cultural systems as well, most especially marriage and the family. Second, since scholarly studies of Burma (at least of the ethnic Burmese) were rare, and since I believe that the anthropologist's first responsibility (when working in an ethnographic terra incognita) is to fill in the ethnographic record, I dutifully collected kin terms and genealogies, along with other ethnographic data. Third, my methods of research inevitably called my attention to kinship and related matters. In following a family through its diurnal cycle, in observing the daily routine of a monastery, in accompanying a village group to a *nat* festival, and most especially, in attending to any event that aroused the special interest or attention of a significant segment of the village (weddings, quarrels, legal hearings, elections, funerals, factional disputes, and so on), the exploration of its background and consequences almost always led into matters related to kinship, even when they were not central to my main interests.

For these three reasons, then, I managed to learn more about kinship than my intrinsic interest in the subject would have warranted. Still, I learned less than I could have, and much less than I should have. Thus, for example, although I dutifully collected kin terms, I did so rather mindlessly, making no attempt while in the field to understand or analyze them, or to relate them to kinship forms and usages. Again, to take a more important example, although I learned about the sororate and levirate, I did not investigate their distribution on the ground, or inquire into the constraints governing the formation of such marriages, or explore their relationship to kinship terms. Since I am now convinced that these secondary marriages, together with sibling exchange, constitute one key to the understanding of the terminological system, this neglect was especially serious.

Still, I was certainly aware in the course of field work of some of the gaps in these data, and it was my intention to attend to them at the end of my stay, or, if time did not permit, during a projected second trip. These plans, unfortunately, did not materialize. In March 1962, the Burmese army staged a coup, and in May (together with most foreigners) I left Burma, some fourteen months after I arrived. By 1969, the military government had still not changed its closed door policy, and from 1969-1972 I conducted research each summer among the recent Burmese immigrants and refugees in Thailand. This work filled at least some of the gaps remaining from the earlier field trip. To be sure, this "study of culture at a distance" has two disadvantages. First, since most of the Burmese émigrés in Thailand are from the wealthy, educated, and westernized segment of Rangoon society, it is difficult to assess the extent to which the findings apply to village Burma. Second, uprooted from the natural context in which their beliefs, values, and customs are embedded and have meaning, the Burmese in Thailand live as isolated families rather than as a genuine community. Hence, the data collected in Thailand consist primarily of informant interviews, unsupported by contextually embedded behavioral observations.

For all these reasons, then, there are important empirical gaps in this volume. Certain important problems are not attended to, and some generalizations are insufficiently supported by the requisite quantitive data. On both accounts, at least some of the interpretations offered in this monograph are less well founded than I would have desired.

The second caveat regarding this study relates not to the conditions of the investigations, but to the professional interests and competence of the investigator. For many years, the study of kinship seemed to me to have increasingly assumed the attributes of medieval scholasticism, characterized by interminable disputes concerning metaphysical essences. In support of this belief, one has only to recall the countless polemical articles on what kinship *really* consists of, what marriage *really* is, whether non-unilineal descent groups are *really* descent groups, and so on. This, combined with the increasingly obsessive concern with kin terms as the core of kinship studies, convinced me that the latter had indeed entered a sterile period.

In retrospect, this judgment strikes me as perhaps unduly harsh. Nevertheless, it had an important consequence for this study: the data were collected and this monograph was written with little more than a passing acquaintance with the current kinship literature. Negatively, this means that many of the current interests of kinship specialists are not addressed, and that the opportunity for illuminating some current kinship controversies by means of Burmese data was lost. As another negative consequence, my attempts to grapple with the theoretical issues posed by the Burmese materials were often pursued without the benefit of recent theoretical advances in the field. A subsequent review of recent kinship literature made me very much aware of the fact that prior knowledge of this field of inquiry would not only have sharpened my analytic tools, but it would have saved much time-consuming analysis and the pursuit of problems that turned out to be blind alleys.

Nevertheless, in rewriting the subsequent drafts of this monograph, I decided—on the perhaps misguided premise that the weaknesses of naïveté are at least somewhat balanced by its strengths—not to reconstitute the first draft in the light of my newly acquired education. (Besides, for the monograph to have really benefited, additional field work was required, and Burma's doors are still closed.) The strengths of naïveté, of course, consist in the absence of any particular intellectual stake or personal involvement in the current controversies that characterize the field, so that I could pursue my own analyses and interpretations in disregard of intellectual allegiance to any particular school or theoretical approach.

Data

Most of the data were collected in Upper Burma as part of an intensive investigation of the village that I call "Yeigyi," about ten miles from the old capital of Mandalay, where in 1961-1962 I made my home for about a year. It should be noted, therefore, that although this monograph is written in the ethnographic present, all statements concerning this village refer to the period prior to the 1962 coup. I do not know to what extent village patterns have been affected by the many new policies of the present government. The data from Yeigyi were, in turn, checked against those collected in spot surveys of other villages in the area, to determine to what extent the former is typical of the villages of that section of Upper Burma which, in many important ways, is the heartland of traditional Burmese culture. Almost always, these two sets of data were consistent.

The village data were augmented by urban data. While working in the villages I made biweekly trips to Mandalay (where my family was living), and was able to compare village materials with those obtained from Mandalay friends. After leaving Upper Burma, I lived for two months in Rangoon where the same procedure was adopted. More important, urban data, as was indicated above, were systematically collected from Burmese informants in Thailand during the summers of 1969-1972. Comparisons of the urban and rural data on kinship, like those concerning religion, politics, and social stratification, confirmed my developing suspicion that there is a genuinely pan-Burmese culture, the more so since the urban sample differed from the rural on variables other than social ecology, the former consisting primarily of the wealthy, highly educated, and highly westernized upper-middle and upper classes. Nevertheless, there are important differences between urban and rural culture patterns, and the magnitude of these differences, interestingly, is greater in the kinship domain than in, for example, religion or politics. Not only are kin —notably uncles and aunts—classified somewhat differently in Rangoon and village terminology, but Rangoon informants are often unclear in their understanding of the stock and the kindred, and in the ways in which they use the terms for designating these groups. In general, consensus in these matters is easily arrived at in the village, which is not at all the case in the city.

For these and other reasons the generalizations reported in this monograph, unless otherwise indicated, apply to village Burma—and more particularly to a small sample of villages in Upper Burma—exclusively. Whenever comparisons and contrasts between the village and the city are theoretically important, they are explicitly noted and discussed. I emphasize again, however, that in the text, "urban" refers primarily to a restricted segment of Rangoon society; I suspect that for the great majority of the population of Rangoon and Mandalay, kinship patterns are highly similar to those found in the village. Most Rangoonians live in "wards" (*yatkwet*) which in most respects resemble juxtaposed villages.

I have already indicated that the material on urban kinship was almost exclusively obtained from informant interviews, while the Yeigyi data were obtained primarily from observations of kinship behavior in various social contexts, accompanied by running questions concerning the meaning of the observed behavior, or followed by sustained interviews designed for the same purpose. Except for data on traditional conceptions of kinship and kinship norms, and for those obtained from the conventional household census, almost every other informant that I interviewed had been, or subsequently became, an actor whose behavior was observed, and it was his own behavior—rather than abstract and generalized cultural statements about kinship—which was the object of inquiry. However, in checking these data against those from other villages, informant interviews alone were used, the informants usually consisting of a village headman and elders.

Many interpretations of these behavioral data are based on personality data, the two sets being related by means of psychodynamic theory. The personality data consist primarily of clinical inferences from behavioral observations, clinically oriented interviews, a preliminary analysis of Rorschach and T.A.T. protocols by James Steele, and the personality findings of other investigators.

Although the generalizations in the text are usually qualified by "some," "many," "most," and so on, when there is insufficient material to specify the provenance of a finding, generalizations take the form, "the Burmese . . ." or "the villagers. . . ." Such statements do not imply that most, let alone all, of the villagers studied believe or act accordingly. Rather, the intended scope of such statements is a social category of sufficient size to constitute a critical social mass, "critical" in that social institutions or cultural beliefs have developed that take account of their beliefs and actions. Quantitatively, such a critical mass need merely comprise a plurality of the social category to which the generalization applies, and when these categories are stratified in complex ways, a plurality may sometimes comprise a very small number.

One final observation. Since, as I have indicated, the intent of this book is theoretical rather than ethnographic, the Burmese data are often compared with those from other societies of similar type (Southeast Asian, peasant, high civilization). Such comparisons, however, are usually random, not exhaustive, and, with some few exceptions, they are intended to be illustrative rather than evidential. That is, they are not intended to "prove" something, but rather to place a seemingly exotic belief or custom in comparative perspective, to document the cross-cultural range of a distribution, or to exemplify or support a theoretical relationship.

Acknowledgements

For making this study possible, I am deeply grateful to the National Science Foundation for its support of field work in Burma in 1961-1962, to the National Institute of Child Health and Human Development for its support of field work in Thailand in the summers of 1969-1972, and to the National Institute of Mental Health for support during part of the writing of this monograph.

For the village phase of the study I wish once again to express my gratitude to the people of Yeigyi, gracious hosts and research partners, and to my two research assistants, U Ba Thaw and U Aung Thein, without whom I could never have worked my way through the complex maze that a new culture poses for the uninitiated field worker.

For the urban phase of the study I am especially indebted to U Zali Maw and U Ye Kyaw Thu, but more particularly to Mrs. Khin Maung Lwin, who became a co-investigator. My wife, Audrey Goldman Spiro, was of invaluable assistance in obtaining information on the sexual attitudes and behavior of urban women. Without her investigations (in the summer of 1972) I would have very little knowledge of these important topics.

I am grateful to F. G. Bailey, Roy G. D'Andrade, Marc J. Swartz, and David K. Jordan for reading parts of the first draft of the manuscript, and to Theodore Stern for reading the entire manuscript. Their valuable criticisms and suggestions importantly improved the final revision. Above all, however, I wish to express my appreciation to F. K. Lehman for providing me with the benefit of his informed and meticulous Burmese scholarship, as well as his superb grasp of contemporary kinship theory. His criticisms reduced the ethnographic error, on the one hand, and strengthened the theoretical argument, on the other. Since, however, I sometimes declined the advice of these critics, the lapses in the text, needless to say, are my own responsibility.

Finally, I am indebted to Mrs. Carolee Johnston, Mrs. Carol Ruffin, and especially Mrs. Sheri Koman, who patiently typed and retyped the many incarnations of the original and subsequent drafts of the manuscript.

Part One. Introduction

1. Towards an Understanding of Kinship

Why Kinship?

Kinship and religion were among the earliest, and have perhaps remained among the most persistent, interests of anthropological inquiry. Whatever the reasons—and a full explanation will require the combined skills of intellectual history, the sociology of knowledge, and the psychology of anthropologists—it is hardly accidental that, having audaciously taken all of mankind as its domain, anthropology should have chosen these two universal systems for special inquiry. To be sure, anthropology has documented the universality of other cultural systems as well, but none is more recognizable across its variable types than kinship or religion. In the case of economic or governmental systems, for example, the polar extremes of any of their recognized typologies, whether evolutionary or formal, are often identifiable as members of the same series only by reference to their intermediate types. One has merely to contrast nomadic, gathering economies with bureaucratic, industrial economies, or small acephalous bands with centralized empires, to grasp this point. In either example it would be difficult to identify the invariant sociocultural core that is shared by all the types in a formal typology, or that has persisted from the earliest manifestation of an evolutionary sequence to its most recent manifestation. The contrary is the case for religion or kinship. Some formidable critics to the contrary notwithstanding, I share with Malinowski, Murdock, and Lounsbury (among others) the view that the nuclear family is the invariant core of every and any kinship system, just as the belief in invisible, superhuman beings, and its associated rituals, comprises the invariant core of every and any religion. It is no wonder, then, that given their evolutionary schemata, the Victorian founders of modern anthropology were as perplexed by the similarities they discovered between their own religious and kinship systems and those of the primitive peoples they studied, as they were intrigued by (and sometimes contemptuous of) the differences.

One of the more significant contrasts between these two cultural systems is that the universality of kinship, at least so far as its family core is concerned, marks man's affinity with many other mammals, while the universality of religion marks his uniqueness (so far as we can tell) in the animal kingdom. The family, sometimes uniparental, sometimes biparental, is phylogenetically rooted, constituting the nucleus, and sometimes the whole, of mammalian societies; and despite the current fashion in some anthropological quarters of minimizing, if not denying, the biological basis of the human family and kinship, it is difficult to escape the conclusion that some of the same biological variables that account for the phylogenetic roots of the family also account for its persistence. It is for this reason that I consider non-kinship relations, more than (as some theorists argue) those of kinship, to stand in need of a high degree of symbolization. That is, the extension of the boundary of the interacting group beyond the network of consanguineally and affinally related kin depends crucially on symbolization for the conceptual basis both of group formation and social identity.

At the cultural level, it is religion which, par excellence, depends on the human symbolic capacity, for it is symbolism that transforms personal fantasy, the wellspring of religion, into culturally constituted reality; it creates being (spirits) out of non-being, and invests words and gestures with instrumental efficacy. This being the case, the universality of religion is not accidental, for as Robertson Smith and Freud (among others) observed long ago, much of religious symbolism is rooted in and is the metaphorical expression of kinship relations. More specifically, religious symbols often represent the transformation and elaboration at the cultural level of fantasies and cognitions at the psychological level, and these in turn are often produced by kinship relations at the social level.

Although kinship is rooted in biology, there is an important distinction between the natural kinship relations of infra-human societies and the culturally constituted kinship systems of human societies. And whatever the shortcomings of *Totem and Taboo*, its important hypothesis that human (culturally constituted) kinship and religion have a common phylogenetic origin is an abiding insight whose implications are yet to be systematically explored.

If, then, kinship is the social domain which most clearly reflects the affinity of human to infra-human societies, and also the domain whose symbolic reflection in religion uniquely differentiates man from the rest of the animal kingdom, its pivotal importance for the study of human society and culture can hardly be minimized. Nor can it be said that anthropology, whose most important technical advances have been made in kinship, has not appreciated this fact. Nevertheless, since anthropology has typically been more concerned with the variability in society and culture than in their regularities, kinship studies too have often concentrated more on the differences in kinship systems or types of systems than on their similarities. Although there can be no denying the importance of these differences, it is also important that their similarities, especially at the interpersonal and psychological levels, be afforded equal recognition.

The roots of these similarities are not hard to discover. However much kinship systems must adapt to and are conditioned by variations in ecology, economy, demography, politics, and so on, they must all deal with certain invariant conditions of human social existence. That is, every kinship system must attend to certain ineluctable biological facts, among which I would stress the following. Human reproduction is bisexual, and conception is effected by means of heterosexual intercourse; humans are born helpless, and they remain physically and emotionally dependent on their caretakers for a prolonged period; children live, minimally, in biparental family groups, so that it is their caretakers (usually their parents) who, for better or worse, satisfy their dependency needs; dependency being the infant's prepotent need, feelings of affectionate attachment develop towards the agents of its satisfaction; satisfaction is always relative to frustration, so that these caretakers are simultaneously the first and most important objects of affection, as well as of hostility; siblings are also part of the family group, and, since affection is a scarce—and therefore competitive—good, they, like parents, are the objects of these same conflicting emotions.

These elementary observations have an important implication for our understanding of human kinship systems. Since all societies have had to respond to and take account of these universal dimensions of human existence, it can be claimed that they represent one set of parameters for the analysis of any kinship system. If so, then in a non-trivial sense it can also be claimed that much of the cross-cultural variability found in kinship systems—differences in the principles of group membership, in the lexical techniques for lumping or differentiating kintypes, in the norms which specify the rights and duties of kinsmen, and so on—represent variable institutionalized responses to this common set of biological, sociological, and psychological parameters. To this extent (but only to this extent) it might be said that, to borrow an analogy from transformational linguistics, these (non-cultural) parameters stand to these (cultural) kinship variables as deep structure to surface structure.

But, of course, the distinction between a variable and a parameter is not absolute; what is a variable in certain contexts and for certain purposes is a parameter in other contexts and for other purposes. Hence, although any elements of a cultural system are variable when viewed either diachronically or cross-culturally, and when they are taken as the *explananda* of inquiry, they become parameters when viewed synchronically and intra-culturally, and when they are taken as the *explanans* of inquiry. That is, when the focus of inquiry shifts from the explanation of cultural systems to the explanation of culturally determined behavior, (diachronic) cultural variables become (synchronic) behavioral parameters. In an intra-cultural, synchronic study, it is behavior, not culture, that is variable. Thus, for an actor in an ongoing kinship system, its norms, terms, rules, and principles are as ineluctable in their "facthood" as is sexual reproduction, biological dependency, and conflicting attitudes towards kinsmen. For although rules of residence, modes of descent, and so on, are cross-culturally variable for the student of culture, they are not variable for the social actor; in *his* "behavioral world" (as Hallowell calls it), residence is virilocal, for example, and descent is patrilineal. This is not true, however, of kinship behavior. Since (as is true for all cultural systems) the elements of a kinship system may produce conflicting behavioral consequences, and since kinship behavior is a product of non-kinship as well as kinship determinants, their interaction is also likely to produce variable behavioral consequences. If this is so, then, confining these remarks to non-cultural determinants, we would expect the invariant determinants of kinship *systems* delineated above to play a prominent role as well in the determination of kinship *behavior*. Thus, however invariable the cultural conceptions of parents within a particular social group may be, or however invariable its cultural norms governing children's duties to parents, attitudes toward parents represent the interaction of culturally specific norms and socially universal emotions. To be sure, to the extent that these emotions and norms are in conflict, we would typically expect the former to be repressed and the latter to be conscious. But unconscious emotions are at least as powerful as, though more devious than, conscious ones. To the extent that emotions and attitudes affect behavior, one would be misguided (if this analysis is correct) to neglect these (universal) non-cultural determinants of kinship behavior, and to attend exclusively to its (particular) cultural determinants.

Lest I be misunderstood, I hasten to introduce an important caveat. In discussing the effects of certain invariant, non-cultural, dimensions of human experience for the understanding of kinship systems, I pointed to certain biological facts (such as sexual reproduction and prolonged dependency) that produce certain sociological consequences (such as a biparental family and socialization) from which flow still other psychological consequences (such as ambivalence to parents). This does not imply, however, that once a kinship system gets started, these factors either retain their initial form or are everywhere the same. On the contrary, they in turn are importantly affected and modified by the resulting kinship system, and by the same feedback mechanism that governs the interaction between man and all of his cultural systems. Thus, sexual norms affect sexual *attitudes* and sexual object *choice;* residence rules affect feelings of *dependency, affection,* and *hostility;* rules of inheritance affect the *cathexis* of parent and *conceptions* of siblings; and so on. In short, since these psychological variables are produced by and vary with different types of social interaction, and since variations in social interaction are a function of variations in social and cultural structures, I would expect these psychological parameters of kinship systems to become psychological variables of kinship behavior, variables which are present in all societies, but which vary cross-culturally along certain dimensions.

If, then, social behavior is governed by attitudes and conceptions, and if the attitudes and conceptions which emerge from social experience are different from those formed by cultural values and norms, it is just as foolish to ignore the former as the latter. Such folly is all the more egregious in kinship studies, for attitudes toward and conceptions of parents, siblings, and some other kinsmen are formed by direct experience with them prior to the acquisition of language, and prior, therefore, to the acquisition of the cultural norms and rules that govern proper interaction with them. To assume, then, as some few kinship specialists do, that kinship behavior and kinship attitudes are exclusively determined by cultural verbalizations of kinship relationships—whether these verbalizations consist of conceptions, values, norms, rules, or terms—and that some type or other of formal analysis of these verbalizations (logical, mathematical, or semantic) is the royal and exclusive road to understanding, is to ignore the lessons of ethology, kinesics, proxemics, and psychoanalysis, among others.

Thus far, then, I have been arguing two theses. First, a phylogenetic understanding of kinship *systems* requires that we attend not only to such variables as economics, ecology, and demography, but also to such parameters as the sociological and psychological consequences of human reproductive biology. Second, a synchronic understanding of kinship *behavior* requires that we attend not only to explicitly formulated cultural norms and rules of kinship, but also to conceptions of and attitudes towards kinsmen and particular types of kin arising in social experience.

The present study attempts to apply these simple theses to the understanding of Burmese kinship, but since its emphasis is synchronic, it is more concerned with the second of these theses than the first. Specifically, this study attempts to explain one set of kinship and kinship-related variables—a sociological set—by means of another set of kinship variables—a cultural and psychological set. The latter set, the *explanans*, consists of three variables, namely, cultural norms of kinship, cultural rules governing kinship behavior, and the actor's conceptions of and attitudes toward kinsmen. The former set, the *explanandum*, consists (among other things) of the composition of the domestic group, the composition of and interaction within the kindred, the differential interaction of kinsmen and non-kinsmen, marriage and mate selection, the relationship between spouses, and so on.

An Approach to the Study of Kinship

If kinship is to be explained in terms of psychological as well as cultural variables—if, that is, the actor's conceptions of and attitudes toward kinsmen are as important for the understanding of kinship as cultural norms and rules—then the anthropological study of kinship behavior must confront the theories and findings of psychoanalysis, a discipline whose focus of inquiry has been the microscopic exploration of such conceptions and attitudes as they relate, at least, to the members of the nuclear family. Following a brief flirtation with psychoanalytic conceptions of family relations—sometimes explicit (as in Malinowski's treatment of the Trobriand family), sometimes bootlegged (as in Radcliffe-Brown's treatment of the mother's brother in South Africa)—anthropological studies of kinship have more or less avoided these conceptions.

Now it might be argued, as some anthropologists do indeed argue, that the claims of psychoanalysis were put to rest as early as Malinowski's research in the Trobriands, and that subsequently there was little point in beating a dead horse. Such an argument is hardly compelling, however, for even if Malinowski's interpretations of the psychodynamics of the Trobriand family are valid, his critical findings would merely narrow the provenance within which the findings of psychoanalysis apply.

Although it has usually ignored the psychoanalytic *theory* of kinship relations, anthropology has not always ignored a psychoanalytic *approach* to their study. Indeed, more than forty years ago Evans-Pritchard (1929) delineated the structure of such an approach with respect to an aspect of kinship studies that remains of prominent anthropological concern, namely the "meaning" of native kin categories. Evans-Pritchard proposed that "patterns of [kinship] behavior" must be sought in the first instance in the "initial situation" of kinship, that is, "in the family organization into which [a child] is born and in which he grows up." (*Ibid.*:191.) This, of course, is the "extensionist" view of kinship, one which is rejected today in many quarters, on grounds, however, which some theorists find less than compelling. When specialists differ, the non-specialist like myself should not take sides; nevertheless, I should like to continue with Evans-Pritchard's explication of *his* version of the extensionist view because it is one which I find entirely persuasive.

Although interested in "patterns of behavior," Evans-Pritchard does not jump from family interaction to extra-familial behavior, as some schools of learning theory might have done. Rather, as he sees it, behavior is determined by "sentiments," and the "initial situation" is important because it creates certain sentiments which in turn affect behavior. That is, "through the sentiments which a child builds up around those who associate most intimately with it . . . it acquires a large number of attitudes towards the extra-family world, *e.g.*, towards authority, towards the opposite sex, and so on. . . . The patterns of behavior which a man observes towards his kin are due in the first place to an extension of his intra-family sentiments to include these people." (*Ibid.*: 191.)

Thus far, then, Evans-Pritchard is arguing that the "meaning" of an extra-family kinsman—I take "sentiment" to refer to a combination of affective and cognitive meanings—is determined in the first place by the meanings which the child develops with respect to his intra-family kinsmen in the process of his interaction with them. So far this is the conventional extensionist view, but Evans-Pritchard departs from that view in two important respects. Although, for A, the meaning of any member of his family, B, is determined by the social relationship between A and B, no dyadic relationship can be understood, he argued, by reference to the dyad alone. Each member of the dyad has a social relationship with a third person, C, and A's relationship to B cannot be understood in isolation from the relationship of both A and B to C. Thus, he writes, "it is difficult to understand the authoritative and estranged attitude of a boy towards his mother [among the Azande] unless we realize that the exclusive attachment to his mother in infancy undergoes a very profound change through daily contact with his father. . . . Therefore to grasp the full meaning of the son-mother relationship, we have [also] to take into account . . . the husband-wife and father-son relationships." (*Ibid.*: 191.) Characterizing this latter notion as "commonplace," he laments the fact that it has nevertheless been "neglected" even by those, like Malinowski, who, having been "richly rewarded by contact with the work of psycho-analytical writers," emphasize the importance of the "initial situation" of kinship.

Now if the meaning for A of an intra-family kinsman, B, cannot be understood by reference to their relationship alone—if, rather, it must be understood by reference to a triad (of which B and A are both members)—then a fortiori, the extension of intra-family meanings to extra-family kin must similarly be based on the meanings developed within these (minimally) triadic relationships. Thus, to understand the meaning of the mother's brother to the sister's son among the Azande, it is not enough, Evans-Pritchard observes, to understand the son's relationship to his mother, for that relationship—and, therefore, the meaning of "mother"—is determined as well by the husband-wife and father-son relationship. By the same token, Malinowski's interpretation of the meaning of the mother's brother in the Trobriands is flawed by the fact that it fails to take into account the "deep and strong jealousy" that obtains between father and mother's brother, just as Radcliffe-Brown's analysis of the mother's brother in South Africa is flawed because it "disassociates" the attitudes of the child to the father and mother when, in fact, these attitudes "interact with and colour each other." In short, all the analyses (to that time) of the mother's brother are suspect, according to Evans-Pritchard, because they neglect to consider the inevitable "influence of the father in the formation of the sentiment towards the mother's brother." (*Ibid.:* 192.)

I have devoted a great deal of space to the explication of this early approach of Evans-Pritchard because in large measure it represents my own late approach. It is an approach, however, which is at variance with, and (in some crucial aspects) in opposition to, a great deal of contemporary kinship theory and kinship research. To be sure, in its stress on meaning it is contemporary, but even here, as we shall see, it diverges in important respects from contemporary approaches. The approach to meaning adopted in this monograph is six-pronged, and although only some of these prongs are explicitly formulated in Evans-Pritchard's paper (1929), all are at least implicit in it. I shall briefly summarize them.

First, the meaning of native kin categories is to be sought more in the social relationships that obtain among kin than in the semantics of kin terms. Second, since the actor's social relationships with his primary kin—those comprising the family—begin in early childhood, the meaning of these kinsmen is to be sought, in the first instance, in his childhood experiences with them. Third, for any actor, the meanings of these primary kin are not to be sought exclusively in his dyadic relationships with them, but the inquiry must include, as well, the relationships that each, in turn, sustains to their other primary kin. Fourth, the meanings of extra-family kin are, to a large (but undetermined) degree, to be sought in the meanings developed in childhood with respect to primary kin. I might add that the meanings of certain non-kin are similarly to be sought in part in this "initial situation" of kinship. Fifth, and implicit in the first four, the meanings which actors attach to both intra-family and extra-family kin are to be sought as much in the "sentiments" (conceptions, attitudes, and feelings) that emerge from their social relationships with them as in their jural norms or in the properties of genealogical space. Sixth, the former meanings are to be sought in unconscious as well as conscious sentiments, as Evans-Pritchard points out in a later paper. Employing "attitude" (rather than "sentiment") as his most comprehensive explanatory variable, he writes: "By attitude is meant an enduring, stereotyped, and socially compelled behavior pattern, together with its concomitant psychological processes both in the *conscious* (sentiments) and in the *unconscious* (complexes)." (Evans-Pritchard 1932:12, italics mine.)

In its emphasis on social experience as a primary determinant of kinship meaning, the approach adopted here does not minimize the importance of kin terms or jural norms as determinants. After all, to the extent that jural norms of kinship are internalized, they govern kinship behavior, and thereby serve to shape those very childhood experiences with kinsmen—and hence the child's conceptions of these kin—to which primary importance is assigned in this formulation. And to the extent that kin term categories reflect socially meaningful classifications of kin, the very acquisition of these terms is accompanied by the acquisition of perceptually significant and behaviorally relevant conceptions of kinsmen. Moreover, even when these cultural phenomena (norms and terms) are not isomorphic with behavior, they nevertheless play an important part in the child's cognitive understandings, if only because those of his conceptions that are acquired in social interaction are filtered through these verbally transmitted norms and conceptions. This being so, the early cognitions of the child are organized and given meaning by these normative and classificatory categories of his society.

Granted, then, that kin terms and norms—but especially the norms —play an important part in shaping the meaning that their kinsmen have for social actors, the approach to "meaning" adopted in this monograph is nevertheless different from the dominant approaches of contemporary anthropology. According to one of these—the symbolist approach (Schneider 1966)—the kinship system is a symbolic system, whose meanings are to be discovered by cultural analysis. Although agreeing that the system is a symbolic one, and that the meanings of kin terms and of kinsmen are primarily symbolic, I do not believe that, without attending to their social and psychological roots, their symbolic meanings are discoverable by means of cultural analysis alone. Although many (but not all) cultural symbols exist outside of social actors, their meanings exist only inside their minds, and if the investigator is concerned with the meanings which cultural symbols have for social actors, he has no alternative but to investigate (as best he can) the minds of those actors. Moreover, since the meanings in their minds are acquired in part as a result of social experience, he must also investigate these social experiences. In short, although agreeing that kinship is a symbolic system, to understand the meanings of its symbols it is necessary, I believe, to study the social and psychological processes from which they arise.

A second approach to the study of kinship meaning is that of ethnosemantics, and, specifically, of componential analysis. Unlike the former, the latter approach is concerned with the referential meaning of kin terms, rather than the symbolic meaning of kinship. Although it believes that the meaning of *kinsmen* must be found in the minds of social actors, it holds that their meaning can be derived primarily (if not exclusively) from a formal analysis of *kin terms*, for—so it claims —componential definitions of these terms correspond to the "cognitive reality" of the native actors. Although agreeing that the meanings we ascribe to kinship must correspond to the actors' cognitive reality, it should by now be apparent that the approach adopted here differs from that of ethnosemantics in a number of ways.

A Critique of Componential Analysis

For componential analysis, the meaning of any kin category is given by a definition whose *definiendum* is a kin term, and whose *definiens* consists of the defining features of the class of kin designated by the term. It will be observed, then, that componential meaning is semantic meaning and, more particularly, the kind of semantic meaning that is derived in accordance with the theory of signs on which componential analysis is based (Scheffler and Lounsbury 1971), namely, referential meaning. According to this theory, the referential meaning of a term (a linguistic sign) in any semantic domain may be either an object (its *denotatum*) or a class of objects (its *designatum*).[1] The members of a class have an attribute or a cluster of attributes that distinguishes each member from its other members, while sharing a common attribute or cluster of attributes. This latter attribute or attribute-cluster constitutes the criterion for class membership, and it distinguishes the class from all other classes of the domain. The distinctive attributes of the individual members of a class are called their *significant features*, while those they share are called the *defining features* of the class. The latter features, in short, comprise the set of necessary and sufficient conditions for class membership. It is these features that a term *signifies*. They comprise the *significatum* of the term

---

1. Componential analysts differ on this matter in one important respect. According to Goodenough (1970:72), the denotata and designata of linguistic signs consist of images or concepts of objects or classes of objects, while Scheffler and Lounsbury (1971:4) view the objects themselves as their denotata and designata. Although this is an important difference, it does not importantly affect my critique of componential analysis, and I have arbitrarily chosen to follow Scheffler and Lounsbury in this brief explication of the theory.

and (to come full circle) the *components* of its componential definition. The meaning of the term is contained in its significatum.

It is evident, then, that the crucial question for the componential analysis of any set of terms is the proper identification of the significant features of their denotata. For componential analysts, the attributes of kinsmen that constitute their significant features for kin classification are the "inherent distinctions" of kintypes—sex, relative age, generation, lineality, and the like—which they conceive to be the "properties of genealogical space." Since kin terms designate kin classes (a class may sometimes comprise only one member), each term signifies those inherent distinctions of kintypes that are common to, and distinctive of, all the denotata of the kin class that it designates. Attending to these inherent distinctions, we can then construct the following definition of what the English kin term *father* signifies: kinsman, male, first ascending generation, lineal. By contrast, the English term *uncle* signifies male, first ascending generation, first degree collateral. Obviously, then, componential definitions of *mother* and *aunt* would merely replace "male" with "female" as significata of *father* and *uncle* respectively.

Now, heuristically, there is nothing wrong with assuming that the significant features of kin consist of the above-mentioned attributes, especially since the definitions that are constructed on the basis of this assumption fulfill the main aims of componential analysis; that is, for any society, they tell the analyst what he must know about any two kinsmen, A and B, such that he can predict that A will refer to B by the kin term x, rather than by y, or z. But componential analysts, as I remarked above, claim much more than this. They claim that componential definitions are (in fact or in principle) "emic" definitions, by which they usually mean that (a) the inherent distinctions of kintypes are, *for the natives,* the variables that constitute the significant features of kin term denotata; (b) as such, they are for the natives the significata of their kin terms, and, hence, the criteria by which they classify their kin; (c) therefore, these significata constitute for the natives the cognitive meaning of their kin term designata.[2] Let us now examine the emic status of componential definitions, beginning with the first of these three premises.

2. "Emic" is a concept still in dispute among the experts, and although the above characterization seems to me to be the prevailing notion, it should be noted that the emic status of componential definitions is still moot. For Wallace and Atkins (1960,1965), a componential definition is emic only if it comprises the "psychological reality" of the native actors, and, in their view, the latter is not a prima facie characteristic of these definitions. In their view most componential definitions comprise "structural reality," but their psychological status is moot until demonstrated by independent techniques of inquiry. For Scheffler and Lounsbury (1971:136-150), on the other hand, componential definitions do in fact comprise the actors' psychological reality, and, hence, for them there is no question about

The claim that the inherent distinctions of kintypes are the variables that comprise the significata of kin terms rests on the *assumption* that they are, for the natives, the significant features of kin denotata, an assumption that few componential analysts have attempted to put to empirical tests. (But see Romney and D'Andrade 1964, Wallace 1965.) To the best of my knowledge, no native speaker has been found anywhere who defines his kin terms by means of these criteria—at least not exclusively. Indeed, native definitions are usually markedly different from those derived by componential analysts. Compare, for example, one native's definition of some few American kin terms with those derived by componential analysis. According to this informant, *father* is defined as "male parent." (It is of more than passing interest to note that at first he included "mother's husband" in the definition, and although, when pressed, he conceded that the latter criterion is not a defining feature of the designatum—there can be unwed mothers and divorced wives—he only reluctantly abandoned this criterion even while admitting that if parents are married, it would be a redundant criterion.) *Mother* is defined as "female parent" (with an initial inclination to include "father's wife" in the definition, and the same reluctance, as noted above, to relinquish it). *Uncle* is defined as "parent's brother or husband of parent's sister" (with *brother* and *sister* defined, respectively, as male and female "who share a common parent" with the target term), and *aunt* is defined as "parent's sister or wife of parent's brother."

Notice that for this native the core terms in the entire set of American kin terms are the sub-set comprising the nuclear family terms (*father, mother, brother, sister*), that all other terms are defined as relative products of these terms, that the significant features of this subset are parenthood and sex, and that the only other feature signified by the relative products is spousehood. For him, then, the variables that comprise the significant features of kinsmen—and, hence, the defining features of his kin categories—are parenthood, sex, and spousehood. They are what *his* kin terms signify. With respect to these variables, "parenthood" includes two relational dimensions, procreation and child care, both of which are criterial. The criterial dimension of "spousehood" is socially approved mating, with the proviso that the reference group for "social approval" might be no wider than the kinsmen of the mates, or any subset thereof, always, however, including ego.

---

their emic status. For Burling (1969), however, componential definitions are emic even though they may not—and he believes that at the present stage of development they do not—comprise psychological reality, because as theoretical statements, separated in certain respects from the observable data, they constitute a means for interpreting and understanding them.

It will be noted, then, that except for "sex," the significata of this native's kin terms do not consist of the properties of genealogical space or of some inherent attributes of alter and ego. They consist, instead, of certain dimensions of the relationship (biological or social) between alter and ego, or between alter and a mediating kinsman of ego, whose relationship, in turn, consists of these relational dimensions.

In this native's schema, finally, the pervasive contrast set in his classification of kin is a parenthood or non-parenthood relationship. Thus, *father* and *mother* are distinguished, respectively, from *uncle* and *aunt* (and from all other kin terms) in that the class of kin designated by the former terms are ego's parents, the latter are not. Similarly, *uncle* and *aunt* are distinguished from all other terms because each designates a class of kin that either shares a common parent, or comprises spouses of those that share a common parent with ego's parent. The kintypes that share a common parent are, of course, "brother" and "sister," and the English terms *brother* and *sister* are distinguished from all other terms in that each designates a class of kin that shares a common parent with ego. Similarly, *cousin* designates a class of kin, one of whose parents shares a common parent with ego's parent, and so on for all the other terms.

I would suggest, on the basis of very little evidence, that the three variables of parenthood, sex, and spousehood universally comprise the core set of kin term significata, and that parenthood or non-parenthood is the pervasive contrast set in most (if not all) systems. Thus, where "father" and "father's brother" are designated by the same term, then, *ex hypothesi*, it is either because both are the children of ego's grandparent, or because they are either actually (in the case of one) or potentially (in the case of the other) ego's parent. Why, if the first alternative is found to be the case, the sharing of a common male parent (rather than being a male parent) should be the criterial basis for their classification is a question that can only be answered, of course, by sociological and psychological investigations. The same would be true, were the second alternative found to be the case, with respect to the significatum of the term by which they are designated. Would it signify "male parent" or "mother's husband," and if the former, *genitor* or *pater?*

Given this assumption about the emic universality of these criteria, it is not surprising that a Japanese informant seems to have perceived these same variables to be the significant features of her categories. This conclusion is suggested, in the first place, by her volunteered definitions of Japanese kin terms (Wallace 1965: table 1). But since these definitions are susceptible of a variety of interpretations concerning their underlying principles of classification, it is suggested even more strongly by what

happened when she was asked to explicate the principles underlying the
following sorting, derived from a componential analysis of Japanese kin
terms:

> elder brother
> younger sister
> niece   cousin
> younger brother
> elder sister
> nephew

She was unable to explain this even after the principles of the componential model had been suggested to her. Instead, she suggested that the
left-hand column did not comprise a homogeneous class, and that "niece"
and "nephew" be placed with "cousin" in the right-hand column. Wallace
argues that this is because she did not have available to her a lineality
dimension, and hence did not perceive that "cousin" is (in his terms)
ablineal, while the others are colineal.

Interestingly, my American informant responded to the sorting (using
the list of English equivalents) in exactly the same way as the Japanese
informant. And it was not because the lineality dimension was not
available to him: he is, after all, an American, and this dimension, it is
claimed, is salient in the psychological reality of American informants. He
observed, rather, that a cousin is the child of a parent's sibling, and a
nephew is the child of a sibling. Hence, nephew and cousin are genealogically isomorphic with each other, both being related to ego through a
sibling of a parent.

My informant's concepts, to be sure, may well subsume the inherent
distinctions of kintypes (the significata of componential definitions), for
since it is in the very nature of biological reproduction for parents to be of
a different *generation* than children, for parents' siblings to be *collateral*,
rather than *lineal*, and so on, these distinctions are of course the properties of genealogical space. This being so, his definitions can easily and
correctly be redefined in terms of these properties, and there is no
question but that the predictive power of the latter definitions is at least as
great as the former. It is not their predictive power, however, but the
emic status of the respective definitions that is at issue, and as a native
informant—for it was I who was the native—I must insist that my
definition of American kin terms (rather than those of componential
analysis) are their emic definitions, at least in my sub-culture. This is not
to say that, as a native, I do not comprehend the componential dimensions, or that I cannot, if instructed, construct definitions of my kin terms
from them, especially since (as derived or induced features) they map the

domain in question exactly as my primary features do. It is to say, however, that they are not for me the significant dimensions—the distinctively relevant features—of the terms, *father, brother,* and the like.

In fairness to componential analysts, it should be noted that they are aware of and have attempted to deal with such challenges to their emic claims. This is especially true in the case of Scheffler and Lounsbury, and if, in the following critique, I single out their recent work (1971), it is because I have found it to be an admirably lucid treatment of the subject, one which is self-consciously aware of its conceptual and methodological problems, and which systematically attempts to resolve them. Let us see, then, how they deal with this problem.

Scheffler and Lounsbury (1971:140) admit that if a "competent" American native were asked for the meaning of *cousin,* he would probably say that "my cousins are the children of my uncles and aunts," rather than "kin of second or further degree of collaterality." Nevertheless, they insist that the componential definition, rather than the native's definition, is emic because the statements of native informants "are not to be taken as sufficient guides to the 'psychological reality' of kinship concepts." (*Ibid.*:141.) Coming from Scheffler and Lounsbury this argument is especially paradoxical because, unlike some componential analysts, they contend that definitions are emic only if they reflect the "psychological reality" of the actors, and that a componential analysis is valid "only to the extent that it replicates the cognitive discriminations made by those who use the system in their daily lives." (*Ibid.*:137.) If so, then if the definitions of the natives differ (as often happens) from componential definitions, why are the latter taken as a more adequate guide to the natives' psychological reality?

The answer, according to Scheffler and Lounsbury, is that componential definitions express the "ground structure and implicit premises that underlie [the native's] discriminations and give shape to his 'world of meanings' "—and so "it is hardly to be supposed that [a native] should be capable of expressing [them] accurately, in ready verbalizations." (*Ibid.*) Now, I would concede that, as a native, I cannot readily verbalize my own conceptions because often there is (as they put it) an "unconcious" dimension in "the underlying premises and the structures of cultural and linguistic behavior, as well as of individual personality." (*Ibid.*) But in the absence of proof, or at least of a compelling argument, I am not willing to concede that underlying my stated definitions of *father, uncle,* and so on, there is an "unconscious" structure of the kind *assumed* by componential analysts, or, if there is, that *it* is the one that gives shape to my "world of meanings." It is true that one may construct question frames which can elicit such definitions from a native, but this is hardly surprising since the properties of geneological space are constituent attributes of all kintype designata. The question, therefore, is not whether they can be elicited from him, but whether they are the salient features which, *ex hypothesi*, his kin terms, howbeit unconsciously, signify for him. Scheffler and Lounsbury claim they are, and the reason that analysis is required to bring them out "is *only* due to the fact that these are not themselves ordinary topics of discourse in everyday life." (*Ibid.*:141, italics mine.)

As I see it, however, the reason analysis is required to bring them out is "only due to the fact" that for the native—any native—they are only incidentally related to the significata of his kin terms, much as Haeckel's componential definition of *God*—"a gaseous vertebrate"—is only incidentally related to its significatum for English-speaking Christians. This is not to say that the properties of genealogical space are not useful *etic* variables, useful for cross-cultural comparisons. But the fact that they happen to be inherent distinctions of kintypes does not ipso facto give them conceptual saliency, any more than the fact that cylinders and pistons, although inherent distinctions of autotypes, are the conceptual basis for the *emic* classification of automobiles.

That componential analysts believe otherwise is an artifact, so I would contend, of their data and methods. Componential analysts, *qua* componential analysts, do not observe kinship behavior, nor do they interview native informants concerning *their* conceptions of their kin categories. Their data consist, rather, of lists of kin terms (often, moreover, collected by other investigators, and contained in ethnographic reports, dictionaries, and the like), and their technique of analysis consists, in the first place, of mapping these kin terms over an etic grid of biological kin types. Now since the properties of genealogical space are the only properties of genealogical grids, and since, therefore, they are the only information contained in such grids, it follows necessarily that they, and they alone, constitute the "components" of componential definitions. In short, given the method, and given the data on which it operates, no other findings are possible. To claim, then, that if a native does not agree with the definitions of componential analysis, it is because these definitions tap "unconscious structures," "implicit premises," and the like, is to view a narrow data base as comprising the parameters of a cognitive system.

In general, componential analysts have not suggested empirical indicators of these "unconscious structures" and "implicit premises" so that they might be checked by direct investigations of the cognitive processes of native actors, much as psychoanalysis attempts to test its claims concerning unconscious psychodynamic processes by such indicators as parapraxes, dreams, neurotic symptoms, projective test responses, and so on. They have, however, offered theoretical and logical grounds for their belief in the emic status of componential definitions. Thus, according to Scheffler and Lounsbury, there are at least two grounds for this belief.

First, it is "extremely difficult to imagine how a truly satisfactory and parsimonious model of the distribution of kin terms over kintypes could help but be anything other than a satisfactory or adequate model of the cognitive system in question." Since, however, the properties of this cognitive system are precisely what is at issue, this argument clearly begs the question. Moreover, since kin terms, as has been demonstrated by Burling (1964) and others, are amenable to a large number of definitions based on these same properties, some of which are equally "satisfactory and parsimonious," how are we to determine which of these definitions reflects the natives' cognitive systems?

The second argument of Scheffler and Lounsbury is also problematic. "We find it difficult to imagine," they write, "how such a model could provide a basis for accurate prediction of usage . . . unless it were 'psychologically or cognitively real.'" Although componential definitions (based on these variables) can undeniably predict the designata of native kin terms, this is not at issue, because, according to the semantic theory on which componential analysis is based, the cognitive meaning of a term is given by its significatum. *Ex hypothesi,* then, what is at issue with respect to the cognitive reality of componential definitions is not what they *designate,* but what they *signify,* so that the claim that they are emic (that they comprise the natives' *significata*) because they predict proper usage (they predict the natives' *designata*) is clearly a non sequitur.

Indeed, if the argument were to be accepted as valid, it would not only confront the empirical challenge presented by other equally satisfactory componential definitions, but, more importantly, it would entail the paradoxical conclusion that avowedly etic models, which are equally precise predictors of usage, also comprise psychological reality.

Nevertheless, I do not wish to get bogged down in problems of evidence and logic, for even if these variables did comprise the significata of kin terms, this would not affect my basic criticism of componential analysis, namely, its assumption that these variables comprise the essential components of the meaning of kinsmen.

The Limitations of Ethnosemantics

In an early paper on componential analysis, Wallace and Atkins asserted that as psychologically oriented investigators they were interested in the "psychological reality" of cultural concepts, which they defined as "the world as [the native actor] perceives and knows it, in his own terms; it is his world of meanings." (Wallace and Atkins 1960:75.) Moreover, though they raised a series of important technical problems which had still to be resolved, they expressed the belief that in principle componential analysis constitutes a powerful technique for discovering the "psychological reality" of cultural concepts. Even if this were true, the meanings constructed by structural semantics would still not discover "psychological reality" in any comprehensive sense, for, as Wallace and Atkins make it clear (and in a later paper, written in 1965, Wallace makes it even clearer) "psychological reality" refers exclusively to the referential meaning of these concepts—that is, to the denotative and designative meanings of words.

Without demeaning the importance of discovering the referential meanings of words, it must be observed that such meanings are not their exclusive meaning; moreover, they are hardly the exclusive meaning of their referents. Thus, when natives (Americans, Burmans, or any other) are permitted to talk freely about their kin (instead of being asked to respond to question frames concerning kin terms), it is apparent that other meanings—love and hate, dependency and nurturance, protection and care, jealousy and rivalry, and so on—are often the most salient.

That it ignores the affective meaning of kinsmen does not in itself, however, constitute a serious criticism of the ethnosemantic approach —after all, a technique cannot be faulted for not doing what it does not claim to do. Hence, my main criticism of ethnosemantics is not that its conception of "psychological reality" is exclusively cognitive, but that it is not cognitive enough. Since, for componential analysis, "cognitive reality" consists of the criteria by which the denotata of a set of terms are differentiated and classified, their cognitive meaning is restricted to the criterial bases that underlie the partition of a semantic domain. That is, cognitive meaning—and hence psychological reality—is confined to the referential meaning of these terms.

The claim, then, that ethnosemantics captures the ways in which "people organize their experience conceptually" and elicits the "principles by which people in a culture construe their world" (Frake 1962:85) is somewhat exaggerated; and the further claim, that it discovers "how different peoples organize and use their cultures . . . the *organizing principles underlying behavior* . . . the way [things, events, behavior, and emotions] are organized in the minds of men" (Tyler 1969:3, italics his) is somewhat extravagant.

Although this judgment may seem unduly harsh, consider only the following. If it is conceded that the cognitive meanings of the objects within any domain are not restricted to their *linguistic* meanings (which even componential analysts concede),[3] and if it is further conceded that

3. For example, Goodenough (1970) concedes, albeit in two footnotes, that "people have concepts that are not represented by the vocabularies of their languages" (*ibid.*:112), and that semantic analysis is not "the only means of getting at emic categories, even of kinship categories" (*ibid.*:114). Nevertheless, since componential analysis is formal linguistic

their linguistic meanings are not restricted to their referential meanings (for words, of course, have connotative and metaphorical meanings as well), it then follows that the taxonomic criteria underlying their latter (componential) meaning constitute a restricted subset of the total set of cognitive meanings that such objects might have for native actors. In the case of kinship, this subset consists of the criteria by which natives assign kin terms to kintypes. If, then, these criteria are comprised, as componential analysis assumes, of the properties of genealogical space —lineality, collaterality, generation, bifurcation, and the like—to contend that they "give shape to [the native] 'world of [kin] meanings,' " and constitute the "principles by which people in a culture construe their [kinship] world," is not merely to restrict the meaning of "cognition" but to trivialize the meaning of "kinship." If this conclusion is not immediately apparent from the abstract character of this discussion, consider whether, for a native speaker of English, the expression "kinsman, female, lineal, first ascending generation" captures non-trivially the conception signified by *mother*, let alone his total conception of "mother." Or, if he is a Catholic, whether this is the conception he has in mind when, by metaphorical extension, he refers to and addresses the Virgin Mary as *Holy Mother?*

If, for kin categories with only one member, the componential or taxonomic dimension of cognitive meaning is unduly restricted, for multiple-member categories it is misguided. For since the taxonomic meanings of class terms consist of the defining features of the class, then *ex hypothesi*, componential definitions render a conception of the class, but not of the separate conception of the denotata that comprise the class. Now, although all classifications are designed for restricted purposes, it is difficult to believe that the significatum of a class term is the natives' most important (let alone their only) conception of the individual members of the class. Yet if "mother" and "mother's sister" are designated by a common term, then, by a componential definition they would have the same cognitive meaning—something like, "female kin of first ascending generation on the mother's side." The assumption that both of these denotata have a common meaning is valid, of course, as long as it is

---

analysis, semantic meaning is the primary component of cognitive meaning, and taxonomic meaning is the primary dimension of semantic meaning.

Even those formal analysts who stress the importance of nonsemantic meaning emphasize the taxonomic dimension of cognition. Thus, when Berlin, Breedlove, and Raven (1968:297) argue that an analysis of unlabeled categories can usually lead to "a more psychologically revealing and culturally meaningful description of the underlying conceptual structure of a particular domain," their notion of "conceptual structure" refers to taxonomic structure exclusively.

recognized that it refers to that dimension of their separate meanings which they share and which constitutes, therefore, the criterial basis for their common taxonomic status. But to contend that because the kintypes "mother" and "mother's sister" are not denoted by separate terms, they have no separate cognitive meanings, reveals the limitation of a theory that confines cognitive meaning to semantic—and specifically, referential—meaning, and that assumes that objects have no conceptual status unless they are named. By attending less to kin terms, however, and more to kin behavior (especially that of children) it can be shown that since conceptions of kinsmen are to a large extent acquired in the process of interaction with them, children's conceptions of kin are often acquired prior to their acquisition of kin terms; that they often acquire these terms in reference to specific individuals whose genealogical relation to them is initially less clear (and less important) than their behavioral relation; and that their conceptual differentiation of the denotata comprising a kin category may remain a part of their "cognitive reality" as adults—that is, much after they have learned that they are undifferentiated terminologically. (Indeed, even at the level of the *semantic* meaning of kin categories, it is obvious that a study of the acquisition of kin terms in childhood would shed important light on this subject, as Burling [1970] has shown.) Thus, to offer a final example, the English kin term *uncle* designates mother's and father's brothers as well as the husbands of mother's and father's sisters (unlike some systems in which these different denotata are, wholly or partially, terminologically differentiated). Nevertheless, it is unlikely that English speakers have the same conception of, for example, "father's brother" and "father's sister's husband."

The Meaning of "Meaning"

Ideally, the total range of emic meanings of kinsmen would include affective as well as cognitive meaning: cognitive meaning would include non-semantic as well as semantic meaning; semantic meaning would include connotative and metaphorical, as well as denotative meaning; and, finally, denotative meaning would include non-taxonomic as well as taxonomic meaning. By singling out taxonomic meaning as the most important type of meaning, componential analysis restricts "meaning" to its narrowest scope. This may be adequate when plants, diseases, color terms, or firewood (some favorite topics of componential analysis) are the objects of inquiry. But for kinship, in which these other types of meaning are of great concern to the actors, such a conception of "meaning" is clearly inadequate.

Ethnoscience justifies its use of taxonomic definitions of kin terms on the grounds that they represent the cognitive reality of the native actors, and this claim rests on the argument that componential definitions predict proper usage of kin terms. Since, however, other types of definitions also claim to represent the cognitive reality of the actors—the type offered by my American informant, for example—and since they also predict proper usage, on what grounds can we choose between them? There are, I think, five grounds for preferring definitions of the type offered by my American informant, all of which are related to the brief discussion above on the meaning of "meaning."

First, with respect to taxonomy, the variables comprising the definitions of the type offered by my informant represent the natives' own taxonomic criteria (which, after all, is what emic definitions of terms are supposed to be).

Second, these variables, though denotative, are nevertheless linked to the connotative and metaphorical meanings of the kin terms. In the case of *father* and *mother*, for example, the variables comprising the definitions of componential analysis—lineality, collaterality, and the like —cannot (except as derived features) be linked, either logically or empirically, to the concepts of authority, nurturance, protection, and so on, which are intimately associated with the connotative and metaphorical meanings of these kin terms in American culture. The variables comprising the definition of my native informant, however—parenthood, spousehood, and so on—have demonstrable logical and empirical links to these metaphorical and connotative meanings, and these, in my view, constitute important cognitive meanings of these terms.

Third, these variables are also related to those cognitive meanings of kinsmen (including their unconscious meanings) that are not signified by their kin terms. Thus, for example, the Oedipal meanings of "father" and "mother" are not part of the semantic meaning of *father* and *mother*, but their theoretical links to the concepts of parenthood and spousehood (the defining variables of my informant's definitions) are easy to forge. The contrary is the case with the componential concepts of lineality, collaterality, and the like.

Fourth, the variables comprising my informant's definitions (especially when they are related to their connotative and metaphorical meanings, and to the non-linguistic meanings of their denotata) can be linked to, and can enable us to understand, the important affective meaning of kinsmen. This function cannot be served by the definitions of componential analysis.

Fifth, the variables comprising my informant's definitions (together with their linked non-taxonomic meanings, non-semantic meanings, and affective meanings) serve as a conceptual bridge from the cultural domain of kinship to other cultural domains. The componential variables, by sealing off the kinship system from all other cultural systems, relegate it to the status of a cultural *Ding an Sich*. My informant's variables, which are conceptually related to such notions as authority, protection, nurturance, and the like, underscore the relationships sustained by kinship to other cultural domains, such as religion and politics. To conceive of the Pope as "the Holy Father," or to George Washington as "the Father of his country," is wholly explicable in terms of my informant's definition of *father*. Such metaphorical extensions of kin terms are inexplicable, however, when *father* is defined as "lineal, first ascending generation" and so on. Viewed through the lens of my informant's definitions, these metaphorical extensions, moreover, are not only explicable, but they underscore the early insight of anthropology that kinship constitutes a core system on which, as a symbolic paradigm, other cultural systems are based.

2. The Village Context of Burmese Kinship

The Historical Context

Yeigyi is a wet-rice village in the dry zone of Upper Burma, approximately eleven miles and four hours (by oxcart) from the former Burmese capital of Mandalay. Although not an isolated village—it is related through kinship, economics, politics, and religion to a large number of regional and national structures—Yeigyi is nevertheless a traditional village, many of its characteristics being little different from those described in the earlier literature on traditional village Burma.

In the history of Yeigyi, two events are especially salient in the minds of the villagers. The first—an external event—not only establishes its antiquity, but it serves to justify the villagers' claim to represent traditional Burmese culture. The second—an internal event—supports the anthropologist's suspicion that the fissionary processes observable in contemporary Burmese society, like those found in other societies, have deep roots in personality as well as in history.

According to older villagers, Yeigyi entered upon the stage of recorded history a little over 200 years ago when a royal prince rested briefly, while on tour, in the mango orchard on the eastern side of the village. Being thirsty, he was offered water by the village women. As a result, the village acquired a special connection to the royal court.

The second historical landmark reported by the villagers was a physical and political split of the village which occurred in the time of U Bou Htei, the great-great grandfather of the present headman. The headman at that time was one U Se, the son-in-law of U Bou Htei, whom some villagers wished to depose from misappropriation of village revenues. To replace him, they chose U Tha Bou, U Bou Htei's son. This conflict led to a bitter factional dispute, which ended with about thirty families (led by U Bou Htei) seceding from Yeigyi to found the village of Nyambin, a few hundred yards away. Subsequently, the (British) government dismissed

U Se from the headmanship of Yeigyi, and appointed U Tha Bou, the headman of Nyambin, as joint headman of both villages. Although they continue to be listed as separate villages in the revenue maps, today Yeigyi and Nyambin are socially, politically, and administratively one village. Physically, however, they remain distinct—they are separated by a three or four minute walk—and they still retain their distinctive names.

The Human Context

In 1961 there were 115 households in Yeigyi, with a total population of 453. The village has witnessed a progressive, and significant, decline in population since the first recorded census in 1891, a decline which is easily documented but difficult to understand. Table 1 compares the official census reports of 1891 and 1901 with the personal census I took in 1961.

TABLE 1. *Population in 1891, 1901, 1961*

Households		Population		
		Male	Female	Total
1891	186	365	383	748
1901	141	294	274	563
1961	115	218	235	453

Compared to other villages in Burma, Yeigyi has always been a large village. Thus in 1891 *(Census Report of India, 1892)*, when the average village in Upper Burma consisted of 44 households and 237 people, and when the figures for the entire country were 105 and 509 respectively, Yeigyi had 186 households and 748 people. Approximately the same relative proportions obtained in the later periods.

The population of Yeigyi is not only large, but it is young. As Table 2 indicates, 44 percent of the population is under 16. Interestingly, there is a preponderance of males over females in the younger age bracket (under 16) but this ratio is reversed in the older (over 16). In Yeigyi, as elsewhere, females outlive males.

TABLE 2. *Population by Age and Sex*

	Under 16	Over 16	Totals
Male	106	112	218
Female	95	140	235
Totals	201	252	453

Of the 202 married adults for whom information is available, 162, or 80 percent, are natives of Yeigyi (Table 3). The small immigrant population comprises in-marrying spouses, refugees from insurgency, and landless workers (primarily basketmakers). Almost all of these in-migrants are from Upper Burma, most especially from villages in the adjacent Mandalay and Sagaing districts. An eighty percent nativity rate is sufficiently high to indicate that the average villager interacts with and is socially related to persons he has known from childhood, and whom presumably, therefore, he knows intimately. This high nativity rate, not unexpectedly, has deep historical roots. Thus, as Table 4 reveals, 87 percent—110 of 126—of all married adults (for whom data are available) are descended from families who have lived in Yeigyi for as many generations as anyone can remember. This means, among other things, that there has been a long period for its culture to become regulated and shared, and its social relationships to become fixed and crystallized. This is one, but not the only, reason that it is necessary to be born in the village in order to be considered a true Yeigyian. In-migrants, as we shall see below, are never entirely accepted as the social equals of the natives.

To some extent, the culture which the villagers share, both with other villagers and other villages, is derived from a common formal education. For the adult generation (age 16 and above) for whom information is available (164 persons), 84 percent of the males and 36 percent of the females have had some formal schooling. These figures compare favorably not only with those for the previous half century (in 1901 the figures were

TABLE 3. *Origin of Married Adults for Whom Data on Nativity are Available*

	Yeigyi	Other	Total
Male	78	20	98
Female	84	20	104
Totals	162	40	202

TABLE 4. *Origin of Ancestors of Married Adults for Whom Data on Nativity are Available*

	Yeigyi	Other	Total
Male	49	7	56
Female	61	9	70
Totals	110	16	126

21 and 2 percent for males and females, respectively), but they compare very favorably with other contemporary peasant communities. Nevertheless, it must be stressed that both quantitatively and qualitatively the level of formal education is low, whether (in the case of males) it is preponderantly received in the village monastery school, or (in the case of the females) in the government school. Thus, although some males spend as many as ten, and some females as many as seven, years in school, the average is four and three years respectively. Moreover, in both cases, "formal education" primarily consists in study of the three R's and rote knowledge of a few Buddhist texts. In both cases, too, literacy is often at a relatively low functional level; some villagers can read only with difficulty because, so they say, they have little occasion to put their training to use.

Although knowledge of Buddhism is a mark of prestige in the village, secular education in itself is of little value, whether as a means to wealth, mobility, or prestige. The only villager who had studied through the tenth standard in the government school in Mandalay—a remarkable achievement for a peasant's son—is today a cultivator whose formal education is of little practical value to him, whose social status is little higher than that of his functionally illiterate peers, and whose income is much lower than any of his fellows who own more land than he.

The Economic Context

Every able-bodied male and female in Yeigyi engages in some occupation, and no one who desires employment is unemployed. There are 21 different male occupations represented in the village, but few demand or engage the full time of their practitioners. Table 5 lists these occupations

TABLE 5. *Male Occupations and Their Distribution*

Occupation	Number of Practitioners	Occupation	Number of Practitioners
Cultivator	87	Milk seller	2
Logger	31	Tea shop proprietor	2
Basketmaker	12	Cowherder	1
Cartman	6	Fisherman	1
Trader	5	Astrologer	1
Monk	4	Actor	1
Carpenter	3	Shampooer	1
Moneylender	3	Field foreman	1
Herbal doctor	3	Shoemaker	1
Exorcist	2	Headman	1
Food seller	2	Total	173

and the number of men engaged in each. Since there are 109 able-bodied men in Yeigyi, and 173 practitioners of the male occupations, it is obvious that few men derive their total income from one occupation exclusively. Nevertheless, although the average man engages in 1.5 occupations, in most cases only one is his primary occupation. Table 6 shows the distribution of those male occupations which engage the primary or exclusive attention of their practitioners. It is apparent that for the great majority of the males—82, or 73 percent—cultivation is the primary but not the exclusive occupation. Indeed, only 51, or 47 percent, of the able-bodied men in the village engage in one occupation exclusively. Their distribution is found in Table 7.

Women, too, engage in a variety of occupations, although the range is not as great as that for the men. As Table 8 indicates, there are only ten female occupations. There being 91 gainfully employed women in the village—only seven women are full-time housewives—it would appear

TABLE 6. *Primary Male Occupations and
Their Distribution*

Occupation	Number of Practitioners
Cultivator (owner, 51; worker, renter, tenant, 31)	82
Logger	10
Basketmaker	10
Monk	4
Basket trader	1
Food-seller	1
Fisherman	1
Total	109

TABLE 7. *Distribution of Males Engaged in
One Occupation Exclusively*

Occupation	N
Cultivator (owner)	27
Cultivator (worker, renter, tenant)	11
Basketmaker	6
Monk	4
Logger	3
Total	51

TABLE 8. *Female Occupations and Their*
Distribution

Occupation	N
Cultivator	92
(owner, 34; worker, renter, tenant, 58)	
Bamboo stripper	23
Basketmaker	10
Tea shop proprietor	2
Storekeeper	2
Seamstress	1
Field foreman	1
Dancer	1
Fisherman	1
Shaman	1
Total	134

that the average woman, like the average man, works in 1.5 income-producing occupations. If, in addition, the non-income producing occupation of housework were included among the female occupations, the average would be increased to 2.5.

Since most villagers are cultivators, it is obvious that land is a villager's most important asset, but—it so happens—it is the most difficult asset to acquire. Land, in Upper Burma, is classified into two broad categories, irrigated and non-irrigated, and the irrigated or paddy land, which is used for the cultivation of wet rice, is the more valuable, since rice forms the staple diet in Burma. Of the 115 households in Yeigyi, 58, or 50 percent, possess only paddy land, eight possess both types of land, while six possess only non-irrigated land.[1] The non-irrigated land, which is used for the cultivation of orchards, sesamum, and some few other products, is much less important than paddy land because, excluded from the irrigation system, in drought years it yields no income, and because (unlike paddy land) its ownership confers little prestige.

Of the 58 households that possess paddy land, 22 received all, and three received some, of their holdings following the post-independence

1. For neighboring Thailand, Piker (n.d., ch. 1, p. 11) reports that 50 percent of the families in a village in the central plains—the same percentage as in Yeigyi—own paddy land. Unlike Yeigyi, however, there are very few tenant farmers in this village, presumably because the other villagers are gainfully employed in non-farming occupations. In a village in the Northeast, however, Tambiah (1970:24) reports that 88 percent of the households own some paddy land. Part of the difference between these two villages is explained, as we shall see below, by the difference in the size of the land holdings, the central plains cultivator owning, on an average, twice as much land as his counterpart in the Northeast.

passage of the land nationalization act, which was implemented in Yeigyi in 1956. (Of the six households that possess non-irrigated land only, four received their plots under the nationalization scheme.)[2] In short, although approximately 50 percent of the households possess some paddy land, only 30 percent possessed such land prior to land nationalization. This does not mean that the others have always been landless. There are, of course, traditionally landless families, but in many cases contemporary landless households are those that had lost (and continue to lose) their holdings through indebtedness. Conversely, formerly landless families have been able to acquire land by dint of hard work and accumulated savings.[3]

In addition to nationalization, there are three ways by which paddy land may be acquired: inheritance, purchase, and gift. Table 9 summarizes the frequency of each of these methods. An examination of those households that acquired all of their land by only one of these methods exclusively reveals that 25 acquired their land through inheritance (these are the traditionally landed families), 22 through nationalization, and 11 through purchase. In short, less than half (43 percent) of those households that possess land today are traditional landowning families. To be sure, some few of those who acquired land through nationalization had been traditional landowning families that had lost their holdings through indebtedness, but even when the latter are included, it is still the case that only half of the present landowning households are descended from traditional landowning families. This important change in the distribution of land holdings is an index not only of the mobility potential in village society, but of the fluidity in its status and prestige heirarchy.

Although 58 households in the village own land, the size, quality, and

2. According to this act, a family was permitted to retain as much of its land, up to fifty acres, as it, together with its close kinsmen, was able to work by itself. Nevertheless, judicious bribery permitted almost all the large *resident* landowners to retain their land, so that all of the 500 acres nationalized and redistributed in Yeigyi by a seven-man village committee had been owned by *absentee* landowners. Moreover, despite nationalization, some villagers still remain landless because land was distributed to former tenant farmers only; nonagriculturalists and part-time, seasonal, farm hands were not eligible. According to government standards, land was distributed according to the following criteria: five acres for a family of three; seven for a family of four; eight for a family of five; up to twelve for a family of eight or more. Technically, nationalized land is owned by the government, and is redistributed upon the death of the incumbent. For this reason, the prestige attached to land ownership does not hold for land acquired by nationalization. Hence, when I conducted a census of landholdings, villagers consistently distinguished between land acquired by purchase, gift, and inheritance, on the one hand, and that acquired through nationalization, on the other.

3. In Central Thailand, too, landless households, according to Piker (n.d., ch. 1, p. 13), are the descendents, only one or two generations removed, of landed families, and, as in Burma, their land was (almost invariably) lost as a result of indebtedness.

TABLE 9. *Methods by Which Paddy Land Has Been Acquired*

Method	Households
Inheritance	25
Nationalization	25
Purchase	17
Gift	5
No information	1
Total	73

value of their holdings exhibit a wide range. Thus, while the average holding is nine acres, the range extends from two to forty-one,[4] and their value varies correspondingly, ranging from K 450 to K 8500. Similarly, the quality of the land, as measured by the market price of its paddy and its yield per acre, also differs greatly. Thus, while the average price per basket is K 3.7, the range is from K 2.5 to K 4.5, and while the average yield per acre is thirty-eight bushels, the range is from twenty to fifty bushels. In short, if paddy land is the villagers' most important economic asset, it is apparent that there are wide differences in wealth in the village.

Non-irrigated land, as already indicated, is economically less valuable because of the much greater risk in its cultivation. Nevertheless, its importance should not be underestimated. Sesamum, for example, brings a much higher price—as much as K 20 per basket—than paddy, so that in good years the annual income of a household can be augmented considerably by these land holdings. As in the case of paddy land, the non-irrigated holdings are highly variable, ranging in size from one to fifteen acres (with an average of seven) and in value from K 100 to K 2300 (with an average of K 690).

If I have devoted more space to the discussion of land than this brief chapter may warrant, it is not only because land is important economically but also because ownership, as we shall see below, is a key variable in the village stratification system.

Another important economic asset of the household—following land and the means by which it is worked (oxen, buffalo, and agricultural implements)—is the house. In Yeigyi every household owns its own

---

4. The average holdings in a second village surveyed was also nine acres, with a range from six to fifty-four. The figures may be compared with those in Thailand, in which the averages are approximately eight for villages in the central plains (Piker n.d., ch. 1, p. 12) and fourteen for villages in the Northeast (Tambiah 1970:24).

house, and although, as we shall see in a later chapter, some are merely bamboo huts, little better than a lean-to, others are large buildings, constructed of teak. Here again, the range is considerable: the value of the average house is K 466, but the range varies from K 30 to K 2000. From Table 10 (based on a sample of 75 households) it is clear that most houses were built by their present inhabitants. If fewer are inherited than might have been expected, it is not only because many families have recently moved into the village, but because an extensive fire in the recent past destroyed many of the older houses.

TABLE 10. *Modes of Acquiring a House*

Mode	N
Built by present inhabitants	49
Purchased	10
Inherited	10
Gift received	6
Total	75

In assessing the standard of living in the village, income as well as assets must be taken into account. Reliable income data are difficult to acquire, but based on a sample of 89 households, I estimated the mean annual household income from all sources in 1961 to be K 1025, with a range from K 180 to K 3660. (At the official rate of exchange, K 4.76 = $1.00.)[5] When income other than cash is included, total consumable income, of course, is appreciably higher. Take, for example, the typical villager who, in addition to his cash income, derives additional non-cash income from working for his fellows during the harvest season. In addition to his noon meal, he receives from the landowner a half bushel of paddy a day, an amount that can sustain a family of four for six days. Hence, two persons working the entire harvest season (about forty days) can accumulate enough paddy to feed a family for an entire year, with enough to spare for their daily food offerings to the monks.

In short, although by western standards the Burmese peasant family is poor, it is not as poor as its cash income would suggest, and it is relatively

5. This figure is less than that in a second village I surveyed, in which the average income was K 1140. Both are considerably higher than the comparable figure for villages in central Burma, where the average for the same period was K 412 (*Report on the Survey of Rural Household Expenditures, 1960-61*). The difference is primarily explained by differences in land holdings (the two upper Burma villages averaged nine acres per household, while in Central Burma the average was only five) and in acre yield (the Yeigyi area is a very fertile one).

well off compared to most other peasant families in Asia. To be sure, the
village has no electricity or running water, let alone telephones or
television, and it is a wealthy villager who owns a bicycle. Moreover,
public facilities are in poor condition, and the one main road becomes an
unusable, muddy lane in which one sinks to his calves during the rainy
season. Nevertheless, the average village family not only has more than
enough food to eat and clothes to wear, but it has sufficient cash for such
occasional pleasures as a theatrical performance, a Buddhist pilgrimage, a
visit to the city, an expensive wedding, and so on. Fytche's (1878:67)
comment is as apt today as it was almost 100 years ago: "All appear well off
. . . two days' labour suffices for three days' bread, and destitution is quite
unknown."

Interestingly enough, this relatively high standard of living—relative,
that is, to Asian peasantry in general—is accompanied by a relatively high
level of indebtedness. At least one-third of all village households are
continuously in debt.[6] The heaviest indebtedness, paradoxically, is found
among landowners, who require loans for agricultural production. In
principle, cultivators can borrow from the government at an annual
interest rate of ten percent a year (which, for Burma, is a very low rate).
In fact, however, most cultivators borrow only from private moneylenders
because they are heavily in debt to the government, and the latter will not
grant them a new loan until they repay the old. Hoping, however, that
the government will sometime cancel their indebtedness, and refusing,
therefore, to repay their previous loans (which the government permits
them to repay in installments), villagers turn instead to private
moneylenders, to whom they must pay usurious rates.

Before Independence it was the "grasping" Indian (Chettiar) who was
blamed for the peasant's woes. Since Independence, however, his op-
pressor is just as likely to be a Burman, and most frequently a fellow
villager, and sometimes a close kinsman. Thus, of the 35 indebted
households mentioned above, 26 borrow from fellow villagers (primarily
from four wealthy cultivators), 9 from moneylenders in Mandalay. In
quantitative terms, the mean annual loan for the 35 indebted households
in Yeigyi is K 545, with a range of K 30 to K 2000. The mean interest rate
for the five month agricultural season amounted to 65 percent per annum,
ranging from 20 to 220 percent.

Typically, the loan is in the form of a mortgage on futures, known as
sabapei. That is, the cultivator borrows from the moneylender at the

6. Describing a village in the Central Plains of Thailand, Piker writes (n.d., ch. 2, p. 44):
"Although many families do not go into debt yearly, there are few which have escaped
indebtedness altogether over the past generation or two; and there are some which are in
debt either more or less continually, or at least for part of almost every year."

beginning of the planting season, with the agreement to repay the loan in paddy at the end of the harvest season. Not infrequently the interest rate is so high—sometimes, as I have indicated, as high as 220 percent—that when he repays his debt, the cultivator's entire harvest is handed over to his creditor, from whom he must immediately borrow again in order to live for the coming year. In short, in the extreme case this system creates the paradox of paddy farmers without paddy, for, having repaid their debt in paddy produced with cash loans, the farmer must again borrow cash from his same creditor to purchase paddy in the market.

If the standard of living in village Burma, though higher than in many other peasant societies, is lower than it might be, the fault cannot be attributed to a malign climate or a dense population. Given its excellent irrigation system (which goes back to the early Pagan period of Burmese history), its high-yielding agricultural land, and its low population density, the agricultural economy might have been expected to produce an even higher standard of living. In part, the lack of economic progress, at least since Independence, can be attributed to the political unrest and insurgency that have had persistent adverse effects on the village economy. In part, too, it can be attributed to the ravages of World War II and the Japanese occupation, which destroyed a large proportion of the national economic infrastructure, and from which the country has never recovered. In no small part, the government, with its confused economic planning and inefficient execution of whatever plans it did have, is also an important contributor (Walinsky 1962).

At the same time, much of the lack of economic progress at the village level can be attributed to the unwillingness of the average villager to exchange leisure for income. Thus, there are two relatively slack seasons in the annual paddy-cultivation cycle—one from the beginning of the transplanting to the beginning of the harvest season, the other from the end of the harvest to the beginning of the planting season—during which villagers enjoy a great deal of leisure. Nevertheless, and despite its promised rewards, most villages (at least in Upper Burma) have resisted all attempts to encourage them to practice double cropping. The Township Officer for the Yeigyi township, for example, had tried very hard to induce the villages in his jurisdiction to experiment with cotton as a second crop. But despite the fact that all the evidence indicated that it would be highly successful, he had little success. The villagers, as he put it, "prefer more leisure to more money."

This preference, to be sure, is not universal. In one village, in which I worked for over a month, an ambitious headman had induced his village to plant a second crop, with the result that it is visibly the most prosperous village in the area. As one member of that village put it, "We want good food and good clothes, and are willing to work for them." In addition to their unusually capable headman, the villagers attributed their diligence to yet another factor. This village is only a short distance from Mandalay, and the villagers are constantly exposed to the many goods and services that, with sufficient cash, might become available to them. "Since," as one of them put it, "we want them all the more strongly, we are willing to work harder for them."

The Socio-Political Context

Political processes at the village level consist in jockeying for influence *(awza)* and prestige *(goun)*. To a great extent, influence is achieved by leadership over a group in which the relationship between leader and follower is a patron-client relationship; and since a local leader has very little largesse to distribute, his patronship is important to the extent that he, in turn, is a client of an important patron outside the village—a Township Officer, a moneylender, a district leader in the powerful national peasant's organization or in one of the political parties, a local MP, and so on. In their struggles for power, village leaders and aspirants to leadership form factions of varying strength, and the resultant factionalism—which is pervasive and often intense—is a constant threat to village solidarity (Spiro 1968).

Most villagers, however, are less concerned with power—except for the power to be obtained through clientship—than with prestige, which is achieved through wealth, and more particularly through conspicuous consumption. Land, as we have already seen, is the most important form of wealth in the village, not only as an economic asset, but as a source of prestige. As such, land ownership is the most important basis for the prestige-based village stratification system.

Roughly, villagers distinguish three social classes. The lower class *(au'tansa)* consists of landless loggers and basketmakers, almost all of whom are relatively recent immigrants. The middle class *(ale-tansa)* consists of two types of small landholders. One type consists of descendants of small landowning families, the other of those who acquired their holdings as a result of nationalization. A similar distinction is found in the upper class *(ahte'tansa)* which, again, is based on land. One type is exemplified by those villagers who, although they do not own much land today, are descended from traditional upper class families—that is, families that had once been large landowners, or in whom the tradition-ally prestigeful offices of headman and elder had been hereditary. The other type is represented by relatively recent large landowners who have no connection with the traditional upper class. These families, despite their greater wealth, tend to be less educated than the traditional upper-class families, lacking their cultural sophistication and social graces. Generally both types are distinguished from the other villagers (by village standards) by their fine houses, in one case inherited, in the other constructed.

Prestige is an all important motive in village society. Jockeying for prestige is not only an important basis for village factionalism, but since prestige enhancement is, to a great extent, a function of conspicuous consumption, it accounts for a significant percentage of household expenditures. Weddings, Buddhist initiations, construction and provisioning of monasteries, and many other forms of Buddhist ceremonies are especially important vehicles for prestige enhancement, so that (with the exception of weddings) they have a dual function: they not only enhance one's (secular) prestige, but they simultaneously contribute to one's store of (religious) merit. Since the latter is the means for a better rebirth, these forms of consumption may be viewed as conspicuous waste in the eyes of the economist, but they are important investments in a better future life in the eyes of the villager (Spiro 1966).

The Administrative Context

Viewed from the outside, the Burmese village is the smallest administrative unit of a political state ruled by a central government in Rangoon. For purposes of administration, the country is divided into districts administered by a District Commissioner; districts are divided into subdivisions administered by a Subdivisional Officer; subdivisions are divided into townships administered by a Township Officer; and townships are divided into villages, each headed by an elected village headman. Viewed from the outside, village government is a means for enforcing the laws and the administrative rules of the higher-order governmental units. Viewed from the inside, however, the village is not the unit of an artificial administrative system, but a natural social system, the unit within which most of the important social relationships of the average villager take place. Hence, from the inside, village government is the vehicle for constraining individual behavior within the permissible limits of village customary law, and for coordinating and facilitating those activities of its members which are beyond their own capabilities.

Although villagers have an opportunity to affect the internal workings of their village by participation in village meetings, these meetings, presided over by the headman, are poorly attended, and their decisions are seldom put into effect. Women never attend, claiming they have no interest in public matters. Monks are disqualified from participating. Older people seldom attend, saying they want to be left alone to think about religious matters. When there is factionalism, as there often is, the faction in opposition to the headman seldom attends. Finally, non-cultivators, who comprise the lower class of the village, never attend on the grounds that their lot could not be affected one way or another by decisions made at these meetings.

The most important of the headman's intra-village functions relate to conflict resolution. Domestic strife, neighbors' quarrels, charges of petty theft, boundary disputes, and so on, are brought to the headman for adjudication, and he usually resolves them informally—by offering counsel, cajoling, pacifying, arbitrating. Sometimes, however, disputes are brought to him for formal adjudication, for villagers are loathe to take their disputes to the courts.

There are a number of reasons why villagers prefer to resolve disputes at the local level. First, they usually do not wish their disputes to be broadcast beyond the village. Second, litigation in the courts can be very expensive, not only because of the ordinary court and attorney fees, but because of the rather extensive bribery (of police, clerks, and judges) which is believed necessary to gain a favorable ruling. Third, based on British-introduced notions of western justice, the courts find for one party only, so that victory for one side means defeat for the other. This notion is foreign to traditional Burmese notions of justice (Furnivall 1948:131-137; Maung Maung 1963:14) still prevalent in the village, in which adjudication involves arbitration—that is, compromise and conciliation. Villagers know that when the village headman and elders sit as a court, they will render a decision that will not lead to the persistence of discord and enmity, and (however strong their case) disputants are committed to the same end. No decision will be rendered that does not, at least to some extent, satisfy both parties.[7] It must be emphasized that this approach to conflict resolution is based not only on villagers' notions of "proper justice" but also on the unwillingness of the judges to render a decision which will offend, and thereby make an enemy of, a fellow villager. A fourth reason for the villagers' disinclination to go into court is based on their conviction that any contact with government means trouble. To go into court means to expose oneself to investigation and interrogation, and there is no way of knowing what kinds of adverse information about oneself might be uncovered. On all accounts, therefore, it is best to keep disputes within the confines of the village. If, therefore, a villager brings a fellow villager into court, it can be assumed that his motivation is usually one of hostility or revenge, and that it is very strong indeed.

7. The same considerations are operative in the traditional sectors of other Asian societies, such as Java (Geertz 1961:47).

But it is not only the litigants who wish to confine disputes to the local level. The village itself has two important stakes in keeping them within the village boundaries. Over and over again, villagers would say how shameful it is for fellow villagers to bring their disputes to the courts. To do so is a reflection on the entire village, for other villages might properly ask: "Are there no elders in that village that these people must go to court in order to settle their disputes?" In addition to such considerations of collective loss of face, the village suffers an economic loss when litigation is taken outside the village. In the case of assault, for example, the accused is punished by fine if he is found guilty by the court, whereas he is ordered to repair the village road or fence if the decision is rendered instead by the headman and council of elders.

Although in some villages the council of village elders is indeed comprised of "elders," men in their fifties and sixties, in Yeigyi they were predominantly young men—in their thirties and forties. In some villages, the elders are appointed by the headman; in others they are self-selected and identified as such by the villagers; in Yeigyi, at the instigation of the new headman, they are elected. Whatever their ages and the method of their selection, village elders are always male, they tend to be of moderate wealth, and they tend to be respected either for their Buddhist learning or for their piety.

Village elders have three functions. First, they assist and advise the headman in decision making. The following were among the problems considered by the Yeigyi elders during my stay in the village. Should an old monastery be restored? Should the materials from a monastery ruin be used to repair the village chapel? How could money be raised to repair the school? Should a villager be granted permission to cultivate public land? Should the village comply with the army's order to repair the village fence? Second, elders act as counselors to villagers. Third, together with the headman, elders serve as judges or arbitrators in disputes, notably those of domestic discord and divorce.

In addition to the council of elders, there are two administrative posts in village government. The village is divided into "wards" consisting of ten contiguous houses, and for each ward there is appointed by the headman a "ten-house head," whose job it is to keep the peace. The headman also appoints a deputy headman who can serve in his stead during his absence from the village.

When the village, collectively, has tasks to be performed, or when it wishes to perform a task for one of its members, it accomplishes these ends by means of both ad hoc and standing "associations" or "groups," each presided over by a "leader" or "head." The "young men's association," consisting of most of the young men of the village, is in charge of all preparations required for village celebrations and religious holydays, as well as weddings, funerals, initiation ceremonies, ordination ceremonies, and so on. The "young women's association," consisting of most of the young women of the village, is in charge of the preparation (but not the cooking) of the food for these affairs. They pound the dry fish, remove the chaff from the rice, filter the water for the monks, and prepare the betel boxes and the plates of pickled tea. The "food group," consisting of twelve men, is in charge of the cooking of the food for these affairs, except for the special curry prepared for initiation ceremonies, which is in the charge of the "curry group," which also consists of twelve men. The "water group" and the "waiters' group" provide the water and serve as waiters and dishwashers, respectively, at initiation ceremonies. Each of these also has twelve members. Finally, the "monks' waiters' group," consisting of fifteen men, serve as waiters and dishwashers at all celebrations in honor of monks. Unlike the first two groups, which draw on almost all the young men and women of the village, membership in the others is by appoint- ment of the head of each of the groups, who in turn is recruited by consensus.

The Religious Context

Since I have already described Burmese religion in the first two volumes of this study (Spiro 1967, 1969), the briefest summary is all that is required here. By any criterion, Buddhism is surely the most important cultural system in village Burma. Buddhist values and metaphysics importantly inform the personal and social lives of the average Burman, so much so that to be a Burman is synonymous with being a Buddhist. Every village has at least one monastery—Yeigyi has three—and although the monk is prohibited from participating in the secular life of the village, the monastery is the focal institution of village life and the celibate monk is the cynosure of village society. Since a better incarnation is the most important aspiration of the average villager, and since this aspiration is achieved by adding to one's store of merit (kuthou), acquiring merit is a primary concern of all villagers. And since they believe that merit is most importantly acquired by feeding monks, provisioning monasteries, and constructing pagodas, a large proportion of village savings, as already indicated, are channeled into these activities. Some, but very few villag- ers, are concerned with accumulating merit to the end of creating a sufficiently powerful karma that nirvana (the Buddhist conception of ultimate salvation), rather than an improved worldly or celestial incarna- tion, might be achieved.

In addition to their Buddhist faith, most Burmese are also involved in the propitiation of various forms of spirits, known as *nat*. These are essentially irascible beings, whose propitiation is required to ward off various forms of trouble which they would otherwise perpetrate. Shamans, or spirit mediums, most of whom are women, are employed to deal with these spirits, and although their function is important, their social status, unlike that of the Buddhist monks, is low.

In their concern to better control, improve, and predict their destiny, the Burmese resort to a variety of other occult practitioners—astrologers, diviners, alchemists, exorcists, and so on. Although their techniques and premises are often at variance with Buddhism, their practices are frequently based on Buddhist beliefs, and they often employ Buddhist symbols to associate themselves and their practices with the power, legitimacy, and prestige of Buddhism.

These religious, supernatural, and occult phenomena are not only persistent features of Burmese life, but they comprise the themes, symbols, and dramatic personae of the Burmese theater, the single most important form of recreation and entertainment in Burma, and its most important vehicle for the transmission and reinforcement of traditional values. Traveling theater troupes move up and down the country, performing in city and village, and villagers travel long distances to watch a dramatic performance which, lasting through the night, combines the varied talents of actors, comedians, musicians, and dancers.

The Psychological Context

In contrast to romantic stereotypes concerning peasant attachment to the soil, most villagers, at least those of Yeigyi, have no such romantic notions about themselves. To work on the soil, they say, is a hard and miserable life, and if it were a realistic alternative they would much prefer to live in the city.[8] Thus, one young man, who had decided to move to Mandalay to become an apprentice stone worker, said he did not want to become a "slave to his fields," as his father had been. Again, a woman enrolled her son in the middle school so that he could become a teacher because "the cultivator's life is a life of slavery." Still another man said he would like to move to the city because the life of the cultivator is "difficult and poor"—he must cut the trees and plow the fields under the hot sun, all the while exposed to stinging insects and poisonous snakes. It is his bad karma, he continued, that destined him to be a cultivator; if his karma changed he might still be able to move to the city.

There can surely be no question about the difficulty of village life. During the planting season, the average male works a fourteen hour day,

8. Ryan and Straus (1954:187) found the same lack of romanticism in Ceylon. In a survey of adult males in one "prosperous and apparently contented locality . . . the majority expressed preference for city life."

rising between four and five o'clock in the morning, and retiring at eight or nine o'clock at night, after eating his evening meal about six o'clock. The harvest season is less demanding, but even then the average male works a ten-hour day. Plowing his fields, one villager suddenly turned to me and said, "I am disgusted with farming. You asked me the other day what nirvana is. I don't know, but I want nirvana so I can avoid this misery." Most villagers express their feelings in an expression that has become a stereotype. "We are," they say, "like oxen, working in the mud and the slime."

Some villagers would like to leave the village, not because of the hardships associated with farming, but because of the poverty associated with it. One woman put it most directly when she said, "I am fed up with being poor." Moreover, the poverty seems endless. As one man put it, "There is no progress. There is no change in your living standards at sixty from what they had been at twenty."[9]

Still other villagers complain about the low social status of peasants. One man noted that no matter what they might do to improve their status, so long as they remain in the village their attempts will be futile. Thus, he himself had educated his sons in Mandalay so that they (unlike him) could become "gentlemen." Nevertheless, he continued, "No matter how rich or educated you are, if you live in a village, you cannot become a gentleman."

It will be noticed from these criticisms that the villagers are not disdainful of village life, as such, but of those characteristics which villagers share with poor people anywhere, whether they be urban or rural: back-breaking labor, poverty, low social status. Sometimes, to be sure, one may hear village-specific criticisms. Village life, one man complained, is monotonous: "one sees the same people and the same scenery all the time." But these criticisms are rare. I wish to stress this point because in attacking the myth of the idyllic village found in certain romantic writers, it is important not to fall into the other extreme of viewing village life, as such, as an unmitigated disaster. There is much about their lives in Yeigyi that the villagers enjoy, and their enjoyment is perceptible to even a casual observer. Even in the absence of their ambivalence concerning the city, the villagers' denigration of their own lives would all but disappear if their hardships were to be alleviated by mechanization, prosperity, and a greater degree of social equality within the larger society.

At the present, however, these hardships are real, and they occasion

9. Pfanner (1962:186) discovered similar attitudes in a village in lower Burma. Eleven of twelve respondents to a questionnaire complained that the cultivator "must work in the hot sun, in the rain and mud," and six complained because it is a "very tiring job."

serious discontent. Why, then, we must ask, do these same villagers, in the face of this discontent, remain in the village? Yeigyi, after all, is not a jungle village, remote from an urban center. On the contrary, it is only a few miles from Mandalay, the second largest city in Burma.

There are at least three answers to this question. First, despite their ambivalence toward their own existence, many villagers are even more ambivalent about the city. Despite its appeals, the city, in their eyes, is morally corrupt, physically crowded, and—what is perhaps even more important—psychologically uncomfortable. Simply put, the average villager feels like a country bumpkin in the city. For other villagers, the city, in spite of its attractions (real or imagined) is not a realistic alternative. Trained for farm labor, they have no readily marketable skills for making a living in the city. Still others, probably the majority, remain in the village because of attachment to friends and relatives. Thus, even after moving to the city and finding gainful employment, some villagers have returned to their village homes because of lonesomeness for their kinsmen. It is for this same reason that many others have never left; although offered better-paying jobs in the city, poor villagers would not accept them because of attachment to their families. One villager drew a philosophical moral from these facts. "As long as there is attachment," he said, "there will be no progress." This comment leads us directly to the subject of the present volume, the role of kinship in village life.

Part Two.   Kinship

3 Cultural Conceptions and Organization of Kinship

The Biological Basis of Kinship Ties

Although, except for primary relatives, Burmese kin terms lump affines together with consanguineal kin, there is little doubt that for the Burmese, it is biology that distinguishes the field of kinship (from other social fields) and that establishes a kinship relationship (in contrast to other kinds of social relationships).[1] Normatively viewed, kinship relationships are permanent because they consist of biological relationships, which can never be destroyed. "Streams may be spoiled," says a Burmese folk saying, "but heredity is never spoiled." Indeed the biological relationships of kinship may supersede even the sacred norms of the monkhood. Thus, although it is contrary to the monastic Rule for a monk to request anything of a layman, it is permissible in the case of a biological relative.

That some shared biological attribute is the essence of kinship is summed up in the proverb, *lu-ma qamyou/kye'ma qayou*, "[One knows] people by their relatives, chickens by their bone [heredity]." That is, the common observation that kinsmen share a common character can be explained by the fact that character is determined by biology, and shared biology is the essence of kinship. This is why the Burmese seldom adopt a child of unknown parents: since its heredity is unknown, its future character is unknowable.

The biological basis of kinship is variously conceived to consist of shared semen, shared blood, and derivation from a common (proximate or distal) womb. On all three accounts, ego is not only related to both father and

---

1. In this regard, as in many others, the Burmese is much like the American kinship system. Thus, commenting on the latter system, Schneider (1968:24) writes: "Two blood relatives are 'related' by the fact that they share in some degree the stuff of a particular heredity. . . . Their kinship consists in this common possession . . . [it] does not depend on intervening relatives, but only on the fact that each has some of the heredity that the other has and both got theirs from a single source."

mother, but he is related equally to the relatives of both. Viewing the kinship field as comprising two descent groups which overlap in ego, then ego is produced by the same ancestral semen that produced his paternal relatives, on the one side, and his maternal relatives, on the other. This notion of semen as comprising the stuff of kinship is supported by the villagers' folk etymological interpretation (there is still another which we shall examine below) of the Burmese word for kinsman, *hsweimyou*, according to which *myou* is derived from *myousei*, semen. On the same view of the kinship field, ego is related to both his paternal and maternal kinsmen because he and they, respectively, are descended from the same ancestral wombs. Hence, kinship distance, as we shall see below, is reckoned by distance from a common womb. Viewing the kinship field as comprising a network (rather than two overlapping descent groups), it is blood which is stressed as the shared biological stuff of kinship. Hence, the Burmese custom—still observed—of forming a blood brotherhood. The way to guarantee permanence and absolute loyalty in a friendship is for friends to become kinsmen, by slashing their arms and exchanging blood.

Since kinship ties are thought to be based on biology, the Burmese kinship system, as I have already implied, is a cognatic system. Since biological descent is reckoned through both parents, every individual is equally related to the relatives of both. Since, however, each group of kinsmen is biologically distinctive in that each has a distinctive set of the three attributes—semen, wombs, and blood—which determine the biological basis of kinship, it is not surprising that maternal and paternal kinsmen are culturally distinguished in the Burmese kinship system. At the most inclusive level, the entire kinship network is divided into relatives related through father (*qahpei hsweimyou*) and those related through mother (*qamei hsweimyou*), and this same distinction, as we shall see, is replicated throughout the entire kinship field down to the smallest circle of the personal kindred. Although there are sentimental, and some jural, differences between maternally and paternally related kinsmen, which we shall describe below, both are equally related to ego since they equally share with him the biological stuff of kinship.

Although maternally and paternally related kinsmen are equally kin, not all kinsmen are equally kin. Since kinship is determined by biology, cross-cutting the maternal-paternal distinction, the kinship field exhibits a kinship gradient along which the degree of kinship distance is a function of the degree of biological distance. Thus, lateral relationships are conceived to be more distant than lineal ones because the biological tie is not as strong in the former as in the latter. Hence, a child is believed to be closer to his parents than his siblings, and closer to his parents' parents than to his parents' siblings. By the same token the kinship bond between genealogically distant kinsmen is weaker than that between those who are genealogically close. Thus, the relationship to a parent is stronger than that to a parent's sibling, the relationship to a parent's sibling is stronger than that to a parent's parent's sibling, and so on. On a more general level, the entire kinship field is divided into genealogically "close relatives" (*nide hsweimyou*) and genealogically "far relatives" (*weide hsweimyou*).

The conception of biological distance as a determinant of kinship distance is reflected in, and emphasized by, the entire kinship terminology. First, generational distance is terminologically marked throughout the kinship field; kinsmen in each generation are differentiated from those in their successively ascending and descending generations. Second, except for the second ascending and descending generations (in which grandparent and grandparent's sibling, and grandchild and sibling's grandchild, have the same terms), lineal kin are systematically differentiated from collateral kin. Thus, parents are terminologically differentiated from parents' siblings, own children from sibling's children, and so on. It is true that collateral and lateral kin of ego's own generation —siblings and cousins—have the same terms, but they are differentiated by the "womb" (*wungwe*) locution: siblings are one's own, or genuine (*qayin*) brothers and sisters—that is, they are from the same womb —while cousins are one or more "wombs removed" brothers and sisters. English-speaking Burmese render this distinction by referring to their siblings as "brothers" or "sisters" and to their cousins as "cousin-brothers" or "cousin-sisters."

This "womb" locution raises an important question about the relationship between biology and kinship to which, however, the answer is ambiguous. Although kinship distance is a function of biological distance, there is some suggestion that within the same degrees of genealogical distance the kinship tie to females is conceived to be stronger than that to males. There is no doubt, as we shall see below, that this is the case at the affective level—although it is not clear whether this is because the female kinsman is a female or a kinsman—but even at the cognitive level there is some reason to believe that, because of the importance of the womb, the (biological) stuff of kinship is thought to be transmitted more through females than males, and that, consequently, more of it is shared with females than with males. Thus, throughout the entire kinship field, degrees of kinship are reckoned, if only symbolically, by distance from a common womb. Beginning with the parents, the child's tie to the mother is believed to be closer than to the father because (among other reasons) the child comes from her womb. Similarly, despite the fact that the father's semen and the mother's womb are equally important in forming their bodies, next to parents, siblings are believed to have the closest kin ties with each other because they are directly descended from the same womb. For the same reason, first cousins are more distant than siblings because they are "one womb removed"—they are descended not from the same mother, but from the same grandmother. Second cousins are even more distant because they are "two wombs removed"—it is their great grandmother who provides their common womb, and so on.

Now in one sense this method of reckoning genealogical distance may only be a symbolic device, in which the womb locution is merely the idiom in which kinship distance is described and discussed. As such, it would have no implication for the relative contribution of the two sexes to the biological stuff of kinship. Its implication, rather, would consist in underscoring the cultural belief that, genealogically, lineal are closer than collateral relatives, that, indeed, collateral relatives are kin by virtue of descent from a common lineal kinsman. Hence, instead of tracing their kinship laterally, cousins, for example, must trace their relationship by going up to a common ancestor and then down again. Nevertheless, we cannot ignore the fact that this emphasis on lineal reckoning is expressed in the idiom of the "womb" rather than of "semen," or for that matter, of both. Of these three possible idiomatic alternatives, is it merely accidental that this one alone is used to express genealogical distance?

There is at least one reason to believe that this choice was not accidental, but that the womb idiom was chosen precisely because of the belief that kinship, viewed as descent, is determined more by the biological stuff acquired from female than from male kinsmen. Thus the biological family, which in one sense may be viewed as a cognatic descent group (of two generations depth), is called a *mitha su*, a "mother-child group." More important, the stock, which is a true cognatic descent group, is also called a *mitha su*, implying that its founding female contributes more than its founding male to its common kinship. To be sure, we must be extremely cautious about such speculations—and additional field work is required before this one can be accepted—but when this semantically based inference is combined with the explicitly expressed belief that children are biologically closer to the mother than the father, it is not entirely implausible to assume that female kin on either side are believed to contribute more of the biological stuff of kinship than their male counterparts, and that one's relationship to female kin, therefore, is closer than that to male kin. In refutation of this

assumption, however, it should be observed that some Rangoon informants use a variant term, *amyou su,* for the cognatic descent group
(though not for the nuclear family), which might be taken to imply that its
founding male (*myousei* = semen) contributes as much of its biological stuff
as his female counterpart. I do not know, however, whether this variant
terminology is a result of urbanism, geography, or acculturation.

But regardless of the validity of these speculations concerning the
relative strength of the tie to male and female kin, there is no question but
that the biological difference between males and females is the basis for a
cultural distinction between male kin and female kin. For almost every
kintype in the kinship field, male kin, as we shall see below, have
different jural norms applying to them from those applying to female kin,
as well as different kin terms. Indeed, in some cases (siblings and
siblings-in-law) this terminological differentiation is based not only on the
sex of the kinsman addressed or referred to, but on the sex of the speaker.
The only exceptions to the terminological differentiation of kin by sex are
found at the fourth ascending (great-great-grandparents) and second
descending (grandchildren) generations, in which, presumably, sex differences for persons of these extreme ages are biologically irrelevant.

Although, to return to the main thesis, kinship distance is viewed as a
function of biological distance, this does not mean that the social or
psychological distance between kin is necessarily a function of their
genealogical distance. The Burmese are well aware of the fact that a close
biological relationship does not guarantee a closer emotional relationship
than a remote one, despite the fact that kinsmen (*hsweimyou*), according
to the folk etymology enunciated by some villagers, are characterized by
an emotional affinity (*hswei*), something like love. But to refer to the
kinship relationship as one of emotional attachment is, at best, a cliché,
and one in which the Burmese place little credence. Indeed, in their
more cynical moods, they say that *hswei* (emotional attachment) should be
pronounced as *shwei* (gold), for kinsmen are attached to their relatives
only if they are rich. Less cynically, they point out that the relationship
between close kinsmen is often characterized by indifference and sometimes hostility, and some even verbalize it as a principle. Thus, one
woman, speaking of a distant relative, said: "Although we are distantly
related, we have love for each other; with some people one can be closely
related, and yet have no love."

The above principle enunciates an important truth about kinship, as the
Burmese conceive of it. Kinship as such is not conceived to be the domain
of love, nor even of friendship—although they may overlap and even
coincide—but of moral obligation. Indeed the whole point of kinship, in
contrast to other kinds of relationships, is that in it, and in it alone, moral

obligations must be honored regardless of one's feelings. One assists non-kinsmen only if one likes (or loves) them; one must assist kinsmen even if one dislikes them. On this dimension, then—the dimension of moral obligation or duty—there is not only a moral dichotomy between the obligations of kinship and non-kinship, but also a moral gradient along which the obligations of close kinship are distinguished from those of distant kinship.

Consanguinity and Affinity

If biologically close kinsmen are culturally distinguished from biologically distant ones, it is not surprising that a conceptual dichotomy is drawn between consanguineal and affinal kin. Strictly speaking, only the former are relatives, *hsweimyou*. If, nevertheless, certain closely related affinal dyads (such as siblings-in-law, or parents- and children-in-law) are accounted as *hsweimyou*, it is only in recognition of some connecting biological link. Thus, both members of the above mentioned first dyad share a blood tie with their common child-nibling (nephew or niece), the second with their common child-grandchild. On this conception, close affines, it will be noted, are scarcely different from the consanguineal kin comprising a kindred. In both cases the criterion for membership is the degree of relationship to a common ego rather than a common ancestor. Nevertheless, even in the case of these closely related affinal dyads, a distinction is made between consanguines and affines. Although the affines may be included in the *hsweimyou*, the consanguines alone are designated by the exclusively consanguineal term *hsweimyou thagyin*.

Given the Burmese restricted conception of kinship, the only affines that can properly be classified as *hsweimyou* or kinsmen—and the only ones for whom there are designated kin terms—are the spouses of one's consanguineal kin, on the one hand, and the primary, consanguineal kin of one's own spouse, on the other. (An important addition to this formulation consists of the parents-in-law of one's child.) Thus, the spouses of the following kintypes and their reciprocals—grandparents' siblings, aunts and uncles, cousins, siblings, and children—are more (the last three) or less (the first two) accounted as kinsmen. Although the reasons are not entirely clear, I think the latter three are viewed as closer because, if affines are either the spouses of consanguines or the primary consanguines of a spouse, then, in these three cases, both criteria are operative in each of the dyads. That is, the reciprocal in a dyad, one of whose members is a sibling's spouse, is a spouse's sibling. (Since cousins, terminologically, are siblings, the same logic applies to them.) Similarly, the reciprocal in a dyad, one of whose members is a child's spouse, is a spouse's parent. Since, then, the siblings and parents of a spouse are the latter's primary consanguineal kin, these dyads have a double, rather than a single, affinal link. This double link, moreover, means that each member of the dyad shares a biological tie with a close consanguine. A parent-in-law and child-in-law both contribute to the biological substance of their common child-grandchild, and both share some of it with him (the same is true of both sets of parents-in-law), and although only one of the siblings-in-law in a dyad contributes to the biological substance of their common child-nibling, both share some of it with him. Now, since biology, in the Burmese view, is the stuff of kinship, this fact invests these particular affinal relationships with a quasi-consanguineal tie, thereby confering upon them a closer kinship bond than the one that characterizes other affinal relationships.

It might also be added, that while the spouses of grandparents' siblings, uncles, and aunts are given consanguineal terms of reference, the spouses of cousins, siblings, and children have special terms of their own. This suggests, as Lehman (personal communication) has observed, that if the former set are *hsweimyou* at all, it is by attachment or assimilation to a proper kinsman, while if the latter are so considered, it is on their own account.

In the light of this analysis it can be seen that in the Burmese system there are three types of kinsmen rather than the two, which according to Schneider, are found in the American system. In Schneider's (1968:52) view, American kinship contains both a "substance" element (shared biology) and a "code for conduct" element. One type of kinsman —consanguines—has both elements, another type—affines—has only the latter. In the Burmese system, too, there is a "substance" and a "code" element, and yet there are three types of kinsmen because, as we have seen, there are two aspects to the element of "substance." With respect to that element, some kinsmen (consanguines) are related because they share some common biological substance with each other; others (the small set of affines discussed above) because they share some common biological substance with a third, closely related, kinsman. The latter comprise a third type which falls between the pure types of exclusively consanguineal kin, on the one hand, and affinal kin, on the other. It will be noted, then, that although the members of this type (siblings-in-law, parents-in-law, and children-in-law) are not—unlike other in-laws —designated by consanguineal terms, they are, with two exceptions, addressed by them. Thus, elder brother's wife and wife's elder sister (male speaking) are addressed as "elder sister," elder sister's husband and husband's elder brother (female speaking) as "elder brother," and so on. Similarly, parents-in-law are addressed as "mother" and "father," and children-in-law as "daughter" and "son." The exceptions (the reciprocal sets of SiHu-WiBr and BrWi-HuSi) are easily explained by reference to their strained relationships, which we shall examine in a later chapter.

Since affines are relatives, in the first instance, by virtue of marriage, their relationship lasts only so long as the connecting link remains unbroken. If, for example, a childless marriage comes to an end by death or divorce, the relationship between ego and his spouse's relatives is also broken: they are no longer *hsweimyou*, and the designated kin term ceases to be operative. As one villager, in answer to a query concerning her new son-in-law, remarked: "Of course he is a 'relative'—he is my *thame?* (son-in-law). But if my daughter dies, my relationship to him also dies; he is then no longer my *thame?.*" This is not the case, however, when there are children, for then the affines, as we have seen, are linked by a shared biological tie to a common consanguine, and their relationship is as perduring as that between two consanguines.

The conceptual distinction between consanguineal and affinal kin is expressed, as I have already noted, in the kinship terminology. In no case do *primary* biological relatives share a kin term with an affine, the former being terminologically differentiated from both the spouses of one's primary kin and the primary kin of one's spouse. Thus, parents are terminologically differentiated from spouse's parents, siblings from both spouse's siblings and siblings' spouses, children from both spouses of children and the children of any affine. Finally, except for the parents-in-law of one's children, neither the primary kin of a spouse of a primary kinsman (for example, the sibling of a child-in-law) nor the secondary kin, affinal or consanguineal, of a spouse (for example, spouse's uncle and aunt, or spouse's sibling's spouse), are even designated by a kin term, for, having no connecting biological link, they are not accounted as kinsmen. If, however, as F. K. Lehman observes (personal communication), certain expressions, such as "wife's uncle," are to be taken in some sense as kin terms, then these more distant affines must be accounted in some vague sense as kin, although their jural dimension is very weak.

On the other hand, affinal kin are frequently designated by the same term as *secondary* biological relatives. Thus, grandparents' siblings and the spouses of grandparents' siblings, parents' siblings and the spouses of parents' siblings, niblings and the niblings of one's spouse—each of these sets shares a common kin term. Despite their common terminology, however, the kintypes in each of these sets sustain different (normative) relationships with ego. Thus, although father's elder brother takes the place of ego's father should the latter die, father's elder sister's husband has no such responsibility. Similarly, although mother's younger sister takes the place of mother should she die, father's younger brother's wife does not have this responsibility. In short, the extension of consanguineal kin terms (in these, and in all other cases) to affines does not carry with them the same normative requirements.

Although consanguineal kin are held to be closer than affinal kin, it must be noted that, just as within the former type social distance is not necessarily a function of genealogical distance, so too (unless jural norms require it) consanguinity does not always take precedence over affinity. In village elections, for example, some villagers supported affinal over blood relatives, while others stressed loyalty to close kin as the basis for their votes. Similarly, in the factional dispute which split Yeigyi during my stay, one prominent woman sided with her brother against her husband, while another sided with a remote affine over a cousin. Nevertheless, when the chips are down—when tragedy strikes or when financial assistance is required—the cultural norm which places biological kinship above all other ties is almost always complied with.

The Moral Dimension of Kinship Relations

There can be little doubt, then, that whatever its behavioral consequences might be, biology is the essential element in the Burmese conception of kinship, as well as being its core symbol and its most important idiom. But if biology is the stuff from which kinship ties are forged, moral obligation, as I have already indicated, is the essence of the social relationships created by these ties. Whether they are liked or disliked, whether they are admired or disdained, whether their interests and values are shared or different, kinsmen are those whom one is obligated to help, to assist, to care for, to be concerned about. When villagers are asked "What is kinship for?" the inevitable response is *tha-hmu na-hmu*, "occasions of pleasantness and pain." That is, kinship is that bond which ego has the right to call upon, and which alter has the duty to respond to, in any life cycle crisis (including rites of passage). In times of economic difficulty (*na-hmu*) it is the duty of kinsmen to assist; for the performance of an illness rite or a funeral ceremony (*na-hmu*) it is the duty of kinsmen to offer financial assistance and to share in the suffering; for the celebration of a birth or for a Buddhist initiation (*tha-hmu*), it is the duty of kinsmen to participate in the rite and share in the joy. And just as it is unthinkable for a kinsman not to offer to share a fellow kinsman's sorrow (*na-hmu*), so it is unheard of for him not to invite a fellow kinsman to share in his joy (*tha-hmu*). It is this dimension of kinship—the obligation to share goods, services, and emotions with a circumscribed set of biologically related individuals, regardless of the personal sentiments which they might feel toward each other—that uniquely characterizes the bond of kinship, and serves to distinguish it from all other social bonds, whether of friendship, religion, business, or politics.

This emphasis in Burma on moral obligation, or duty, as the essence of the social bond created by kinship ties seems, at first blush, to differentiate the Burmese from the American kinship system. According to Schneider (1968:40), it is not duty but "love" which "is what American kinship is all about." Now Burmese not only has indigenous terms expressive of both sexual and affectionate love, but it also contains numerous Pali loan words which mark many other distinctions among different types of love, and yet no informant even suggested that (except for parents and children, and for spouses) love, in any of its meanings, is what uniquely distinguishes kinship from non-kinship. Indeed, when one attends to Schneider's (1968:40) definition of "love"—"enduring, diffuse solidarity"—one wonders whether duty, rather than love, is not the distinctive feature of American kinship as well. Surely, this is a definition neither of *eros* nor *agape*, the two traditional conceptions of love in Western culture, whereas it is a remarkably good definition of "duty."

That duty is conceived to be the essential characteristic of Burmese kinship may not only be inferred from behavioral observations (to be described below), but it is explicitly stated (in the course of interviews) by the villagers themselves. In order to uncover the essence of the kinship bond, I asked the villagers to compare kinship with friendship, two affective and positive types of social relationships, which, however, are polar opposites on other important dimensions. Friendship, in contrast to kinship, is freely chosen and freely broken, it is initiated by shared interests and sentiments, and it is based exclusively on personal regard and even affection. A few villagers—and many urbanites—said they preferred their friends to their relatives, especially because they shared more interests with their friends. It is all the more striking, then, that in a random sample of twenty-two villagers, only one said that friendship is the stronger tie, and only two believed friendship and kinship to be of equal strength. All the others viewed kinship as the stronger. Even more striking are the grounds on which these nineteen based their judgment. In one form or other, and without exception, they all stressed what I am here calling "moral obligation," the obligations of kinship being categorical, those of friendship being optative. That is why, many went on to point out, that one must be concerned with pleasing a friend, but not a relative, for the latter must willy nilly come to your aid. That is also why, they again observed, one may visit a friend's house more often than a relative's. Since the relative, but not the friend, will always come to you when you have a crisis, kinship can be neglected, but friendship must always be cultivated.

I have already observed that some urbanites, particularly the younger, upper middle class, say that they prefer their friends to their relatives. In this group, especially, there is a social and cultural gap between the modern young people and their more conservative parents. Hence, it is understandable that, as one recent graduate of Rangoon University put it:

Friends are better than relatives. If I tell my relatives that I am unhappy, they may ask why, but they often do not understand, or they may ignore my answer, but my friends will understand. Moreover, friends will not betray a confidence, but this is not true of relatives. If my cousin knows, my aunt will know, and if my aunt knows, my parents will know.

Nonetheless, even this girl's conception of the moral dimension of the kin tie is no different from that of the villagers. You may *like* a friend more than a kinsman, but your *duty* to your kinsman supersedes all other relationships. Urbanites, like villagers, agree that although friends are fine, in time of trouble one can rely only on relatives, they alone are dependable. As the proverb has it, *qayei kyi/thwei ni:* "In matters of urgent importance, blood is closest" (relatives alone will help).

As if to underscore this moral dimension of kinship, and to differentiate it from all other social relationships, all close kinsmen—those within the core kindred at least—are always and only addressed by their appropriate kin terms. Not only are kinsmen as a group thereby cognitively differentiated from non-kinsmen, but within the kinship group, the terminological system, which carefully differentiates kintypes according to such distinctive features as relative age or generation, serves further to cognitively underscore the differential moral obligations found within the kinship field. Like sex, which is an equally pervasive distinctive feature—indeed, in a few limiting cases, sex or generation are the only distinctive features—relative age and generation are not distinctive features uniquely of Burmese *kinship;* rather, distinctions based on relative age and generation, like those based on sex, are generic distinctions which pervade all of Burmese *culture.* Hence, when they are used as distinctive features in the terminological system of kinship, they distinguish kinsmen not so much as kinsmen but as people. Despite the fact that sex is as pervasive a distinctive feature as relative age and generation, I am not concerned with it here because, unlike the latter two, it is not germane to this discussion of the moral dimensions of the kinship system. Sexual differentiation reflects a dimension of the Burmese stratification system, whereas age and generation distinctions reflect a dimension of the Burmese ethical system.

In Burma, as is true throughout traditional Asia, it is morally incumbent upon the young to render esteem and offer homage to their elders. This holds not only for kin, but also for non-kin, and it applies not only to members of different generations but to age differences within the same generation, even—as the Burmese say—if the difference in age is a difference of only one day. Hence, in the Burmese address system, the honorifics which precede proper names are systematically age-graded (and sex linked), depending on whether the person addressed (or referred to) is of a lower, the same, or a higher age grade than the speaker.

This same attention to absolute and relative age is found in the kinship terminology as well. Generation is a distinctive feature of every kin term; every term—through at least the first five ascending and descending generations—is generation specific. More than that, all kinsmen within the same, the first ascending, and the first descending generations are also differentiated according to relative age. Thus, father's elder brother has a different term from father's younger brother, older sister has a different term from younger sister, and so on. Within the same generation, even finer distinctions can be made, if necessary, by means of morphemes which, however, are not kin-specific. Thus, if ego has more than one elder sister, each in turn is differentiated by appending "eldest," "middle," or "youngest" to the kinship term for elder sister. The same technique is used at the first ascending and descending generations.

The importance of age as a distinctive feature can be gauged by its relative imperviousness to the inroads of change. Thus, although traditional collateral distinctions have been eroded to a great extent in modern Rangoon terminology—the matrilineal siblings of parents and grandparents are seldom differentiated from the patrilineal—the distinctions based on relative age remain in full force.

To a large extent, of course, the non-kin terms for the designation of relative age are merely descriptive and classificatory, carrying no honorific or moral implications as such. To some extent, also, even the kinship specific age-graded terms primarily reflect differences in the rights and duties associated with elder and younger kin. But these very differences are based on moral obligations. A younger brother, for example, has the moral obligation of paying homage to an elder brother, and the elder, in turn, has the moral obligation of caring for the younger's children during his absence or after his death. Hence, not only are older and younger brothers designated by different terms, but so are father's older and younger brothers, and for exactly the same reasons. The same is true for the other kintypes whose kinship terms embody age as a distinctive feature.

Thus far I have been discussing the kinship field as if it comprised an undifferentiated set of moral relationships, based on a homogenous set of cultural norms. But, as we have already seen, this is not at all the way in which the Burmese conceive of the social field of kinship. Indeed, if this were the case, then, given that the Burmese kinship system is cognatic, everyone would be potentially involved in a continuously ramifying and unwieldy network of moral relationships. If this network is less extensive and less unwieldy in practice than its potentiality for expansion permits, it is because (as we have already seen) the Burmese recognize greater and lesser degrees of kinship, and hence of moral obligation, as a function of the relative closeness or remoteness of genealogical relationships. Given this conception of genealogical distance, the kinship field exhibits, as it were, a conceptual—and hence a moral—gradient, extending from the closest biological ties at its core to the more remote genealogical ties at its peripheries. This gradient is reflected institutionally in a configuration of three concentric kin groups which, for lack of standarized terms, I shall call (beginning with the smallest) the family, the core kindred, and the extended kindred.[2] Hence, I now wish to turn from a discussion of generic conceptions of kinship to an examination of these kinship groupings and the relationships which they comprise; in short, from cultural conceptions of kinship to its social organization. Social organization, of course, is also based on culture, for the social organization of kinship is determined by cultural conceptions of kinship distance, and by cultural criteria by which the kinship field is properly sliced. Nevertheless, the focus of the subsequent discussion is on the cultural *organization* of kinship *groupings,* rather than the cultural *meaning* of kinship *ties.*

The Family (*Mitha Su*)

The Nuclear Family

In Burma, as in almost all other societies, the closest ties of biological kinship are those found among the members of the nuclear family—the "primary" relatives of parents, children, and siblings. The exceptions to this generalization consist of those few societies that do not necessarily recognize parents as *genitor* or *genitrix*. Because of the incest taboo, however, the nuclear family also includes an affinal dyad, the two spouses. Hence, there is an important difference in the kinship composition of the two nuclear families to which any Burman belongs during the

2. The situation in Java (Geertz 1961:18) and Central Thailand (Piker n.d.: Ch. 2, p. 19-20) are very much the same as in Burma.

course of his life cycle. His so-called family of orientation—the nuclear family into which he is born—consists exclusively of kin related to him consanguineally; his family of procreation—the nuclear family which results from his marriage—consists, as well, of one person related to him affinally, his spouse. Since I am concerned here with biological kinship, the marriage relationship will be treated in a separate chapter.

Because residence in Burma is typically neolocal, the nuclear family, known as the *mitha su* (mother-child group), is transformed in the course of the domestic cycle from a domestic or residential group to a dispersed group. To be sure, the youngest daughter typically remains with her parents after her marriage, but the other married children usually leave their natal household (*qeindaung su*) and set up their own households. As each married child leaves, he is called a "household split-off" (*qeindaung kwe*) with respect to his natal family. He is said to "live separately" (*qeindaung kwe neide*) or to have "gone to a separate household" (*qeindaung kwe thwalei*). Given this type of domestic cycle, the sequence from co-residence to dispersal is repeated in every generation. Hence, just as ego and his siblings are household split-offs from their common family of orientation, so too their children will become household split-offs from their respective families of procreation (their children's families of orientation), and so on for their children's children.

But since the stuff of Burmese kinship is biology, and since biological ties persist even after co-residence is dissolved, the rights and duties that characterize the relationships between the members of the nuclear family are not altered by their dispersal. These relationships remain the same whether the members comprise a domestic group, or whether, as household split-offs, they are dispersed across separate domestic groups. In short, the family's dissolution as a household group (*qeindaung su*) does not affect its individuals' membership in, or their collective identity as, a family group (*mitha su*). I shall deal with each of these variables separately.

Their dispersal does not affect the individuals' membership in the family because the cultural norms which uniquely govern the relationships of its dyads—parents and children, on the one hand, and siblings, on the other—are the same whether they live together or separately. Nor does their dispersal affect their collective identity, because so long as the parents are alive the nuclear family which they founded—their family of procreation—remains a distinctive social group, in at least two senses. First, it is a corporate group in that the parental estate remains intact so long as either parent is alive; only after the death of both parents is it divided in more-or-less equal parts among their children, the siblings.

Given this type of inheritance, then, so long as either parent is alive, the siblings share a common interest in the family estate.

The dispersed nuclear family is a social group, in the second place, because its members periodically assemble for common purposes, most especially for religious ceremonies and rites of passage, but also for cooperative labor or for the discussion and solution of common concerns and problems. To be sure, since the siblings may be accompanied by their spouses, such gatherings do not consist exclusively of family members, but these affines are included as a gesture of courtesy—they are, after all, the relatives (*hsweimyou*) of their spouses' siblings and parents—and not because they are conceived to be members of the family (*mitha su*). Sometimes, however, the integrity of the family as an exclusive group is emphasized by the fact that spouses are not invited even as a courtesy. When, for example, questions concerning the marriage of an unmarried sibling, or the disposition of property, are to be discussed at a family council, the siblings may be instructed by their parent(s) to leave their spouses behind, even though they are free to discuss these matters with them later on.

The Stock

Although siblings' spouses, whether or not they are invited to its gatherings, are not included in the dispersed family, siblings' children are included so long as the family retains its separate and collective identity, which is to say, so long as at least one of its founding parents remains alive. As the siblings marry and have children, the *mitha su* is expanded to include the original couple and all of their lineal descendants—their children, grandchildren, and even their great grandchildren if, as infrequently happens, either member of the original couple is still alive. In short, the *mitha su* includes—and the term is used to refer to—not only a nuclear family, but also (what is variously called), a "stock" (Fox 1967:169) or a "lineal family" (Murdock 1960:4).

A stock, like a nuclear family, comes into potential existence with each marriage; it comes into actual existence with the demise of the founder of either spouse's stock of orientation; and it comes to an end with the demise of its founding couple. In short, the stock consists of a couple and their direct descendants. In addition, then, to the kintypes comprising the *mitha su* viewed as a nuclear family, as a stock the *mitha su* also includes the following additional kintypes: great-grandparents and great-grandchildren (if, as infrequently happens, the former survive), grandparents and grandchildren, uncles and aunts, nephews and nieces, and cousins. Excluding great-grandparents, the full *mitha su* is depicted in

Diagram 1. As a nuclear family, the *mitha su*, both before and after its dispersal, is comprised of kintypes 1,2,3, and 4. As a stock—and as a stock it is always dispersed—the *mitha su* includes the children (but not the spouses) of 3 and 4, namely, kin types 5, 6, 7, and 8.

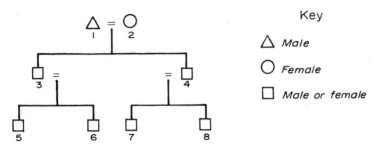

Key

△ *Male*

○ *Female*

☐ *Male or female*

Diagram 1. The family *(mitha su)* as nuclear family and as stock.

In short, the *mitha su*, as a stock, is a cognatic descent group, typically of three generations' depth. I say, "typically" of three generations, because when the grandparents die—and they usually die during the lifetime of their grandchildren—and the family estate is divided among the children, the stock, viewed as a corporation (with respect to the estate), is dissolved. However, at about the same time that this happens, the siblings of the original dispersed nuclear family have typically become grandparents themselves, and, with the dissolution of their parents' stock, they have each become the head of their own stock, distinct and separate from those headed by their siblings. It must be noted, however, that the stock remains a referential category for its members even after it ceases (with the demise of its founder) to be a corporation.

Let us, then, summarize the developmental cycle of a *mitha su*. As a nuclear family, a *mitha su* is formed when a married couple has children. When the children marry, the *mitha su*, as a residential family of procreation, is dispersed. As a stock, a *mitha su* is formed when the children marry, and the nuclear family of procreation of each of the dispersed siblings (exclusive of their spouses) is joined to their family of orientation. The stock is dissolved, and each sibling (together with his spouse) forms a new stock, when his parents die, and the children of his dispersed family of procreation establish their own families of procreation. For any ego, then, the developmental cycle of the three stocks to which he belongs as a descendant of one grandparental pair, beginning with his status as a grandchild and ending with his status as a grandparent, is depicted in Diagram 2.

Ego as child

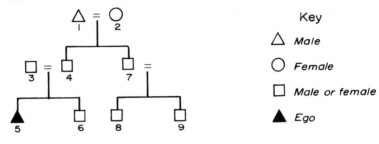

Key

△ Male

○ Female

☐ Male or female

▲ Ego

Ego as parent

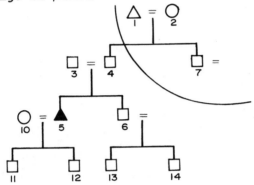

Ego as grandparent

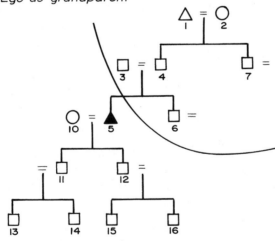

Diagram 2. Stock *(mitha su)* formation and segmentation in the life cycle of ego.

In the life cycle of the individual, as the diagram shows, each of ego's successive stocks is formed by the progressive sloughing off of collateral relatives. As a child in his grandparent's *mitha su*, his stock includes not only his parents and grandparents, but also his collaterals in his own and the first ascending generations (cousins and aunts and uncles, respectively). As a parent in his parents' *mitha su*, it includes his collaterals in the first descending generation only (nephews and nieces). As a grandparent, and the founder of his own *mitha su*, it includes no collaterals at all. This emphasis on lineal relationships is consistent, of course, with the point made earlier that, in Burmese kinship, lineal kinsmen—beginning with the nuclear family—are conceived to be closer than lateral, let alone collateral, ones. Thus the spine of the *mitha su* consists of its lineal kin; collaterals must trace their relationships by going up to a common lineal ancestor and then down. With the death of the common living ancestor, a descent group as shallow as the *mitha su* necessarily comes to an end because the collaterals no longer share a living lineal ascendant.[3]

As a kinship group, the stock is second in importance only to the nuclear family so far as the rights and duties of kinship are concerned. Moreover, since its membership comprises a dispersed nuclear family plus the children of its siblings, its collective identity during its (typically) three-generation duration is assured for the same reasons that the identity of the nuclear family is assured. First, whenever the core members—the dispersed nuclear family—of a *mitha su* assemble, its peripheral members—the children of its sibling group—automatically join them. Indeed, the father or mother of the former is known as the "leader" (*lugyi*, or "big person") of the latter. Moreover, whether a *mitha su* is taken as a dispersed nuclear family or a stock, its members comprise a corporate group, for as long as either of its founders is alive, the family estate is the potential inheritance (in equal parts) of their children, and the latter's children are, in turn, the potential heirs of that part of the estate inherited by each of their parents.

Since, in the Burmese, as in any cognatic kinship system, descent is reckoned equally through males and females, in principle every ego is at birth a member of two stocks, one founded by his father's parents and one founded by his mother's. Hence, although the kintypes in both are the same, the grandparents, uncles, aunts, and cousins comprising the former

3. In Western society, the relationship to collaterals is even more seriously impaired when the parent, through whom the link is traced, is no longer alive. This is the case at least in Bethnal Green, a working class section of London, where the death of a parent, and especially the mother, weakens the ties between siblings and effectively dissolves the relationship with uncles, aunts, and cousins to whom the parent was the connecting link (Young and Willmott 1965:78-85).

stock are related to ego through common descent from his father's parents, while the analogous kintypes comprising the latter are related to him through common descent from his mother's parents. Since these are two different descent groups, ego has different membership in each. Thus, when his mother's sister, for example, celebrates the initiation of her son, or when his mother's father calls a family council to discuss the marriage of his mother's brother, ego and his siblings are invited to join a group which consists of their mother's stock (and, sometimes its in-marrying spouses). The converse is the case when ego and his siblings participate in some event or celebration as members of their father's stock.

Although their recruitment principles and their personnel are different, maternally and paternally related stocks cannot be distinguished in terms of any of their group functions. From a formal, cultural, point of view, there is only one difference between them, and this relates, as we shall see below, to membership in the spirit cults. With respect to all other cultural criteria, including jural norms, there are no important differences between the paternal and maternal segments of the kinship field: since, in both cases, membership is determined biologically, and since in both, therefore, members are equally close or remote, the jural norms which govern their behavior are the same for both.

At the dyadic level, on the other hand, there are some important cultural differences between the maternal and paternal sides, although on balance they do not add up to a preference for the one or the other. Thus, there are important differences between maternal and paternal uncles and aunts, especially when their nephews and nieces are young children. The mother's (younger) sister and the father's (elder) brother are jurally responsible for their sibling's children should anything happen to their sibling. Where possible, their role as parent surrogate is institutionalized, as we shall see in a later chapter, in the form of the (posthumous) junior sororate and senior levirate.

The jural differences between paternal and maternal uncles and aunts find a parallel in their terminological differentiation. Thus, *Mo*Br is terminologically differentiated from *Fa*Br, and *Mo*Si from *Fa*Si. These distinctions, moreover, are replicated at the next ascending generation, as well, where Mo*Mo*Br and Fa*Mo* Br are differentiated from Mo*Fa*Br and Fa*Fa*Br, Mo*Mo*Si and Fa*Mo*Si from Mo*Fa*Si and Fa*Fa*Si. Even more striking is that in a terminological system in which relative age is almost always a distinctive feature, the collateral distinction in the uncle and aunt terms is even more strongly marked than that of age. That is, each of the collateral distinctions is designated by a unique word, while their further distinctions of age are indicated by productive affixation. It need only be added that where there are no jural distinctions between paternal and

CHART 1. *Kin Terms Used in Yeigyi*

Omitted in the text, the Burmese tones are indicated in this chart by a transcription devised by Lehman (1970). Every syllable has one of several tones. The First tone (high pitched and short) is marked by a subscript dot (.); the Second tone (middle pitched), by a hyphen (-); the Third tone (high pitched, long, and dropping), by a postponed colon (:).

Kin Type	Reference	Address
GrGrGrGrPa (lineal & collateral)[1]	*bin*	—
GrGrGrPa (lineal & collateral)[2]	*bi.*	—
GrGrFa (lineal & collateral)	*bou:*	*hpou:hpou:gyi*
GrGrMo (lineal & collateral)[3]	*bwa:*	*hpwa:hpwa:gyi*
GrFa, GrFaBr, GrFaSiHu	*qahpei-gyi:*	*qahpei-gyi:*
GrMoBr, GrMoSiHu	*qahpou:*	*qahpou:*
GrMo, GrMoSi, GrMoBrWi	*qamei-gyi:*	*qamei-gyi:*
GrFaSi, GrFaBrWi[4]	*qahpwa*	*qahpwa*
Fa	*qahpei*	*qahpei/qaba/ ,ˈ hpeihpei/baba*
Mo	*qamei*	*qamei/meimei*
Fa(eld)Br, Fa(eld)SiHu[5]	*ba.gyi:*	*ba.gyi:baba*
Fa(yng)Br	*ba.dwei:*	*ba.dwei:*
Mo(eld)Br, Mo(eld)SiHu[6]	*qu:gyi:*	*qu:gyi:*
Mo(yng)Br, Mo(yng)SiHu,Fa(yng) SiHu[7]	*qu:lei:*	*qu:lei:*
Fa(eld)Si	*qayi:gyi:/qayi*	*qayi:gyi/kyi:gyi:*
Fa(yng)Si, Mo(yng)BrWi, Mo(eld)BrWi	*qayi:*	*qayi:*
Mo(eld)Si, Fa(eld)BrWi[8]	*kyi:do*	*kyi:do*
Mo(yng)Si, Fa(yng)BrWi[9, 10]	*qado*	*qado/dolei*
(eld)Br, (eld)male cousin[11]	*qakou*	*qakou/kou kou*
(yng)Br, (yng)male cousin[12]		
male speaking	*nyi*	*nyimaun/nyilei*
female speaking	*maun/hnamaun*	*maun/maungalei*
(eld)Si, (eld) female cousin[13]	*qama.*	*qama.*
(yng)Si, (yng) female cousin		
male speaking[14]	*hnama.*	*hnama.*
female speaking	*nyi-ma.*	*nyi-ma.*
son[15]	*tha:*	*tha:*
daughter	*thami*	*thami*
nephew, spouse's nephew	*tu*	*tu/tha:*
niece, spouse's niece	*tūma*	*tūma/thami*
Grandchild (and their classifica- tory siblings)	*myi:*	*myi:*
GrGrandchild (etc.)	*myi?*	*myi?*
GrGrGrandchild (etc.)	*ti*	—
GrGrGrGrandchild (etc.)	*htut*	—
parent-in-law[16]	*yaukkhama*	*qahpei,gamei*
Hu[17]	*yau kya:/lin*	*qakou/etc.*

CHART 1 Continued

Kin Type	Reference	Address
Wi[18]	mein:ma./maya:	mein:ma/mein:mayei
(eld)BrWi, Wi(eld)Si (male speaking)	ma.yi:	ama./etc.
(yng)BrWi, Wi(yng)Si (male speaking)	hke-ma.	hnama./etc.
(eld)SiHu, Hu(eld)Br (female[19] speaking)	hke:qou	qakou/etc.
(yng)SiHu, Hu(yng)Br (female[20] speaking)	ma'	maun/etc.
SiHu, WiBr (male speaking)	yau'hpa.	yau'hpa (SiHu addressing WiBr) personal name (WiBr addressing SiHu)
BrWi, HuSi (female speaking)	yau'ma.	ama./nyi-ma.
Parent-in-law of one's child[21]	hkami.hkame	personal name
SoWi	kywe:ma.	thami
DaHu	thame	tha:

1. Colloquial: "My grandmother's grandmother," etc.
2. Colloquial: "My mother's grandmother," etc.
3. Burling (1965) records bin and bi. for my bou: and bwa:
4. Rangoon informants, who say they also apply to Mandalay, use the following terms:

GrFa	qahpou:	qahpou:
GrMo	qahpwa:	qahpwa:
GrPa(eld)Br, GrPa(eld)SiHu[a]	qahpei-gyi:	qahpolei/hpolei
GrPa(yng)Br, GrPa(yng)SiHu[b]	qahpoulei:	hpolei
GrPa(eld)Si, GrPa(eld)BrWi	gamei-gyi:	hpwalei
GrPa(yng)Si, GrPa(yng)BrWi[c]	qahpwa:lei:	hpwalei

(a) Burling (1965), whose terms were collected in Rangoon, does not include the in-laws in this and the following three entries.
(b) Colloquially, both are qahpoulei; qahpei-gyi: is not used.
(c) Colloquially, both are qahpwa:lei; gamei-gyi: is not used.
5. Here, and in all other contexts, "Br" and "Si" include both siblings and cousins.
6. For Rangoon informants, ba.gyi: is used exclusively, although the ba.gyi:-qu:gyi: distinction is known.
7. For Rangoon informants, qu:lei: is used exclusively; the ba.dwei-qu:lei: distinction is not made.
8. For Rangoon informants, kyi:do is used exclusively; the qayi:gyi-kyi:do distinction is not made.
9. For Rangoon informants, qado is used exclusively; the qayi:-qado distinction is not made. Burling, however, records dolei for both.
10. A Rangoon informant, a native of Upper Burma, supplied a variant set of maternal uncle and aunt terms, possibly letal-formal, for Upper Burma.

Variant maternal uncle/aunt terms

Mo(eld)Br	wa.yi:gyi:
Mo(yng)Br	wa.yi:lei:
Mo(eld)Si	mi:gyi:
Mo(yng)Si	mi:dwei:

maternal relatives there are, correspondingly, no terminological differentiations. Thus, paternal and maternal grandparents both have the same terms, as do matrilateral and patrilateral cousins, and matrilateral and patrilateral nephews and nieces.

To be sure, jural norms do not necessarily determine personal sentiment, and the fact that kinship distance is the same for both maternal and paternal kin at the cultural level does not mean that it is the same at the social and psychological levels. In fact, at the latter levels they are not equally close, for the Burmese say that they *feel* closer to their maternal kinsmen, and this feeling has certain social consequences, as we shall see in a later chapter.

I have already indicated that in terms of their collective behavior there is one difference between the maternal and paternal stocks, and this relates to the spirit cults, which we must now examine briefly. Among the various spirits *(nat)* propitiated by the Burmese, there is a category of hereditary spirits whose propitiation, unlike all the others, is mandatory, at pain of supernatural punishment. Their inheritance is determined by descent; all persons in a particular descent group make offerings to the same hereditary spirit. Although they are known as "mother's side-father's side" spirits *(mizain-hpazain nat)*, the hereditary principle is unilateral and specifically patrilineal, rather than bilateral. (See Spiro [1967:97-103] for a full discussion.) This means that although the stock itself is cognatic, its hereditary spirit is inherited (by males and females

---

11. Informants say that the royal term *naun-do-gyi:* is used among some commoners even today in Mandalay.

12. Uterine siblings are distinguished from cousins by adding *ayin* (true, genuine) in the former case and *wungwe* (of a different womb) in the latter. First, second, and third cousins are differentiated by specifying the number of wombs by which they are removed.

13. Eldest, middle, and youngest of the elder siblings are differentiated by the suffixes *gyi:, lat,* and *lei:/nge:,* respectively.

14. Burling does not distinguish sex of speaker. In both cases his term is *nyi-ma.*.

15. Relative age for both son and daughter is distinguished in the manner indicated in footnote 13.

16. When it is necessary, Fa-in-law and Mo-in-law can be distinguished by adding *yau kya:thu* and *mein:ma.thu* (literary) or *qahti:* and *qama.* (colloquial) respectively to the generic term. Alternatively, the Mo-in-law term becomes *kaukhama.* Burling distinguishes them by recording *yaukkhama qahpou:* as the Fa-in-law term. In early middle age the terms of address ("father" and "mother") are dropped in favor of personal names (plus the normal honorific).

17. The legal term is *hkin-bun:*.

18. The legal term is *zani:.* Spouses frequently address each other by personal names (plus the normal honorific).

19. Sometimes *hke:quo* is used to designate (eld)SiHu only, Hu(eld)Br being designated as *hke:qougyi:*.

20. Burling records *hke:qou.*

21. Male and female can be distinguished by adding *qahti:* and *qama.* respectively.

alike) only from and through males. In short, although the stock is a *bilateral descent* group, its agnatically related members comprise a *patrilineal cult* group. On the local level, this group, together with other agnatic groups who have the same hereditary spirit, make periodic offerings to their spirit, either collectively, or through a delegated representative. It need only be added that, unlike the cognatic stock, the unilineal cult group is, of course, much more than three generations in depth. Indeed, each of the local cult groups can be viewed as a minimal (cult) lineage, a true segment of a maximal (cult) lineage whose members are spread throughout the entire country.

This patrilineal principle may rest on the traditional distinction between the two kinds of substance that make up heredity, "bone" *(ayou)* and "blood" *(thwei)*. Traditionally, as Lehman has observed (personal communication), bone counts over blood and it is this consideration that might account for the (cult) lineage being patrilineal. This is consistent, too, with the weak agnatic bias that Lehman finds in his analysis of the system of categories.

The Kindred (*Hsweimyou Thagyin*)

The Core Kindred (*Nide Hsweimyou*)

Every sibling group, as we have seen, is born into two separate stocks. In addition, every sibling group is a member of a stock formed by their own parents. Finally, each ego in the sibling group, together with his wife, forms his own stock. Each ego, in short, belongs to, and is related to all the members of, each of these four stocks. But although ego is related to all of them, they, in turn, are not all related to each other. Rather than constituting separate segments of a larger descent group, each stock is an independent descent group. Nevertheless, since ego has membership in all four stocks, for *him* they do constitute one large kinship group—not, to be sure, a descent group, but nonetheless a kinship group—for although not all of them are related to each other, they are all related to him. This ego-oriented kinship circle—"circle," perhaps, is preferable to "group"—is itself part of a much larger circle of kinsmen that the Burmese call *hsweimyou* (or *hsweimyou thagyin*), and anthropologists call a personal kindred—that is, a kinship group that is recruited "on the basis of the degree of relationship of its members to a common ego rather than a common ancestor" (Fox 1967:164). The ego-orientation of the *hsweimyou*, in contrast to the ancestor-orientation of the *mitha su*, is emphasized by the very term itself. We have already noted that, according to some villagers, *myou* (in *hsweimyou*) is taken as an ellipsis for *myousei* (semen), so that when the kinship field is viewed as two descent groups which overlap in ego, the latter is related to relatives in both by descent from a common ancestor in each. According to other villagers, however, *myou* is best glossed as "to branch out, as from one source," much as the boughs of a tree that branch off from its trunk. Hence, when the kinship field is viewed as a network of ego-centered kindreds, each ego is the source —like the apex of an inverted triangle—from which a segment of the kinship field radiates bilaterally and symmetrically.

Folk etymology aside, and whatever its external boundaries may be, the kindred consists of distantly, as well as closely, related cognates. For the Burmese, the cognates in the kinship circle comprising ego's four stocks constitute his closely related, or (as they call them) his "near" kindred (*nide hsweimyou*). Their relationships are depicted in Diagram 3.

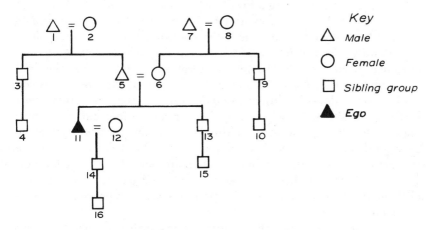

Diagram 3. The core kindred (*nide hsweimyou*).

In Diagram 3, figures 1, 2, 3, 4, 5, 11, 13 comprise ego's paternal stock. Figures 6, 7, 8, 9, 10, 11, 13 comprise his maternal stock. Figures 5, 6, 11, 13, 14, 15 comprise his parental stock. Figures 11, 12, 14, 16 comprise his and his wife's stock. Together they comprise his *nide hsweimyou* or—as I shall call them—his core kindred. In other words, in addition to the members of his nuclear families—parents (5,6), siblings (13) and children (14)—and stocks—grandparents (1, 2, 7, 8) and grandchildren (16)—the core kindred consists of ego's maternal and paternal uncles and aunts (3, 9), cousins (4, 10), and nephews and nieces (15).

As in the case of the stock, the core kindred remains relatively constant in size because of the system by which successive generations drop the collaterals of each previous generation. Thus, for example, figures 3 and 4 in Diagram 3—ego's father's siblings and his father's sibling's children —are part of ego's core kindred, but not of his children's. Since for the latter (figure 14), these collaterals are not once but twice removed—for them they are father's father's siblings and siblings' children—they are extended (rather than core) kindred. The same is true of the other members of ego's own core kindred. The system, then, works rather simply. For each ego, the collaterals of the stocks into which he is born are dropped during his own life cycle, and become, instead, his core kindred. For each sibling group, the collaterals of the core kindred of each of their parents are dropped and become, instead, their extended kindred. Viewed in this light, the relationship between stock and kindred becomes clearer. The stock may be seen as cross-cutting the kindred, so to speak, rather than being a lower-order component of it.

Since, as we have seen, every ego (or, more properly, every sibling group) has a unique kindred, the latter—unlike the stock—has no collective identity, nor can it in any sense be a corporate group. As I have already explained, and as Diagram 3 indicates, one third of ego's kindred (those on his paternal side) are not at all related to another third (those on his maternal side)—the former are *qahpei hsweimyou*, the latter *qamei hsweimyou*—although each is related separately to the remaining third (ego and his siblings and their children). It is because of this interlocking network that ego's full core kindred is a periodically visible group despite the fact that two-thirds of its membership are not related to each other. For since they are all closely (and equally) related to ego, they are all invited when, for example, he performs some important life cycle ceremony.

Notice, however, that when ego performs such a ceremony for his children, rather than for himself, the assembled group is doubled, for then his spouse's kindred—who are equally close to his children—are also invited. Nevertheless, although both kindreds are periodically joined physically, they are conceptually distinguished. For the husband, the wife's kindred are *meinma hsweimyou* (wife's kindred); for the wife the husband's kindred are *yau'kya hsweimyou* (husband's kindred). In short, most of the kindred of his closest affine—his spouse—are no more members of ego's core kindred than are the kindred of his consanguines' affines. This cannot be said, however, of those whom we might term his "core affines," namely, the parents and siblings of his spouse, the spouses of his siblings, and the spouses of his children and their parents. Both because of their quasi-kinship tie, which we noted above, and because of the special norms which govern their interaction, they share, in part, in both the "substance" and "code" of biological kinsmen. In short, those affines that are members of his spouse's, his siblings', and his children's families are also members of ego's core kindred.

If, then, primary consanguines are members of the family and the stock, and if secondary consanguines are members of the stock and the core kindred, these core affines are members of the core kindred (but not of the family or the stock).

The Extended Kindred (Weide Hsweimyou)

The core kindred, or "near relatives" (nide hsweimyou), are distinguished by the Burmese from remote, or "far relatives" (weide hsweimyou).[4] They are thought of as related to each other, much as two concentric circles, each with its own set of normative requirements. The differentiation of core from extended kindred—as I shall call these more distant kinsmen—is physically evident to even a casual observer when the entire kindred assembles for a celebration or commemoration. At weddings, for example, the extended kindred both of the bride and the groom are invited to the reception, but only their core kindred are invited to the wedding ceremony. Again, at various religious celebrations, the core kindred are invited to the meal which accompanies the ceremony, while the extended kindred are served only tea and cakes following the meal.

Although the distinction between nuclear and extended kindred is physically evident and, as we shall see, conceptually and socially relevant, the boundary which separates them is very hard to draw in fact, although it is easy in principle. If the core kindred, as we have seen, includes the primary relatives of ego's primary relatives—his maternal and paternal grandparents, uncles, aunts, and cousins, as well as his nephews, nieces, and grandchildren—then the extended kindred includes at least the primary relatives of the core kindred—the maternal and paternal grandparents, uncles, aunts, and cousins of ego's parents, as well as the nephews, nieces, and grandchildren of ego's children. Although this is a perfectly sound and clearly distinguishable genealogical boundary, it is nevertheless not entirely consistent with the boundary—or boundaries—which the Burmese themselves, or at least Burmese villagers, demarcate. The reason is simple. A genealogical principle alone fails to take account of the strong blurring of the distinction between nuclear and extended kindred produced by the interaction of cognatic descent and village endogamy. Let us see.

---

4. They are also variously designated as hsweimyou qayin qacha (alternatively, hsweimyou yincha) and hsweimi myousa, respectively.

In Yeigyi, at least, 80 percent of the married adults are natives of the village. Even more important for our present purposes is that in 82 percent of all marriages both spouses are natives of Yeigyi, and in only 18 percent is only one of the spouses a native. When such a high incidence of village endogamy[5] is combined, as it is in Burma, with a bilateral kinship system, the result is a complicated network of cross-cutting kin ties, so complicated that sometimes villagers themselves cannot specify the links by which they are related to particular kinsmen even when they designate them by a specific kin term. For example, although Ma Thein Khin calls Daw Kyi, *kyido* (Mo [eld] Si/Fa [eld] BrWi), she could not trace the genealogical ties which make this the appropriate term. Similarly, Daw Myan vaguely knows that she is related to Kou Swe, but she did not know what the relationship is, even though, as in the previous example, he calls her *kyido*.

These cross-cutting kin ties have the further consequence, as I have contended, of blurring the distinction between close and remote kin because a remote tie traced through one part of the network may be a close tie through another. Consider, for example, the following slice of an actual kin network in Yeigyi. (To facilitate understanding, alphabetic symbols are substituted for Burmese proper names.)

Mr. *A* is related to Mr. *B* because *A*'s father and *B*'s wife are classificatory siblings. Hence, Mrs. *C* is related to both because she is the niece of Mr. *B*'s wife. But Mrs. *C* is also related to Mr. *D* (who is also related to Mr. *A* and *B*) not only because Mr. *A*'s mother is Mr. *D*'s (classificatory) sister, but also because her brother-in-law is Mr. *D*'s (classificatory) brother. All of the above relatives, in turn, are related to Mr. *E* because his grandmother is the sister of Mr. *D*'s grandmother. But now it gets even more complicated. Since Mrs. *C*'s father is the (classificatory) brother of Mr. *D*'s wife, and since the latter's paternal grandfather is also the grandfather of two village monks, it follows that Mrs. *C*, like the others mentioned above, is also related to these monks. But the monks' mother . . . and so on in a continuously widening network!

If, then, such cross-cutting kinship networks often make it difficult to differentiate close from remote kinsmen, this conceptual distinction often

5. Village endogamy is reported elsewhere in Burma, Nash (1965:70) reporting an endogamy rate of 93 percent for a village in Upper Burma. The picture in Thailand is mixed. Tambiah (1970:15) reports an almost equally high rate for a village in the Northeast, but the obverse has been reported for the Central Plains where, according to Piker (n.d.: Ch. 2, p. 3) more than half of the married males in the region he studied have married exogamously. Indeed, in this region marriage rules prohibit matrimony between persons for whom a genealogical connection can be "specified exactly," although they sometimes do occur. The absolute cutoff point, according to Piker, is second cousinhood.

becomes socially useless precisely when it would be most useful—to help decide, for example, between conflicting loyalties. Consider the following divorce dispute which took place while I was in Yeigyi. The wife, who initiated the divorce, is the niece of U Lum Byei's sister. But U Lum Byei, an important man in the village, is also the son-in-law of Daw Kyi, the mother-in-law (by a second marriage) of the accused husband's mother. Who, then, was U Lum Byei to support—the husband or the wife—when both sides asked him to intercede on their behalf? Whatever the basis for his decision—and he finally decided to support the wife—it could not be, and it was not, based on considerations of genealogical distance.

Since, then, the distinction between core and extended kin is often difficult to make on the basis of genealogical relationships alone, the distinguishing criteria are often particularistic. In short, the basis for inclusion of a particular kinsman in one or the other groups is to no small extent optative. Moreover, this may be the case even when the genealogical relationships are unambiguous, so that a genealogically close kinsman may sometimes be classified with one's extended kindred, and a genealogically remote kinsman may sometimes be included in one's nuclear kindred and sometimes dropped altogether. As one shrewd villager put it, "Whomever you like [within the recognized bonds of kinship] is your *hsweimyou*." Thus, for example, my landlady included the distantly related, but highly prestigeful, village headman among her nuclear kindred, while neglecting to include a more closely related kinsman who happened to be poor and non-prestigious.

Even in this kind of system, however, one cannot create a kinship bond out of whole cloth; one can only decide whether an existent bond should be permitted to die or whether it should be continued—and, if the latter, whether it should be viewed as close or remote. In either event, these decisions, as we have seen, are determined by considerations of personal benefit. Relationships with kindred that are useful—economically, politically, and so on—persist because they are continuously activated. Those that are not useful, and therefore not activated, are soon dissolved.

On the basis of observations made in another Burmese village, Nash (1965:59) arrived at the identical conclusion.

A person has the option of building a structure of reciprocity between himself and a kinsman or the alternative of ignoring the relationship. If the genealogical relationship is not cultivated between kinsmen, it is no different than a relationship between neighbors, covillagers, and casual friends. Without special cultivation, a man will expect and receive no more from a kinsman than he would from a neighbor or fellow villager.

To put the Burmese situation in proper perspective, it is important to emphasize that this optative dimension of the Burmese system is hardly unique to Burma. It is found in most cognatic systems in which, in the absence of well-bounded unilineal descent groups, the opportunity for manipulating a genealogical map is readily available. Where, as in Central Thailand, village endogamy—the other putative determinant of the Burmese situation—is also present, the construction of the kindred is exactly as it is in Burma, as Piker (n.d., ch. 2:3-4) indicates. "Although ties to minimal kin units (usually households) are generally more binding and enduring than any other social relationships undertaken by the individual, villagers feel they may be dissolved—temporarily or permanently—if expediency so dictates." Tambiah (1970:17) echoes these remarks in his comments concerning Northern Thailand: "Close kin are naturally more important than more distant kin, but which of the close kin (outside the nuclear family) depends on situational circumstances and not on jural norms."

But this optative aspect of kinship is found not only in Burma and the other so called "loosely structured" societies of Southeast Asia; it is present in the much more structured society of India as well. According to a Gujarati saying, "a useless brother is a stranger" which, according to Mandelbaum (1970:153), means that "even the brother bond is subject to differing interpretation and that a kinship relationship is valid only to the extent that it is activated." Later, summarizing the work of A. Mayer, Mandelbaum writes that many villagers consider that "kinship is defined more by social interchange than by remembered connections through descent or marriage." (*Ibid.*:154.)

It may be concluded, then, to return to Burma, that the distinction between core and extended kindred is often optative, being determined as much by psychological and situational, as by genealogical, criteria. This is one (but not the only) reason that knowledge of the jural norms related to each kintype, or of the manner in which the terminological system differentiates some kintypes and lumps together others, is not sufficient to predict behavior within the kindred. Except for a few highly specific patterns, such as the levirate or the sororate, differences in interaction within the kindred depend less on the formal attributes, jural or terminological, of the kintypes than on the affective and structural relationships that obtain between the kinsmen that embody these types. Thus, it is all but impossible to predict from these formal attributes alone whether it will be a brother or a cousin, a mother's brother or a sister's daughter, a younger aunt or an elder nephew, that in any specific situation will come to a particular actor's assistance. The system, as they say, is loosely structured, as it is almost everywhere in Southeast Asia. As Nash (1965:64), from his independent studies in Upper Burma, has observed: "One hardly ever finds the same range of kinsmen assembled as one moves from activity to activity or from kindred to kindred. . . . The personal and particular circumstances of each person determine what part of his kindred he will use, and for what ends kinsmen will invoke their particular bond."

If, nevertheless, I now propose to examine the jural and other formal dimensions of kinship it is because, first, they do comprise one of the determinants of action, and second, because an analysis of the discrepancies, when they occur, between the normative and actual dimensions of kinship interaction tells us a great deal about Burmese society and personality.

4. Cultural Norms of Kinship Relations

A kinship system is much more than a conceptual and classificatory system. To be sure, kintypes are classified in certain ways and the kinship field is partitioned in a certain manner, but any classification and categorization, whether at the individual or the cultural levels, are always means to some other end—if only (to take the most trivial example) the anxiety-binding end of the category system of an obsessive compulsive neurosis. Hence, although kinship classification, like all other classifications, is in the first instance a system of thought, it is not (as some structuralists seem to believe) merely that. If all classifications are means to, and in the service of, some type of "work," then the "work" of Burmese kinship classification—and, I would contend, all other kinship classifications—is, as I have already indicated, moral "work." If kinsmen are classified in certain ways, it is because they are believed to stand to each other in certain relationships, and in the Burmese kinship system these relationships, as we have seen, entail (among other things) moral obligations.

But every moral obligation, every duty, implies its converse. To say that A has a moral obligation to help B is also to say that B has a right to receive help from A. Every duty, in short, has its reciprocal right, and vice versa. Since the kinship system is a cultural system, the rights and duties of kinship are cultural, that is, they are defined by jural norms. As in the case of American kinship, we can say that Burmese kinship includes what Schneider (1968:52) has termed, a "substance" element—in both systems, the substance is shared biology—and a "code for conduct" element. Although this "code" is derived from jural norms, these norms, as we saw in the last chapter, are not uniformly distributed over the entire kinship field. Rather, their distribution takes the form of a moral gradient, beginning from the nuclear family as its core and radiating by progressive attenuation to the extended kindred at its periphery. This being the case, any systematic discussion of these kinship norms must deal separately with the kinsmen comprising the nuclear family, the core kindred, and the extended kindred, respectively.

The Nuclear Family (*Mitha Su*)

Parents and Children (*Miba-Thathami*)

The parent-child bond is unique in Burmese kinship. In it, and in it alone, are the obligations of kinship expected to be honored categorically. In it, and in it alone, the expression that I so frequently heard in the village, "Kinship is kinship, and business is business"—economic gain supersedes kinship obligations—does not hold. If you can't rely on the relationship created by this bond, you can rely on no other.

The uniqueness of the parent-child dyad is expressed in a variety of cultural symbols and forms. Thus, for example, while terms for some other close kinsmen—great-grandparent, uncle, aunt, brother, and sister—are used as honorifics in addressing non-kinsmen, the terms for parents and children are unique in that they are not and cannot be used in this way. Similarly, while all other consanguineal kin terms are "classificatory," the terms for parent and child are "descriptive," at least as terms of reference. Thus, sometimes a sibling's child may be addressed as "son" or "daughter," or (less frequently) a parent's sibling as "father" or "mother," but they are never used in that fashion in reference. In short, terms for parents and children are unique in that they never designate, nor can they be used to designate, anyone else.

The uniqueness of the parent-child relationship is found again in the configuration of rights and duties that characterize it. Since parents, as we shall see, are held to be sacred, these rights and duties are not always symmetrical. Thus, while it is the parent's right to receive, it is the child's duty to give, honor, and respect. These sentiments are expressed not only in the usual ways in which—as described in a later chapter—inferiors show deference to superiors, but they are displayed in the custom of physical prostration (*shihkou*), a form of ritualized deference, or "worship"—because, together with the Buddha, His Teaching, His monastic order, and one's teachers, one's parents are one of "Five Objects of Worship." Beginning in early childhood, when children prostrate themselves before their parents upon returning from school, worship of parents continues throughout life. As adults, this ritual is performed most elaborately three times a year—on the days before the Festival of Lights, New Year, and Lent—in (what is known as) the *gado* ("to beg pardon") ceremony. On these days, children bring presents of food to their parents,[1] present them with cool water (symbolic of their desire that their relationship be "cool" or peaceful), and, prostrating themselves before them, beg their forgiveness for whatever offenses they might have committed, and then ask for their blessing. In response to this request, the parent intones the following formula: "May you have long life, beauty, pleasantness, and energy." He may also add: "May you be wealthy, and well, and may you live, together with your family, to an old age, and may all demerit acquired from wrongs committed against your elders be wiped out by this act of merit."

Since children are obliged to respect their parents, it comes as no surprise to learn that to insult, abuse, or disobey them is considered a heinous act. Indeed, contemporary Burmese belief, like seventeenth-century Christian belief (Laslett 1971:178), holds that a child who commits such an act will be punished by a short life.

Other aspects, however, of the parent-child relationship are more symmetrical. In times of trouble, for example, parents are expected to come to the assistance of their children, and children to their parents, and this expectation is almost never violated. Thus, when Daw Tin required immediate funds for a lawsuit, she encountered considerable difficulties in obtaining them. Since, as a non-native, she had married into the village, the villagers felt little responsibility to assist her. Since her husband, moreover, had become a monk and was technically no longer married to her, his relatives felt no obligation to help her. She could have asked her relatives in her natal village for help, but since they had not offered voluntarily, she would not do so. On the other hand, her parents and her (married) daughter came to her immediate assistance, giving her money of their own, and raising additional funds through loans.

Financial assistance is but one kind of aid. There are others. If, for whatever reason, a person cannot care for himself, his children or his parents are expected to take care of him and, if necessary, take him into their home.[2] And these normative expectations are honored. Although (as we shall see in the following chapter) parents and adult children prefer typically not to live with each other, there is, nevertheless, no hesitancy about inviting a widowed child or a widowed parent to live in one's home. (The hesitation, if there is any, comes not from the potential host, but, as

1. This ritual is performed, however, for all elder kinsmen—uncles, aunts, grandparents, and so on—and, in theory, it should be performed for any elder in the village or in one's neighborhood.

2. For aged parents there used to be a formal ceremony known as *nobo-sat*, in which children formally invite their parents to be in their charge for the remainder of their lives, just as they, as children, had been in their parents' charge. Reported by the Ferrars (1900:192), no contemporary informants, however, have heard of it.

we shall see, from the potential guest.) In Yeigyi, for example, our household census reveals that, *without exception*, widows or widowers who cannot or will not live alone, live in the home of either a parent or a child. Again, if a young child requires a home, either because of the death or divorce of his parents, it is the latter's parents who, *without exception*, undertake this obligation.

The uniqueness of the parent-child bond, and of the rights and duties that characterize it, is indicated by, and institutionalized in, customary inheritance laws. On the death of a parent, the latter's spouse inherits his property, but after the demise of the surviving parent, the children, and they alone, inherit the parental estate. As long as any children are alive, no other kinsman has any rights in it. This is not only the norm, but, as the data on land inheritance in Yeigyi show, in that village, at least, it is scrupulously followed (Table 11). Of the seventy-three landowning households in Yeigyi, twenty-five acquired at least part of their holdings through inheritance, five as a gift. (The others acquired their land by purchase and nationalization.) The gifts, however, can also be viewed as (what might be termed) anticipatory inheritance since they are accounted as part of the inheritance of the recipients when the estate is eventually divided. It will be seen, then, that except for bequests of land to a spouse—which is ultimately inherited by the children—all inherited land is inherited by children and bequeathed by parents.

TABLE 11. *Land Bequests*

Recipient	Gift of		Bequeathed by		Total
	Parent	Parent	Spouse	Unknown[a]	
Son	1	11	0	1	13
Daughter	4	7	0	1	12
Spouse	0	0	5	0	5
Totals	5	18	5	2	30

[a]This means that the data are missing, not that the recipient does not know whether the land was received from parent or spouse.

The same generalization, as Table 12 indicates, holds for the inheritance of houses. Of a total of seventy-five cases of house ownership in Yeigyi, in ten, the house was acquired by inheritance, and in six by gift (the others were built or purchased); and in all these cases the transactions were between parents and children exclusively.

The jural importance of the parent-child tie is seen most clearly in the rules governing inheritance in the event that a widow or widower

TABLE 12. *House Bequests*

Recipient	Gift of Parent	Bequeathed by Parent	Total
Son	4	1	5
Daughter	2	9	11
Totals	6	10	16

remarries. Should the widow remarry, the property she had inherited from her deceased husband is divided in equal parts among their children. Should the widower remarry, half the property he had inherited from his wife is divided in equal parts among their children, while the remaining half is held in reserve for those he might beget in his second marriage. In neither case does the parent bring the inherited property to his new marriage to become (as it ordinarily would) his and his spouse's joint property.

In short, and with the sole exception of bequests to pagodas and monasteries, a person's ultimate heirs are his children. Should he have more than one child, the property is divided in equal shares among them. These rules of equal inheritance cannot be circumvented by means of a will since the Burmese do not recognize the validity of a will. Hence, if, as Tables 11 and 12 indicate, sons are more likely to be given, and daughters bequeathed, houses, with the reverse being true in the case of land, it should not be assumed that these differences are discriminatory; rather, they are based on expected sex differences in the domestic and life cycles. Since youngest daughters, as we shall see, tend to remain with their parents even after they marry, their share of the land is often given to them while the parents are still alive, the sons and other daughters inheriting after the parents' death. That daughters acquire the parental house, either through gift or inheritance, much more frequently than sons is explained by the same fact: in compensation for caring for their parents, the house also is bequeathed to the youngest daughter.[3] These rules are so firmly accepted (according to the village headman) that there has never been any litigation in Yeigyi involving sibling conflict over property inheritance.

In the village, the reciprocal of property descending to children occurs

3. Similar rules of inheritance are found in Central Thailand, as Mentzer (1972:88) indicates: "The most frequently expressed opinion about distribution of property is that land and money should be divided equally among all children, and the house should belong to the youngest child who stays with and cares for elderly parents. However, there is a recognition that parents often do not make this choice, but rather give most or all property to the child who treats them best and, therefore, whom they love the most."

in the case of childless couples, that is, their parents become their heirs. Similarly, if a widow or widower and their children move in with parents, the parents become their heirs upon their death. The principle here is the reciprocal of that which provides for the inheritance of the parental estate by the youngest child: since the parents take care of the child, they are entitled to his property. In fact, however, this latter procedure, regardless of the principle on which it is based, is in violation of Burmese customary (and now codified) law. For, in law, property must always descend, never ascend, in accordance with the principle that "the waters of a stream flow down, they never flow up" (*qauk kou tha sounde/quahtet kou masounbu*). Legally, then, the property of childless couples should be inherited by their siblings or their nephews and nieces, and the property of widows and widowers, even when they live with their parents, by their children.

Although villagers usually comply with the cultural norms which define the rights and duties of parents and children, it would be false to suggest that they always do so. Either because of their ambivalence (to be described in the next chapter) or because of self-interest, they sometimes neglect to carry out their parental or filial obligations. Hence, although the following examples are by no means typical, to ignore them would result in an exaggerated picture of the extent to which cultural norms determine parent-child behavior.

Daw Kyi is the wealthiest woman in Yeigyi. Rather than wishing to leave her property to her children, she has given it to the village monastery, thereby hoping to enhance her karma and improve her rebirth. Her children, she explained, "will have to fend for themselves. I have to be concerned about my future birth. My major aim is the acquisition of merit for myself. What happens to them [her children] is their problem."

In an obverse case, the parents of U Kant had bequeathed him ten acres of paddy land on the understanding that he would use the income to construct a monastery in their name. Instead of complying with their request, he has used the income for his own needs. Although U Kant did not tell me of this incident, and therefore I could not query him about it, other villagers commented that he will always be bothered "in his mind" because of his disobedience, for he will surely be punished for it in his next existence. Others observed that his life would be shortened because of it.

Again, when the widower, U Sein, asked me to lend him money to repay his debts, I asked him, out of curiosity, why he had not asked his daughter. He laughed, bitterly, saying she would give him nothing.

More extreme is the case of Maung Bo Shi. Five years in the army, he never once returned to the village to visit his elderly parents, nor, despite their poverty, did he send them any money during the entire period. Understandably, his parents' resentment was very strong.

If these examples (together with the parent-child tensions discussed in the following chapter) caution us neither to romanticize the parent-child bond, nor to confuse cultural norms with social relationships, they should not, on the other hand, obscure the fact that normatively and behaviorally it is the strongest of all kinship bonds. Very few villagers complained about maltreatment on the part of their parents, and fewer yet would characterize their children as invidiously as Thai parents (from a village in central Thailand) characterized theirs. Few children, they claimed (Mentzer 1972:101-102), reciprocated their parents' love and concern:

Parents *must* rear children, but when children are grown they leave their parents behind. A mother always pities her children. But children try to shift the responsibility for parents from one to another. . . . As long as parents have property, the children will be attentive and helpful, but when property is gone, children pay no more attention to them. And if children inherit no property from parents, they simply would not help them.

Burmese parents are not only the child's most important kinsmen, but they are the fulcrum for the rest of the kinship system. It is the bond with his parents that forges the child's bonds with other kinsmen, that recruits him to membership in his stocks, and that creates for him a network of bilateral kindred. On a cognitive level, it might be said that to some extent at least the very design, as well as the use, of the kinship terminology compels the child to perceive his kinship field through his parents' eyes.

So far as its design is concerned, I have already pointed out, to offer but one example, that the differentiation of matrilateral from patrilateral *parental* siblings is replicated at the next generation by the differentiation of matrilateral from patrilateral *grandparental* siblings. This means that the child is compelled to cognitively parse a kinship sub-field in the same manner as his parents, for, of course, his grandparents' siblings are his parents' parental siblings. Although the terms which the child uses are different from those used by his parents, they designate the same semantic kinship space, and they slice it up in exactly the same way. More directly, however, the use of kin terms in address may even result in the child's using the same terms as his parents. Thus, for example, ego's MoMoSi, who is his grandmother and his mother's aunt, is ego's *ameigyi* and his mother's *kyido*. Frequently, however, ego addresses her not as *ameigyi*, but as *kyido*, using the kin term that his mother uses.

Returning to the parent as kinsman, rather than as a link to other kinsmen, I have already said that the parent-child bond is the strongest of all kinship bonds. It must now be added, however, that its strength varies according to the various dyads—father-son, father-daughter, mother-son, mother-daughter—that comprise it. This being the case, we must now shift our attention to these dyads. Again, however, the focus at this time will be on the cultural norms and expectations which govern these dyadic relationships, rather than on their expression (or non-expression) in behavior.

For both parents, the attachment (*thanyozin*) to the daughter is held to be stronger than to the son, a belief which parents generally explain by reference to the daughter's greater attention to them as they grow older. Daughters, they point out, often cook for them, care for them when they are ill, do their washing, and so on. Regardless of sentiment, this greater attention on the part of the daughter is culturally constrained by the sexual division of labor, on the one hand (the above tasks being female specialties), and by prescriptive institutional arrangements on the other. The latter arrangements, moreover, not only determine certain forms of parent-daughter interaction, but they themselves are institutionalized expressions of the cultural conception of, and the normative emphasis on, the strength of the parent-daughter bond. Since these institutions will be described in detail elsewhere, I shall only outline them here.

There is the custom, for example, of newlyweds residing postnuptially, for a smaller or larger period, with the bride's parents. There is also the custom of the youngest married daughter living permanently with her parents and caring for them until they die. Sentimental ties aside, there are therefore more households of parents and married daughters than of parents and married sons. The same pattern is found in the other societies of Southeast Asia as well. (See Tambiah [1970:12] and Piker [n.d.:5] for Thailand, and Geertz [1961:45] and Jay [1969:68] for Java.)[4] In addition, in inter-village marriages, it was the custom in the past—one which today, however is no longer observed—for the husband to move to the wife's village (Furnival 1911:24).[5] Finally, when a villager (the custom is

4. In Thai villages, to take only one example, there is a strong tendency for married daughters to set up house in their parents' compound. Hence, although the marriage is neo-local with respect to the parents' home, it is matrilocal with respect to the compound. Looked at from the latter perspective, the Thai nuclear family might be said to be embodied in a matrilocal joint family (compound). Moreover, while in Burma, property (as we have seen) devolves equally on sons and daughters, in Thailand it is inherited primarily by the sisters (and their husbands) who live in the matrilocal compound, while their brothers acquire property through their wives from the estate of the wives' parents. This, at least, is how it is described by Piker (n.d., ch. 2:4) and Tambiah (1970:12) for the Central Plains and the Northeast, respectively. In yet another Central Plains village (Sharp 1953:82-83), however, the situation is similar to what I have reported for Burma.

5. Of the seventeen cases of inter-village marriages found in Yeigyi, the wife is from the outside in eleven, the husband in six. In short, in most of these cases residence is virilocal.

not found in the city) is very sick and thought to be dying, he often requests to be moved to his daughter's house to spend his last few days or hours on earth.

If these various institutionalized arrangements symbolize the greater strength of the parent-daughter bond, the following folk saying articulates it directly. "When children marry," the Burmese say, "one loses a son, but one does not lose a daughter."

Despite these cultural conceptions of, and parental expectations concerning, the daughter, it should be noted in passing that parents claim that sons are preferable to daughters. In the first place, sons bring them merit. For sponsoring their son's Buddhist initiation (a ceremony almost every boy undergoes) and monastic ordination (which many men undergo if for only a short time) parents acquire much merit. There is, in addition to this religious advantage, a more mundane reason for preferring sons. The latter are easier to raise since there is much less concern about leaving them alone or supervising them. Daughters are believed to be in constant danger of being seduced or sexually compromised, and since a daughter's sexual purity is a persistent concern of her parents, she must be kept under rigid surveillance, a nuisance at best.

If the parents' relationship to the daughter is conceived to be closer than that to the son, the relationship of children of both sexes to the mother is thought to be more intimate than that to the father. From earliest childhood, the father is more remote than the mother, and since, normatively, he is the primary locus of authority, he often engenders a feeling of fear which sometimes persists into adulthood. Indeed, the father is characterized as the *ein-u-nat*, "the lord who lives in the front of the house." And in fact, to turn to actual behavior, his authority is often expressed in a painful fashion. Thus, although both parents may punish and even beat their young children, fathers do so more frequently and severely. On both accounts, teenagers still living at home will seldom go to father when they have a problem, or when they are in trouble, for his initial response is expected to take the form of criticism if not punishment. Often, they approach their mother, or an aunt or uncle, instead, and the latter will then broach the matter to the father for them. Sometimes the reluctance to approach the father is extreme, as in the case of the young man who, when he wished to marry his present wife, asked his older brother to speak to his father on his behalf. This, of course, is an extreme

---

This is most probably related to economic considerations, the groom's parents providing land as part of the dower. In Northeast Thailand, on the other hand, where land is inherited (primarily) by daughters, it is understandable that most inter-village marriages are uxorilocal (Tambiah 1970:15).

case, but even in the more typical cases the child's relationship to the father includes a greater degree of respect and deference than of intimacy and affection.

As I have already implied, however, these attitudes apply more to the son than to the daughter. The daughter, especially during latency, may spend much time with her father, going about with him almost as a companion. It is only when she enters puberty, and the strong Burmese incest taboo interferes with further expressions of affection and intimacy, that the father-daughter relationship becomes reserved.

If the father is viewed more as a figure of authority, one who must be treated with deference,[6] the mother is viewed more as a source of affection. The mother-child bond is conceived to be an intimate one, and the mother is the object of greater affection than the father. Consistent with the belief that the strength of a kinship tie varies with the strength of the biological tie, the Burmese attribute this conception of the mother-child bond, in part, to the early biological relationships that obtain between mother and child—the mother carries the fetus inside her body, and nourishes the baby from her breasts. The biological unity of mother and child, which is believed to be established through nursing, is exemplified in the following anecdote. When I told a mother I could not give her the medicine she requested for her nursing baby, because it was too potent for an infant, she said: "Never mind; I'll swallow the medicine, and he can drink it with my milk."

It is in partial exchange for her nurturance that, in the Buddhist initiation, the son "worships" his mother before his father, and that the merit he acquires from becoming a novice is transferred to the mother. Even then, say the Burmese, this merit does not compensate her for the milk he imbibed from even one breast. It is for this same reason, they also say, that the Buddha preached his first sermon in heaven to his mother. Interestingly, the Chinese and Hindus attribute the special relationship and duty of the son to the mother to the same biological factors. In the Chinese view, the mother's hold over her son is due to "the great physical debt the son owes his mother who carried him, gave birth to him, and nursed him." (Hsu 1963:29). And according to at least one classical Hindu source, in her relationship to the son, the mother is one thousand times more venerable than the father (who in turn is one hundred times more

6. This deference is even greater among the Shans of Burma. "A girl or woman must dust the father's seat with respect. Shans are most particular that no stranger, or wife or child, should ever sit in the father's place. It may be a chair, it may be a bamboo seat, it may be only a mat on the floor: however humble it is, it must be treated with veneration, and the girl or woman who dusts it should do so with her body politely bent; she must not stand upright until the sweeping of the sacred place is finished." (Milne 1910:42.)

venerable than teacher) because the mother "bears him in her womb and rears him up." (*Ibid.*)

For the Burmese there is yet another, but related, biological reason for the strength of the child's obligation to, if not affection for, the mother. Childbirth, according to traditional notions, is a drain on a woman's health and vitality, and it thereby hastens her death. Since, then, as the proverb has it, "with each pregnancy, a woman progresses three times daily to the grave," a child's gratitude to his mother can hardly be minimized.

The mother-child bond is not only conceived to be stronger than the father-child bond, but, if cultural expressions are to be taken seriously, the mother may be said to be viewed as the pivotal person in the family. We have already noted, for example, that the term for the nuclear family and the cognatic stock, *mitha su*, means the "mother-child group." Similarly, the Burmese term for parent is *miba*, "mother-father," the prior designation of mother being a symbolic indication, villagers contend, of her primary influence on the children. This notion finds expression, too, in a proverb. "If the son commits evil, the mother [not the father] is to blame." (*The Lokaniti*, p. 285). Because of her greater importance to the child, it is also believed, as we shall see, that a child should not be deprived of his mother. Hence, in the case of divorce, children (with rare exceptions) are given to the mother, not the father.

Although the tie to the mother is held to be an especially close one for children of both sexes, its behavioral expression is particularly evident in the mother-daughter relationship. Even when they live in separate households, mothers and daughters are constantly visiting each other, daughters go to their mothers above all others with their problems, mothers and daughters are close confidants, mothers take care of daughters' children, and so on.[7] To care for her daughters' children is the mother's responsibility, but the care of her son's children, as one woman put it, is the responsibility of his wife or her mother.

In short, the mother-daughter bond, as Nash (1965:51) says, is the "keystone" of the Burmese family:

The notion of keystone is a simple architectural analogy. It refers to a social relationship which supports others. Without it, the whole edifice collapses. . . . In the village family the mother-daughter bond may be considered the keystone relationship. Marriage does little to attenuate it, and it serves as the chief linkage between households.

It is precisely because of the strength of the mother-child relationship

7. It is of interest to note that in other societies, as widely distributed as Java (Geertz 1961:78-79) and working class London (Young and Willmott 1965:46-50), this same conjunction of the nuclear family household and bilateral descent, together with the primacy of the mother-daughter tie as the basic kinship bond, is a prominent feature.

that, as we shall see, it is potentially disruptive of other relationships. Given the daughter's strong tie to her mother, she may sometimes be neglectful of her husband; that, at least, is the way he often perceives it. As in working-class London (Young and Willmott 1965:64-65), this not only creates resentment on the part of the husband toward his mother-in-law, but it is a source of conflict between husband and wife. That the wife sometimes resolves the conflict by returning to her mother is yet another index of the strength of this bond.

The special bond between mother and daughter is best illustrated in the living arrangements of widowed parents in Yeigyi. As Table 13 indicates, when they live together with their adult children, widows almost invariably live with daughters, widowers with sons. The five mother-son households are based on necessity, not preference, brought into being either because the mother had no daughter, or because the latter was unmarried, and the mother required a male to work her land. To be sure, there are important social and cultural constraints on the reverse arrangements, such as suspicion of incest when a father lives with an unmarried daughter, or conflict with the daughter-in-law when a mother lives with a married son. Nevertheless, our data indicate that the mother-daughter preference obtains even when the father-daughter incest problem does not arise (where the daughter is married) and when the daughter-in-law problem does not arise (where the son is unmarried). In any event, since there are as many mother-son as father-son households in Yeigyi, the important finding in Table 13 is the discrepancy between the large number of mother-daughter households (eleven) and the small number of father-daughter households (one). (And the latter case, strictly speaking, does not count since the woman is in fact a daughter-in-law.)

In stressing the parallelism between the cultural emphasis on the importance of the mother-child bond and the importance of the social relationship between mother and daughter, I do not wish to suggest that the mother-son relationship is at variance with this cultural emphasis. For

TABLE 13. *The Pattern of Parent-Child Households*

Household Pattern	N
Mother-daughter	11
Mother-son	5
Father-son	5
Father (in-law)-daughter (in-law)	1
Total	22

d.f. = 1; X^2 = 4.9; p = .05.

if the former is more evident behaviorally, the latter (for reasons discussed elsewhere) is at least as important emotionally. If its behavioral expression is less evident, it is because of its troublesome Oedipal overtones. These, to be sure, are equally troublesome in the father-daughter relationship, but the emotional intensity of the son's feeling for his mother is publicly recognized and openly expressed. The son clings to and longs for his mother, the Burmese say, as one might long for a gift or the fulfillment of a wish (*taun ta-de*). Hence, they point out, it is no accident that the son's first and unthinking reaction to a harmful or frightening stimulus is to cry, *amei!* or *ameilei!*—"Mother!" On the mother's side, the most obvious indication of her feelings for her son is her reluctance to relinquish him to his wife which, as we shall see, is a great point of tension between mother-in-law and daughter-in-law.

Siblings (Nyi-akou maun-hnama)

Second in importance only to the parent-child bond is that between siblings. If mutual aid and assistance are normative expectations in all kin relationships, they are especially strong in the sibling relationship. In addition to the generic responsibilities inherent in the sibling relationship, there are sex-specific responsibilities, such as those entailed in the levirate and sororate. There are, too, age-specific responsibilities, and it is hardly surprising, therefore, that younger and elder siblings are terminologically differentiated.

In childhood the elder sister is important for younger siblings of both sexes, and in adulthood, the elder brother is especially important for his younger sister. In childhood the elder sister is a surrogate mother for her younger siblings. When mother is absent, it is she who cares for them, nurtures them, and disciplines them. A typical village scene is a young girl, even of six or seven, carrying a younger sibling at her hips, giving him food, or preventing him from toddling off into the neighbor's compound. Hence the traditional couplet, *amagyi/ami-aya*, "elder sister [takes]/mother's place." Although, as an adult, the elder brother is a surrogate father, he seldom plays that role in childhood since he is either at school or helping his father in the fields. During adolescence, however, he has the duty to watch over his sister and guard her virtue. Should she lose her virginity or be sexually compromised in lesser ways, it is the elder brother who is held responsible and he must bear the brunt of the inevitable criticism. Hence, he is expected to keep his younger sisters under constant surveillance.

On all accounts, then, the relationship between siblings of opposite sex is especially close; to some extent they are confidants. The elder brother gives advice to his sister, but the sister is not free to advise her brother unless he requests her advice. In a sharply age-graded society, it would be unacceptable for a junior to tender unsolicited advice to a senior.

These special relationships aside, siblings have the strongest obligations to appear at those occasions and in those events in which kinship is, par éxcellence, brought into play: the crises and rites of passage of the life cycle. More than any other kinsmen (except parents), siblings are expected to come to each others' assistance in time of need (especially economic need), and to participate in the celebrations and commemorations associated with birth, marriage, death, and so on. Even if they see very little of each other at any other time, they are expected to be prominent in these *tha-hmu na-hmu* ("joy and suffering") contexts. And it is rare that these expectations are not honored. Both physically and financially, the assistance and participation of siblings at a wedding or funeral, at a Buddhist initiation rite or an exorcistic séance, is all but automatic.

It should be noted that the duty of participation applies equally strongly to both giver and receiver. It is not only a breach of duty for a sibling to refuse to participate in a rite of passage, it is a breach of the same magnitude not to invite his participation. This is true even of ordinary events, such as sharing in a common meal. Thus, if only certain siblings are invited, although it is to pursue a common interest not shared by the others, the latter, as one informant put it, "will be very hurt," and even when the reason is explained, they will still "feel pain inside."

The sibling relationship is a special one for another reason. In it, as in the parent-child relationship, the norms of kinship almost always supersede those of the market. Take, for example, the following typical cases. When Kou San Hla wanted a desirable plot of land which was owned by his brother and sister, they did not, to be sure, offer it to him as a gift, nor did they reduce its sale price from the normal market value. But they did do something they would not have done for other kinsmen, let alone a non-kinsman: instead of requiring immediate full payment, or, alternatively, interest on the mortgage, they sold him the land on credit, asking neither a down-payment nor interest. Similarly, when Daw Thi Hla required a set of poles for the construction of her new house, she purchased them from her brother who charged her only the price which he himself had paid, or half the price he would have charged a non-sibling. Again, when U Ba Thaw constructed a new house, he was assisted without payment by four relatives, to whom, however, he supplied meals. But when Daw Myan, a poor widow, required a new house, her brothers (and her sister's husband) not only worked without payment, but they even provided their own meals.

For the rest, siblings are little different from the members of the core kindred, and their other relationships can be described together with the latter group.

The Core Kindred *(Nide Hsweimyou)*

Consanguines (Hsweimyou Thagyin)

The core kindred, it will be recalled, consists of those kinsmen whose genealogical distance from ego is one degree removed from those comprising his family. Lineally, then, it includes grandparents and grandchildren; collaterally it includes uncles and aunts, cousins, and nephews and nieces. From the point of view of participation in life-cycle crises and rites of passage, the members of the kindred are interchangeable, but certain norms (and sentiments) are specific to various of its dyads.

The relationship between grandparents and grandchildren, over and above the fact that the former are the founders and leaders *(lugyi)* of the stock, is an especially close one. Among the grandparent-grandchild dyads, the grandmother-grandson relationship is particularly close. Since, as often happens, newlyweds may live with the bride's parents for a few years following their marriage, since the youngest married daughter takes up permanent residence with her parents, and since in general married daughters are closer than married sons to their mothers, it is the maternal grandmother with whom the grandson has this preferential relationship. Villagers are not blind to the fact that the results of this preference are, on the one hand, a "terribly spoiled" grandson, and, on the other, a "very resentful" granddaughter.

At a normative, rather than sentimental, level, the important relationships within the kindred are found in the uncle-aunt and nephew-niece dyads, and these are not only connected with the levirate and sororate. Father's elder brother, for example, is addressed by a quasi-paternal term, and, indeed, he is expected to be a father surrogate to the children. Similarly, although she is not addressed by a maternal term, mother's younger sister is expected to be a mother surrogate to her sister's children. These special relationships, of course, are dissipated over time, and they are not operative when the nephews and nieces are adults.

The members of the kindred are also differentiated at a group level. As in Java, the women of the maternal matriline comprise an especially close group, one, however, which is primarily affectively rather than normatively based.[8] The mother-child relationship, as we have seen, is the closest of all kin relationships, and the child's tie to the mother extends to her sisters, nieces, mother, and aunts. In childhood, this extension holds

---

8. Geertz (1961:78) describes the Javanese situation as follows: "These are the people with whom the most mutual aid is exchanged; these are the people who are more often secondary members of the household; these are the people whose children are taken into the household; these are the people with whom the warmest relationships are maintained. Thus, while primary structural emphasis is on the nuclear family, there is a secondary, supplementary structure—that of the network of ties between related women."

for sons and daughters alike. As the boy grows up, however, and forms his own family, he drops out of this special network, so that in adulthood only the women of the matriline comprise an especially close circle, as indicated by both the frequency and the quality of their interaction.

This special relationship between the women of the mother's matriline is explained by the Burmese as a function of the specially close biological tie of mother and child. Because of this strong element of biological kinship, the child is said to *feel* closer to his mother than to his father. This feeling, they add, is intensified by the additional (non-biological) fact that the father is usually a remote figure in the family, so that it is only natural that the children feel closer to the mother who is much more available to them. On both accounts, then, the feelings for the mother automatically generalize, they say, to her relatives, so that they feel closer to mother's kin than to father's. But this generalization, despite what the Burmese say, is, of course, not that automatic. It is more plausible to believe that children in the first instance are closer to the women of the mother's matriline because they see and interact with them more frequently. The father is not only a remote figure in his family of procreation, he is also removed from his family of orientation, whom he visits less frequently than his wife visits hers. The wife not only visits her mother more frequently, but she takes her children with her; and since her sisters are equally close to their mother, the children frequently encounter their mother's sisters and the latter's children, as well as their mother's mother, during these visits. As the children grow up, the boys become "remote" from these, and other family, ties, but the girls continue to maintain the close relationships that are first forged in childhood.

Whatever the grounds may be, the norms which govern relationships within the kindred are more likely to be honored within the maternal matriline, not because the norms are different or stronger, but because of the especially strong affective bond that obtains between and among them. This bond is reflected—at least it could be so interpreted—in the asymmetrical way in which kin terms are applied as respect terms in non-kin contexts. Thus, persons of a different generation from ego (or of greater power and prestige regardless of generation) are addressed by the respect terms *qu* and *do,* for males and females respectively. These are kinship-derived terms which, in their pure form, designate *maternal* uncle and aunt, respectively.[9] Given the special quality of the maternal matriline, it is significant that the idiom which is used to invest all

9. As kin terms, *qu* and *do* are never used as separate terms; rather they are combined with a form designating relative age, and it is this combined term which constitutes the kin term. Thus, for example, mother's brother is never *qu*; he is *qugyi* (elder) or *qulei* (younger). Similarly, mother's sister is never *do;* she is either *kyido* (elder) or *qado* (younger). In short, as respect terms, *qu* and *do* are not kinship, but kinship-derived, terms.

relationships with a quasi-kinship quality—a quality of trust—is one associated with maternal aunts and uncles.

We can now turn from these special relationships to the normative expectations which are general to the core kindred. The following examples of kindred behavior, selected from different classes of events observed during my study of Yeigyi, exemplify these norms in practice.

Kindred are expected to come to one's assistance in case of sorcery. Thus, when A was believed to have been bewitched, his brother and his cousin's husband arranged to bring an exorcist to the exorcistic rite; another cousin paid the exorcist's fee.

Kindred are expected to help when kinsmen have encounters with the law. When B was accused of murder, the following relatives helped him raise funds to hire an attorney: mother, mother's sister, mother's brother, and mother's brother's son. In a similar case, and for the same purpose, C was assisted by father's brother, brother, brother-in-law, and sister.

Kindred are expected to help in time of illness. When D's baby was ill, his cousin and the latter's wife cared for it when D and his wife had to be away. Again, when E was hospitalized, her brother's daughter attended her during her stay.

Kindred are expected to offer assistance in farming. When F had to spend the night in Mandalay, his father's cousin looked after his cattle. Again, when G threshed sesamum he used his cousin's threshing floor, not having one of his own.

The kindred, as already indicated, are particularly important in life-cycle and Buddhist ceremonies, especially weddings, Buddhist initiations, and funerals. Nor does their responsibility end with death: for they continue to perform ceremonies whose function it is to transfer merit to the deceased to enhance their chances for a better rebirth. The magnitude and organizational complexity of this assistance may be gauged from the following Buddhist initiation ceremony, which H and his wife performed for their son. (When, in this example, a kintype is listed below more than once, it indicates a different, not the same, person, so that the number of kin involved in this ceremony was much larger than the indicated kintypes.) The master of ceremonies was paid by H's FaBrSo. The pavilion in which the ceremony was held was brought in carts supplied by three BrSo, WiBr, WiSiSo, four WiSiHu (and four non-kinsmen); it was returned in carts supplied by SiHu, WiSiHu, two Wi(classificatory)SiHu, four WiSiSo, WiBr, two Wi(classificatory)Br (and one non-kinsman). The costumes were paid for by Wi(classificatory)Si, transported by Wi(classificatory)Br, and returned by Wi(classificatory)Br. Ponies were supplied by Wi(classificatory)Br. The papier maché elephant was brought by BrSo, WiMoBr, Wi(classificatory)Br. The elephant was returned by two BrSo, and WiSiHu. Guests from other villages were brought by three BrSo, and returned by two BrSo and WiBr. Mats were brought by Wi(classificatory)Br (and one non-kinsman). Food purchased in the city was transported by Wi(classificatory)SiHu. Firewood was brought by BrSo, two Wi(classificatory)Br, BrSo, and paid for by (classificatory)Br (and a non-kinsman).

The kindred are not only expected to *do* certain things for their members, they are also expected (and this is just as important) to refrain from doing other things. Thus, to take one example, kindred are expected to refrain from taking punitive action in situations where, were the culprit a non-kinsman, they would certainly take it. Thus, when *I* discovered three young women stealing his bean plants, he ordered that they be returned, and from two of the three, but not the third, he also took the sheaves of grain that were theirs. When asked why he refrained from taking any from the third, he said he could not do so because she was a relative (FaBrSoDa). Similarly, although *J* claimed to have proof that the village headman, a political opponent, had absconded with village funds, he said he could not report this fact to the authorities because the headman was his wife's relative (FaSiSo).

In stressing the obligations of kinship, note must be taken of the constraints on, and the limits of, these obligations. Thus, all things being equal, close kin who are geographically distant do not have the same obligations as distant kin who are geographically close. Thus, when *K*'s wife was ill, his second cousin (extended kindred) took care of her when he was away from the house because his genealogically closer (core) kindred lived far away, whereas this cousin lived close by. The obverse also holds. *L* did not prosecute a distant kinsman, his FaFaBrSoSo, who had stolen a tool, not merely because they were kinsmen, but because they were neighbors. Were he to prosecute, he said, the latter fact would create no end of embarrassment.

Reciprocity is another constraint on the obligations of kinship. When, for example, relatives offer financial assistance to ego for the celebration of a wedding or an initiation, the exact value of their contribution is recorded. (In the cities, where, for example, wedding presents are offered to a newly wedded couple, each of the presents is recorded after the guests have departed.) Ego can then calculate whether his obligations to them have been consequently wiped out—he and they are now even—or whether the balance has shifted and he is now obligated to them. Should he then ignore the imbalance, he will eventually discover that they refrain from assisting him.

Reciprocity obtains no less between siblings than in any other kin relationship. Although one can generally turn to a sibling when in need, his assistance is typically but one transaction in an ongoing system of exchanges. Thus, if ego helps his sibling in the harvesting of his crops, it is with the expectation that the latter will help him for the same number of days. One morning, for example, M became extremely angry with her brother because he insisted that she drop everything that very morning to help harvest his paddy in exchange for the two days he had helped harvest M's sesamum. M told him she could not help him on such short notice, but that she would give him the equivalent of her labor in cash that he might hire a laborer in her place. He demurred, saying that it would take him time to find laborers, and the paddy had to be harvested that day. The conflict was resolved only after M prevailed upon her husband and her mother to take her place in her brother's field.

There are limits as well as constraints on kinship obligations. Thus, in an example given above, when E was hospitalized, she was attended by her brother's daughter. Since the latter is poor, and could ill afford to lose her regular wages, E compensated her by the equivalent of her daily earnings.

At the most general level, we might say that the outside limits on kinship obligations are met when kinship norms conflict with market norms, for then the hard-headed considerations of business and profit sometimes prevail. Consider the following examples. At the end of the agricultural season, when his financial reserves are depleted, N, like almost all villagers, must borrow on agricultural futures, and usually he borrows from the weathiest woman in Yeigyi. Although she is his cousin, he must nevertheless pay her the going interest rates, which means that if he repays the debt on time, the interest rate is ten percent, but if he is derelict, it is doubled. When I asked why he continues to pay these usurious rates, N said: "That's fine, but how will I get other loans in the future?" "Well," I asked, "since she is your cousin, why don't you ask her to show greater sympathy, and lower the interest?" "That would be useless," he answered, "for when property is involved, one doesn't talk about kinship."

Despite the fact that market considerations set a limit to kinship norms, there is still a difference between the treatment of kindred and non-kindred in favor of the former. Thus, although N was charged the going interest rate by his cousin, it would be unthinkable for her to seize his land for arrears on his interest payments, as she would if he were not a kinsman. And not only the interest, for, his cousin complained, her kindred seldom repay their debts, and, unlike the situation with non-kinsmen, kinship norms prevent her from doing anything about it. In short, even for this grasping moneylender, kinship sentiments serve to qualify the market character of a business transaction. She may not grant him a second loan, but she will not bring legal action against a kinsman for welching on his debt. In the same vein, O's wealthy aunt insisted that he pay her for a sack of rice despite the fact that his savings were exhausted because of illness. On the other hand, she agreed to accept deferment until the end of the harvest season when he would have the money.

Kindred, then, are persons who stand to each other in a special, but limited, relationship of rights and obligations. But this relationship (like any relationship) is ultimately guaranteed only by a sense of mutual trust, and there are at least some villagers who view their kindred as no more trustworthy than non-kindred. For them, the distrust and suspicion that informs such a large part of Burmese social relations (as it does every-where among peasants) holds for the kindred as well. Thus, one important (and wealthy) villager said that were he to ask any of his kindred to act as a trustee for the estate he would leave to his young daughter, he could not at all be sure that they would not abscond with it. It is best, he said, to tell no one about one's business affairs, because none, kin included, are trustworthy.

An extreme, and probably a limiting, example of the untrustworthy character of kinsmen was experienced by P. Possessed by a maleficent spirit, and unable to work for three months, P not only used up his reserves, but he was forced to liquidate most of his assets. When his health was finally restored, he brought a cart-load of bamboo to the broker with whom he had always done business. The latter said he could not buy his bamboo because Q, a close kinsman of P, had told him that P had given up his bamboo business; consequently he had bought all the bamboo he needed from Q. Although a member of P's kindred, Q had no compunction about taking advantage of his illness to deprive him of his sole means of livelihood.

The following case of perfidy, involving the wealthy widow R, is almost as revealing. Motivated by jealousy and rivalry, she falsely accused two young men, S and T, of molesting her granddaughter, hoping thereby to send them to prison. Now these two young men are no strangers to R: S is the husband of another of her granddaughters, and T is the son of her former daughter-in-law (the step-son of her own son). (When T's mother, incidentally, asked her husband to persuade his mother to withdraw her accusation, he refused to do so.) R's accusation against S was instigated in the first place by U, the cousin (classificatory brother) of S's wife, who was angry at S because the latter prevented him from swindling a great deal of money when they were in partnership. Despite these kin relationships, R swore that, if necessary, she would sell her entire estate in order to prosecute this case to a successful conclusion.

These examples of breach of trust, including the expectation (at least in some persons) that such breaches will occur, do not negate the thesis that at the *cultural* level (the level of norms) the core kindred is the group within which trust and solidarity are supposed to obtain. It might be argued that this normative expectation is symbolically expressed in the convention, mentioned above, of using kindred terms as honorifics for addressing non-kindred. Thus, all males, depending on age and status, are addressed (and referred to) as "uncle," "older brother," and "younger brother"; similarly, females are addressed (and referred to) as "aunt" and "sister." It is as if, by the lexical imputation of kinship status to everyone, the minimal bonds of loyalty, trust, and solidarity that, normatively at least, characterize the kindred, might then extend to all social relationships. It is because the normative relationships within the core kindred are taken as ideal-typic social relationships that, so I am suggesting, they constitute the model for all other social relationships. F. K. Lehman (personal communication) suggests, however, that the extension of kin terms is not so much an extension of the norms of trust as of *formal* respect and status. As he sees it, kin relations are the model for formal relations, not (or not only) in their positive *normative* dimension, but in all their ambivalence.

Affines (Hsweimyou)

For all practical purposes, the affines that are truly part of one's kindred are, as we have seen, the parents and siblings of one's spouse, the spouses of one's siblings, and the spouses and parents of the spouses of one's children. These "core affines" not only share a quasi-biological tie, but the norms which govern their relationships are similar to the consanguineal members of the core kindred. Hence, if Burmese kinship comes into operation especially in life-cycle ceremonies, these core affines have the right to be invited. Even if the affine's marriage link to ego is broken by the death of a sibling or spouse, they still have a right to be invited because the quasi-kinship tie remains so long as they share a common child-sibling.

Ego may interact in these contexts with his extended affines as frequently as with his core affines. Thus, they may be invited by ego to his own rites of passage, not because they are ego's kindred, but out of courtesy to his spouse, to whom they are related as core affines. Moreover, when ego and his spouse perform a rite of passage for their child, his spouse invites them as members of her kindred. In either event, since they are husband's kindred (*yau'kya hsweimyou*) or wife's kindred, (*meinma hsweimyou*), they assemble at ego's house just as his own kindred do, which means that in these contexts ego's kindred interact with his spouse's kindred as frequently as they do among themselves.

If core affines have some of the rights of core kindred, they also have some of their duties. They have not only the right but also the duty to participate in rites of passage. They also have the duty, though it is not as strong as that of consanguines, to assist each other in times of need and crisis.

As in all societies, relations between affines are often characterized by tension, including hostility, jealousy, and suspicion. This is not to say that similar tensions are absent among consanguines. On the contrary, they are found, as we shall see in the next chapter, even in the core consanguineal relationships, those between parents and children, and between siblings. The difference, however, is that tensions are both conscious and explicit in the case of affines, whereas they are either unconscious or denied among consanguines, especially among the core consanguines whose relationships are conceived to be unambivalently solidarious. Given this kinship ideology, one may admit (to oneself as well as to others) that one does not like one's sibling, for example, but it would be almost impossible to admit to hostility to him, or that one's behavior to him was instigated by non-solidary intentions. This is not the case with affines, concerning whom the kinship ideology does not stress solidarity. Hence, affines are quite prepared to admit to such non-solidary sentiments such as hostility, jealousy, and suspicion toward each other.

Since jealousy and hostility are not unexpected from them, affines are often wary of each other. Thus, one frequently hears comments of the following type: "The things we say among ourselves (consanguines) we have to be careful in saying among in-laws." It is in three dyads especially that these sentiments are both expected and prominent, namely, in the two sets of parents-in-law, same-sex siblings-in-law, and parent-in-law plus sibling-in-law. The tensions among these dyads are, as we shall see, stereotypic, and in one case they are institutionalized. Unlike consanguines, in which such sentiments occasion guilt feelings—and are therefore denied, repressed, or rationalized—their cognitive and behavioral institutionalization in the case of affines obviates the need for guilt. Let us now briefly examine these dyads.

With respect to the two sets of parents-in-law (*khami-khame*ʔ) it is assumed that they will compete with each other over relative status in the non-kinship field, that they will compete for the respective loyalties of their children in the kinship field, and that, moreover, they will criticize each other for not treating their respective son and daughter properly. As for the various parent-in-law and child-in-law dyads, the one which exhibits the greatest tension, and which is explicitly recognized as a stereotypically tense relationship, is the mother-in-law and daughter-in-law dyad. Among the sibling-in-law dyads, the tension between brothers-in-law (SiHu-WiBr) is equally strong and equally stereotyped. Inasmuch as their relationships importantly affect Burmese residence patterns and the composition of the household, they will be treated separately in the next chapter.

Before concluding this section, it might be observed that there is one affine whom I have neglected to mention, namely, the step-parent. As the spouse of a consanguine, the step-parent is not only an affine, but, by the criteria used for its definition, a core affine. This is one case, however, in which sentiment overrides the usual structural criteria. The sentiment between step-parent and step-child, at least stereotypically, is so negative that step-relatives are excluded from both the core and the extended kindreds. I shall have more to say about them in the following chapter.

The Extended Kindred (Weide Hsweimyou)

If, as I argued in the last chapter, the interaction in Yeigyi of village endogamy and cognatic descent produces *diffuse* kin ties, thereby reinforcing the tendency to blur the distinction between core and extended kindred, their interaction also produces *pervasive* kin ties which reinforce the tendency to blur the distinction between kin and non-kin. As a result of the interaction of these two variables, nearly everyone in the village is related, either consanguineally or affinally, to almost everyone else. Thus, when U Shin's mother-in-law died, U Chan, a man I did not take to be a relative, went to inform the monk to be in readiness for the funeral. When I asked him why he, rather than a relative of U Shin, had gone to the monastery, he replied, *ya ywa ya hsweimyou*, "To take on the village [is to] take on kin." That is, by the mere fact of living in a community, one acquires kin.

In short, the web of kinship in a Burmese village is so pervasive that it has the effect of minimizing the importance of kinship beyond the core kindred as a basis either for social differentiation or group organization. In the Yeigyi headman election, for example, a large percentage of the electorate were related either by marriage or by blood to all three candidates, and kin ties in themselves could not (and they did not) form the basis for choosing among candidates. This is also the case when villagers try to decide where their loyalty lies in factional disputes, or which, among various cooperative work groups, they should join, and so on. This characteristic of Burmese kinship is found throughout Southeast Asia and it is probably another basis for the "loose" structure of the societies in the area.[10]

Still, it would be false to conclude that extended kin ties serve no function at all. Their very pervasiveness, which reduces their value as a

10. For Java, Geertz (1961:2,3) writes: "From the point of view of the functioning of the society, the Javanese kinship system . . . makes relatively few contributions . . . kinsmen

basis for social differentiation, increases their value as a basis for social integration. Indeed, it is primarily because of their mutually felt kin ties that Burmese villagers view themselves as not merely comprising a *territorial* group, but as constituting a *social* group. For to the extent that they feel a sense of mutual responsibility and an identification with the other members of their village, as fellow villagers, such a feeling primarily derives from sentiments of common kinship. Lest I be misunderstood I hasten to add the obvious point that fellow villagers have many bases for identification with each other—they are all peasants, Buddhists, Burmese, and so on. Since these latter bases, however, are common to all villagers in Burma, they establish their identity as *Burmese* villagers, not as *Yeigyi* villagers. It is the latter identity, the one which differentiated the species from the genus, that is at issue here; and—this at least is my argument—this particularistic identity is derived from the fact that, in a very broad sense, each village is a relatively distinct kinship group. Hence it is that only if he comes in as a kinsman, as a spouse, or as a relative of a native, that a stranger who settles in a village can ever truly become a member. Should he come without such ties, he will always be suspect because, as the Yeigyi headman put it, villagers like to feel that their co-residents are reliable, especially in periods of crisis. They cannot feel this way about strangers because the latter, he emphasized, have no kin-relationships to other villagers, and while "non-relatives might put you in trouble, relatives will not."

Even in-marrying spouses sometimes have difficulties in overcoming their status as "strangers," or *qethe* (literally, visitors or guests) to the village despite their affinal links to it; and without such links it can almost never be overcome. To be an integrated member of village society, it is necessary to have been born in the village, or, short of that, to have married one of its members and to have demonstrated, by conforming to its kin-like norms, that there are no grounds for being suspect. The immigrant without such a kin tie is not only suspect, but his status as "stranger" often places him outside the pale of mutual sympathy, responsibility, and cooperation. Thus, for example, when a young man from a village near Yeigyi was in prison, waiting to be tried for murder, his mother and wife could raise few funds for his defense in his own village

---

are not organized into corporate groups of any sort, and [even core kindred] serve primarily as sources of aid in trouble and of pleasurable companionship." Similarly, for Central Thailand, Piker (n.d. ch. 2: 18-19) writes: "Except for ceremonial assistance, this circumstance of widespread relatedness, however, has little social significance for the villager. The mere fact that two people are *jad* tells us nothing about the actual social relationship, if any, between them. In fact, the overwhelming probability is that there is none except the most casual acquaintanceship."

because his father's relatives were dead, and they themselves were immigrants from other villages. They raised the funds, instead, from relatives in their natal village.

In short, it is the ties of kinship that constitute the cement of social relationships in a Burmese village. Without such ties, life can sometimes be literally rendered impossible, as the following cases testify. When Ma Shi married Maung Youn, she moved to Yeigyi from her natal village, and when she was three months pregnant, her husband took ill. Since Maung Youn's parents were dead and his other relatives too poor to support them both, and since Ma Shi's relatives were living in her natal village, there was no one in Yeigyi to care for them: having no kin ties in the village, the other villagers felt little obligation to them. Hence, Ma Shi had no alternative but to return to her own village, for, as Maung Youn explained, "If you have no relatives, you have no support."

The following case is even more telling. Driving from Yeigyi one morning, I stopped to speak to a village friend who was on his way to a nearby village to assist his wife's sister, who had been bitten by a poisonous snake. This woman and her husband had lived in the latter village for only one year, having moved there from another district. Being strangers, and without kin, there was no one in the village to take her (by bullock cart) to a doctor, or, as she herself wanted, to a certain pagoda famous for curing snake bites. Although she had been bitten in the early hours of the morning, she was still waiting, seven hours later, for the arrival of her sister's husband (my friend from Yeigyi), who was to transport her. All of this he related to me without indignation; for him these were self-evident and accepted facts of village life.

In the cities, where the urban ward *(yatkwet)* is the functional equivalent of the village, the situation of the "stranger" is similar. If he is in need, the neighbors, according to urban informants, expect his relatives to help him. If the latter do not appear, the neighbors might then offer their assistance—on condition that it does not cause them too much trouble. If, however, it entails serious effort or inconvenience, the urban stranger, like his village counterpart, is usually left alone to handle the problem as best he can.

The Burmese, of course, are not the only people who, though living in a politically organized, non-kinship based society, nevertheless distinguish kin from non-kin on a scale of moral obligation. Among the Sarakatsani of Greece, to take but one example, this distinction is even more sharply marked. For them, not only are blood kin alone trusted, but even within this category, it is only within the family that true cooperation and assistance are to be found. As for non-kin, they are viewed as "almost [as] enemies. A man would be foolish and weak to trust them, unmanly not to exploit them within the limits conventionally allowed." (Campbell 1966:142.) In this society, then, the family is the primary, perhaps the only solidary group, a "social isolate facing the majority of the community on terms of hostility and mistrust," receiving only "qualified support" even from kinsmen. (*Ibid.*) A recent description of life in a southern Italian town portrays an almost identical situation, one in which the boundary of solidarity is narrowly confined to the family (Davis 1969).

In this comparative perspective, the Burmese situation is expansive and inclusive. To be sure, since almost all villagers are related, either consanguineally or affinally, kinship ties beyond the nuclear kindred are an unimportant basis for *differential* behavior. They are a crucial basis, however, for the undifferentiated exchange of those rights and duties which define the village as a social (in contrast to a mainly territorial) group. It is their common membership in a cross-cutting network of extended kin that constitutes the main basis for the villagers' sense of trust, shared identity, and mutual responsibility which, after all, is the very basis for group life. In time of need, one can count on one's fellow villagers because they are kinsmen, and kinsmen, normatively if not actually, are those who care.[11]

11. Different commentators (personal communication) have suggested that too much is made here of the moral-affective dimension of kinship. Thus, F. K. Lehman holds that the in-marrying stranger validates his membership in the village not (as I have claimed) by conforming to its kin-like norms, but by following the right forms; he believes that, in effect, kinship establishes status relations rather than normative sentiments. F. G. Bailey makes a similar point in claiming that the normative sentiments (of trust, responsibility, and so on) which I emphasize are better construed as "a language of claims than a guide to behavior." I would not dispute either contention, but I would suggest that even when viewed merely as a language of claims, available to villagers who sustain a given status relationship, these normative sentiments have a genuine moral force. Hence, even if the normative expectations are not always fulfilled, they are difficult to evade.

5. Kinship Attitudes and the Composition of the Domestic Group

Introduction

Thus far we have been primarily concerned with cultural conceptions of kinship and kinsmen, the kin groupings that are produced by these conceptions, and the cultural norms and values that are expected to govern kin relations, both dyadic and collective, within these groupings. Although he may not conceptualize them in precisely the same manner that I have, the average Burmese villager has acquired, from childhood on, the conceptions, values, and norms of kinship delineated in the previous chapters. Moreover, he has not only learned about them, but at some cognitive level he believes them to be correct and proper, and at some affective level he is motivated to act in accordance with them.

But action in any social domain is governed not only by the norms and values that comprise a society's cultural heritage. In the case of kinship, for example, the child not only learns (through the process of enculturation) the jural norms and formal values of kinship, but, since he grows up with them, he also learns (through the process of socialization) a great deal about his own kin. He learns what kinds of persons they are, what they will do and not do for him, under what conditions they will reward and punish him, how they differ in their treatment of him, and so on. Although these two sets of conceptions are empirically inseparable, it is important to distinguish them analytically, if only because they are often discordant.

The latter conceptions of kin are acquired rather differently from those acquired through the learning of the formal cultural norms and values pertaining to them. That is, they are acquired not by tuition from kinsmen ("enculturation") but as a consequence of social interaction and experience with them ("socialization"). By being suckled and toilet-trained in certain ways, by being praised for working hard and punished for neglecting a chore, by being encouraged to study his lessons and restrained from talking throughout a long and tedious ceremony, the child not only learns about food and feces, work and duty, study and religion, but he also acquires conceptions of his parents and other kinsmen, and of their attitudes to and relationships with him. These experientially acquired conceptions may or may not be consistent with the cultural values and norms of kinship which are explicitly transmitted to him, but they are at least as important in informing his conceptions of kinship and kinsmen because they are associated with and give rise to intense affective reactions and responses. Thus, the child who develops conceptions of his parents as brutal and punitive will harbor rather different attitudes to them from one who perceives them as nurturant and benign, even though the cultural norms and values associated with them might be the same for both. If this is so, then surely kinship *behavior* is as much determined by these experientially acquired conceptions of kinship and kinsmen, and their associated affects, as by the culturally constituted conceptions. Kinship behavior, I would contend, is the product of the interaction of these two sets of cognitive determinants, as a kind of parallelogram of forces. Since the culturally determined conceptions have been described in the previous chapters, this chapter will deal with the kinship conceptions acquired through the experience of domestic living.

Now the kinship experiences of the Burmese child—"child" here includes anyone who is still in a status of jural subordination to his parents—fall well within the normal range of such experiences, cross-culturally viewed. Burmese parents, like parents in most (perhaps all) societies, are at times both kind and unkind, affectionate and aggressive, permissive and punitive, and so on. As a result, Burmese children, like children in most (perhaps all) societies, acquire conflicting conceptions of and ambivalent emotions toward their parents (and their other close kinsmen), many of which comprise that constellation of conceptions and emotions which comprise the normal Oedipus complex. Kinship behavior necessarily reflects these conflicting conceptions and ambivalent emotions, even when the culturally constituted conceptions and attitudes are—if they ever are—unambiguously unidimensional. Hence, although solidarity with certain kin may be a norm, it can never be a categorical attribute of kinship behavior.

With these rather obvious, perhaps banal, comments, I now wish to examine certain kinds of kinship, and kinship-related, behavior in Burma, with the intention of elucidating the relative contribution of the two cognitive determinants of kinship relations, the cultural and the experiential or social. In short, I wish to elucidate the relationship between the sociology of kinship, the *explanandum*, and the cultural and experiential conceptions of kinsmen, respectively, the two *explanans*.

Although there are any number of points of entry into the domain of sociological kinship, the domestic group seems to be better than most. First, it is universal. Second, it is the single most important social group (kin or non-kin) in village Burma. Third, being a residential group, it is typically the one in which kin interaction is the most frequent and intense. Fourth, it is in this group, primarily, that cultural conceptions, norms, and rules of kinship are transmitted to the child, and attitudes toward kinsmen are acquired by him. And fifth, in village Burma, at least, it is an exclusively kin-based group, and one in which the degrees of kinship are generally close; for, although the household may sometimes include kinsmen less closely related to ego than parents, grandparents, and siblings, it rarely includes anyone outside the core kindred, and it never includes non-kinsmen. (This is not true in the city, where the household may include servants or distant relatives, who in effect function as servants.)

Although the domestic group is universal, its composition is cross-culturally (and to some extent intraculturally) variable. Thus, although the bi-parental nuclear family is a universal, biologically based, sociological unit, it is not necessarily—as, for example, the Israeli kibbutz, the Indian Nayar, and the African Nyakyusa, prove—a domestic group. Moreover, where, as is the case in most societies, this elementary family does constitute a domestic group, it is very often a part of a larger residential unit. Thus, in societies with an extended family system, the domestic group may consist of two or more biologically related, nuclear families. In short, although in all societies, every typical social actor is a member, *seriatim*, of at least two nuclear families—his family of orientation in which he is born and raised, and his family of procreation which he forms when he marries and has children—in many of these same societies approximately half their members, namely, the married males or females in societies with matrilocal or patrilocal joint family households, respectively, belong to only one domestic group. Only in societies with nuclear family households is the typical social actor a member, *seriatim*, not only of two nuclear families, but of two domestic groups—the household in which he is raised as a child, and the household which he forms as a married adult.

In societies characterized by prescriptive residence rules, the composition of the domestic group is a consequence, to a large extent, of compliance with these rules. If, then, rule-conforming behavior is taken for granted, what is to be explained in these cases is not the composition of the domestic group, but either the origin or the persistence of the rule; the former inquiry would attend to diachronic social causation or synchronic social functions, the latter to actors' motives. In societies, however, where there are no residence rules—where residence, in short, is optative—the composition of the domestic group is in itself an important problem for a kinship investigation. For whatever type or types of domestic groups might be found in such societies, it is difficult to imagine that kinship conceptions, norms, and attitudes would not play an important role in the explanation. I would put it even more strongly: in societies such as Burma, in which residence is optative, the distribution of household types provides an important, perhaps unique, key to the understanding of conceptions of and attitudes to kinsmen and kinship. I now wish to explore these notions in village Burma, where the household, or domestic group, is the building block of village society.

Although, on the one hand, it is internally differentiated, and although, on the other, it is related by a variety of cross-cutting ties (economic, political, religious, kinship) to other groups, it is the domestic group, *qeindaung tasu*, (*qeindaung*=household, *tasu*=one group) which constitutes the social, economic, religious, and administrative unit of village Burma. This is true even in the case of extended family households, which in Yeigyi comprise 25 percent of the total. Thus, unlike some other societies, such as Ceylon (Kandy), in which each nuclear family within an extended family household owns and works its own lands, retains its own income, and cooks at its own hearth, in Burma the entire household shares and pools these activities and resources.[1] Contrariwise, if the domestic group is smaller than a nuclear family, if, for example, the household consists of a widow (or a divorcée) and her children, it is still the case that, rather than joining forces with a larger kinship-related group, it maintains its autonomy as a social and economic unit.

This same characteristic applies to the religious and political dimensions of the household. The domestic group maintains its own Buddhist and spirit shrines, and it is responsible for offerings to the Buddha and the spirits, for the feeding of monks, and for the upkeep of the monastery. Similarly, it is the domestic group which is the smallest unit of government administration. The Burmese village is divided into groups of ten households, each headed by a "ten-household leader," and each household, taken as a unit, is responsible for its proportional share of village

1. Yalman's description of the situation in Kandy (Yalman 1967:102-103) stands in sharp contrast to that in Burma. "The 'unit of food consumption' in the Kandyan village consists of a wife, unmarried children, and a husband. It always has separate granaries, and it has a separate cooking place. Every married woman has her own pots and stones in a particular part of the house where she cooks. The cooking area is private and other women may use it only with express permission. . . . Thus the nuclear family, the basic commensal group, is the most clearly drawn cell in the village. It is referred to as a *ge* in Sinhalese. A dwelling may have a number of *ge* in it. They may live under the same roof, but they are distinct units. Their separateness is brought out by the fact that when one asks the number of 'families' (*pavula*) in a village, the answer will refer not to the number of 'houses' or to the number of 'kindreds,' but to the number of *ge* in the community."

taxes, corvées, and village defense. (In this regard, it is of interest to observe that these same characteristics, with minor exceptions, are found in urban Burma as well. Except for their westernized sections, Rangoon and Mandalay are divided into wards, within which it is the household which is the social unit.)

Whatever the size and composition of the domestic group, it is, by definition, not only a social group, but also a physical group; that is, it comprises a household. This means, to put it in its simplest form, that as a physical group it is distinguished (and separated) from other domestic groups by its sharing of a common compound and, more specifically, a common house within the compound. In Yeigyi, with only one exception, the house is jointly owned by a married couple, and, when one of the spouses dies, its ownership becomes the sole possession of the living spouse. Ownership of the house and compound confers more than economic title on its owner(s); the houseowner is always the jural head of the household, whether the latter consists of a nuclear family or a joint family. If, in the latter case, therefore, a parent or parents live with a married child, and if the child and his spouse have title to the house, it is they, and not the parents, who exercize authority within the household. Hence, whatever its composition, a household is always referred to as the household of A and B, the names of the husband and wife, respectively, who hold title to the house.

The house, then, is more than a physical building and it is more than an economic asset. Ownership of the house symbolizes the locus of jural authority within the household. The house itself symbolizes marriage, not only the marriage of the couple who own it, but that of any other couple that might reside in it. To be married is to live under a common roof; a formerly married adult (widowed or divorced) may live alone, but an unmarried adult, regardless of age, lives with a married or formerly married member of his or her natal household. Finally, the house symbolizes the unity of the household. It is in the house that the domestic group is spatially separated from the rest of the village; it thereby provides it with its physical unity and symbolizes its social unity.

As a physical structure, the house is usually a modest building, and, except at the polar economic extremes, there are few differences among village houses. Usually built on stilts for protection against the annual monsoon-produced flooding, the typical house consists of one, or at most two, rooms (with an attached cooking shed) constructed of coconut-thatch walls and bamboo slit-floors. An expensive house, on the other hand, is constructed of wood, with floors of teak, and though it may often have no more rooms than the thatched house, it is typically considerably larger. The house is usually empty of furniture, since people sit, eat and sleep on the floor—if, that is, these activities occur in the house—and one always, therefore, removes one's footgear before entering the house.

The house is usually not regarded as an aesthetic object; typically, it is dusty, often disorderly. Nor is the interior of the house regarded as a place in which to spend time, not, at least, during the day. Social life, for the most part, takes place in the courtyard outside the house, or—in the case of the majority which stand on stilts—underneath it. The house is rarely used for eating, nor, in the heat of the summer, for sleeping. Typically, meals are eaten either in the cooking and/or eating shed attached to the house, or (especially in hot weather) outside. Although villagers sleep inside during the cold and rainy seasons, in the hot summer months they prefer to sleep on low platforms either beside the house or underneath it. Finally, except for those few houses not built on stilts, the house is not often used for protection against the elements; not being insulated, it affords little protection from the summer heat. Rather, the open area underneath the house is usually used for protection against the sun (and rain).

What then is the house used for? Primarily it is a place in which clothing and valuables are stored, in which the Buddhist shrine is kept, in which the symbol of the house spirit (a coconut) is hung, and in which private activities, such as sex or privileged conversations, take place. But the notion of the house as "hearth and home," as a physically enclosed space within which one "lives," is not found here. Even the wealthy build their teak-constructed houses primarily for conspicuous consumption, and sometimes for larger and more secure storage space.

This characterization of the house holds regardless of the size and composition of the household that resides in it, for despite the centrality of the domestic group, there are no residence rules by which its size and composition might be determined, or by virtue of which a more or less uniform household type might result. Residence, on the contrary, is optative, and if, as we shall see, the nuclear family household is both the most frequent and also the ideal type of domestic group, it is because both are the consequence of that parallelogram of conflicting and competing cultural norms and psychological attitudes which was alluded to above. It is this parallelogram of forces, rather than the domestic group as such, which I hope to elucidate in this chapter, for these forces (as I have already suggested) provide the anthropologist with a sharply focused lens for examining those aspects of kinship which elude an exclusively cultural analysis.

Types of Domestic Groups

All other things being equal, the Burmese village household is believed ideally to consist of one nuclear family (*mitha su*)—a married couple and their minor children. Burma shares this ideal with most of the societies of lowland Southeast Asia, not only the other bilateral and kindred based societies (Ceylon, Cambodia, Java, Laos, Malaya, and Thailand), but even the one patrilineal, patrilineage-based society (Vietnam). This household ideal is one of the features that differentiates the civilizations of Southeast Asia from their two giant neighbors (and most important cultural benefactors) on the North and West. For in China and in India, the household ideal is the extended (patrilocal joint) family, although in pre-Communist China only a small percentage of peasant households—less than 10 percent in one study (Fei 1939:28)—were of this type, and in India, where the percentage is larger, it still represents a minority (Kolender 1968). In practice, then, the typical Chinese and Indian domestic group, like that of the Burmese, consists of a nuclear family.

Discounting perturbations in both the life cycle of the individual (occasioned by death or divorce) and the developmental cycle of the domestic group (occasioned by the rule, for example, that newlyweds live temporarily with the bride's parents), both of which necessarily affect its empirical expression, the actual distribution of household types in village Burma exemplifies this nuclear family ideal. Typically, married couples set up their own household either at, or shortly after, marriage. This pattern of neolocal residence, which necessarily produces a nuclear family household,[2] is the prevalent (and preferred) pattern in contemporary peasant societies throughout the world (Wolf 1966:65-73), and despite the conventional wisdom to the contrary, it was also the case in preindustrial Europe (Laslett 1971: 90-91).[3] If, nevertheless, the nuclear family households in Yeigyi comprise only 62 percent of the total (72 of a total of 115), this is because of a variety of countervailing forces which will be examined below. First, however, the other types must be enumerated.

2. Cross-culturally viewed, the direction of this relationship is variable. In some cases the residence preference determines the household types; in others, the household preference determines the residence type. In village Burma, as we shall see, it is the former which is salient—that is, the preference relates to residence, not to household composition.

3. Contemporary historians of the European family have all but demolished the earlier picture according to which the European nuclear family is a relatively late institution which, produced by industrial capitalism, succeeded a pre-industrial joint family. For all the seventeenth-century communities in England which have now been studied, the highest proportion of extended families found in any of them was 20 percent, and in most the percentage was less than half of that. As Laslett (1971:91) comments, "Unless all these communities happen to have been very exceptional indeed, living with in-laws can only have been occasional in the [preindustrial] world we have lost." This is so, according to Laslett, because the size and constitution of the family were governed by the following "general rule," which, except for the last two lines, applies without change to contemporary Burma. "No two married couples or more went to make up a family group; whether parents and children, brothers and sisters, employers and servants, or married couples, they associated

In addition to the nuclear family household, there are, as Table 14 indicates, four other types of domestic groups in Yeigyi. Second to the nuclear family, the most frequent household type is the "truncated stem family," consisting of one parent and his or her adult children (and grandchildren). In a few cases these began as genuine stem families, in accordance with the custom of the youngest daughter remaining with her natal family after her marriage, and they only later became "truncated" by the death of one of the parents. The great majority, however, are not only "truncated" but "pseudo" stem families, because they were formed only after the death of the parent's spouse, in accordance with the obligation of the adult child to care for his surviving parent. In short, most of the truncated stem family households entered in Table 14 are a consequence of a perturbance in the life cycle of one of its members rather than an enactment of a joint family ideology.

TABLE 14. *Household Types*

Household Type		N = 115
Nuclear Family		72
married couple and young children	60	
married couple	7	
married couple and young children of deceased/divorced relatives	5	
Truncated Stem Family		25
widow/widower and adult children (single, married, divorced, widowed with or without children)	24	
widow and widowed father-in-law	1	
Single Member		11
widow	7	
widower	3	
bachelor	1	
Stem Family		4
temporary	3	
permanent	1	
Truncated Nuclear Family		3
widow/divorcée and young children	3	

only for convenience. When a son got married he left the family of his parents and started a family of his own. If he was not in a position to do this, then he could not get married, nor could his sister unless the man who was to take her for his bride was also in a position to start a new family." (Laslett 1971:90.)

The third most frequent household type consists of a single member. With only one exception (a bachelor), its member is a widow or widower who prefers to live alone, rather than with parents or children. Since, except for widows, it is highly unseemly for unmarried females, whether of marriageable or post-marriageable age, to live alone, none of these single member households consists of spinsters.[4] They live either with parents or with married siblings.

The next most frequent type is the stem family household, of which there are in Yeigyi only four cases, of which only one is a genuine or permanent case. The others represent that transitional phase in the developmental cycle of the domestic group in which a newly married couple lives temporarily with the parents of the bride or groom (usually the former). Nevertheless, these figures do not reflect the true incidence of this type because, as has been indicated above, some of the "truncated" stem families in Table 14 began as genuine ones. It might be added that, contrary to accepted doctrine, stem families, at least in Burma, are more common in urban than in rural settings, especially at the polar ends of the economic scale. Thus, rich parents hold their married children by holding out to them the expectation of wealth, poor ones by the children's difficulties in buying or renting a separate dwelling.

The least frequent household type in the village (there are only three cases) consists of the "truncated" nuclear family, one in which a normal nuclear family has been reduced, as a result of death or divorce, to one parent. As in the case of the single-member household, the existence of this type is another measure of the strength of the neolocal preference, the remaining spouse deliberately rejecting incorporation into his parents' household. That in all three cases the head of these households is a female is not accidental; it is a result of norms (to be discussed below) concerning the proper residence of children following the death or divorce of their parents.

To summarize, despite the nuclear family ideal, almost 40 percent of the households in Yeigyi do not conform to this type; instead of one, there are five household types in this village. A discrepancy of similar magnitude between the actual and the ideal household types is characteristic of Southeast Asia (and probably everywhere else). Despite their nuclear family ideal, nuclear family households constitute only 56 and 77 percent of the total in two villages in Upper Burma (Nash 1965:45, 247), 59

4. The Burmese distinguish between two types of unmarried persons: those who have not yet married, but are still of marriageable age, and those, past the usual marriageable age, who will probably remain unmarried. The former, those in the fifteen to thirty age range, are *lubyou* and *qapyou* ("young males" and "young females"), the latter are *lubyougyi* and *qapyougyi* ("bachelors" and "spinsters").

percent in a Javanese village (Geertz 1961:32), 51 percent in a South Vietnamese village (Hickey 1964:92), 72 percent in a Sinhalese (Kandyan) village (Yalman 1967:173), 55 percent in a Central Thai village (Piker n.d.:16), and 65 percent in a Northeast Thai village (Tambiah 1970:12).

Since most of these non-nuclear family households consist of domestic groups larger than the nuclear family, it must be observed that throughout Southeast Asia a not insignificant percentage of villagers have domestic ties with a variety of kinsmen, a conclusion which is not predictable from such bald cultural tags as "the Southeast Asia nuclear family ideal" or "the Southeast Asia custom of neolocal residence." To be sure, such tags convey the valid notion the the *typical* domestic group in this area is small. In Yeigyi, as Table 15 indicates, the average household contains either three or four members, depending on whether the median or the mode is used as the measure. From these figures one would hardly imagine, however, that 30 percent of its children below the age of sixteen live in households that include, in addition to their parents, at least one other older relative (typically a grandparent), or that, to take another example, 40 percent of its households (excluding the eleven single-member households) include at least one representative of the following kintypes (identified in relationship to the household head): grandchild, spouse of grandchild, spouse of child, great-grandchild, sibling, parent, grandmother, brother's child, sister's child, parent of deceased spouse.

Despite the fairly large percentage of non-nuclear family households in Yeigyi, very few, as I have already emphasized, represent a rejection of the nuclear family ideal. Most of them represent instead either a temporary phase in their developmental cycle,[5] a structural solution to the disruption of an existent nuclear family caused by inevitable (death) or contingent (divorce) events in the life cycle of the individual; or a countervailing cultural norm, such as, for example, that the youngest daughter remain with her parents. If this point has been unduly and tediously emphasized, it is because, when overlooked, it has led to serious misinterpretations of Southeast Asian social structure, whether taken as a conceptual model or as a description of actual arrangements "on the ground."[6]

5. I am especially indebted to Fortes' seminal paper (1958:1-14) for my understanding of the domestic cycle.

6. In commenting on studies of Thai social structure, Evers (1969:120), for example, is impressed by what he sees as a "discrepancy" between the "anthropologist's model" and the "statistical model" of Thai society, a discrepancy which he infers from the fact that despite their nuclear family ideal, as many as 35 percent of the households in Thai villages studied consist of "extended families." From this he concludes that Thai society is not as "loosely structured" as most anthropologists have claimed, since, so he argues, the existence of such a high percentage of extended families indicates that corporate (highly structured) groups

TABLE 15. *Frequency Distribution of*
Household Size (N = 115)

Number of Households	Household Members
11	1
13	2
25	3
23	4
22	5
12	6
6	7
2	8
1	9

Median = 4; mode = 3.

Thus far, however, I have left unsaid much more than I have said, and I have left unexplained far more than I have explained. To say, for example, that most households in Yeigyi conform to a nuclear family ideal, leaves unsaid both the grounds for the conformity and the characteristics of the ideal. And to explain the four other household types as solutions for problems that are found in all human societies is to leave unexplained why these, rather than a variety of other known solutions, have been chosen. Thus, to return to the first point, when we say that a certain structural type is a widely shared cultural "ideal," we can mean that it is an attribute of a cultural heritage (in which case "conformity with an ideal" means behavior constrained by a cultural norm), or we can mean that it is an attribute of social actors (in which case "conformity with an ideal" means behavior motivated by a personal preference). The nuclear family household in village Burma is the ideal domestic group in this second sense. As such, it is the preponderant household type not because actors are constrained in their choice by a cultural norm (the norm of neo-local residence), but because newlyweds and their natal families alike, except under specified conditions described below, prefer to live separately from each other. Indeed, this preference is reflected in the very term for marriage, *qein-daung pyu*, "to set up a household." Moreover, this is a

---

are an important part of Thai social structure. The "loose structure" thesis aside, these extended families are *not* an index of the importance of corporate groups in Thai social structure, for (as in Burma) they are typically ad hoc and temporary solutions to interferences in life and domestic cycles, rather than prescriptive or preferential arrangements, based on normative, structural principles. The same explanation applies to the other societies in Southeast Asia, in all of which (as we have seen) the deviations from their nuclear family ideal represent for the most part structural solutions to problems created by death and divorce, aging and poverty.

deep-seated, not a capricious, preference, one which is motivated by the desire to avoid the tensions that are typically found in an extended family household.

This being so, the key to the Burmese preference for neo-local residence is primarily to be sought in the relationships that obtain within and between the domestic groups of the newlyweds. This does not mean that the tensions in these relationships are uniquely characteristic of Burmese kinship. On the contrary, most of them are characteristic of peasant families everywhere (Wolf 1966:65-73), and, more generally, they are probably universal, since, as we shall see, they relate to those feelings, sexual and aggressive, which derive from normal Oedipal and sibling relationships. If, then, these tensions do not produce the same institutional arrangements—after all, the nuclear family household is hardly universal, even among peasants—it is because institutions are responsive to other determinants as well, which may be more compelling. Thus, the different types of households which are associated with different peasant societies—patrilineal stem, patrilineal joint, and nuclear—can be explained, as Goldschmidt and Kunkel (1971) have suggested, by different combinations of political, legal, and economic determinants which override the affective relationships among kinsmen. Only when these latter determinants are absent, or not compelling, can household composition be determined primarily by such affective considerations as kinship tensions.

But though these tensions may be overridden, this does not mean that they therefore subside, let alone disappear. On the contrary, they are at least as acute in China and India, with their extended family households, as in Burma or Thailand with their nuclear family households. It may mean, rather, that (like other universal tensions) their expression as well as their resolution admit of a variety of cultural forms and institutional arrangements, and in both India and China other institutional arrangements have been evolved, in part, to deal with them. But only "in part," for as we shall see, the tensions that are avoided in the Burmese nuclear family households are very much present in the Chinese and Indian extended families, leading to a great deal of unhappiness, and even despair, in certain of the family members. In short, when these tensions are overridden, it may also mean a decrement in human happiness as the cost of achieving solutions for other problems, political and economic. It is difficult to judge which is the greater cost; one can only point out that cost-free solutions are as rare in the social as in the economic domain.

Before examining the kinship tensions in Burma, and the manner in which they are both expressed and resolved, it might be valuable, in order to place the Burmese case in its proper comparative perspective, to examine the types of tensions that are theoretically expected in any extended family household, and which can, in principle, be avoided in the nuclear family household.

A Theoretical Excursus

To simplify what is a much more complicated picture, I have restricted this excursus to the kintypes that are found in the nuclear families of any social actor (the "ego" of kinship analysis) and his spouse. Thus, if the domestic group of a married ego were always and only to consist of a nuclear family, then, as Diagram 4 indicates, ego would live successively in two domestic groups, none of whose members would overlap. In the first, ego's family of orientation, ego is a child and a sibling (and nothing else) and he or she lives with parents and siblings (and no one else). In the second, ego's family of procreation, ego is a spouse and a parent (and nothing else) and he or she lives with spouse and children (and no one else). In short, although ego lives with them as a minor, as a married adult he or she does not live with (1) father, (2) mother, (3) brother, (4) sister. Moreover, if ego does not live with siblings, neither does he or she live with (5) brother's wife and (6) sister's husband. Furthermore, since ego's spouse also lives neolocally, ego does not live with (7) spouse's father, (8) spouse's mother, (9) spouse's brother, (10) spouse's sister. Finally, since ego's children also form separate households when they marry, ego does not live with (11) married son or (12) married daughter nor with (13) son's wife and (14) daughter's husband.

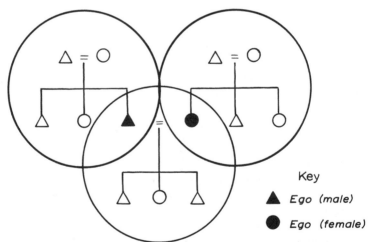

Key

▲ Ego (male)

● Ego (female)

Diagram 4. Composition and relationship between ego's families of orientation and procreation taken as separate households.

To put it differently, if all newlyweds form their own households, the domestic group cannot include any of the following fifteen adult dyads: (1) father-son, (2) father-daughter, (3) mother-son, (4) mother-daughter, (5) father-in-law and son-in-law, (6) father-in-law and daughter-in-law, (7) mother-in-law and son-in-law, (8) mother-in-law and daughter-in-law, (9) brother-brother, (10) sister-sister, (11) brother-sister, (12) sister's husband-wife's brother, (13) brother's wife and husband's brother, (14) sister's husband and wife's sister, (15) brother's wife and husband's sister. In sum, even when the analysis is confined vertically to two generations, and horizontally to the primary relatives of each spouse, fifteen kin dyads are automatically excluded from the domestic group if newlyweds form their own households.

Now, obviously, there can be a variety of reasons for the nuclear family household which are not necessarily related to the presence or absence of any or all of these dyads. But if, as in the case of village Burma and numerous other societies, the nuclear family constitutes the ideal household type precisely because the members of some or all of these dyads prefer not to live with each other, the grounds for such avoidance, even when all fifteen have such a preference, can be shown to comprise a relatively small theoretical class.

Theoretically, avoidance of any kind can be motivated by positive, as well as by negative, sentiments toward the avoided object. Since the latter are the more obvious, let us begin with them. Typically, the negative sentiments which lead to avoidance are fear and dislike (including a variety of stronger emotions such as disgust, hatred, and so on). If an object is feared, it may be avoided for self-protection. If it is disliked, it may be avoided (as in the case of foul odors or offensive people) out of disgust or antipathy, but it may also be avoided (as in the case of people we hate) because of possible temptation to harm or injure the object. Sometimes, however, it is not the object itself, but an attribute of the object which is disliked, in which case it is avoided (as in the case of a river about to overflow its banks) only when it is likely to display that attribute, and again the motivation may be fear, antipathy, or temptation to injure.

Avoidance motivated by positive sentiments is only slightly more complicated. If one likes or wants some object, but knows that such an emotion or desire is inappropriate or forbidden, the object may be avoided so as to preclude the arousal of the emotion or the temptation to act upon the desire. Thus a cardiac patient may avoid football games because the excitement is bad for his health, or a dieter may avoid candy shops so as not to be tempted to violate his diet.

This typology of the grounds for avoidance in general can easily subsume those on which kinship dyads might wish to avoid living with each other. The latter grounds, however, can only be understood with reference to the structural and cultural dimensions of the relationship of the dyads to each other or to a third kintype. This being so, one would expect the grounds for consanguineal and affinal avoidance, respectively, to be influenced by different structural and cultural factors.

With respect to the consanguineal dyads (those consisting of the various kintypes comprising the nuclear family), neo-local residence means that siblings who had lived together when they were unmarried minors, do not live together when they are married adults, and parents and children who had lived together when the latter were unmarried minors, do not live together when they are married adults. If, then, neo-local residence is motivated by the desire to avoid joint family households, the above two consequences of neolocality suggest that there are at least four conditions which might create such a desire in one or more of these dyads. (1) Tension produced between the members of a dyad by the relationships characteristic of their former statuses. Thus, for example, the relationship between siblings when unmarried minors might have been characterized by rivalry, or the relationship between parents and their unmarried children might have been characterized by hostility. (2) Tensions produced between the members of a dyad by a change in an ascribed status of one or both members so that their previously nonconflictual relationship is now characterized by conflict. Thus, for example, when a child becomes an adult, conflict might arise between him and his parents because of his desire to change his role, in accordance with the change in his ascribed age status, and their opposite desire that he continue in his former role. (3) Tensions produced within one or more members of a dyad by a change in their ascribed status(es) because the norms governing the new status(es) are incompatible with previously acquired drives or desires. Thus, for example, when children become sexually mature, conflict might arise between their libidinal desires with respect to a sibling or parent and cultural taboos that prohibit them. (4) Tensions produced between the members of a dyad by a change in an achieved status of one or both members because the role associated with the new status of one member frustrates the expectations of the other. Thus, for example, conflict might arise between a parent and a married child because the latter assigns higher priority to the requirements of his spouse than of his parent. Alternatively, conflict might arise between brother and sister because one or the other shows greater concern for his spouse than for his sibling.

With respect to the affinal dyads (those comprising the kintypes of the respective nuclear families of the two spouses), neo-local residence means that a dyad that had not lived together when one or both members were minors continues in not living together when both are adults. In this case the motivation for avoidance of joint family households must derive from

tensions produced by their new statuses, and, discounting such idiosyncratic factors as personal antipathy and the like, these tensions can only be
produced by (1) a discrepancy between the present and the past relationships of one or both members of the dyad to a third kintype, or (2)
incompatibility between some aspect of the dyadic relationship and the
cultural norms which govern it. With respect to the first, tension in a joint
family might develop, for example, between a child's parent and an
in-marrying child's spouse because of rivalry for the affection or the
loyalty of their common child-spouse. Similarly, tension might develop
between a sibling's spouse and a spouse's sibling because of rivalry for the
affection or loyalty of their common sibling-spouse. With respect to the
second, tension might be created, for example, because of sexual attraction between affines of the opposite sex and cultural rules concerning
incest or adultery.

Proceeding, now, from these theoretical expectations, let us examine
the tensions, the desire for whose avoidance constitutes at least a partial
explanation for the nuclear family household preference in village Burma.

Determinants of the Nuclear Family Household

Parent-Child Tensions

Although, as we have seen, the norms governing the parent-child
relationship stress respect and deference as obligations of children to
parents, and affection and assistance as mutual obligations of children and
parents, and although, as we have also seen, these norms are usually
expressed in action, it would be naive to assume that the parent-child
relationship in Burma, anymore than elsewhere, is unidimensional.
Intimate relationships are characterized everywhere by ambivalence,
and to stress exclusively the positive dimension of the parent-child
relationship—as is true of those anthropologists who attend to cultural
ideals alone—not only gives a false picture of that relationship, but
it impedes an understanding of the behavior that flows from the
ambivalence.

To say that a relationship is ambivalent is merely to say that, in addition
to the positive sentiments which ego and alter feel toward each other,
they also experience (consciously or unconsciously) negative ones. Some
Western writers have neglected to see the hostility-based tensions in
Oriental families either because, impressed by their normative expressions of solidarity, they have tended to sentimentalize them, or because
they have confused formal deference patterns with actual sentiment.
Viewed psychodynamically, customs of formal deference may not only,
however, express respect, but they may also serve as constraints on the
expression of hostility and other negative sentiments. Often, such cus-

toms are as much an index of tension as of respect. That this is so is suggested on the macroscopic level by the acting-out behavior of post-war Japanese youth and the Chinese Red Guards, and on the microscopic level by the tensions revealed by studies of family interaction in a variety of Oriental societies.

In Burma, tensions between parents and children relate, in the first place, to problems of autonomy and independence. This, at least, is how it is articulated on a conscious level in Yeigyi. Negligible in the cross-sex relationships, and submerged in the especially close mother-daughter relationship, these tensions are especially prominent, as they are else-where in Southeast Asia, in the father-son relationship. (For Java, for example, see Jay 1969:106.) The following example, though hardly typical of father-son *behavior,* is illustrative of the potentially explosive *tension* that is often found below the surface. When U Htin, a respected village elder, discovered that his (twenty-year old) son had stolen food from a village shop, he struck him with the palm of his hand. Furious, his son picked up a knife and, threatening his father, dared him to strike him again. Shaking and (obviously) frightened, U Htin walked away.

Usually under control, and therefore invisible, tensions between father and son only infrequently erupt in such a disruptive and (to the Burmese) shocking form. Nevertheless, so long as the son remains in a subordinate status, the tensions engendered by his struggle for autonomy persist.

Although somewhat less pronounced, the mother-daughter relation-ship often exhibits similar characteristics. As long as the daughter lives with her, she must remain subordinate to her mother. As one mother put it, she would have no objection to her divorced daughter living with her because, though she is an adult, "I can order my daughter to do whatever I like." This same theme, from the obverse position, was stressed by a young widow who refused to move in with her parents after her husband died. "At times," she said, "they will be good [they will not try to dominate], but at times they will be bad."

This desire for autonomy is by no means one-sided. Parents are just as keen to avoid subordination to their children as the latter are to escape from the domination of their parents. This desire emerges in sharpest relief in the comments of those widows and widowers (and divorcées) who, despite their option of living with their children, have nevertheless chosen to live alone. Their choice is based on the *personal* expectation, reinforced by the *cultural* premise, that living with children (like living with parents) is a source of trouble. Thus, one widow, who lives apart from both a married son and a married daughter, said simply: "It is not easy to live with [married] children. They tell you what to do." Another, with only a married son, said that if she lived with him, he would "try to squeeze money from me." The widowers echo the sentiments of the widows. One, an older man with married sons and a married daughter, said: "If I lived with my children, they would try to govern me." Another said, "If you live with your children, they try to control you."

Parent-child conflict can be explained not only in terms of the Burmese (personality) need for autonomy, but also in terms of Burmese (cultural) values regarding deference and respect. Normatively, the young offer deference and respect *(nei-ya htade)* to their elders, especially to their parents, whether they live with them or not. But since authority *(awza)* in the household resides with the one who owns the house and controls the income, the children have the authority when their parents live with them, and although they may continue to treat them with formal defer-ence, the parents no longer occupy a superordinate status. Their position of respect, the Burmese say, is destroyed *(nei-ya matu-bu).*

If, as I have already noted, parent-child conflict is especially prominent in the relationship between parents and children of the same sex, then it may not only be explained in cultural, but also in social terms. In general, it is the parent of the same sex who is the greater frustrator of the young child. The father, as we have seen, is both authoritarian and punitive, and his punishments more frequently fall on the son than the daughter, if only because the son is more frequently in his physical presence, and because his chores are assigned by the father rather than the mother. It is natural, then, that dereliction of duty or acts of irresponsibility are punished by the father. Although the mother is less punitive toward the daughter, at least physically, than the father is toward the son, she is nevertheless a frustrating figure. The daughter is inducted into the work force at an earlier age than the son, as is appropriate to the sexual division of labor characteristic of an agricultural economy, in which a great deal of un-skilled female work can be turned over to the daughter at a relatively early age. It is the mother, then, who imposes chores on the daughter, who consequently keeps her confined to the family compound (while her brother can freely wander about the village), and who punishes her for lack of attention to her responsibilities. For children of both sexes, then, parents (and especially same-sex parents) are frustrating figures, and the consequent hostility and rage of the Burmese child no more disappear in adulthood than those of other children anywhere else in the world.

But childhood punishment and restraint is not the only social basis for parent-child conflict in adulthood, nor for the special conflict that obtains between same-sex parents and children. The latter conflict, especially, may be explained not only in uniquely Burmese terms, but in more general, pan-human or Oedipal terms. Our data suggest that part of the parent-child conflict is an expression of normal, pan-human, Oedipal hostility, and that this dimension of the conflict is especially prominent in the son-father relationship.

Since, as we shall see in a later chapter, the husband-wife relationship takes precedence over all others, and since the son resents the father's privileged position vis à vis his mother, this resentment is an especially important basis in Burma for the son's hostility. The Burmese psychologist Sein Tu emphasizes this process when he writes of the son's "perception of the importance of the father to the mother, and of his prior and more powerful claim to her attention and love." (Sein Tu 1964:276.) This situation, according to Sein Tu, generates "great aggressiveness" in the son, so that the deference required in interaction with parents (and elders in general) serves as a defense against these aggressive impulses which "have to be kept rigidly in check." *(Ibid:* 283.)

At the adult level, the Oedipal basis for the son's hostility to the father emerges most clearly in the vehemence with which sons attack philandering fathers. In those cases which I know of personally, some sons refused to have anything to do with their fathers when they discovered their infidelities. Others, while not severing their relationship, spoke of their "hatred" for them. The following comment of one son, describing how he felt when he first found out about his father's infidelity, is not atypical. "I really hated him, sometimes I wanted to kill him."

The Oedipal-based father-son hostility is reflected, at the cultural level, in a prominent and widely known myth. That this myth originated in India—villagers take it to be a *Jātaka,* and although it is not included in the standard Cowell collection, it is found in both the *Dipavamsa* and the *Mahāvamsa*—does not diminish its psychological force in Burma; it has not only been incorporated into Burmese mythology, but its theme is the basis for a pervasive element in Burmese religious art and architecture, it is recounted as well in Burmese literature and classical drama, and it is an official government emblem.

As told in Yeigyi, the tale begins with a young princess, who was a nymphomaniac. As a young woman, her sex drive was insatiable; once she was abducted by 500 robbers in the forest, and although each of them had sexual intercourse with her, she was still not satisfied. Her father, ashamed of his daughter's nymphomania, banished her from the court. While wandering in the jungle, she met a lion, with whom she had intercourse, and since he alone could satisfy her sexually, she married him. Eventually they had two children, a son (who was eventually to become the Buddha) and a daughter. The son, Thihabāhu, was ashamed that his father was a lion, and he persuaded his mother and sister to abandon him. They left the jungle while the lion was away, and eventually returned to the court where the princess' father, the king, warmly welcomed them.

In the meantime, the lion, who was filled with grief, set out to find his family. As he wandered through the villages, the people were frightened and asked the king for protection. When the king asked his court whether any would volunteer to hunt down the lion, Thihabāhu, realizing that the lion must be his father, volunteered to kill him. So he set out for the jungle, and eventually found his father. Although the father was over-joyed to see him, the son slew his father with a bow and arrow.

As a reward for slaying the lion, Thihabāhu was made king of a new kingdom. However, shortly after ascending the throne he was struck blind, and the court physicians were unable to cure him. One day, however, a hermit came to the court and informed Thihabāhu that his blindness was retribution for his parricide, and that his sight could only be restored if he would repent of this sin. He told him to construct an image of a lion in honor of his father, and that he pay homage to it. Ashamed to be seen doing homage to a lion image, Thihabāhu ordered the image to be placed in front of a pagoda where, if he did obeisance to it, people would think that he was really worshiping the pagoda. This done, Thihabāhu prostrated himself before the image, and his sight was restored.

That is why, the villagers say, a leogryph *(chinthei)* stands at the entrance of large and important pagodas. (Actually, there are two of them, one at either side of the entrance.) Indeed, this symbol of the slain father is ubiquitous in Burma, the lion image being portrayed graphically, as well as plastically, in a variety of contexts—official documents, coins, formal invitations, dust jackets, and so on.

A more remarkable Oedipal tale, remarkable for reasons which will soon become apparent, was recounted by an American-educated woman from Rangoon. When I asked a group of westernized Rangoonians whether the Oedipus complex was found in Burma, they expressed surprise that I should have asked the question—of course the Oedipus complex is found in Burma!—and they then proceeded to give all kinds of examples. When I then asked if they knew any Oedipal legends or myths, they knew only the Thihabāhu myth. However, the above-mentioned woman said she knew of yet another, but after thinking a few moments she expressed surprise that she had characterized it as Oedipal. When she recounted the tale, it became apparent that on the manifest level it indeed is not an Oedipal tale, for although the theme is Oedipal, the dramatis personae are not. That, however, she had originally offered it as one suggests that this is what it signifies to her at a latent level.

The tale concerns one Maung Ba Kyein, a traveler, who comes to a certain kingdom and is told that a Nāga, a mythical serpent, had killed the king, taken the queen as his wife, and satisfied his hunger by eating the people. After hearing this tale, Maung Ba Kyein decides that he would become king. One night he entered the queen's chamber, and placed a banana stalk in the queen's bed, so that, when both were covered with a blanket, it would appear as if the queen were sleeping with a man. Hiding behind the curtain, Maung Ba Kyein then waited for the arrival of the Naga. When he entered the chamber, the Naga, seeing what he took to be the body of a sleeping man, pierced it with his sword. Just as Maung Ba Kyein had planned, the sword stuck in the banana stalk, and, as the Naga attempted to extricate it, Maung Ba Kyein stepped from behind the curtain and slew him. He then took the queen as his wife and he himself became the king.

I would suggest, then, that one of the reasons for the Burmese preference for nuclear family households, and their avoidance, whenever possible, of joint family households, is their desire to avoid the conflict that is found in the parent-child relationship, a conflict which, in large part, reflects normal Oedipal hostility. But the libidinal component of the Oedipal relationship is just as important as the aggressive for this neo-local residence pattern. Although Sein Tu, whose research was primarily concerned with male personality, stresses the sexual element in the mother-son relationship only—"The child comes to regard the womenfolk (mother and sister) in the house as dispensers of nurturance and objects of sex desire" (Sein Tu 1964:280)—it is just as prominent in the father-daughter relationship. In both of these dyads, I would suggest, the desire to avoid the tension produced by the incompatibility between a personal desire (incestuous attraction) and a cultural prohibition (incest taboo) constitutes one of the motives for the avoidance of extended family households.

So that I not be misunderstood, I wish to stress that these libidinal ties between parents and children are normal. They are found in all societies, and are in fact weaker in Burma than in many. Thus, to take but one example, the erotic overtones in the parent-child relationship in South Asia are much stronger than in Burma. In India (at least in the urban, upper-middle class, Bengali family) the father-daughter bond is highly eroticized, according to the compelling data presented by Roy (n.d.), and it has a strong influence on the daughter's entire life cycle. In India, father and daughter are separated when, following her marriage, she moves into her husband's natal home. Although the mother-son relationship is equally eroticized, the son remains with his mother when he marries, and, if I may extrapolate from Roy's data, his strong Oedipal tie to his mother is rarely severed. This is also the case in Ceylon, as Obeyesekere (n.d.) has shown in convincing detail.

That, in Burma, the avoidance of joint-family households is motivated, in part, by avoidance of incest temptations is a thesis which the Burmese themselves, the villagers at least, consciously verbalize. Although villagers know of no cases of parent-child incest, they (unlike most Westerners) acknowledge the presence of libidinal feelings in the parent-child relationship, and the daughter, especially, is trained from a relatively early age to avoid physical intimacy with her father (and brothers). Beginning at about the age of ten, girls are forbidden to sit on their father's lap or to cuddle with him, in order to prevent the arousal of erotic feelings. To act upon such feelings (at any age) would be monstrous, even though no well-conceived grounds for the incest taboo was ever adduced by the villagers. Mother-son incest is prohibited, they contend, because one should not have intercourse "in the same hole from which you were born." That mothers are conceived as potential inciters of incestuous feelings in their sons is suggested by the *Dhammathat* which include the following acts among the list of "female improprieties": When she caresses her grown-up son with feelings other than those of maternal affection," and, again, "When she artfully evidences lustful feelings even for her grown-up son." (Gaung 1905:17, 18.)

Father-daughter incest is even more heinous, so that reasons are neither required nor offered. As the village headman put it, it is so evil "you shouldn't even think about it."

The enormity of parent-child incest is reflected in its punishment. Today, villagers say, parent-child incest would be punished by a physical beating of the culprits, followed by their banishment from the village (and, if their deed were known, they would be barred from any other village). In traditional Burma, according to Daw Than Than Ohn (personal communication), the punishment was even more severe. The offenders were forced to eat "like dogs and pigs"—for so they were viewed —following which they were deported from the country. In addition to social punishment, the karmic retribution for incest is rebirth in hell, but only after the male has been reborn as a female, and the female as an animal. (The discrepancy between the respective punishments of males and females is in accordance with Buddhist folk belief in which one can fall only one step at a time in the ladder of existence. Hence, given the Buddhist value hierarchy, males fall to a female, females to an animal, status.)

If insults and accusations can be interpreted both as expressions of anger and as techniques of aggression, then the fact that incestuous insults and accusations are viewed by the Burmese to be the gravest of all, may be taken as yet another measure of the horror attached to incest. The rage evoked by such taunts as, "mother-fucker" (*mei-qei lou*), or, embellished, "You return to your mother to fuck" (*nin qamei nin pyan lou*), has been known to provoke murder. If the reaction is so strong, it is perhaps plausible to infer that it touches a raw nerve, the intensity of the reaction concealing the intensity of the desire to commit the very act with which he is taunted.

Perhaps, too, a similar explanation accounts for the rage aroused by another form of insult, one in which another is alleged to have intercourse with the parent, usually the mother. Thus, "I fuck your mother" (nint qamei nga lou), or as embellished, "I stretch and fuck your mother's large cunt" (nin qamei saukpat-kyi nga hpye lou), or, again, "mother-giver!" (me-ei pei), meaning, you offer your mother to others for fornication. Rage is aroused in these cases, I would suggest, because (among other reasons) others are fantasied to commit the very act which the victim of the insult is prohibited from committing.[7]

Thus far, then, I have suggested that the avoidance of joint families is motivated, in part, by the conflict between incestuous desires and incest prohibitions. This suggestion is confirmed by the explicit statements of the villagers. Somehow, these desires are not seen as a problem so long as the spouse of the child or both of the child's parents are alive; it is as if the presence of these other dyads serves as a powerful counter-influence to incestuous desires. When they are present, then, the problem is merely anticipatory—it might arise should the other spouse die, and parent and child of opposite sex are left alone in the house. It becomes actual, however, in those cases in which a married child, who had been living neo-locally, loses his spouse, and the question of co-residence with his widowed parent arises. Here, the evidence is very clear. Although there are cases of mother and son living together, there is only one case—and this, as we shall see, is the exception which truly proves the rule—of father and daughter. That father and daughter do not live together is explicitly related to village notions concerning sex and incest. Father and daughter cannot live alone together, so it is assumed, without being susceptible to either the temptation or the suspicion of incest. The exception noted above consists not of a father-daughter dyad, but of a father-in-law and his daughter-in-law, who are above suspicion because the woman is in her fifties and the man in his nineties.

It should be noted that urban informants typically deny that incestuous feelings or suspicions play a role in the determination of residence or household composition. Nevertheless, I know of one case, a widower and his spinster daughter, in which the father demanded that his daughter-in-law visit them every day. His alleged reason was that his daughter "should not be lonely." But the real reason, according to his grand-

7. All of these examples, it will be noted, are parent-directed. I have never heard any incestuous insults that are child-directed, such as "son fucker," or "daughter fucker." It is my impression that this is characteristic of most societies, and although one might speculate on the reasons, I can think of none that is especially compelling.

daughter, was to forestall gossip and suspicion of incest. And suspicion of this kind is easily aroused. In the village, once the daughter has reached puberty, father and daughter will not remain alone in the same room. This, too, is viewed as a quaint notion by their city cousins, although the latter are shocked by events to which Westerners would pay little or no attention. Thus, some Rangoon friends recounted the shock of the members of a sophisticated Rangoon club when a father and daughter sang a popular duet which describes how a couple behave when the lights go out. The same sophisticated group were even more shocked when a father and daughter danced together at a ball.

To summarize, then, temptations or accusations of incest constitute one of the grounds for the avoidance of parent-child (or, at least, father-daughter) households. Why this reason applies more strongly to father and daughter than to mother and son is a question to which, unfortunately, I was not alert when conducting field work.

Tensions Between Parents-in-Law and Children-in-Law

Tension between parents-in-law and children-in-law, which may be even stronger than tension between parents and children, is another motivational basis for the formation of nuclear family households. Of the various parent to child-in-law relationships, conflict between daughter-in-law and mother-in-law is the most acute. Villagers take it for granted that (as they say) "It is in the nature of their relationship for mother-in-law and daughter-in-law to quarrel." The tensions between them are exacerbated by, but not confined to, joint living. When I remarked to Daw Myan, an elderly woman, on how hard she worked in the paddy fields, she said bitterly: "Yes. It is because my son married early, and is supporting his wife instead of helping us. So now, we can rely only on ourselves." Her comment echoes the Burmese belief that when a boy marries, his family loses a son for—as the proverb has it—"the son follows along after the wife" *(tha meinma laik thwathi).*

Although Daw Myan's bitterness indicates that at least part of the tension between mother-in-law and daughter-in-law is induced by their struggle for the allegiance of the husband-son, when they live together there are two additional bases for tension. First, there is their struggle for domination, a struggle which is reflected in the traditional couplet: *kyweima mahkweima/yaukhama htaukhkwa.* "The daughter-in-law acts like a bitch/the mother-in-law like a [crooked] *htaukhkwa.*" The *htaukhkwa* is the pole used to steady the yoke before the oxen are harnessed; if crooked, the yoke will not be balanced. (It is significant that the villagers' interpretation of the proverb is rather different from its literal meaning. According to the proverb, in which the daughter-in-law acts the bitch while the mother-in-law is the prop of the family, the daughter-in-law is the culprit. In the villagers' interpretation, in which the "ox pole" becomes the "[crooked] ox pole," mother-in-law and daughter-in-law alike are the culprits.)

But the daughter-in-law has an additional reason to resent a co-resident mother-in-law. Since, typically, the son is strongly attached to his mother, he may sometimes pay her more attention than the wife deems desirable, and the latter's jealousy may lead her to attempt to disrupt their close relationship, and, if unsuccessful, to return to her natal home. The mother-in-law, resenting her daughter-in-law's attitude, may explicitly tell her that she has no business interfering with the mother-son bond. But that is not all. Often, the mother-in-law does not hesitate to criticize her daughter-in-law for not performing her wifely duties as well as she should. Thus, a dutiful wife, as we shall see in a later chapter, is expected to rise in the morning before her husband, prepare his food, and have everything in readiness for him. Should she be lax, a critical mother-in-law (and sometimes even a mother) is quick to bring the wife's dereliction to her attention.

For both reasons it is easy to understand why Burmese folk etymology interprets the term for daughter-in-law, *hkyeima*, as referring to the pain she suffers in this subordinate role. Since the term for son-in-law is *thamet*, one would expect the daughter-in-law to have a parallel term; instead, it is *hkyeima* because, it is said, the latter is the woman *(ma)* who must sweat *(khywei)* in trying to please her mother-in-law.

Since resentment and jealousy, clearly, are poor sentiments on which to base a solidary household, it is little wonder that mother-in-law and daughter-in-law prefer to avoid extended family households. If, nevertheless, one is formed, it typically occurs when a weak son submits to a domineering and possessive (as well as wealthy) mother. The prior struggle between mother and wife in attempting to influence his decision is viewed as a zero-sum game, analogous to a competitive Burmese athletic match. Indeed, it is said of the victorious mother-in-law (as it is said of a victorious athletic team) that she has "dominated" *(nainde)*, and that henceforth it is she who will "rule" *(kyizoude)* the family.

Conflict between mother-in-law and daughter-in-law, is of course a "type" conflict in many, perhaps most, societies; and since it is especially prominent when they are co-resident, it is one of the factors predisposing for nuclear family households, or at least for the avoidance of patrilocal extended family households. This is true for societies as widely separated as Java (Geertz 1961:29; Jay 1969:145-147) and Kandyan Ceylon (Yalman 1967:119), on the one hand, and England on the other. In England, for example, married couples in working-class London (Bethnal Green) avoid living with the husband's parents because the "tension" between co-residing mother-in-law and daughter-in-law, produced by their "rival(ry) for a stove and a sink—and maybe for a man," is "sharp" (Young and Wilmott 1965:32). Hence, if newlyweds are too poor to set up housekeeping, they live preponderantly with the bride's, not the groom's parents.

But kinship tensions are not, of course, the only determinants of household composition, and patrilocal extended family households may exist despite acute tensions between mother-in-law and daughter-in-law, as, for example, in India and China, where the tension between these affines is much more acute than in Burma. The result, however, is proverbial: the suffering of the daughter-in-law, constantly subject to the authority and domination of the mother-in-law, is a well-known and often commented upon theme. (See Mandelbaum [1970:91-92] for India, and Hsu [1971:64] for China.) In both, moreover, the wife is not only oppressed by the husband's mother, but, as among the Arabs (Patai 1971:443-444), she is secondary to her in the affection of her husband. Since, to quote a Chinese authority, the welfare and happiness of the married couple must be subordinate to that of the parents, marriage must not be allowed "to transfer the center of affection, loyalty, and authority from the parents to the new couple." (Yang 1969:23.) Hence, in China and India alike, display of affection between husband and wife are discouraged, and in the former, concubinage and prostitution are encouraged as a means of diverting the husband's romantic love from his wife. (*Ibid.: 24.*)

At the same time, and despite the fact that the mother-in-law is structurally the dominant of the two, in China, at least, she is not much happier with the arrangement than the daughter-in-law, and she often attempts to mitigate her problem by the practice of "adopting a daughter-in-law" (Wolf 1968)—bringing a very young girl into the household, who, when she attains her majority, becomes the wife of the son.

If the relationship between mother-in-law and daughter-in-law is the most conflictful of the parent and child-in-law dyads in Burma, the other three also exhibit varying, though lesser, degrees of tension. As already noted, the relationship between daughter-in-law and father-in-law is not an exceptionally conflictful one. Hence, although married sons do not live in the home of a widowed mother, they may do so with a widowed father, especially when it is to their economic advantage. Even then, however, there may be opposition from the wife for, with widowhood, the father often becomes closer to his son, and may attempt to exert greater influence over him than is enjoyed by his wife.

Induced by their rivalry for the loyalty of the daughter-wife, the tension between son-in-law and mother-in-law, though less intense than that between daughter-in-law and mother-in-law, may yet be strong enough, and this tension is one of the factors which opposes the formation of matrilocal extended families. Generally, the son-in-law is the subordinate person in this relationship; in some cases, it is said, he may fear her power. The tension between them is stronger when the discrepancy in their ages is small, so that their rivalry for the loyalty of the wife-daughter is accompanied by underlying sexual tensions as well. But tensions between mother-in-law and son-in-law are not the only constraint on the formation of matrilocal extended families, for the rivalry between father-in-law and son-in-law serves as another constraint. Since, as we have seen, the father-daughter relationship is often very close, the rivalry of husband and father for the loyalty of their wife-daughter may not only lead to tension, but also to overt conflict (Nash 1965:50). Although such formerly extreme measures, as the taboo proscribing conversation between son-in-law and parents-in-law (Ba Aung 1914:225), are no longer operative, I suspect that this avoidance custom was instituted to prevent the overt expression of the tension which exists between them, as were the customs of respect which are still practiced among these same affines in Java (Geertz 1961:29).

Thus far this discussion has been addressed to the rivalry between parent-in-law and child-in-law for the loyalty of their child-spouse, a rivalry which, either potentially or actually, is always present in joint family households. But if these rivals sustain a relationship of *inter*personal conflict, the object of the rivalry, the child-spouse, is subject to *intra*personal conflict in attempting to decide where his or her primary loyalty lies. In uxorilocal residence, it is the wife, and in virilocal residence, the husband who is caught between the conflicting demands of the spouse and the parents (although typically, according to informants, it is most acute in the wife). These incompatible loyalties are acute enough when they live neo-locally—they are, as we shall see, the second most frequent cause for divorce—but they are especially difficult under conditions of joint living. Even while I was in Yeigyi, a couple was divorced for this reason. Caught between the demand of his sick father to be cared for by his wife and the wife's persistent refusal to comply with the demand, the son-husband finally resolved his conflict of loyalties by siding with his father, whereupon his wife left him. The villagers, incidentally, sided with the husband. They pointed out that if he had had a sister, she, rather than his wife, would have been expected to nurse his father, but since the husband was his father's only child, filial piety required that his father (rather than his wife) receive his primary loyalty.

Sibling Tensions

Extended family households based on the sibling bond are even rarer in Yeigyi than those based on the parent-child bond. Thus, there is only one case in Yeigyi of a widower living with a married brother, and there are no cases of two (or more) married siblings living together, with or without their parents. (Urban informants, however, report a few such cases, admittedly rare.) The explanation seems to be two-fold: tensions between siblings, on the one hand, and siblings-in-law, on the other. Although the sibling relationship, to begin with the former, entails mutual responsibilities, and although it is sometimes one of affection and even intimacy, it is also productive of conflict. As one widow (who lives alone) said, she could not reside with her married sister because "we could not live together peacefully."

If parent-child conflict is usually related to struggles over autonomy, sibling tensions, particularly between those of the same sex, are primarily related to rivalry and envy. Sisters are rarely envious of a more successful brother because they acquire prestige from the latter's success, but they may be envious of a sister whose husband has higher status than their own. It is among brothers, however, that this particular basis for sibling rivalry is especially acute, and in the city, as well as in the village, one can even find cases of men who became monks as a result of this problem. Although brother-sister envy, as I have mentioned, is less frequent, it is most often, according to informants, a reflection of the brother's persistent resentment, traceable to their childhood, that the sister (as is often the case) was the father's favorite. Indeed, this particular basis for tension can be more broadly generalized. Much of the rivalry between siblings, regardless of sex, can be traced, according to informants, to childhood rivalry. This rivalry, according to my observations, is generally related —as it is elsewhere—to competition for the love and affection of parents, and since in the village it is the younger child who is generally favored, the younger child is more frequently resented by the elder. Their rivalry is reflected in the Thematic Apperception Test in which children are often seen as "threatening rivals for a marginal amount of food or parental love" (Steele n.d.).

Rivalry between childhood siblings, whatever its causes, is taken for granted, and its expression in overt aggression is not only observable, but it is taken to be self-evident. Indeed, one of the reasons for never leaving a baby alone is the fear that he will be harmed by an elder sibling. In one (admittedly extreme) case, a two-year-old girl, ostensibly combing her baby brother's hair, pushed a hair pin into its tender skull, and only the sudden arrival of the mother prevented her from causing him serious injury. As they grow older, girls (but not boys) undergo an important structural change, for at the age of five or six they are expected to care for their younger siblings, and at this time their behavior becomes maternal. As part of the maternal role, they can sublimate much of their hostility to their young charges by scolding and punishing them for wrong-doing.

Even in adulthood, sibling rivalry, whatever its sources, may sometimes erupt into overt aggression and conflict, as the randomly chosen cases cited below indicate. The citation of these cases, it must be emphasized, should not be taken to mean that conflict is typical of the sibling relationship, for, in fact, its incidence is small. I, at least, observed only a few cases. These isolated cases of sibling conflict are cited, rather, as an index of their more extensive rivalry which is usually kept under control, but comes to the surface under special circumstances. This is not to say that cases exemplifying the reverse process—one in which conflict produces, rather than expresses, tension—do not also occur. Such cases, however, are also infrequent, and they are not discussed here because they are not germane to the present argument concerning neo-locality. That is, since both types of sibling conflict are rare, it is not their conflicts but their tensions that are germane to the preference of siblings for neo-local residence. Indeed, it is precisely because of their avoidance of co-residence that siblings—so my argument goes—are able to maintain relatively non-conflictual relationships despite their rivalry. Let us now examine some of these cases of conflict.

U Kant and U Thant, brothers living in adjacent houses, quarreled over the ownership of a gourd, whose economic value was trivial. Unable to resolve their dispute, they brought it to the village elders for adjudication. U Kant claimed the gourd because it was growing in his compound, U Thant because he had planted it. Unable to effect a compromise, the elders resolved the problem by declaring that the gourd would belong to the village, and its fruit would be used for feeding the monks.

U Sa Mya, a widower, and Kou San Hla, his married younger brother, live together intermittently in the house owned by their Mandalay-residing parents. Each works his own fields, and each assists the other in working his. Although the elder brother frequently requested his sister-in-law to feed his laborers, he persistently resisted providing her with sufficient funds to defray the expense. Since U Sa Mya's resistance evoked obvious distress in his brother—more than once it reduced his brother and sister-in-law to tears—it seemed like a direct expression of his resentment of his brother, almost as if it were calculated to provoke conflict. And this indeed is exactly what happened. For a long time, given the deference pattern expected of a younger brother, Kou San Hla found it impossible to criticize or demand additional payment from his older brother. Finally, however, his (and his wife's) resentment could no longer be contained, and he told his parents that he intended to move from their house. The latter eventually prevailed upon him to remain, but only after they ordered U Sa Mya to honor his obligation.

Ma Nain and her husband, Kou Sein, returned from Mandalay where they had bought food for offerings to the monks. Ma Nain's younger sister, Ma Hlain, asked her if they could make a joint offering so that she too might acquire merit. Ma Nain refused, saying she wanted the merit entirely for herself. At this, Ma Hlain became enraged, and demanded that her sister repay the debt which, so she claimed, she owed her. Ma Nain denied the existence of the debt, insisting that it had in effect been repaid when her sister, having sold the harvest from their jointly owned mango orchard, had not given her an equal share of the proceeds. Their quarrel escalated into a shouting and screaming match which, punctuated by verbal abuse, could be heard across the village. Finally, exhausted, they each walked away. In the meantime, the conflict between the sisters provoked their husbands into a quarrel. Ma Hlain's husband told his brother-in-law that if he and his wife believed they had not received their fair share of the mango sale, they could go to the headman for adjudication. The latter, in a rage, struck him twice with his fist, and when his brother-in-law dared him to strike again, he turned and walked away. Two months later, the brothers-in-law were reconciled, but the sisters still refused even to talk to each other, each accusing the other of selfishness and deceit. It might be pointed out that this is a case in which tension produces conflict—Ma Nain's resentment of her sister was openly expressed in her almost unheard of refusal to share her merit—and the conflict, in turn, exacerbates the tension.

To take a final example, let us consider the case of U Cit Hti, a man generally knowledgeable about Buddhist matters, who became deeply envious of his younger brother's suddenly acquired reputation as an expert on Buddhist metaphysics and meditation. His brother, U Cit Hti said to me, had become selfish and arrogant; he talked about meditation, but did not practice morality. People admired his brother, he continued, because he tells them what they like to hear, but they dislike him (U Cit Hti) because he is honest, and says exactly what is on his mind. His brother, he claimed, is a pretender, and pretenders are more to be feared than enemies, for since one never knows what they are about, one cannot deal with them. U Cit Hti's envy of his brother (combined with some other frustrations) eventually led him into an acute depression, and finally into the yellow robe.

Sibling rivalry, like the tension observed between other kinsmen discussed earlier in this chapter, is probably no more acute in Burma than it is elsewhere. If it is one of the constraints on the formation of extended family households, this does not mean that societies characterized by such households do not have such friction. Rather, in the latter societies, a variety of social and cultural structures serve to contain the conflict that might develop from it. Nevertheless, these structures are not always effective, and often these households do not survive the death of the parents. In India, for example, patrilocal joint families tend to persist only for as long as the father lives. After his death, the rivalry between the brothers, which is muted by the father's presence, usually breaks into the open and leads to the splitting of the family as a normal (and final) stage in the domestic cycle (Mandelbaum 1970: 66, 125-126). In China, too, although the "big family ideal," as Hsu calls it (Hsu 1971:108-122), is found everywhere, it is rarely practiced. Friction between brothers either leads to family fission when they marry, or, if they stay under the same roof (as they do in Hsu's West Town), the household property is split, and the nuclear family of each brother becomes in effect a separate social unit. As the people of West Town put it, "Few families with three generations can eat from the same kitchen; they can't get along together." (*Ibid.*: 121.)

Thus far we have been primarily concerned with siblings of the same sex, whose tensions are generally related to rivalry. Rivalry between cross-sex siblings, as I have aready noted, is much less frequent, their tensions being related more importantly to sex. Unlike same-sex siblings who are occasionally co-resident, cross-sex siblings never live together, and one of the reasons offered by informants is the explicit (and stereotypic) tension between wife's brother and sister's husband, which is consciously related to the former's resentment of the latter for having taken his sister. Like most motives, this resentment no doubt is over-determined, but one of its components, as we shall see below, probably relates to the unconscious sexual overtones—the incestuous residues—in the brother-sister relationship. The Burmese are well aware of the possibility of erotic feelings between siblings, and just as girls, as they approach puberty, are forbidden to cuddle with their father, they are similarly forbidden to do so with their brother. One informant reports that when, at the age of ten, she was told by her mother to avoid such physical intimacies with her brother, and she asked the reason, her mother said, "Would you want to marry one of your brothers when you grow up?" This, she said, struck her as an awful thought at the time, and she said that she did not. "If so," her mother replied, "stay away from your brothers."

As in other societies, sibling-incest impulses are not extinguished, though they are repressed or sublimated, and avoidance of the intra-psychic conflict produced by them is probably another reason for the complete absence of households of cross-sex siblings in Yeigyi. Indeed, adult cross-sex siblings not only do not live together, but (like cross-sex parents and children) they are not permitted to be alone together at night where no one can observe them. The reason for the prohibition relates to temptations or accusations of incest, a reason which is summed up, so the villagers say, in the following proverb: "Pots placed together touch/ropes placed together become entangled."

But these are not the only indications of the erotic element in the brother-sister relationship. There are some suggestive behavioral and cultural indications as well. While these do not prove anything, either individually or collectively, they are consistent with all the other data. At the cultural level, one can hardly overlook the fact that husband and wife frequently address each other as "brother" and "sister,"[8] nor can one ignore the additional data supplied by Sein Tu, who, in research unrelated to my own, arrived at the same conclusion concerning the erotic component in the brother-sister relationship. In the Burmese court, he points out, princes and even commoners addressed their wives and mistresses as "royal sister."[9] He also cites the eighteenth-century poem which advises that if one desires to pluck two desirable varieties of shrub, it should be done in the month of Wazo, but if one desires his "youngest sister, [he should] come and pluck her in the early months of Tabaung or Tagu." (Sein Tu 1964:280.)

The most important cultural evidence is found in (what is probably) the best known myth in Burma, that concerning the most famous spirit in the pantheon of the Thirty-Seven Lords (nat). (For details of this nat and a more complete narrative of the myth, see Spiro 1967:92-95.) Min Mahagiri is the only pan-Burman spirit in the pantheon; his symbol (and residence) is a coconut, which hangs from the rafter of every traditional household in Burma. In addition, his statue, and that of his sister, are enshrined on Mt. Popa, the national center of the nat cult.

Min Mahagiri was a blacksmith, one U Tin De, who lived in the ancient Burmese kingdom of Tagaung. Fearful that this powerful blacksmith would raise a rebellion against him, the king of Tagaung took his sister, Shwei Myet Hla, as his queen. Then, as a ruse, he asked the queen to summon her brother to the palace, and, when he arrived, the king ordered that he be thrown into the flames. When his sister was informed

---

8. In those few cases of cousin marriages, spouses are kin who, by extension cousin-sibling , address each other by sibling terms. Nevertheless, it is suggestive that non-cousins also use these terms, and that, even in the few cases of cousin marriages, other terms are not used to express their affectionate (in contrast to their kinship) bond.

9. Because of the legal preference for royal half-sibling marriages, some of the court marriages at least would have been contracted between half-siblings. Nevertheless, one cannot dismiss the facts that commoners, as well as those princes that did not contract such marriages, also used the same terminology of address, and that those princes that did contract such marriages had no term to express their affectionate (in contrast to their legal) relationship other than the sibling terms.

of his fate, she threw herself into the flames with her brother, and, except for their heads, they were consumed by the fire.

After their deaths, brother and sister became *nat*, inhabiting the tree under which they had died, and eating those who came to rest in its shade. The king had the tree uprooted, and cast into the Irrawady, where it floated to the medieval capital of Pagan. The king of Pagan appointed them as the guardian spirits of Mt. Popa, placed their heads in a shrine on the mountain, and ordered that an annual festival be held in their honor. In commemoration of their subsequent assistance to the monarchy, a later king ordered that a coconut be hung, and propitiated, in every house in the kingdom in their commemoration.

Here, then, is a myth of a brother and sister whose love was so great that the sister sacrificed her life rather than live without him. The sexual overtone in their relationship is implied in two taboos which are still observed today. When a woman goes into labor pains, the coconut must be removed from the house since childbirth is offensive to them. More important, spouses never sleep on the southeastern side of the house, the side at which the coconut is hung, because these brother and sister spirits are especially offended by the sight of sexual activity. Now in Burmese belief all pure beings are offended by sex, and in this case the Brother-Sister Nat, just because they are siblings and living together have all the more reason, as Lehman observes (personal communication), to insist on their abhorrence of sex. For unless they are asexual, they cannot be *pure* nat.

I would finally mention a behavioral indication of the libidinal tie between brother and sister. I have already observed that the brother is the designated protector of his sister's virtue, a role which he zealously performs. As some villagers put it, a brother whose sister's honor is sullied can be led to murder against her lover. Viewed psychodynamically, the brother's exaggerated defense of his sister's virginity, especially when combined with his rather exaggerated rage to taunts by others of having had sex with her—"[I] fuck your elder sister" *(nin qama lou)*, or "[I] fuck your younger sister" *(nin hnama lou)*—suggests that an (unconscious) erotic attachment is not unlikely. The stereotypic resentment of the sister's husband importantly strengthens the plausibility of this inference, as we shall see in the following section.

Sibling-in-Law Tensions

The relationship between cross-sex siblings-in-law is more or less affectively neutral. This is not the case, however, in the relationship between those of the same sex. Among the same-sex dyads, the most tense relationship—and one of the most tense in the entire kinship system—is found in the *yaukhpa,* the wife's brother-sister's husband dyad. Theirs is a stereotypic, culturally expected tension, allegedly motivated by the brother's resentment of his sister's (especially his younger sister's) husband. "Until her marriage," as one villager put it, "she has been his. Hence, he is jealous if she shows affection to anyone else," let alone marries him. His (putative) feeling is reflected in the proverb, "When the sister takes a husband, her brother's arse burns" *(hnama lin nei/maun hpin kyein).* The second line of the couplet is intended as a double entendre—it pains the brother to lose her, and it arouses pangs of sexual longing for her. (Although *maun* is the term for younger brother, informants quoted the complet in discussing the attitudes toward the sister of the elder brother. Following their understanding—or, at least, their use of the couplet—I have rendered *maun* as "brother," not "younger brother.")

The brother's feelings are reflected in the way in which kin terms are exchanged between him and his sister's husband. Whereas all other siblings-in-law address each other by sibling (not sibling-in-law) terms, the sister's husband addresses his wife's brother as "brother-in-law" *(yaukhpa),* and the latter does not even use this affinal term in addressing his sister's husband. Instead, he addresses him by his proper name, a usage which (in Burmese) connotes an inferior or subordinate status. Since this cultural expression reflects essentially unconscious, rather than conscious, tension, informants—as would be expected—offer various ad hoc (and sometimes not very convincing) explanations for it. Piecing them together, one can construct the following synthetic explanation.

Since the brother is both "embarrassed" by and "resents" his sister's marriage, "he simply cannot call her husband *yaukhpa.*" To do so is to underscore the painful fact that the latter is married to his sister, whereas by addressing him by his name he is treating him, as it were, as a stranger, not an affine. The brother "resents" the marriage because, being a wife-giver, he loses a sister, while his brother-in-law gains a wife. He is "embarrassed" by the marriage because he views the dower which his sister receives from her husband's family as, in a sense, the brother-in-law's payment for her sexual services. This is "humiliating" for him.

All of this tends to support the thesis that the brother's attitude toward his sister's husband is primarily motivated by his (unconscious) libidinal tie to his sister. This interpretation is further supported by the fact that a male with an unmarried sister reacts with rage to being addressed as *yaukhpa,* "wife's brother," even in jest and in a context which is culturally defined as ritual license. Thus during the Water Festival, the otherwise circumspect relationship between the sexes is relaxed, and sexual obscenities (both verbal and gestural) which are usually strictly prohibited are both permitted and expected. But to address a man with an attractive sister as *yaukhpa* is to court trouble, for the implicit meaning "I want your sister," is rage-producing. If it is a serious offense even during the carnival-like atmosphere of the Water Festival, it is understandable that a man is never addressed as *yaukhpa* in any other context.

Related to this seemingly harmless appellation is the enraging insult, "you give your younger sister [to another for coitus]" *(hnama bei)*. This is a generic, not a brother-in-law specific, insult, but it is an indication of the brother's attitude to his sister's sex. When she marries, the brother does not exactly "give" his sister for coitus, but he allows her, albeit legally, to be used for sexual purposes.

To conclude, then, the tensions between brothers-in-law, which in part are related to the sexual overtones in the brother-sister relationship, constitute another basis for the avoidance of brother-sister households. The same holds, though to a much lesser extent, for the relationship between brother's wife and sister's husband *(yaukma)*. Since, typically, brother and sister (especially younger sister) sustain an intimate relationship, the sister—even ignoring the unconscious incestuous elements in the relationship—often resents the brother's wife for having displaced her from the special place in her brother's affection. Hence, many Burmese say, the sister prefers that her brother marry one of her friends. "She does not like to give him to a stranger." On the wife's side, even ignoring her possible resentment of her husband's lingering attachment to his sister, there is a special problem in connection with her husband's elder sister. For, given the importance of age in the Burmese social structure, the wife may feel (sometimes with justification) that her sister-in-law has more influence than she over her husband. In this case, resentment flows from a structural rather than an affective determinant. On either account, since the brother-sister relationship is close, conflicts may occur between spouses because of their respective attachment to brother or sister. Unlike the situation among the Arabs (Patai 1971:444), however, the husband is not expected to side with his sister in the event of a conflict between her and his wife.

The hostility between these two sets of same-sex siblings-in-law, it should be noted in concluding this section, is formally reflected in the kinship terminology. Relative age is a distinctive feature in all kin terms in ego's and the first ascending generations, with the sole exception of these same-sex siblings-in-law. By ignoring age, and merging elder and younger brother-in-law and sister-in-law, respectively, in one term *(yaukhpa* and *yaukma)*, it is as if the overriding dimension of their relationship —rivalry—supersedes all other considerations, even that of age-respect.

Since relative age is otherwise universally recognized, not only in the kinship terminology, but in the respect terms which are used for non-kin, it is difficult to escape this conclusion.

Determinants of the Stem Family Household

Thus far I have argued that the Burmese preference for neo-local residence derives in part from tensions between ego, his own, and his spouse's primary kin. This explanation also accounts, of course, for two other types of domestic groups found in the village—the single-member household, and the truncated nuclear family household, both of which are the result of changes in an original nuclear family household brought about by perturbances in the life and domestic cycles. This explanation does not account, however, for the rather large number of extended family (stem and truncated stem) households, as well as the small number of nuclear family households which include children who are not the biological offspring of the married couple. The former in particular must be explained since it most clearly violates the (putative) preference for neo-local residence. Actually, there are two types of stem family households in Yeigyi, temporary and permanent, and since the former type is merely an interlude in the developmental cycle of the domestic group, I shall begin with it.

In our previous discussions, it was pointed out that parents prefer to avoid co-residence with their married children if this means that the parents must live in the home of the children, for in such cases the children are the household heads and the parents must consequently come under their domination. But since they have no fear of this occurring when the children live in their (the parents') house—for then, the parents, as the household heads, have jural authority over the children —they prefer that their children live with them rather than establish their own household. In the first place, they enjoy the economic advantage of their children working their land. Second, if the child is a daughter, they (and the daughter, too) have yet another motive. Since, as we have seen, the bond between daughter and parents is an intimate one, both are often reluctant to separate. Burmese customary law seems to have struck a compromise solution by prescribing that newlyweds reside with the bride's parents for the first three years of their marriage. This prescription was almost invariably followed in the past (Sangermano 1893:165, Forbes 1878:65, Malcolm 1839:194),[10] and it is still practiced in Burma today—as

10. According to Malcom the period was three years, three months, and three days. If the groom preferred not to follow the custom, and if the bride agreed, he had to pay 60 *ticals* to his in-laws. If, having agreed to the custom, they then departed before this minimum period, the groom had to pay "such a proportion as can be agreed upon."

it is in Thailand (Piker n.d., ch. 2:59; Tambiah 1970:13; Blanchard 1958:424), with some variation. First, the three-year period is not insisted upon; typically it is much less. Second, residence is not always uxorilocal; a survey of Yeigyi and five adjacent villages revealed that only 60 percent of couples who lived with parents before forming their own households live with the bride's parents, though this is lower than comparable data reported for both Burma and Thailand.[11] If the groom's parents are large landowners, if the groom is an only child, or if the bride's house is too small, the newlyweds live instead with the groom's parents.

That newlyweds are willing to live with either set of parents indicates that from their part, too, there are reasons for complying with this post-nuptial residence custom, and these will be discussed below. Sometimes, however, they remain even longer, and given their desire to become independent of their parents (and parents-in-law), the primary inducement to extend the period or to make it permanent, is, as Nash (1965:49) points out, a large parental estate. Few, if any, villagers possess enough property, however, to make this a desirable (or, for that matter, a possible) option. In addition, a married daughter must eventually leave her parental home to make room for her younger sisters when they marry, for very few parents (however much they may desire it) have sufficient land to support a large extended family household.

It is evident, then, that despite the children's preference for neo-local residence, this post-nuptial residence custom means that parents with many daughters, and especially if they also have large landholdings, seldom live alone. As soon as one married daughter completes her temporary residence, another is ready to take her place. Structurally, such parents may be said to maintain a serial stem family household—that is, a stem family in which the personnel of the younger generation changes periodically. But this serial stem family comes to an end with the post-nuptial residence of the youngest daughter, for either she then forms her own household or she remains with her parents to constitute a permanent stem family. Almost without exception, the latter is the way in which genuine stem family households are formed, and it is they that constitute a clear violation of the generalization that parents and married children prefer to live apart.

There are at least three mitigating circumstances that serve to override this preference. For the children there is the strongly held kinship norm, according to which it is the special obligation of the youngest child, and especially the youngest daughter, to care for aged parents, and this

11. In two other villages in Upper Burma, the uxorilocal percentages are 72 and 74, respectively (Nash 1965:45 and 247). For Thailand the percentage is 71 and 85, respectively, for villages in the Central Plains (Piker n.d., ch. 2:59) and the Northeast (Tambiah 1970:12).

obligation is not easily shirked in a culture which emphasizes filial piety.[12] The motive of the parents is less altruistic, for this arrangement is for their benefit. They not only have their daughter with them, which assures them of support and care in their old age, but they enjoy these pleasures without suffering the most important privation of (and the basis of their normal opposition to) co-residence, namely, loss of dominance. As the owners of the house, it is they who are the household heads, thereby retaining their authority over their daughter and son-in-law. Since it is precisely this latter condition, however, that renders co-residence with parents unsatisfactory to their children, one would expect that, in addition to the daughter's sense of filial duty, the couple would have other incentives for living with her parents, and, indeed, there are. In addition to sharing the income from the parents' agricultural lands, the daughter is often given her portion of her inheritance at this time as a pre-death gift. This custom is observed in the cities, as well, where (according to Rangoon informants) it may sometimes lead to resentment, even to litigation, on the part of the other siblings. Moreover, in exchange for caring for them, her parents (in compliance with customary law) bequeath their house and their entire agricultural equipment to their daughter. In short, the main incentive for the couple to live with the wife's parents is the considerable economic advantage which they enjoy in this arrangement.[13]

Determinants of the Truncated Stem Family Household

When one of the parents in a genuine stem family dies, the household may then be characterized as a truncated stem family. As I have already indicated, however, most of the households so classified in Table 14 are truncated stem families structurally, but not genetically, because gener-

12. More than one informant commented on the discrepancy between the normative injunction, according to which the wife follows the husband, and the actual practice (exemplified both in this custom and in the temporary post-nuptial residence custom) by which it is consistently violated. The injunction is contained in the proverb: "Let the hair bun [woman] follow the hair knot [man]" (*yaun nauk sadoun laikpa*). This is but one example, as we shall see, in which the norm of male dominance is contradicted—if only because wife givers have an edge over wife receivers—by the reality of female dominance.

13. The same custom and the identical economic advantages are found in Thailand, both in the Central Plains (Sharp 1953:82-83; Piker n.d., ch 2:3; Mentzer 1972:84-87) and in the Northeast (Tambiah 1970:13). Mentzer writes: "It is apparent that inheritance of house and land is the crucial factor in determining ultimate residence, and the dominant pattern (78 percent) is for the youngest child to remain in the natal home. Presumably, the child who remains with the parents will inherit the house, and that plot of house land. The youngest child and his spouse, then, is ensured of a residence after marriage. . . . [Hence, although] the quality of the personal relationship between child and parent is just as frequently expressed as the determining factor in marriage residence as the practical economic circumstances of the situation, access to property is recognized as the single most important consideration" (Mentzer 1972: 83-84).

ally they are formed after the dissolution of a nuclear family household (through death or divorce), when the remaining spouse forms a joint household with parent(s) or a married child. Since, however, the spouse could have chosen to live alone (as indeed a minority do), these pseudo-stem family households, as they might be called, constitute another violation of the generalization that parents and married children prefer not to live with each other. As in the case of the genuine stem families, however, this normal preference is balanced by other incentives.

The incentives for the parents have already been discussed in the discussion of the genuine stem family. That is, widowed, divorced, or married, parents object to living with a married child if it means living in the latter's home, in which, since the child is the head of the household, the parent is subordinate to the child and his spouse and subject to their authority. This is not the case when the child and his spouse live in the parent's home, for then the parent is the household head, and they are subject to his authority. Under these circumstances, the parent prefers —for the reasons emphasized in the discussion of the stem family—to live together with his married children, and this preference is not diminished by the fact that he is widowed or divorced.

This abstract discussion can be concretized by examining the residential arrangements of the truncated stem families in Yeigyi. As Table 16 indicates, of the eighteen households containing a widow or divorcée,

TABLE 16. *Structure of Truncated Stem Family Households*

Widows and divorcées live with			Widowers and divorcés live with		
Adult children		16	Adult children		5
Children live in			Children live in		
their home	13		their home	3	
They live in			They live in		
children's home	3		children's home	2	
Parents		2	Parents		1
They live in			They live in		
parents' home	2		parents' home	1	
Parents live in			Parents live in		
their home	0		their home	0	
			Adult siblings		1
			Siblings (brother)		
			live in their home	1	
			They live in siblings'		
			home	0	
Total		18	Total		7

there are only three in which the mother lives in the home of the children. Similarly, of the six households containing a widower or divorcé, in only two do the fathers live in their children's home. (In the one case in which a widower lives with a sibling, they share the house of their absentee parents.) In general, then—I shall turn to the exceptions below—a parent is quite content and usually prefers to live with his children so long as he is structurally superior, a status which is assured when he is the household head. If, in addition, he is also a landowner—as is true of nine of the thirteen widows and all of the widowers—his preference is strengthened because his children are then dependent on him economically as well.

The five exceptions in Table 16 also have an economic explanation. In four of the five, the parents are landless and their children are land-owners. If parents have no means of support, they will live with children even if, as they put it, the latter "try to govern" them.

What, then, governs the children's willingness to live with their parents? The first reason, of course, is filial duty. In addition however, they are governed by the same motives that are operative in their parents. In those few cases in which the parent lives in the child's home, the child and his spouse have little fear about being relegated to a subordinate status since, as household heads, they are structurally superior. In the majority of cases, however, the child lives in the parent's home. Nevertheless, since in twelve of the sixteen cases the parent is a land-owner, the child's loss of autonomy is balanced by the incentive of economic advantage. In exchange for caring for the parent and working his land, the child and his spouse not only share in the income from the land, but, upon his death, they inherit the bulk of the land and the house. It might be added that in the cities, where housing is scarce and expensive, the saving on rent, especially for a young couple with moderate means, is another important economic incentive.

Despite these economic advantages, in some cases the impediments are too powerful to permit the formation of such households. Thus, in the sixteen cases in which a widow and her adult children live together, every possible combination is found, as Table 17 reveals, except one: a *married son* living in the home of his mother. The daughter-in-law's fear of being dominated by her mother-in-law overrides any economic advantage that might be gained by such an arrangement. Nor, it might be added, are there many cases of a married daughter living in the home of the mother, despite the fact that (there being no struggle over the son-husband) the tension between them is relatively slight. In most cases, it will be noted, it is an unmarried daughter (single, widow, divorcée), prevented by custom or economic circumstances from living alone, who lives in the home of the mother.

TABLE 17. *Composition of Truncated Stem Family Households*

Residence when widows and children live jointly			Residence when widowers and children live jointly		
Widow lives in child's home . . .		3	Widower lives in child's home . .		3
Son (and daughter's son)	2		Son		2
married	2		married	2	
unmarried	0		unmarried	0	
Daughter		1	Daughter		1
married	1		married	0	
unmarried	0		unmarried (widowed		
Child lives in widow's home . .		13	daughter-in-law)	1	
Son (and son's son)	3		Child lives in widower's home . .		3
married	0		Son		3
unmarried (bachelor,			married	2	
widower, and			unmarried	1	
divorcé)	3		Daughter		0
Daughter (and child's			married	0	
daughter)		10	unmarried	0	
married	4				
unmarried (spinster,					
widow, and					
divorcée)	6				
Total		16	Total		6

But tension between mother-in-law and daughter-in-law is not the only obstacle to the formation of a truncated stem family even when it is clearly economically advantageous. As Table 17 indicates, widowers do not live with daughters; they live only with sons. (The seeming exception to this generalization is a household consisting of a father-in-law and daughter-in-law, both of whom are very old, and therefore not an exception.) Here, too, economic advantage is not sufficient incentive to balance the obstacles—conflict with son-in-law, if the daughter is married, and incest accusations if she is not.

Thus far, most of the pseudo-stem families have been explicable by reference to such variables as economic advantage, sexual norms, and filial duty. There still remain, however, three unexplained configurations. If children are reluctant to be subordinate to their parents, why are there four cases (out of sixteen) in which a child lives in the home of a widowed parent despite the fact that (the latter having no property) it is not to his advantage? Again, why is there one case each of a widow, a divorcée, and a widower living in the home of parents, when (since both parents are alive) none has a special filial obligation to do so? Finally, why are there three cases of a widow or divorcée living alone with young children, whereas widowers and divorcés with children live with their parent(s)? To answer these questions we must turn to still other Burmese customs and beliefs.

The first two questions have one answer. Whatever their obligations to their parents, and whatever the parents' economic situation, unmarried women, as well as young and childless widows and divorcées, have no option but to live with their parent(s) because of cultural beliefs concerning sex. It would be unthinkable for them to live alone because of the supposed danger of sexual assault/or allegations of sexual impropriety.

Widowers and divorcés with children live with their parent(s), whereas widows and divorcées with children live alone, because of various cultural beliefs concerning children. The belief that young girls (and to a somewhat lesser extent, young boys) should always be raised by an adult female means that a widower or a divorcé with a young daughter always lives in a household with an older woman, preferably his mother. The belief that a father and a daughter past puberty should not live alone under the same roof (because of incest temptations or accusations) means that a father with a teenage daughter either moves in with his parent(s) or he requests a close female relative (MoSi, FaSi, Si), usually a widow, to care for her.

Cultural beliefs concerning children, specifically in relation to step-parents, account for the last unexplained household configuration —nuclear family households which contain the young and adolescent children of relatives (Table 14). The relationship between step-parents and step-children is (or is believed to be) especially stressful. For a girl, life with neither step-parent presents a pleasant prospect. Whatever the girl's age, it is believed that her step-mother will mistreat her, and this theme is echoed in folktales (Htin Aung 1954:114ff) and folk songs (Myint Thein 1970:44, 47) as well. If, however, she is pubescent, it is believed that her step-father will attempt to seduce her, a fear which is supported by numerous newspaper accounts of step-father seductions. Based on these beliefs and fears, the girl is always sent to live with a relative if her divorced or widowed mother remarries. In addition, cases were reported to me in Rangoon of widows or divorcées who, instead, force their daughters to marry when they re-marry.

For a boy, the situation is somewhat different. Although not believed to be the target of a seductive step-mother, his relationship to the step-father is thought to be tense because the latter is resentful of his obligation to support him. Nevertheless, boys are not sent to live with relatives when their mothers remarry, although they often leave voluntarily when they are old enough to work. However, in at least two cases known to me, young boys were taken in by grandparents even prior to their ability to support themselves because of alleged mistreatment by a step-father.[14]

Most of these problems, as we shall see in a later chapter, are obviated if the widow or widower enters into a levirate or sororate marriage.

Summary

Let us now summarize this lengthy argument. The affective relationships among primary relatives are such that, almost anywhere, conflicting impulses lead to both an attraction for, and an aversion to, the combining of parents, married children, and married siblings into one household. In peasant societies, at least, in which, typically, households are either patrilocal joint, patrilocal stem, or nuclear, the decision to act upon one rather than another set of impulses seems to be related to a variety of extra-familial political, legal, and economic conditions (or a combination thereof), but especially to intra-familial rules of inheritance. (Goldschmidt and Kunkel 1971.) Thus, holding these external conditions constant, patrilocal stem families are associated with impartible inheritance, patrilocal joint with patrilineal partible inheritance, and nuclear with bilateral partible inheritance. In short, in the absence of economic advantage, residence seems to be a function, as it is in Burma, of those various affective conditions which, as outlined in this chapter, lead to the avoidance of extended family households, and, therefore, of the tensions which almost universally characterize this household type. Although most Burmese households are of the nuclear family type, there are other forces—economic advantage and filial responsibility, mainly—which nevertheless override the desire to avoid the tensions found in the extended family household.

When these overriding forces prevail, and extended family households are established, the anticipated tensions are not overcome, neither in Burma, where such households are a minority, nor in other societies, such as India, in which they are the majority. In identifying the affective grounds for the Burmese neo-local residence preference, I was not, therefore, pointing to tensions which are unique to, nor even especially strong in, Burmese kinship relations. Rather, I was pointing to kinship affects which are more or less universal and which, in most societies, lead to the same institutional consequence to which they lead in Burma—the

14. Burma is not the only Asian society with the wicked step-parent theme. In Java, one of the few other societies in Southeast Asia for which we have information, the wicked step-mother, but not the wicked step-father, is an established belief. (Geertz 1961:41-44). The same emphasis is found in East Asia, at least in China (Hsu 1971:256).

nuclear family household. That these tensions are no more intense in Burma than in other societies, and less intense than in many, can be inferred from the fact that in those (minority) cases in which extended family households are established in Burma, it is the extended family, not its constituent nuclear families, that is the household unit. In some other societies, such as Ceylon (Kandy), the same tensions are sufficiently strong that peace can be maintained in the extended family only by emphasizing its constituent nuclear families as the household unit, each having its separate hearth, working its own land, and so on.

In general, however, the hostile and erotic components of kinship tensions are neither stronger nor weaker in Burma than they are elsewhere. In Lebanon, to take a Near Eastern example (Khuri 1970:597-618), the erotic component in the relationship between father and daughter, father's brother and brother's daughter, father-in-law and daughter-in-law, son-in-law and mother-in-law seems to be more pronounced than it is in Burma, as is the hostile component (derived from problems of power and control) in the father-son, and mother-in-law plus daughter-in-law relationship. The Burmese, like the other societies in Southeast Asia, escape both the direct and indirect consequences of these tensions by the institutionalization of neo-local residence and, hence, by the avoidance of the extended family household which produces these consequences. The Indians and Chinese, on the other hand, escape most of the direct consequences of the patrilocal joint family by various other institutions which circumvent them, but they have not been able to escape their indirect consequences—their high social and psychological cost. This cost is paid in the coin of hostile mothers-in-law, depressed and resentful daughters-in-law, mother-son fixations, sexual frustrations of various kinds, and so on.

Part Three. Kinship and Marriage

6. Kinship Institutions and Marriage Choice

Introduction

Structurally, marriage is the point of intersection between kinship and the basic unit of Burmese society, the domestic group. In the first place, the conjugal family (which is either the core of, or coterminous with, the domestic group) is incipiently created by marriage, which serves to legitimize the offspring of the married couple. Second, the domestic group in itself comprises both consanguineal (parents-children, sibling-sibling) and affinal (husband-wife) kinsmen. Third, each domestic group constitutes a node in a network of domestic groups, a network that is the very basis for the persistence of the kinship system. Fourth, the normal dissolution of the domestic group, for reasons other than death or divorce, is caused by the marriage of its children and their attitudes toward their domestic kin; together, they are the basis for the formation of a new domestic group. Fifth, if the domestic group is incipiently brought into being by marriage, the marriage relationship, in turn, is affected by a complex of kinship-determined activities and sentiments—such as family-monitored premarital sex taboos, attitudes toward parents and siblings, parental attitudes towards the importance of the wedding and dower, and so on.

In short, in referring to marriage as the point of intersection of kinship and the domestic group I am alluding to the fact that, on the one hand, kinship norms and domestic group relationships create marriage, and that marriage, on the other hand, creates the domestic group and sustains the kinship system. In this chapter, however, I am concerned with only one facet of this reciprocal relationship, namely, the influence of kinship—and especially kin relations in the domestic group—on the inception of marriage and, hence, on the formation of new domestic groups.

In the pursuit of this concern, I shall attempt to elucidate, in chronological sequence, the kinship determinants of the process of marriage formation, beginning with the motivation for entering into a marriage and ending with the wedding ceremony. In Burma (as in many societies) this means attending to the following key variables, each of which will be dealt with separately: the importance of marriage to the aspiring couple, constraints on marriage, the patterning of secondary marriages, the ways of initiating a marriage, the engagement, the dower, and the wedding. Before examining these variables, however, it is necessary to assess the importance of the marriage institution within the Burmese social system and, more particularly, for the couple contemplating marriage.

The Desirability of Marriage and its Structural Transformations

That marriage is a highly desirable institution in Burma may be inferred from a number of quantitative measures. In the first place, the percentage of bachelors and spinsters is very low, at least in village Burma. In Yeigyi, for example, only one male (aged 62) and three females (aged 35, 40 and 54) had never married. (There is some suggestion that the females, daughters of wealthy landowners, have remained spinsters because there were no males of either sufficiently high social status or sufficient wealth to be viewed, in their own or in their parents' eyes, as eligible spouses.) The small percentage of unmarried adults in Yeigyi is duplicated in seven other villages in the area. In village A, there were none; in B, there was one bachelor (mentally defective); in C there was one spinster (a female who came from another village to care for her younger sister who had married into the village); in D there was one bachelor and one spinster; in E there were three spinsters; in F there were two spinsters and one bachelor; in G there was one spinster. Now, however else one might wish to interpret this high rate of marriage, it cannot be attributed to the stigma of the unmarried state. Not only is bachelorhood, like almost every other aspect of one's life fate, assumed to be an (involuntary) consequence of karma (over which one has no present responsibility), but, even more important, the highest status in village society is that of the unmarried, celibate monk.

Another index of the desirability of marriage is the early age at which it occurs. According to the *Dhammathat*, parents should attempt to marry their children before the completion of their sixteenth year "so as to prevent their falling into sin" (Lahiri 1957:11), and although this rigid injunction is not complied with in Yeigyi, marriage is fairly early. Thus, out of seventy-three (first) marriages, the mean age of the groom was 21, the bride 17.8.[1] Since, however, only slightly more than half of the

1. It is difficult to explain the difference between Yeigyi, an Upper Burma village, and Mayin, a village in Lower Burma, in which the average ages are 25 and 20 for males and

present 16-20 age group are married, it would seem that the mean age at marriage may be increasing. In any event, in order to better interpret these figures, it should be noted that the age range for first marriages is wide, 14-41 for males and 11-25 for females. It should be noted, too, that in general cultivators marry at a later age than basketmakers. Thus, of the ten unmarried females under twenty, only one is a basketmaker's daughter; and of the seven unmarried males under twenty, none is the son of a basketmaker. To put it differently, the children of cultivators tend to delay their age of marriage somewhat longer than those of basketmakers, suggesting a clearcut occupational and social class difference.

Another measure of the desirability of marriage, especially in a society such as Burma, in which divorce is easy to obtain, is the infrequency of divorce. Of the eighty-seven marriages in Yeigyi, there have been only ten divorces—a divorce rate of only eleven percent—and, as we shall see in the following chapter, the rate is even lower in some other villages.

A final measure of the desirability of marriage is the high rate of remarriage, both for the widowed and the divorced. Some 50 percent of the widows, and 66 percent of the widowers in Yeigyi have remarried, and although none of the divorcées has, 50 percent of the divorcés have also remarried. The absence of remarriage among the divorcées does not, moreover, contradict the generalization about the desirability of marriage. Rather, it reflects the difficulties, for reasons discussed in a later chapter, of divorcée remarriage.[2]

It is of interest to observe that these quantitive indices of the desirability of marriage were commented on by earlier observers of Burma. "In this happy land," wrote Fytche (1878:70) almost a century ago, bachelors

---

females respectively (Pfanner 1962:136). These figures are about the same as those reported by Rangoon informants: 26 for males and 20-21 for females.

2. Widows and widowers also encounter obstacles to remarriage, which partially explains why twenty-four of the thirty remarried widows and widowers in Yeigyi married each other. The obstacle to their remarriage does not relate (as it does in India or China) to the near-prohibition on widow (but not widower) remarriage, for (as the above figures reveal) there is no such prohibition in Burma. It relates, rather, to the cultural attitude of the Burmese to the state of widowhood and their consequent reluctance to marry a widow (*muhsouma*) or widower (*muhsou*). Literally, these terms denote a hunter or killer, but some informants derive the terms from *amuhsoude*, "that which is bad." On either account, widowhood connotes an immoral status, with the implication that in some fashion the surviving spouse is responsible for his or her spouse's death. Alternatively, the "deeper meaning" of the terms, as one informant put it, is "bad luck." Accordingly, the widow or widower is not so much the agent of evil, as the victim of misfortune, and since his or her unfortunate state can spill over onto any close relationship, there is a reluctance to marry them. Either interpretation accounts for the fact that in the village (though not in the city) *muhsou*, but especially *muhsouma*, is almost never used in public; the more euphemistic *tahkulat* ("having lost once"), is used instead (for divorcées, as well as widows).

and spinsters "are unknown, and the widowed seldom remain long in that state."[3]

If my interpretation of these quantitative measures is valid, it can be concluded that marriage in Burma is indeed a highly desirable state. In order to understand its desirability it is necessary to understand the structural effects of marriage on the newlyweds. Structurally, Burmese marriage represents a threefold passage from one status to another. First, it represents a formal transfer of primary loyalty and commitment from one's family of orientation to one's family of procreation. Second, it represents (especially for the girl) a transition from a non-sexual to a sexual role. Third, it represents a formal change from subordination to the authority of the parents to independence from them. It is the last two changes which account, almost entirely, for the view of marriage as a highly desirable state. I shall examine each of these changes *seriatim*, beginning with the last.

It will be remembered that, even after he is married, a child who lives in the home of his parents is subordinate to their authority; how much more so, then, if he remains unmarried. His subordination is financial, as well as social. Even in the cities, let alone the villages, unmarried children turn over their earnings to their parents (usually the mother) who then doles out money to them when and as it is needed. In the village (but not in the city) this financial control applies even to widowed and divorced children who live with parents. My widower landlord, for example, was the joint owner, with his parents, of rather large holdings in paddy land. Although he managed the estate, they retained all the profits, granting him only a small allowance for spending money. Again, when my neighbor's wife died, and he moved in with his mother, he regularly turned over his cash income to her.

In short, for males and females alike, it is not age, but marriage—the formation of a separate household—that severs the child's subordination

---

3. This early comment, which indicates the historical continuity for the contemporary data from Yeigyi, renders all the more surprising the discrepancy between the Nashs' data (Nash and Nash: 1963) and my own. From their six-village survey in Upper Burma, they write that the marriage age is late, the proportion of bachelors and spinsters is high, and the widowed only infrequently remarry. Part of the difference between us is interpretive. Thus, if 50 percent of the widowed and divorced men and 26 percent of the women remarry (their Table 4), then, given that a large percentage are widowed or divorced at a relatively late age, I would consider this to be a high rate of remarriage. Again, if 66 percent of the males and 68 percent of the females have been married by age twenty-five (their Table 3), I would not consider this a late marriage age. (In Ceylon, to take a comparable situation, the median age of marriage in the Low Country is 28 and 22 for males and females respectively [Ryan 1953:153].) Part of the difference between the Nashs' data and mine, however, is genuine, and remains unexplained.

to his parents, and renders him structurally independent of them. Marriage entails the setting up of a separate household, and it is the latter condition which is essential for the child's independence.

To be sure, emancipation from subordination to parents may be purchased at the price of subordination to the spouse. Thus, for the wife, marriage signifies a passage from formal subordination to her father to formal subordination to her husband. Informally, however, it may represent (as we shall see below) a passage from subordination to dominance. For, as a daughter in her natal household, she is subordinate by virtue of age (as well as sex) to almost all of its other members, but as a married woman in her husband's household, she is not only formally superordinate to her children, but informally she may also be dominant over her husband. For the husband, whatever its informal dimensions, marriage represents a passage from formal subordination in his family of orientation to formal superordination in his family of procreation.

Since the reluctance to remaining subordinate to the parents is, as we saw in the last chapter, the major motive for neo-local residence, it is understandable that the achievement of independence should be an important reason for the desirability of marriage. This reason is even stronger in the cities, at least for the girls, than it is in the villages, for until she is married, a city girl may not even leave her house without a chaperone. To be sure, this anticipated autonomy is not the only reason for its desirability. As I have noted, marriage also signals the beginning of the villager's sexual life, and this motive is at least as strong. In one sense, of course, these reasons are interrelated. If parents, and other members of the domestic group, restrict the child's autonomy, it is they who also exercise the greatest surveillance on the child's sexuality. (For a girl, the brother is as important as the parents in this regard). To become independent of one's parents, therefore, means to achieve not only social and economic but also sexual autonomy. Since, however, the social dimension of this autonomy has been discussed in the previous chapter, and since the sexual dimension will be discussed in a separate chapter, they need not be discussed here.

Although husband and wife alike achieve sexual independence from parental control, it must be emphasized that for the wife this control is transferred from parents (and brothers) to her husband. In the Burmese view of marriage, a wife—more specifically, her sex—is the "property" of her husband. The husband is said to "own the wife" (meinma painde), which, as a principle in Burmese customary law, is taken to mean that he is the owner of her sexuality (Ikama painde lin)—that is, he has exclusive rights in her sexuality. Given this asymmetrical conception of sexual rights, it is another accepted principle of customary law, that the wife alone can commit adultery, for "adultery" is defined as the violation of a property right. Since the wife has no property right in her husband's sex, his extramarital affairs may be considered immoral or sinful, but they do not constitute "adultery." Since "adultery" is a violation of a property right, it is considered to be both a civil and a criminal offense. Considered as a civil offense, the husband may obtain a divorce from his wife and obtain damages from her lover. Considered as a criminal offense, the lover may be imprisoned for his action.

Burmese customary law regarding adultery is used as the basis for interpreting the third of the Five Buddhist Precepts. This precept, which enjoins "wrong conduct with respect to sexual pleasures" (kāmesu micchācāra), has been interpreted by most scholars to enjoin whatever sexual behavior is enjoined by the secular sexual mores of each Buddhist community. So far as the choice of a sexual partner is concerned, the Burmese interpret this injunction to refer to intercourse with a minor without the consent of his or her parents or guardians, and with another man's wife without the consent of her husband. Presumably, if the minor has parental permission, neither the minor nor his or her seducer would be in violation of the precept, and (to return to the subject at hand) if the wife has her husband's consent, neither she nor her lover would be in violation. Indeed, this *is* the Burmese presumption, though informants hasten to point out that although the precept is not violated thereby, the wife and her lover are in violation of a lesser sin, that of *paradāra kan*, an illicit sexual act.[4]

To summarize the Burmese view of the marriage bond, "adultery" always and only means sexual relations between a man, whether married or unmarried, and a married woman. Relations between a married man and an unmarried woman (widows, divorcées, and spinsters) is not "adultery," although the lover is said to be faithless *(thissa mede)*, and the behavior of both is accounted as a demerit *(akuthou)*, entailing karmic retribution. Still, for a husband, adultery consists in seducing another man's wife; for a wife, it consists in infidelity to her husband. Since, however, the husband violates no property rights by infidelity to his own wife, he does not commit adultery by sleeping with an unmarried woman. Similarly, since the unmarried woman violates no property rights in sleeping with another woman's husband, she also has not committed adultery. In Yeigyi, for example, it is well known that the unmarried girls from remote villages, who are hired as seasonal farmhands, are regularly

4. The *Pali-English Dictionary* of the Pali Text Society defines *paradāra* as "the wife of another, somebody else's wife," and *pāradārika* as "an adulterer." That my informants construe the expression differently presents a problem which at this time cannot be resolved.

seduced by the married (and the unmarried) men, and neither are viewed as adulterers.

In the Burmese view, then, a man can commit adultery only with another man's wife, a woman can commit adultery only if she is a wife. This conception is reflected in the many Burmese terms for an adulterer and adulteress—there is no term for the abstract concept, "adultery"—all of which emphasize the adulteress' infidelity to her husband, and the adulterer's infringement on the rights of the woman's husband.[5]

We may now turn to the third structural change which is brought about by marriage. This one, like the other two, is importantly implicated in the kinship system. Whatever the relationship between parent and child, and however strong their emotional attachment, marriage represents, at least formally, the transfer of the child's primary commitment from parents (and siblings) to spouse (and children). This change, as we saw in the last chapter, is expressed in three ways. It is symbolized by the neo-local residence pattern; it is institutionalized in customary law according to which spouse (and children), not parents (or siblings), are one's heirs; and it is articulated in cultural norms which stress that, in the event of conflict between loyalty to parents and to wife (and children), loyalty to the wife and children ought to take precedence. In short, just as the primary obligations of ego's father and mother were to each other (and their children), so, too, ego's primary obligations are to his spouse (and his children). As the proverb has it, "As for the husband, [it is] the wife [who is most important]; as for the wife, [it is] the husband." (*Linthi mayalmyathi lintha.*)

To be sure, cultural norms and personal sentiments are not always consistent, and despite the normative primacy of spouse over parents, the latter, as we have already seen, resent their children's fulfilling the norm, and the former, in turn, resent their spouse's violating the norm. We have seen, too, that most of the resentment toward children (especially that of mothers toward sons) and between mothers-in-law and daughters-in-law flows from this conflict. Having already discussed this conflict, our present concern is with the cultural norm which attempts to resolve it by assigning primacy to the husband-wife over the parent-child relationship.

But this norm has yet another implication for the cultural and structural

---

5. The following are the main terms for an adulteress. "[A wife who] keeps a spare [or reserve] husband" (*lin saun htathi*); "[a wife who] enjoys a monkey" (*myauk mweithi*); "[a wife who] breaks up [a home] and goes against [her vows]" (*pouthpyat*); "[a wife who] lives with [both a husband and] a lesser husband" (*lin linnge neide*); "[a wife whose] lesser husband [sneaks into her house by means of] the rear door light" (*naukmi linnge*). The main terms for an adulterer are: "[a man who] keeps [a married woman] on the sly" (*qamhyaun tadi*); "[a man who] steals [another's] wife" (*maya hkhoude*); "[a man who] steals into [another man's] opening" (*kya hkhoude*).

importance of marriage; for the primacy which it accords to the husband-wife relationship holds not only with respect to their parents, but also with respect to their children. Thus, although one's children are one's ultimate heirs, the immediate heir is the spouse, the children inheriting only after the spouse's death. Thus, the couplet quoted above (linthi maya/myathi lintha) is also used as a legal principle of inheritance: if either spouse dies, the remaining spouse is his heir. The primacy of spouse over children is seen even more strongly in the case of a second marriage, in which the obligations to the new spouse take precedence over the obligations to the children from the first marriage. This explains, in part, the tensions (alluded to previously) between step-parents and step-children.

Spouse Selection: Freedom and Constraint

Freedom of Choice

Kinship plays a not inconsiderable role in the initiation of a marriage and in the choice of a marriage partner. The incest taboo constrains the choice of a partner in a first marriage, and the levirate and sororate, though to a lesser degree, constrain choice in secondary marriages. In addition to these formal constraints, parents may attempt to influence the choice of a spouse, and in some cases they may go so far as to arrange a marriage. Leaving the formal constraints aside for the time being—I shall return to them below—let us begin this discussion with the role of the parents.

Essentially, the choice of a spouse is voluntary for both boys and girls. To be sure, there are a few arranged marriages, but these are confined to the very wealthy, serving to create or cement economic alliances. By "arranged marriage" I do not merely mean a marriage in which, as sometimes occurs in Burma, the parents take the initiative in introducing the future spouses to each other and attempt to influence them to marry. I mean, rather, a marriage in which the children have little or no option but to accept their parents' choice. It is in this restricted sense that it can be said that arranged marriages are very infrequent, although in the past, according to older villagers, their frequency was much higher for "children obeyed their parents." (For the same reason, so they allege, the frequency of divorce was also lower: since the parents arranged the marriage, it was an insult to them to dissolve it.) My strong impression, however, is that in the past, as now, arranged marriages were confined to a small number of wealthy families. This impression is supported by the available Western sources on marriage in traditional Burma. Except for Trant (1827:210) and Symes (1800:239), who allude to a form of wife purchase,[6] the early writers on Burma describe a system in which marriage is voluntarily entered into by the two partners (Sangermano 1893:165; Malcom 1839:194; Fytche 1878:69-70), and in which arranged marriages take place primarily between families of wealth and social position (*Census of India* 1912:146).

Of course, in the past, as in the present, parents were concerned that their children make "good" marriages, boys' mothers, especially, being on the lookout for a good match for their sons. But then, as now, children could enter into marriage "without the consent of the parents of either party, and even in direct opposition to their wishes." (Sangermano: *ibid.*) To be sure, according to the Laws of Manu (Maung Maung 1963:55), marriage was traditionally effected in three ways: by parental arrangement, by a go-between, and by mutual consent. But these are complementary, not mutually exclusive, practices. Parents, for example, may indeed attempt to arrange a marriage, but unless the children consent, they will drop it. Conversely, even when a marriage is based on free choice, the consent of the parents is almost always requested. Moreover, whether the one form or the other is practiced, a go-between is almost invariably used to make the initial contact and the early arrangements.

Although a marriage may be initiated by the parents, it can be effected only with the consent of the children because neither in law nor in custom can parents impose their will on their offspring. What is meant by "parental arrangement," therefore, is that the parents—and it is almost always the boy's parents who make the first overture—initiate the negotiations, subject, however, to the approval of the children. The same finding is reported by Nash (1965:248) in another district in Upper Burma, and it is true in Thailand, at least in the Central Plains (Piker n.d., ch. 2:43-44), as well. In this respect (as in many others) Burma and Thailand present a striking contrast to their neighbors, for not only in India and China, as well as in Malaya, Java, and Ceylon, marriages are uniformly arranged by parents, with little consideration for the wishes of the children.

Not only do parents not compel a child to accept a spouse, but they usually accept the child's choice even when they disapprove of it. Indeed, they have little alternative because, provided they are not under age—a girl under twenty may not marry without her parents' consent, while a boy need only attain puberty to do so—children can marry without

6. Thus, Symes (1800:239) refers to the custom of "selling women to strangers," but he himself notes that this was restricted to the "lowest classes of society" and was a "consequence of heavy pecuniary embarrassment." He adds, however, that it was not "considered as shameful, nor is the female dishonoured."

parental consent; and elopement, as we shall see below, is a source of great shame for parents. Just as parents will not, and cannot, compel a child to marry against his will, children are similarly loathe to choose a spouse against their parents' will, and although the latter happens more frequently than the former, it is not done lightly, even among highly westernized, urban youth. To marry the man with whom she was in love, said a university lecturer from a highly placed family, "would have given me great pleasure," but because of her parents' disapproval, she did not marry him. Had she done so, "I would not have what I want even more—a *peaceful* life and a *cool* mind." It is especially difficult for a girl to marry in opposition to parents because, in addition to the stress entailed by parental disobedience which affects boy and girl alike, the girl's is exacerbated by the fact that an elopement is particularly shameful for the girl's parents.

Idiosyncratic factors aside, parental approval or disapproval of a marriage depends to a large extent on the degree to which the child's choice is consistent with the following criteria, listed in descending order of importance. First, it is preferred that the intended spouse should be a Burmese Buddhist. The Burmese are no less ethnocentric than other people—though they are far less so than Indians, for example—and village parents, at least, strongly oppose marriage to a non-Burman and especially a non-Buddhist. In fact, there are no inter-ethnic or interreligious marriages in Yeigyi, but this is hardly surprising because neither in Yeigyi nor in the surrounding villages are there any non-Burmese or non-Buddhists.

A second preference is that the intended spouse should, roughly, be of the same or superior socioeconomic status. In the village stratification system, the basketmakers, as we have seen, form a class apart, and cultivator families especially oppose the marriage of their children with them. Again, however, it should be stressed that compared to some of their neighbors, class endogamy is not as strong in Burma as in Java, for example (Geertz 1961:57), and it does not even begin to approximate the caste endogamy of India (Mandelbaum 1970:98-104). Nevertheless, most marriages are in fact class endogamous. Thus, in a sample of 52 marriages in Yeigyi, only four occurred between children of basketmakers and cultivators, and in 32 marriages that occurred between children of cultivators, in 26 children of landed cultivators married children of landed cultivators, and those of landless cultivators married those of landless cultivators. Moreover, and consistent with marriage in other stratified societies, almost all of the marriages that occurred across class lines were hypergamous. This same pattern of class endogamy and (in interclass marriage) hypergamy emerged in a survey I conducted in seven other villages in the area.

Despite these very clear patterns, many villagers—but especially the basketmakers—resist any social class interpretations of their marriage choices. Basketmakers explain the low incidence of intra-class marriage by arguing that people marry whom they love, and love depends on contact and familiarity which, in turn, depend on contiguous residence. Hence, basketmakers say, their children tend to marry each other because they live together and therefore know each other best. Cultivators are much more ready to concede the relationship between marriage and social class. Many state flatly that they would disapprove of the marriage of their children to lower class spouses, which, in the village context, refers almost exclusively to basketmakers. The disapproval is much stronger in the case of daughters than of sons for in the former case, so they say, their disapproval would take the form of active opposition. The following comments of a small landholder are typical. He would not object, he said, to his son's marriage with daughters of poor or landless, families, but basketmakers are "different." Cultivators and basketmakers, he tells his son, occupy totally different and unequal statuses. "We don't know where they [basketmakers] came from; they have no status (*qasin qatan*). If you fall in love with one of their daughters, know that you will have to live with her. You cannot live with us." There are no circumstances, he said, in which he would accept the bride in his house.

Although the number of upper class families is small—and hence generalizations are difficult—it can be said that their objection to marriages with the middle class is almost as strong as middle class objections to marriages with the lower class. When the son of one of the two upper class families in Yeigyi married the daughter of a poor and landless cultivator, his parents not only disinherited him, but when he was severely bitten by a dog and without funds for medical treatment, they refused to call a doctor, although they were told he would be crippled for life.

Parental opposition to inter-class marriage is especially strong in the case of parents whose daughters wish to marry hypogamously. Daughters are told that they not only risk a lowering of living standards by such a marriage, but—and even more important—that they bring a stigma upon their parents. As the expression has it, they "smear soot on the face of their parents." In one case, which occurred during my study, the daughter's middle class parents sent her to live with relatives in Mandalay in order to separate her from a poor orphan boy whom she wanted to marry.

The third criterion for parental approval of a marriage is that the intended groom should be older than the intended bride by at least two or three years (Urban informants say that a six- or seven-year difference is even better). Thus, even nephew-aunt marriage is opposed not so much because of the extension of the incest boundary, but because in such a marriage the wife would (typically) be older than the husband. Aside from important differences in sexual maturation between males and females, a marriage in which the wife is the elder spouse is considered inappropriate because it would cause important confusion in the sex and age respect categories; on the one hand, females are expected to show respect to males, but, on the other, the younger are expected to show respect to their elders. Preponderantly the ages of spouses in Yeigyi conform to the expected pattern. Thus, in a sample of sixty-four first marriages, the husband was older in fifty, the wife in seven, and in seven they were the same age. The same pattern holds for the twenty-three second marriages, the husband being older in sixteen, the wife in six, and in one they were the same age.

A fourth parental preference in regard to a child's marriage is that the latter's intended spouse be a fellow-villager. This emphasis on village endogamy is based on at least four considerations. One does not know a stranger as well as a fellow villager; the out-marrying spouse (which, in effect, means his parents) may pay a rather substantial "entry-fee" for permission to live in the village of his spouse; parents prefer that their child live close to them; finally, a stranger (as we have seen) is never fully integrated into his spouse's village.

There is a fifth and final basis for parental approval or disapproval of a marriage, which is astrological auspiciousness, but this criterion does not arise until much later, when final negotiations are entered into and the couple's horoscopes are read.

Based on the degree of parental approval or disapproval, and the extent of their interference or non-interference, the Burmese classify the ways in which marriage may be contracted into four types: (1) the couple fall in love, and arrange the marriage by themselves with or without parental consent (*lunge qahkyin gyin*); (2) the parents grudgingly consent to their children's choice (*miba thabo kyade*); (3) the parents happily approve of their children's choice (*miba thabo tude*); (4) the parents arrange the marriage, with or without their children's consent (*miba peizade*).

Incest Taboos

Although incestuous desires, as we have seen, are as prevalent in Burma as anywhere else, there is no word in Burmese for "incest" (so far as I have been able to determine), so that incest taboos are subsumed by villagers under the more general rubric of prohibited marriages or illicit sex. In the latter case, the reference is always to the Buddhist precept interdicting illicit sexual behavior, which, however, does not explicitly mention incest. Hence, although everyone agrees that incest prohibitions are few, the incest boundaries are not entirely clear. Thus, villagers, in agreement with the *Report of the 1911 Census of India* (IX, Pt. I: 149-150), say that marriages with parent, child, sibling, half-sibling, uncle, aunt, nephew, niece, grandparent, and grandchild are forbidden. On the other hand, the Burmese scholar and jurist, Maung Maung (1963:56-57), writes: "the union of uncle and niece, nephew and aunt, half-brother and half-sister, was permitted. . . . As regards cousins, generally speaking, union with agnates is strongly deprecated, while that with other cognates is not looked upon with disfavor, provided the woman is on the same line as the man or below it."

Agreeing with Maung Maung, Rangoon informants say that except for marriage with parents, grandparents, and siblings, all other marriages between kinsmen are permitted and occur, even though some (cousin-cousin, uncle-niece, aunt-nephew) are frowned upon. They also agree with him that, traditionally, the prohibited degrees were stronger on the father's than on the mother's side, although this distinction is not observed today. Traditional norms (they say) interdicted marriage in the patriline up to two degrees removed, whereas it was permitted in the matriline when the partners are only one degree removed.

In some important respects, then, these urban views do not agree with those found in the village. Villagers strongly contend that uncle-niece and aunt-nephew marriages are prohibited. They disagree among themselves, however, concerning (first) cousin marriage, some claiming that it is prohibited, others claiming (in agreement with Rangoon informants) that though it is not approved, it is nevertheless permitted. Villagers, however, do not distinguish (as do Maung Maung and urban informants) agnates from other cognates.[7]

These differences concerning the incest taboos, especially those concerning cousins, are of more than passing interest, and I shall return to

7. Not surprisingly, in Thailand, too, there are important, seemingly regional, differences in these matters. Tambiah (1970:18), writing of the Northeast, places marriage between first cousins at the outward limits of the incest taboo. Piker, on the other hand, writing of the Central Plains (n.d., ch. 2, p. 3), says that marriage even between second cousins is prohibited, and that marriages "between people so closely related that genealogical connections can be specified exactly are frowned upon." This, of course, accounts in part for the tendency toward village exogamy in Central Thailand, in contrast with the tendency toward village endogamy in Upper Burma.

them below in the discussion of the kinship terminology. In the meantime we can hold them in abeyance and turn, instead, to other considerations of these taboos. Unless otherwise indicated, the rest of this discussion will refer to village attitudes and beliefs exclusively.

Explanations for incest prohibitions vary according to the relationship that is prohibited. I have already discussed the villagers' attitudes toward and the grounds for their opposition to parent-child incest. So far as other relatives are concerned, the "womb" idiom (wombs removed), together with notions concerning the evils of the mixing of generations, are the stated reasons for incest prohibitions. Thus, sibling marriage is prohibited because "those from the same womb should not marry." Those who believe that cousin marriage is prohibited say that even those one womb removed may not marry—first cousins, it will be recalled, are terminologically classified as siblings. Those who believe that cousin marriage is permitted say that the one womb removal applies only if the couple are of different generations (uncle-niece, aunt-nephew), but not if they are of the same generation (cousins). Even the former agree, however, that relatives two wombs removed may marry—so long as they are of the same generation—but a small minority hold out for a distance of three wombs.

In general, the incest taboos are observed. In the genealogies, there are cases of marriage between cousins two wombs removed, but there are none at a distance of only one (let alone from the same) womb. On the other hand, informants report isolated cases, known to them from other places, of incest and even marriage between first cousins, uncle and niece, and aunt and nephew.

Villagers agree that the sanctions for violating incest taboos vary according to the degrees of consanguinity. I have already described the severe punishment—legal, physical, social, and karmic—for parent-child and sibling-sibling incest. Most other forms can apparently be practiced with legal, physical, and karmic impunity, though the couple would be exposed to social censure.

Preferential Marriage

Brother-Sister Exchange

Although it occurs infrequently today, older informants say that brother-sister exchange traditionally constituted the preferred form of marriage. Given the proviso that the husband be older than the wife, typically this form of marriage is one in which an elder brother and younger sister pair are exchanged for an elder sister and younger brother pair (though, in principle, the exchange can be between elder brother-younger sister pairs). Although this form of marriage (termed *maun le hnama le*, or *peizade*) is practiced only rarely in contemporary Burma, the kinship terminology suggests that it may not have been infrequent in the past, or, at least, that it may have been normatively preferred. For on this assumption the terms for same-sex siblings-in-law and their correspond-ing terms as aunts and uncles fall neatly into place, the sororate and levirate are more readily explained, and the importance of the dower can be better understood. (Indeed, when the dower is taken into account, "sister exchange," or, even better, "daughter exchange" is a preferable expression). On the further assumption that the levirate and sororate were (as they still are) preferred, if not required, secondary marriages, then much of the remaining terminology—the remaining aunt and uncle terms, and the terms for opposite sex siblings-in-law, cousins and niblings—also fall neatly into place. In short, given these two assumptions about preferential primary and secondary marriages, the traditional (and much of the modern) classification of the kindred may be explained as logically entailed by the marriage system. Correspondingly, the changes that have occurred in the modern terminological system are likewise explicable by the gradual decline in the normative salience and, hence, in the persistence of this marriage system. Before explicating this thesis, we must first, however, describe these marriages and their possible manifest functions, for the latter, of course, provide the incentives to enter into such arrangements.

In the Burmese context, marriage based on sibling exchange can be shown to have at least two functions, one economic, the other psychologi-cal. The economic function relates to the dower, and since this will be examined in detail below, it need only be stated here that the parents of the groom bestow a considerable amount of property on the bride. This being the case, this form of marriage serves to balance what is otherwise a one-sided property transaction, for while family A gives property to a girl from family B, family B, in turn, gives property to a girl from family A. Thus the dower becomes a form of property exchange rather than a one-sided transaction.

Psychologically, sibling exchange marriage may be shown to be related (as some informants explicitly recognize) to the brother-in-law (*yau*'*hpa*) tensions discussed in the previous chapter. The wife's brother, it will be recalled, resents losing his sister to her husband. This resentment is exacerbated by the fact that, in some sense, the latter's payment of a dower implies that he is paying for his wife's (the brother's sister's) sexual services. On both accounts the sister's husband is viewed as having the "upper hand" over the wife's brother. Sibling exchange serves to balance this account, for in this form of marriage each brother-in-law loses a sister to the other, and each "pays" for the sexual services of the other's sister. In short, to the extent that the wife's brother is disadvantaged by the sister's husband, each brother-in-law (who, in this form of marriage, occupies both kin types simultaneously) experiences the advantage of the one, as well as the disadvantage of the other, type: the ledger, as it were, is balanced.

But there is another ledger which must be balanced in the case of sibling exchange. If one of the partners in such an exchange should die, the remaining spouse has a claim on a new partner. This claim is best honored by his right to marry a sibling of his deceased spouse—that is, by a levirate or sororate marriage. Although these forms of secondary marriage occur independently of sibling exchange, their continuing practice in Burma (albeit with diminished strength, both normatively and statistically) lends some support to the assumption that sibling exchange, though infreqent today, may have been a preferred form of marriage in the past.

Levirate and Sororate

So that their form be better understood, it should be noted that these marriages differ from sibling exchange not only because sibling exchange is a primary marriage, and they are mostly a secondary form of marriage; they differ in another important respect (which follows from this one). In sibling exchange, a sibling of one sex within a sibling set is *exchanged* for a sibling of the *opposite* sex in another sibling set. In the levirate and sororate, one sex in a sibling set is either *substituted* for or *added* to a sibling of the *same* sex. Where, as in some societies, the husband marries his *living* wife's sister in a sororate marriage, the latter is added to a same sex sibling. In Burma, where only the *posthumous* sororate is practiced, then, in the sororate and levirate alike, the secondary spouse is substituted for his deceased sibling.

The sororate and levirate are always secondary marriages for at least one of the partners, because both involve the remarriage of a widow (levirate) or a widower (sororate). In Burma, in which the senior levirate alone is practiced, a levirate marriage is usually a secondary marriage for the husband, as well, because as the elder brother he is usually already married—polygyny is permitted in Burma— widowed, or divorced when he marries his younger brother's widow. Since, on the other hand, the Burmese only practice the junior sororate, the younger sister is usually single when she marries the husband of her deceased elder sister. Hence, the sororate is usually a primary marriage for the woman, except in those few cases where she may have been married, and subsequently divorced or widowed. Since polyandry is forbidden in Burma, she cannot contract a sororate marriage if she is already married.

The levirate and sororate, of course, are widespread forms of marriage in the ethnographic record: in Murdock's cross-cultural sample of 250 societies (Murdock 1948:29), the levirate is reported for 127 societies (with no data for 65), and the sororate for 100 societies (with no data for (91). Both are also found among Burma's neighbors in mainland Southeast Asia, as well as in many parts of India and China.[8]

Institutions which are so widely distributed, and which are found in such a wide diversity of structural and cultural settings, are not, it may be assumed, practiced capriciously, and before inquiring into particular explanations for their practice in Burma, we might first examine the generally accepted explanations. Westermark (1922:210-216, 264) examines four types of explanation for the levirate, and I can do no better than summarize them.

One explanation for the levirate is that it is a means by which the givers of bridewealth or dowry (dower) protect their investment, for it guarantees that both wife and property remain within the wealth-giving family. This is especially the case in the junior levirate, the type in which the younger brother inherits his elder brother's property (including his widows). A second explanation is found in those societies in which the levirate is a duty rather than a right (as is implicit in the above explanation). Here the reason offered is that the brother has an obligation to care for the wife and children of his deceased sibling. A third explanation, one familiar to us from the Biblical levirate, is also based on duty: it is the living brother's duty to "raise up seed" to his dead brother should the latter die without issue. A fourth explanation relates to the wish to "preserve the union" between the two families.

The last two explanations have no relevance in the Burmese context; the Burmese themselves do not refer to them. But the first is offered by the Burmese as an explanation not only for the levirate but for the sororate, as well. Westermark, too, includes it among the explanations for the sororate, and he mentions two others, as well (1922:264), namely, to preserve the union between the families, and to provide the sister's children with an appropriate mother surrogate. Again, the latter, but not the former, is also stressed in Burma.

8. LeBar et al, (1964) record the practice of the levirate among the Nosu, South China Miao, Indochina Miao, Thailand Meo, Burmese Shan, Trung-Cha, Li, and Rhade, and the sororate among the South China Miao, Jarai, and Rhade. Their distribution in India is summarized in Karve (1968:65-66, 133, 193, 226).

In Burma (and elsewhere) there are advantages for both parties to a levirate marriage. For the husband's brother there is the advantage of acquiring the use of the dower (and of keeping it within the family), for if his brother's widow were to have married outside, she would take the dower with her, and he (and his family) would lose it. This, however, is a minor advantage, unless the family is wealthy and had paid a very large dower, and it must be balanced against the problem created by taking another wife if he is already married. If, moreover, he is willing to face that problem, he would prefer to marry a virgin. To the extent that he feels obliged to care for his brother's children, he can do so without marrying their mother. For the widow, the advantage of the levirate is much greater, for in a society in which widow remarriage is extremely difficult, as it is in Burma, she almost automatically acquires a husband, an economic provider for herself and her children, and a father surrogate for the latter. ("Almost automatically" because if her original marriage was part of a sibling exchange, her husband's brother is obliged to marry her in order to redress the balance occasioned by her husband's death.)

In the sororate, the advantage is even more one-sided. The girl has little to gain from a marriage to the husband of her deceased sister, and she must be viewed primarily as a pawn in an exchange system whose balance, if the original marriage was based on sibling exchange, must be redressed. The only advantage for the girl (and her parents) is found in those cases in which her brother-in-law is wealthy, or in which her parents had provided him with a large dowry (for then both types of wealth remain in the family). Otherwise the incentives for the girl are slim, and it is hardly surprising that a girl who enters into a sororate marriage is either very young (and therefore susceptible to parental influence) or in her late twenties (and therefore in danger of becoming a spinster.)

For the man, however, the advantages of the sororate are considerable. First, there is the twofold economic advantage of not having to pay a new dower (which he would have to do were he to marry outside) and of retaining full possession of his original dower (which he could not do if he married outside, for half the dower would become the immediate possession of his children who would probably not be living with him). Second, there is a considerable sexual advantage. Widowers, like widows, have difficulty in remarrying, and in this case, he not only almost automatically acquires a wife, but (usually) a virgin to boot. Finally, he acquires a difficult-to-obtain mother-surrogate for his children, for most other women would not look kindly at the prospect of raising another woman's children. It is little wonder, then, since it is the male who must initiate a marriage, that the sororate is more frequently practiced than the levirate.

Although I have thus far stressed the advantages of these secondary marriages for the spouses, the advantages to the children are at least as important. The levirate and sororate not only provide the orphans with a father- and mother-surrogate, respectively, but in doing so they simultaneously solve the difficult step-parent problem. Step-parents, it will be recalled, are both stereotypically and actually a serious problem for their step-children: the step-father is hostile to the step-son and a seducer of his step-daughter, and the step-mother is especially hostile to her step-daughter. In the levirate and sororate, the step-parents are consanguineal uncles and aunts with whom, it can probably be assumed, they have had fairly affectionate relationships. In addition to the hostility dimension, these marriages also solve the sexual dimension of the step-parent problem. Since the step-father is now her uncle, the girl is doubly protected from his seductive advances: first, because of their previous relationship, second, because of the incest taboo.

Although this analysis of their functions explains the differential motivation and reluctance of the various siblings to enter into the sororate or levirate, it does not account for another aspect of these marriages as they are practiced in Burma, namely, their asymmetrical form. For, as we have seen, it is not just any kind of levirate and sororate that are practiced in Burma, but only the *senior* levirate and the (posthumous) *junior* sororate. As the Burmese say, "*hkeqou* always marries *hkema, ma*' never marries *mayi.*" This means, as Chart 2 indicates, that a male practices the levirate and sororate, respectively, only with a sub-set of the set of sisters-in-law, namely, the wife of his (deceased) *younger* brother and his (deceased) wife's *younger* sister *(hkema)*; and that a female practices such marriages respectively, only with a sub-set of the set of brothers-in-law, namely, the husband of her (deceased) *elder* sister and her (deceased) husband's *elder* brother *(hkeqou)*.

That the Burmese practice these particular asymmetrical forms of the levirate and sororate is perplexing on two accounts. Not only do the Marma—who, it is generally assumed, retain the old Burmese kinship system (Bernot 1967)—practice the reverse form of the levirate, but the reverse form of both practices are preponderant in the cross-cultural record (Westermark 1922:207-220). The Burmese, however, have a ready answer to this problem. Since, as we have seen, a major reason for these secondary marriages is to provide the deceased parent's children with a parent surrogate, then, in marrying his wife's younger sister *(hkema)*, a widower is marrying a woman who, with respect to his children, is their mother's younger sister. Now, in theory, at least, mother's younger sister *(qado)* is the children's sentimentally appropriate mother surrogate, for,

CHART 2. *Sibling-in-law Terms*

Term	Kin Type	Sex of Speaker
mayi	eld-BrWi/Wi-eld-Si	male speaking
hkema	yng-BrWi/Wi-yng-Si	male speaking
yau'hpa	SiHu/WiBr	male speaking
hkeqou	eld-SiHu/Hu-eld-Br	female speaking
ma	yng-SiHu/Hu-yng-Br	female speaking
yau'ma	BrWi/HuSi	female speaking

so the Burmese say, "Children feel especially close to their *qado.* "(Indeed, in the traditional terminology, she is called *midwei,* "little mother.") That this is so derives, in part, from the residence rule by which, it will be recalled, a couple resides post-nuptially with the wife's family, often until her younger sister gets married. As a result of this rule, young children often reside in the same household as their mother's *younger* sister—typically the *elder* sister is already married and gone —and since she often takes care of them, they become especially attached to her. Moreover, even prior to their mother's marriage, their mother's younger sister had had a special relationship to their mother, for the elder sister plays a maternal role vis à vis her own younger siblings: she cares for, nurtures, and disciplines them when their mother is absent. A typical village scene is that of a young six- or seven-year-old girl carrying a younger sibling astride her hips. Hence, the proverb, *qamagyi qamiqaya,* "The elder sister [takes] mother's place." In short, a younger sister has a special regard for her elder sister from earliest childhood, a regard which, so it is argued, she transfers to the latter's children. For both reasons, then, the junior sororate provides the widower's children not merely with any mother-surrogate, but with the sentimentally appropriate one.

The senior levirate is explained on similar grounds. In marrying her husband's elder brother, a woman marries a man who is, with respect to her children, their father's elder brother. The latter, *bagyi* ("big father"), is the children's jurally (and sometimes the sentimentally) appropriate father-surrogate. Kinship norms decree that it is *bagyi* who must take father's place even when the latter is alive; how much more so when he is dead. This obligation is so strong, villagers claim, that even if the elder brother is already married and his wife objects, he is nevertheless permitted to perform a levirate marriage.

But consideration of the children is not the only reason for the *junior* sororate and the *senior* levirate. Another, and perhaps equally important, reason relates to the importance of relative age, and the deference patterns associated with it, in the Burmese social structure. Since they are typically his elders, the sisters-in-law who are disqualified as spouses in these secondary marriages—elder brother's wife and wife's elder sister —are addressed by the male as "elder sister," *ama,* and they, reciprocally, address him as "younger brother," *maun.* On the other hand, he addresses the sister-in-law whom he may take in the levirate and sororate—younger brother's wife and wife's younger sister—as "younger sister," *hnama,* and they address him as "elder brother," *qakou.* Corresponding to these linguistic usages, the younger show those signs of deference and respect (in word and in duty) to their older siblings-in-law that any junior normally displays toward his senior.

Given these considerations, if a man were to marry his wife's elder sister, or a woman her husband's younger brother, the respect system based on age (which, in the case of these particular dyads, has been established for some time) would come into sharp conflict with that based on sex, in which the wife offers respect to the husband. In such a marriage, then, the person superior in the age-based respect system would be inferior in the sex-based respect system, and vice versa, and the resulting intrapsychic conflict, both cognitive and emotional, would, as the Burmese point out, be almost impossible to handle. In the senior levirate and junior sororate, on the other hand, the sex and age respect patterns run parallel to each other. In both cases, a man receives conjugal deference from a woman from whom he has always received both age— and sex-based deference, and a woman offers conjugal deference to a man whom, on both accounts, she has always tendered deference.[9]

To be sure, a man's elder brother's wife is not necessarily his elder, and it might be argued that in such a case the junior levirate might be permissible. Even then, however, the problem remains (though to a lesser extent) because the wife tends to acquire the status of her husband, and the deference which ego displays to an elder sibling is transferred to his spouse even when the latter is younger than ego. Nevertheless, there are cases in which this form is permitted. If a man should die, leaving young children but no elder brother, there is no objection to his widow marrying his younger brother *(ma')*, so long as he is her elder. Under the same circumstances and for the same reason a widower may take his wife's elder sister *(mayi)* in a sororate marriage.

---

9. These arguments concerning the difficulties of status reversal would presumably have had force in the past as well, and yet historically Burmese law has permitted the marriage of a younger brother to an elder brother's fiancée and spouse. Thus, according to the *Dhammathat,* "If either of the betrothed dies, *his younger brother* and her younger sister shall be given as substitute." (Gaung 1905: 44, italics mine.) Again, "If the bridal present has been paid, and the husband disappears, then after three years *his younger brother* can take her as wife." (*Ibid.*:76.)

Preferential Marriage and Kinship Terminology

I have already noted that sibling exchange is only infrequently practiced today, although, according to older informants, it was a preferential form of primary marriage in the past. I have noted, too, that the levirate and sororate, though not prescriptive, are certainly preferred forms of secondary marriage even today (although, unfortunately, I have no data on their prevalence). I have noted, finally, that on the assumption that these were traditionally the preferred, if not prescribed, forms of marriage, much of the Burmese kinship terminology, especially in its grammatical (and, to a lesser extent, its semantic) dimension, can be shown to be logically derived from, and systematically related to, this marriage system. The expression "marriage system" must be underscored because it is the configuration of the three practices—sibling exchange, the sororate, and the levirate—which according to the argument explains the kinship terminology. As secondary marriages, the sororate or levirate in themselves could hardly be expected to motivate the classification of kin—and, indeed, Murdock (1948:175-177) has shown that they do not. When, as in the case of Burma, however, both these forms of secondary marriage are practiced conjointly, and—what is more important—when they are part of a total marriage system in which sibling exchange is the preferred form of primary marriage, then, so I am contending, this marriage *system* provides the most plausible explanation for the kinship terminology.

I hasten to add, however, that I am not contending that marriage systems invariably explain terminological systems, for of course there are too many exceptions to support a theory of that scope. But, as we shall see, the detail and scope of the systematic relationships they sustain in Burma renders any other explanation for the Burmese system much less plausible. Indeed, were it not for the curious anthropological assumption that theories must possess a nomothetic character to be valid, I suspect that the cross-cultural evidence is sufficiently strong to support the contention that this theory is statistically valid—valid, that is, under certain kinds of conditions and for certain kinds of social systems. If this is true, then our strategy ought to be to explain those cases—the Dravidian is usually cited in this connection—that are inconsistent with the theory, rather than explaining away those that are consistent with it.

Turning now to the Burmese case, we shall begin our analysis with the terminological correlates of the primary marriage form, sibling exchange. In this form of marriage, as Diagram 5 indicates, the two types of siblings-in-law, sibling's spouse and spouse's sibling, are one and the same person. Thus, for any male ego, his wife's brother and sister's husband, and for any female ego, her husband's sister and brother's wife, are, respectively, one and the same person. This being so, one would expect both types of brothers-in-law and both types of sisters-in-law to be designated, respectively, by one and the same term. As the chart of sibling-in-law terms (Chart 2) reveals, this is indeed the case in the Burmese system: both of the former types are *yau'hpa,* both of the latter are *yau'ma.* Thus, in Diagram 5, figure 4, who is simultaneously the wife's brother and sister's husband of figure 1, is the latter's *yau'hpa* in both of these statuses, and vice versa. Similarly, figure 5, who is simultaneously the husband's sister and brother's wife of figure 2, is the latter's *yau'ma* in both these statuses, and vice versa.

Sibling exchange marriage not only explains the same-sex sibling-in-law terms,[10] it also explains a sub-set of the aunt and uncle terms, namely, those by which these siblings-in-law are designated in their statuses as uncle and aunt. (The remaining uncle and aunt terms are explained, as we shall see below, by other marriage forms). The classifications of both sets of kin types, the siblings-in-law and the aunts and uncles, are systematically related to each other, in that the terminological merging of the two types of uncles and aunts, the consanguineal and affinal, parallels the merging of the two types of same-sex siblings-in-law. This can easily be explained by sibling-exchange marriage.[11] Since in this type of marriage, each spouse occupies the two types of (same-sex) sibling-in-law statuses simultaneously, it necessarily follows that, as aunt or uncle, each also occupies a simultaneous consanguineal and affinal status. This being so, it might be expected that the classification of this sub-set of uncles and aunts would both reflect this latter contingency and also conform to their classification as (same-sex) siblings-in-law. Both expectations are borne out.

As Diagram 5 reveals, sibling exchange produces four pairs of simultaneously occupied consanguineal and affinal uncle and aunt statuses. The two males, respectively, simultaneously occupy the statuses of Mo-eld-Br/ Fa-eld-SiHu (figure 1) and Mo-yng-Br/Fa-yng-SiHu (figure 4); the females, Fa-eld-Si/Mo-eld-BrWi (figure 2) and Fa-yng-Si/Mo-yng-BrWi

---

10. F. K. Lehman (personal communication) sees the relationship between sibling exchange and same-sex sibling-in-law terms as merely a special case of a more general structural situation, namely, WiBr and SiHu are structurally equivalent because "(a) both are in the residual system of families not 'mine', and (b) in a structurally and affectively-compensatory way, one gives me my wife and I give the other my sister."

11. Again, F. K. Lehman (personal communication) offers a different interpretation. As he sees it, based on the principle of "residuality" of "outside families" (enunciated in the previous footnote), FaSi is compensation for Mo. That is because MoBr, as it were, gives her (to Fa), so FaSi goes to his structural equivalent. Hence, MoBr gives Mo, and someone gets FaSi in return. It is this, he argues, that explains the terminological equivalent of MoBr and MoSiHu (*qu*), and FaSi and MoBrWi (*qayi*).

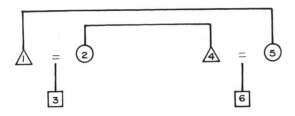

Diagram 5. Sibling-exchange marriage and same sex
sibling-in-law terms.

(figure 5). Although each kin type in each of the paired statuses is different from the other types in the pair, to differentiate them terminologically would result in cognitive chaos if, as happens in sibling-exchange, one and the same person represents both types. One obvious, and efficient, solution is to designate both by the same term, and, as Chart 3 reveals, this is the case in the two traditional terminologies; for the contemporary terms, it holds for the aunts, but not the uncles. It will also be noted from Chart 3 that the terms of this set, and for the remaining set of aunt and uncle terms, are not only mutually exclusive, but that, semantically, the latter terms alone *(ba* and *mi)* carry the meaning of parent or parent-surrogate. It is from this latter set of uncles and aunts that the eligible spouses for the levirate and sororate are drawn.

Returning to the former set—those that participate in sibling exchange—Diagram 6 readily demonstrates that their classification as uncles and aunts parallels their classification as (same sex) siblings-in-law. Before examining this diagram in detail, however, it should be observed that the two classifications, though parallel, are not equivalent. The aunt and uncle terminology is more proliferated than the sibling-in-law terminology, as would be expected in an age-asymmetrical exchange system such as the Burmese. Although relative age is ignored in the sibling-in-law terminology (for the reasons explained in Chapter Four), it would be rather surprising if (in a system in which relative age is otherwise a pervasive distinctive feature) it were ignored in the uncle and aunt terms. Nevertheless, the parallelism, as Diagram 6 indicates, is evident.

In Diagram 6, for the sibling set represented by figure 6, figure 1 is *wayigyi*, both as Mo-eld-Br and Fa-eld SiHu, and figure 2 is *qayigyi* both as Fa-eld-Si and Mo-eld BrWi. Similarly, for the sibling set represented by figure 3, figure 4 is *wayilei* both as Mo-yng-Br and Fa-yng-SiHu, and figure 5 is *qayilei* both as Fa-yng-Si and Mo-yng-BrWi. Since the suffixes *gyi* and *lei* merely designate "elder" and "younger," respectively, it is apparent that the classification of the aunts systematically parallels the

CHART 3. *Classification of, and Terms for, Aunts and Uncles,
Traditional and Contemporary*

Kin types	Judson's Terms[a]	Traditional Upper Burma Terms[b]
Fa-eld-Br, Mo-eld-SiHu	*bagyi*	*bagyi*
Fa-yng-Br, Mo-yng-SiHu	*badwei*	*badwei*
Mo-eld-Br, Fa-eld-SiHu	*qugyi*	*wayigyi*
Mo-yng-Br, Fa-yng-SiHu	*qumin*	*wayilei*
Fa-eld-Si, Mo-eld-BrWi	*qayi*	*qayigyi*
Fa-yng-Si, Mo-yng-BrWi	*qayi*	*qayilei*
Mo-eld-Si, Fa-eld-BrWi	*migyi*	*migyi*
Mo-yng-Si, Fa-yng-BrWi	*midwei*	*midwei*

Kin types	Contemporary Terms[c]
Fa-eld-Br, Fa-eld-SiHu	*bagyi*
Fa-yng-Br	*badwei*
Mo-eld-Br, Mo-eld-SiHu	*qugyi*
Mo-yng-Br, Mo-yng-SiHu, Fa-yng-SiHu	*qulei*
Fa-eld-Si	*qayigyi*
Fa-yng-Si, Mo-yng-BrWi, Mo-eld-BrWi	*qayi*
Mo-eld-Si, Fa-eld-BrWi	*kyido*
Mo-yng-Si, Fa-yng-BrWi	*qado*

[a] Judson, a missionary in mid-nineteenth century Burma, compiled a Burmese English dictionary, from which these are taken.

[b] These were collected from a native of Mandalay, (Upper Burma) now resident in Rangoon.

[c] This is the classification and the terms current in Yeigyi.

classification of the reciprocal sisters-in-law, and the classification of the uncles that of the reciprocal brothers-in-law: every *yau'pa* is a *wayi*, and every *yau'ma* a *qayi*. And this parallelism makes sense only in a system of sibling exchange, for the latter entails that the two distinctive types of sibling-in-law are embodied in one and the same person. This, in turn, entails that in their statuses as uncles and aunts, each sibling-in-law is simultaneously a consanguineal and affinal uncle or aunt. Hence, these contingencies require that the consanguineal and affinal member of each pair be designated by a common term, and that the classification of this set of uncle and aunt terms parallel the classification of the sibling-in-law set.

Before turning to the contemporary terms, I wish to stress that this argument concerning the terminological correlates of the forms of mar-

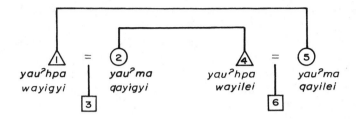

Key

Upper terms are sibling-in-law (same sex) terms
Lower terms are aunt and uncle terms

Diagram 6. Sibling exchange, the classification of same-sex
siblings-in-law, and their corresponding classification as uncles and aunts.

riage (or any other structural form) does not require that the form in question be prescribed and, therefore, be widely, if not universally, practiced. It only requires that it be preferred, so that the contingencies discussed here (overlapping kin domains and simultaneously embodied kin types within each domain) occur with sufficient frequency that they cannot be terminologically ignored without producing cognitive confusion even for a minority. In short, this explanation for the kin terms does not assume normative prescription or statistical generality of the marriage form. It merely assumes a sufficient degree of preference and practice that these contingencies occur with some minimal probability (whose value cannot at this time, be stipulated). This assumption underlies the analysis of the other terms (discussed below) as well.

Turning, then, to the contemporary aunt and uncle terms, it can be seen that they exhibit the same pattern as the traditional terms, with one important exception. As Chart 3 reveals, Mo-eld-Br is *qugyi* while Fa-eld-SiHu is *bagyi*—a disjunction which poses an obvious problem for the siblings of a sibling-exchange marriage: does the sibling set in figure 6 of Diagram 6, for example, refer to figure 1 as *bagyi* (Fa-eld-SiHu) or *qugyi* (Mo-eld-Br)? Merely to raise the question indicates that the contemporary terminology could have replaced the traditional one only after a steep decline of sibling exchange, both normatively and statistically. And, as I have already observed, both types of decline have occurred: sibling exchange has no normative salience in contemporary Burma, and its occurrence is merely fortuitous. That this change has been accompanied—albeit less rapidly—by corresponding changes in the uncle terminology supports the thesis adopted here: that the classification of kin is determined by jural norms and structural arrangements (in this case, marriage form) rather than by arbitrary cognitive rules. To uncover the reasons for the change in marriage form would, of course, constitute an important discovery for the light it might shed, on Burmese kinship and on general kinship theory as well. It is most unfortunate, therefore, that (kin terms not being of interest to me at the time I was engaged in field work) I neglected to look into this question.

In this system, in which the levirate, the sororate, and sibling exchange form a configuration of related practices, then, just as the terms for the same-sex siblings-in-law, and their corresponding uncle and aunt terms, are explicable by reference to sibling exchange marriage, so the terms for opposite-sex sibling-in-law, and their corresponding aunt and uncle terms, are explicable by reference to the sororate and levirate. Let us begin with the sibling-in-law terms.

It will be noted from Chart 2 that, just as for those of the same sex, so too for those of opposite sex, both types of sibling-in-law—sibling's spouse and spouse's sibling—are designated by one and the same term. Unlike the former, however, relative age is a distinctive feature in the latter, one which is marked not merely (as it is in many uncle and aunt terms) by the addition of age-designating suffixes to a shared term, but by the use of separate terms. For these siblings-in-law the significant dimension is whether they are qualified to contract a sororate or levirate marriage, and it is along this dimension that they are classified. Thus, a male calls his elder brother's wife and his wife's elder sister (neither of whom is available to him in a secondary marriage) by one and the same term, *mayi*. He calls his younger brother's wife and his wife's younger sister by another term, *hkema;* these are the sisters-in-law he is permitted to marry in the senior levirate and junior sororate, respectively. Reciprocally, the female calls her elder sister's husband and her husband's elder brother by one and the same term, *hkeqou;* these are the brothers-in-law she may marry in the sororate and levirate, respectively. She calls her younger sister's husband and her husband's younger brother by another term, *ma'*, and neither is available to her in a levirate or sororate marriage.

The classification of opposite-sex siblings-in-law provides us with a ready explanation for their classification in their statuses as uncles and aunts, and this, in turn, enables us to account for the remaining core kindred. Although father's brothers, elder and younger alike, have a modified father term *(ba)*, the elder alone participates in these secondary marriages, and, as Chart 3 indicates, he is terminologically distinguished from the younger brother. The former is *bagyi*, or "big father," and, moreover, he is often addressed as *baba*, "father." Similarly, although in the older system, mother's elder and younger sister are both designated by a modified mother term (*mi*), the younger sister alone participates in these marriages; correspondingly, she is terminologically distinguished from her elder sister, and designated as *midwei*, "little mother." To be sure, the contemporary term for mother's sister does not incorporate the semantic feature of the traditional term—*do* is not "mother"—but, what is more to the point, it does incorporate the latter's structural feature. That is, mother's younger sister (*qado*), the potential surrogate mother, is distinguished from the elder sister (*kyido*), who is not a surrogate mother. But this is not all. Affinal aunts and uncles, as Chart 3 reveals, follow the same paradigm: those that qualify as spouses in the levirate and sororate are merged with the corresponding consanguineal aunts and uncles, and vice versa. Thus, father's younger brother's wife and mother's elder sister's husband are merged, respectively, with father's elder brother and mother's younger sister. Although they are different kintypes—the former affinal, the latter conjugal, kin—they appropriately share the same term for both are parent-surrogates in a levirate or sororate marriage.

Finally, as Diagrams 7 and 8 reveal, the aunt and uncle terms are systematically related not only to each other but also to their correspond-ing terms as siblings-in-law. That is, the classification of potential spouses (siblings-in-law) and potential parents (uncles and aunts), on the one hand, and non-potential spouses and parents, on the other, systematically parallel each other. A man, it will be recalled, performs the levirate and sororate, respectively, with his younger (but not his elder) brother's wife, and his wife's younger (but not her elder) sister. It will be remembered, too, that the children's sentimentally appropriate mother surrogate is

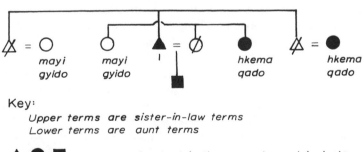

Key:
Upper terms are sister-in-law terms
Lower terms are aunt terms

▲ ● ■ Kin types involved in the sororate and levirate

⚥ ∅ Deceased

Diagram 7. The sororate and levirate and the classification of a man's sisters-in-law and their corresponding classification as aunts.

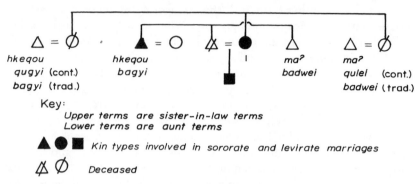

Diagram 8. The sororate and levirate and the classification of a woman's brothers-in-law and their corresponding classification as uncles.

mother's younger sister. Hence, as Diagram 7 indicates, for male ego (figure 1) the two sisters-in-law who are his potential wives are both *hkema,* and both are *qado* to his children. In short, we now see why Fa-yng-BrWi is classified with Mo-yng-Si. Although father's younger brother's wife is not an especially sentimentally appropriate mother —and, indeed, since their own mother is usually living when father marries her, she does not play the maternal role—since she is father's *hkema;* and since any *hkema* is potentially their father's wife, consistency requires that she be *qado* to the children.

Correspondingly, the two sisters-in-law who are disqualified to be ego's wives are both *mayi,* and since neither, therefore, can be a mother-surrogate to his children, neither is the latter's *qado;* both on the contrary are *gyido.* Again, we can see why these two different kintypes—one affinal, the other consanguineal—are classified together: Fa-eld-BrWi = Mo-eld-Si because neither is a potential step-mother.

The same paradigm holds for the classification of a woman's brothers-in-law and their corresponding classification as uncles. A woman, it will be remembered, performs the levirate and sororate, respectively, with the elder (but not the younger) brother of her husband, and with the husband of her elder (but not her younger) sister. It will be remembered, too, that the children's jurally, if not always sentimentally, appropriate father-surrogate is father's elder brother. Hence, as Diagram 8 indicates, for female ego (figure 1) the two brothers-in-law who are her potential husbands are both *hkeqou.* In the contemporary terminology, these brothers-in-law have separate terms as uncles (Fa-eld-Br=*bagyi,* Mo-eld-SiHu=*qugyi*), whereas in the traditional terminology they have the same term *(bagyi).* Either classification, however, is compatible with the argument of this section, although the traditional classification is more rigorously so. Let us begin with the latter.

A woman, as I have already observed, rarely has children when she enters the sororate, but since it sometimes happens—if, for example, she has been widowed or divorced—then, when she marries her elder sister's husband, not only does she acquire a husband, but her children acquire a father. Under the circumstances, although Mo-eld-SiHu is not (like Fa-eld-Br) an especially jurally appropriate father-surrogate, he is nevertheless their mother's *hkeqou*, and since any *hkeqou* is the potential husband of their mother, consistency requires that he (like Fa-eld-Br) be designated *bagyi*.

The contemporary terminology does not reflect, nor the contemporary situation require, such a consistency. Since a woman who enters the sororate is only rarely a mother, and since in any event the practice of both the sororate and the levirate are in decline in modern Burma, the conjunction of both contingencies is so rare that the disjunctions of these two types of elder uncle is unimportant. What is important, however, is that the elder uncles, the potential step-father(s), be distinguished from the younger uncles, who are disqualified from performing the paternal role. The latter disjunction is a requirement of both systems if the brother-in-law and uncle terms are to be structurally parallel, and indeed this disjunction is found in both. In the more rigorously systematic traditional system, both types of younger uncles are *badwei*, which corresponds to their merging as brothers-in-law. (Both are *ma?*). Although, in the contemporary system, these two types of younger uncle are disjoined (one being *badwei*, the other *qulei*) the important thing is that neither is merged with elder uncle. Neither, that is, is *bagyi* or *quji*. In short, even in the contemporary system, the parallelism between brother-in-law as mother's potential or non-potential spouse, and uncle as children's potential or non-potential father-surrogate, persists.

That the grand-uncle and grand-aunt terms do not duplicate those of the uncles and aunts is a puzzling finding, especially since the children often call their parents' aunts and uncles by the same terms which their parents use. Although their duplication is neither required nor predicted by the theory upon which this analysis of kin terms is based, it is puzzling, nevertheless, on more general cognitive grounds.[12] The important pre-

---

12. In the village system, both grandfathers, their brothers, and the husbands of their sisters are distinguished from the brothers of the grandmothers and their sisters' husbands. The former set are *qahpeigyi* ("big father"), the latter are *qahpou*. Similarly, both grandmothers, their sisters, and the wives of their brothers are distinguished from the sisters of the grandfathers and the latter's brothers' wives. The former set are *qameigyi* ("big mother"), the latter *qahpwa*. In neither case is relative age indicated; younger and elder are merged in a single term. In short, all at the second ascending generation are either *qahpeigyi* or *ahpou*; the former are married to *ahpwa*, the latter to *qameigyi*.

The urban (Rangoon) system is even more simplified. Although, formally, relative age is distinguished, colloquially, elder and younger are merged. Moreover, the village distinction

diction from this theory is that the traditional marriage system (sibling exchange as primary, and sororate and levirate as secondary, marriage) explain the traditional classification of cousins. This it does; and, by implication, the changes in the system explain the ambiguity (discussed in the previous section) concerning the extension of the incest taboo to cousins. Some informants and some published sources contend, it will be recalled, that marriage between cousins is permitted (though frowned upon), others contend that it is prohibited between agnatic cousins only, and still others contend that marriage between all cousins is prohibited. Since the Burmese are in agreement on almost all other kinship matters, it is strange that there should be such important disagreement over this matter. It is less strange, however, if we assume that the present freedom in marriage choice represents a historical change from the traditional marriage system. For then, some informants could be stressing the incest norms logically required by the traditional marriage system; others, those consistent with the new marriage system; and still others, a combination of the two.

The above conclusion follows from the deduction that under the traditional marriage system cousins were classified rather differently from the way they are classified today and that this classification constrained marriage choice. For when sibling exchange (marriage between two sets of siblings of opposite sex) is the preferred form of primary marriage, each sibling in the exchange is the cross-uncle or cross-aunt of the children of the opposite-sex sibling in the sibling set. And when the sororate and levirate (marriage between siblings-in-law of opposite sex) are preferred forms of secondary marriage, the substitute siblings (elder brother and younger sister) are not only the parallel-uncle or parallel-aunt of the children of their same-sex siblings, but, in addition, they are their actual or potential parent-surrogates. It is not surprising, then, that parents' same-sex siblings (and they alone) are designated by a modified father and mother term, and under the circumstances one would expect the parallel niblings (and they alone) to be designated, reciprocally, as "son" and "daughter." This is, indeed, the case, as Judson indicates: sons and daughters, together with parallel nephews and nieces, are *tha* and *thami*, while cross-niblings are *tu* and *tuma*. With the breakdown of the traditional marriage system, this is no longer the case: instead of merging own children and parallel siblings, the latter are merged with cross-niblings (both are *tu* and *tuma*) and differentiated from own children.

---

between the grandfather's and grandmother's side is eliminated. Instead grandfather and grandmother have one term (*qahpou* and *qahpwa*, respectively) and all other male and female siblings and siblings-in-law, respectively, have another term. Males are *qahpolei* ("small grandfather"), females *qahpwalei* ("small grandmother").

On the basis of the same logic, one would expect that in the traditional system cross-cousins would be distinguished from parallel cousins, while the latter would be merged with siblings. For given the regular practice of the sororate and levirate, parallel cousins are potentially, if not actually, half-siblings, since they share a common father-stepfather and a common mother-stepmother. Thus, the husband in a levirate marriage is not only the father of his own children, but he is the step-father of his brother's children, and his new spouse (his brother's wife) is not only the mother of his brother's children but also the step-mother of his children. The analogous situation obtains in the sororate. Cross-cousins, on the other hand, are never half-siblings, because under the system of sibling exchange they are the offspring of a marriage between two sets of opposite-sex siblings. Although this expectation is not supported by direct evidence—for even in Judson's terms all cousins are classified with siblings—it is supported by the indirect evidence of the Marma terminology. For on Bernot's assumption that the Marma terms represent the archaic Burmese terms, then in an even older period than Judson's, not only were parallel cousins differentiated from cross-cousins and merged with siblings, but cross-cousins, in turn, were (as they are in the Marma) merged with siblings-in-law. This implies that the former (like the latter in contemporary Burma) were potential spouses, while parallel cousins (who, as half-siblings, are merged with siblings) were not.

Against this background it is at least conceivable that the contemporary classification, in which parallel and cross-cousins alike are merged with siblings, originated as the merging of siblings and parallel cousins only, and that, as the traditional marriage system declined, the parallel cousin vs. cross-cousin distinction became socially and therefore cognitively irrelevant. Under these circumstances parallel cousins could have been classified with cross-cousins, or the latter could have been classified with the already merged parallel cousins and siblings. That the latter, rather than the former, option was ultimately adopted remains unexplained, although I suspect that its adoption is related to the incest taboo. Since the Burmese village, as I have noted, represents a relatively closed kinship network, the classification of all cousins with siblings places a brake on the even greater restriction of the size of the endogamous group.

This diachronic speculation is consistent with the various disagreements alluded to above concerning the appropriate boundary of the sibling incest taboo. Although all cousins in the modern system are classified with siblings, the urban attitude toward cousin marriage is much more permissive than the rural. This is explicable by my suggestion. Since the large population of the city decreases the probability, and lessens the concern over, excessive endogamy, cousin marriage, though frowned upon in the city, is not prohibited. To be sure, cousin marriage is not prohibited in the village either, but it is very strongly disapproved, so that its incidence approaches zero. Moreover, since villagers strongly disapprove of any form of cousin marriage, it is understandable that the village attitude, unlike that of the city, is not more restrictive toward agnates than other cognates. In the city, however, where this distinction is made, it is entirely consistent with what I have said above about the differential incidence of the levirate and sororate. Since the former is the more widely practiced, agnatic cousins are the more likely to be half-siblings, and it is their marriage, therefore, that causes the greater concern.

To conclude, then, the logical requirements of the traditional Burmese marriage system enable us to explain almost the entire set of terms comprising the traditional terminology of the core kindred, and the changes in the marriage system enable us to explain the changes that have taken place in the terminological system. This analysis suggests that kin terms are not determined, as some theorists contend, by arbitrary cognitive rules, but by jural norms and the structural arrangements attendant upon compliance with these norms—in this case, norms governing marriage. If this analysis is correct, the overriding criterion in the classification of almost all the kinsmen comprising the Burmese core kindred is eligibility of siblings and siblings-in-law for primary and secondary marriages. All else follows as links in a logical chain from that single criterion. It is this criterion (and not the dimensions abstracted by componential analysis) that provides the emic definition of these kin terms. Kin terms, to be sure, are cognitively mapped, but the key to the mapping, to reemphasize the thesis of this section, consists of the jural norms governing marriage. For an understanding of these terms, therefore, one must first look to the sociology of kinship. Only then do the cognitive rules emerge as predictable (because logically entailed) means for ordering social life, rather than a set of rules invented out of whole cloth which, like the rules of some parlor game, operate in a social vacuum.

This analysis underscores, too, the importance of diachronic data for the analysis of synchronic processes. It was only while pondering the historical changes that have occurred in the Burmese uncle and aunt terms, as well as those that have occurred in the Burmese marriage system, that the present hypothesis suggested itself. That is, since aunts and uncles are also siblings-in-law, it seemed not implausible that Burmese kinship terms may be related to the norms governing marriage. Had these historical data not been available, the kin terms could have been explained, of course, by the usual rules discovered by componential analysis, but the rules themselves would have remained inexplicable.

7. Kinship Institutions and the Consummation of Marriage

Initiation of Marriage

Although marriage based on sibling-exchange and the levirate and sororate are ethnographically and structurally interesting, as well as theoretically challenging, it must be emphasized that today most marriages in village Burma are based on free choice, the only kinship constraints consisting of informal pressure by the parents of the children to make a "good" marriage—one that is socially and economically beneficial. This being the case, we must now examine the procedures by which the typical marriage is initiated.

It should be noted, in the first place, that the initiative for establishing a relationship between a boy and a girl is exclusively the boy's, for however much she may be attracted to a boy, there is no socially approved means by which a girl can take the initiative. Even among modern urban youth the girl, according to university students, can take the initiative only indirectly. Thus, if she likes a boy, she may talk admiringly about him to her girl friends, with the expectation that they, in turn, will report her feelings to him. In village and city, alike, even the boy seldom attempts to contact the girl directly. Although attracted by a girl (by having observed her at the village well, or in the fields, or at a Buddhist festival) there is no acceptable way by which he can approach her directly or talk with her in private. To tell her directly of his love would be unthinkable, for that is tantamount to saying he wishes to have intercourse with her; and to seek her out in private is equally impossible for, until they are engaged, the girl will avoid him because, should he as much as touch her, her "name is destroyed" (na-me pyette).

For all these reasons, the boy must approach the girl through a go-between (qaungthwe). Generally, he chooses the girl's (but sometimes his own) elder sister or aunt for this function. He may either instruct her to tell the girl of his love, or he may ask her to deliver a love-letter (*yiza sa*) to her. In the cities, of course, the love letter is usually sent through the mail, but in either case its content almost always conforms to a rather stilted stereotype: "I love you. I will love you until death. I want to marry you. From the very beginning, when I first saw you, I loved you. I will serve you forever," etc. If the girl does not reciprocate his feelings, she tells him so through the go-between, and, typically, that ends it. Thus, an important (manifest) function of the go-between is its face-saving value for the boy, sparing him the humiliation of a direct rejection.

If the girl reciprocates the boy's feelings, the go-between arranges a meeting at the girl's house, but if the parents disapprove of the boy, they may meet in the go-between's house. However strong her feelings, the girl even then seldom tells the boy that she reciprocates his love, or that she wishes to marry him, lest he think her cheap. Hence, although she continues to meet him, she may sometimes delay giving him an answer for as long as six months.

During this interval, the couple are never permitted physical privacy. The boy visits the girl only in her home where, although they may be alone in a room, the girl's parents are close by, usually in the next room. Sexual contact of any kind is strictly prohibited, and even the appearance of a sexual relationship must be carefully avoided. When the girl finally agrees to the boy's proposal, the next step is for his parents to approach the girl's parents, usually through an intermediary, to obtain their approval for the marriage. (The use of an intermediary seems to be a standard practice in Southeast Asia, including Thailand [Piker n.d., ch. 2:36-37], and Vietnam [Hickey 1964: 100], as well as in China [Hsu 1971:85]). Should her parents give their consent, the only remaining obstacle is astrological: it is necessary that the horoscopes of the couple match. Since Burmese astrology forms a complex belief system, and since, in any event, it would take us far afield to examine the many astrological beliefs concerning the marriage, I shall summarize only those that are commonly held even by those who are not deeply involved in astrological matters.

Although certain marriages are auspicious (the marriage of Sunday-born through Monday-born to Tuesday- through Thursday-born, Monday- through Sunday-born to Wednesday- through Saturday-born, and so on for seven combinations), the Burmese are not so much concerned with arranging auspicious combinations as in avoiding inauspicious ones. Traditionally, inauspicious marriages are those between Saturday-born and Thursday-born, Friday- and Monday-born, Sunday- and Wednesday-born, and Wednesday afternoon- and Tuesday-born.

Although, if parents are opposed to a marriage on other grounds, they may base their public opposition on such astrological grounds, it is commonly accepted that these unfavorable signs can be overcome by a variety of means, astrological and religious. Thus, assuming that parents favor the marriage, they can ask the astrologer to calculate an auspicious time for the wedding, and this auspiciousness can counterbalance the possible dangers attendant upon the inauspicious combination. In addition, a Monday-born, for example, can overcome the dangers involved in marriage with a Friday-born by making offerings (in consultation with an astrologer) at the Monday-born corner of a pagoda. These are only some of the means by which the dangers of poorly matching horoscopes can be circumvented. In general, ill omens of this kind are considered insuperable obstacles to a marriage only by the few persons who are rigidly bound to astrological belief.

To summarize, then, although individuals are free to choose their spouses, their marriage is dependent upon the approval of both sets of parents. To be sure, they may marry by elopement without parental consent, but this is considered a drastic course, one on which, as we shall see, few couples are willing to embark.

Engagement and Wedding

Anywhere from a few weeks to a year after their initial meeting, the boy's parents call again on the girl's parents to arrange for the engagement, which typically preceeds the wedding. The engagement ceremony—known variously as *kyaung lande* (to be put on the path together), *sei sat gyin* (to be brought into a relationship), or, as combined in the engagement invitation, *sei sat kyaung lande*—is a public event, held in the presence of invited guests, and always including the headman, village elders, and the kindred of the engaged couple. The expenses are defrayed by the parents of the boy, despite the fact that the ceremony is usually held in the house of the girl. (In the city, however, the parents of the girl defray the expenses.) Prior to the ritual, the guests are entertained by music piped through a loud speaker, and they are offered food and drink. The ritual itself is brief. A master of ceremonies, usually the headman or a village elder, announces the amount and content of the dower (of which more later) which had been agreed upon by the parents. Usually, too, that part of the dower which, like jewelry, is for the use of the girl alone, is transferred to her at that time. (In the cities, there is no transfer of property at this time, nor is the amount of the dowry—the dower is seldom practiced—ever announced, though, of course, it may be leaked.) The master of ceremonies then describes the splendid qualities of the future bride and groom, announces the date of their forthcoming wedding, and gives them his blessing and avuncular advice (the latter known as *sounma saga*).

Brief as it is, the engagement has at least three important functions (in addition to the announcement of the dower and the setting of the wedding date which, of course, can be performed without an engagement ceremony). First, and foremost, it establishes the serious intentions of the boy, so that thereafter he may, with impunity, go in and out of the girl's house. Before the engagement, suspicious that he may only be interested in a casual affair, the girl's parents not only keep the young couple under surveillance, but they may also make trouble for the boy. Since, related to this first function, the declaration of intent to marry is tantamount to marriage, a second function of the engagement in some, but not all, families, is to permit the couple to have sexual relations. (Since, however, they still do not live together, sexual intercourse usually takes place in the fields or the woods.) Finally, in the event that the engagement is broken or her fiancé dies, the girl (in the former families) is not viewed as promiscuous or immoral for having lost her virginity.

Since none of these conditions obtains in the city where, despite their engagement, fiancees may not be alone together, let alone commence sexual relations, the functions of the urban engagement ceremony are obscure. Formerly, its main function was the announcement of the impending marriage. But since increasingly the wedding is held very shortly after the engagement—so that nothing should intervene that might break the engagement and thereby "destroy the girl's name"—the wedding is usually announced (by written invitation) prior to the engagement. Hence, the urban engagement ceremony seems to serve primarily as a vehicle for conspicuous display.

The wedding *(mingala hsaung* = to carry out an auspicious ceremony), which takes place anywhere from a month to two years following the engagement, can be performed at any time of the year, except during the three month Buddhist lent *(Wa)*, providing it is held on an astrologically auspicious day. Unless her mother is pregnant, the wedding, like the engagement, is held in the home or compound of the bride's parents, although the expenses, at least in the case of village weddings, are defrayed by the parents of the groom. In city weddings this is not necessarily the case, and the two sets of parents must reach an agreement concerning which will defray the expenses of the ceremony, the reception following the ceremony, the furnishings of the bridal chamber, and (if the couple intends to set up house immediately) the furnishings of the house. Typically, however, it is agreed that the bride's parents defray these expenses, although this is by no means an automatic assumption, and often agreement is reached only after prolonged negotiation. Sometimes, the agreement is to share expenses, one side paying for the ceremony, the other for the reception, or one paying for both of these and the other for the linen, bedding, and other furnishings *(hkanwin pyitsi)* of the bridal chamber or the new household. Sometimes, however, agreement cannot be reached, and urban informants recount cases of wedding arrangements being canceled because of parental recalcitrance over these financial arrangements. Obviously, these disagreements seldom arise if either set of parents views the intended spouse of their child as an important catch.

Although the wedding, like the engagement, is an entirely secular ceremony—Buddhist monks do not officiate, nor may they attend even as guests—it is framed by religion, a Buddhist ceremony being performed in the morning prior to the wedding, and a spirit *(nat)* ceremony in the evening (or the following morning) after the wedding. Thus, on the morning of the wedding day, Buddhist monks are offered a special meal at the home of the bride, for Buddhists believe that offerings to monks are a most important means for acquiring merit, and in this case the merit is intended to improve the karma of the couple, as well as of their parents. At this time, too, the monks chant passages from Buddhist *Sutta* (known as *pareitta*), whose purpose is to ward off any dangers that might befall the newlyweds. (The most important *Sutta* for this purpose is the *Mangala*, or Auspicious, *Sutta.*) Wealthy families offer food to the monks on the morning after the wedding, as well.

The spirit *(nat)* ceremony, which takes place at the shrine of the village guardian spirit, consists of offerings by the mothers (but not the fathers) of the newlyweds, and by the bride (but not the groom) to their respective hereditary spirits and to the village guardian spirit. These offerings (like the *pareitta*) are intended to ward off danger to the newlyweds, particularly the danger that might otherwise be caused by the spirits themselves.

The wedding takes place in the morning—so that "the karma of the couple [should] rise like the rising sun"—but the festivities usually begin the night before when recorded music, piped through a loudspeaker rented for the occasion, is played continuously throughout the night. (The louder the volume, and the more people who hear it, the greater the prestige for the groom's family, who defray the expenses). The ceremony is performed in the presence of numerous guests including the kindred and friends of the bride and groom, one representative each from every household in the village, and the village headmen and elders. As the guests, dressed in their holiday finest, enter the wedding pavilion, each makes a cash contribution, which is used to help defray the expenses. (In the cities, wedding presents are offered instead.) The amount of each contribution is recorded so that the delicately balanced system of reciprocity may be maintained. The guests then proceed to mats or tables where food is laid out. If the couple's parents are poor, the food consists of tea and cakes; wealthy parents, however, lay out a banquet. Only after everyone has eaten does the simple ceremony begin.

At this ceremony the bride and groom sit facing both sets of seated parents. Between them is a ritual offering *(gado bwe)* to the parents. The officiant—who may be an honored guest, village elder, headman, or professional master of ceremonies—instructs the bride and groom to "worship" *(shikkou)* their parents—to prostrate themselves before them, to request their formal approval for their marriage, and to beg their pardon *(gado)* for any offense they might have dealt them. Following this they are instructed to "worship" the Buddha, His Doctrine, the Order of Monks, and their teachers. The parents signify their approval by reciting the traditional blessing which expresses their hope that health, wealth, longevity, and nirvana be vouchsafed to the couple. As in the engagement ceremony, the officiant recounts the many qualities of the couple and of their parents, and offers them words of advice for a happy marriage *(sounma saga)*. At the conclusion of this simple ceremony, the father of the bride announces the amount of the dower (the marriage payment offered the bride by the groom's parents) and, where one is given, of the dowry (the marriage payment offered the groom by the bride's parents).[1] Then the hands of the bride and groom, which are held together (sometimes, too, their hands or their thumbs are tied) are dipped into a bowl of water. This is symbolic, so it is sometimes said, of their union, which should be "as indivisible as water." With this, the wedding is over and the guests begin to wander out.[2]

When the guests depart, it is the custom for the boys and young men of the village to assemble at the house in which the newlyweds will sleep, and to beat on the walls with sticks, until they are offered some of the choice food left over from the wedding feast. This custom (known as *mingala taung*) is a tame reflection of an older, and dangerous custom (described by Scott, among others) in which, on the wedding night, young bachelors would shower sticks and stones on the roof of the newlyweds'

---

1. As already indicated, there is no announcement of the dowry in the cities where, however, the wedding is not complete until two married women, relatives of the bride, walk up and down the aisles scattering a mixture of rice and coins over the heads of the guests. (This ceremony is called *shwei mou ngwei mou ywade.*) Following the wedding, city families typically have a banquet-like reception, either in the afternoon or the evening.

2. Burmese villagers offer neither congratulations for achievements, nor sympathy for sorrows. At funerals, for example, no one offers condolences to the bereaved. Similarly, at weddings, congratulations are offered neither to the bride and groom, nor to the parents and families.

house, refusing to leave until paid a ransom in money (Shway Yoe 1896:58). Although neither the beating nor the stoning of the bridal chamber is practiced in the cities, the sexual consummation of the marriage is delayed in a manner which is not unrelated to this practice. Groups of young men and women, from the parties both of the bride and groom, obstruct the passage of the couple to the bridal chamber until they are paid a ransom. The obstruction, especially in the case of the groom, may be strenuous indeed. Sometimes, he may be delayed for hours before being allowed to proceed, and in some cases he succeeds in reaching his bride only after the use of considerable physical force. Since the ransom is termed "stone price" (gebou)—because if it is not paid, the couple will, in theory, be stoned—it seems not unlikely that this urban practice is the successor to the earlier custom of stoning, which is still prohibited in the villages.

In the cities this is not the only ceremonial obstruction to the completion of the wedding. Even before the wedding begins, the groom and his party are prevented by the bride's party from entering the wedding hall until they are paid a ransom. Since this practice is reported in Shway Yoe (1896:58), it is surprising that, although it is still performed in the cities, it is no longer found in the villages (not, at least, in those which I studied).

The custom of interrupting a ceremonial event until a ransom is paid is not confined, it should be noted, to the wedding. It is also found, for example, in the Buddhist ordination rite in which the procession of the young novice is obstructed until a ransom is paid (Spiro 1971:240). As in the case of the wedding, this obstruction is known as *kyou tade*, since the procession in both cases is held back by a rope.

Rather than speculate on the origin or functions of this stoning custom, I shall merely summarize the origin myth, as recounted in Yeigyi, which serves as its charter.[3] According to the myth, this custom originated after one of the recurrent destructions of the earth and all its inhabitants by fire, water, and wind. Sometime after this destruction, four gods (*samma deva*), beings without sex organs, descended to the earth where, finding no food, they discovered that soil was a source of nourishment. Having ingested this terrestrial matter, they became more material and were thus unable to ascend to their heavenly abode. Soon after, they discovered a certain wild-growing root, as well as wild rice, which they added to their diet. As a result, they began to develop sex organs, as well as those

3. Although the villagers did not identify this myth as scriptural, and although it differs from the following scriptural version in some respects, it is almost certainly taken from the *Aggañña Suttanta* of the *Dīgha Nikāya* (in *Dialogues of the Buddha*, Part III). A slightly different version is given by Shway Yoe (1896:58-59).

"mental impurities" *(kilesa)* which Buddhism identifies as greed, anger, and lust; and this in turn led them to the practice of sexual intercourse. When the higher gods *(brahma deva)* observed them engaging in sex, they became angry and stoned them.

The moral, at least by implication, seems to be very clear: sex is a gross and material thing, inspired by gross and material impulses *(kilesa)*, and its inception, at least, should not go unpunished. This does not mean, of course, that this constitutes the motivation for the current custom of pounding or stoning the house of the newlyweds, which, unfortunately, I did not investigate. That something of this kind is, at least in part, in the villagers' minds may be inferred, however, from their recounting of the myth when I inquired about the custom.

Functions of the Wedding

Unlike some other cultures, in which the wedding is the instrument which creates a marriage, the Burmese ceremony (as it is understood at least in the village) has no such power or effect; the wedding is merely a public announcement of the couple's intention of living together as man and wife. This function, however, is of paramount importance because the one necessary condition for a legally constituted marriage is, precisely, that it be based on a public declaration of intent to live together as husband and wife.

Important as it is, however, this function cannot in itself explain the practice and persistence of the wedding because there are other recognized means for making this declaration. Thus, if a couple, with or without the approval of their parents, openly live and eat together under the same roof, jointly participate in sabbath observance, pagoda worship, and so on, their status as husband and wife is legally valid and publicly assured. Indeed, in the case of previously married couples *(qeindaungyi)*, who are prohibited from having a wedding (because a woman may have only one marriage ceremony), the above expressions of intent can be the only signs of a valid marriage.

Although there are, as we have seen, a number of indicators of a valid (common-law) marriage, the most important is commensality. "To eat [from the same dish]" so that, as the Burmese say, "the hands [of husband and wife] come together" *(thamin letsoun sade)*, is the essential instrument and symbol of marriage. In the past, commensality was even more binding than it is today. If, for example, it could be proved that a couple had eaten from the same dish, they could be compelled to live together as man and wife (Malcom 1839:194). The importance of commensality is reflected in lexical usage. Thus a parent who marries off a child is said, colloquially, "to give [his daughter] a husband for eating" *(lin peisade)*, alternatively, "to give [his son] a wife for eating" *(maya peisade)*.[4] (These expressions have sexual overtones as well. *Sade* means to eat, but colloquially it can also mean to copulate.) Similarly, some informants claim that the daughter-in-law is called *hkyweima* because she is the woman *(ma)* who is fed *(kywei)*. Like all folk etymologies, this one is culturally illuminating even though it may be linguistically useless.[5]

If commensality, as well as the other indicators of common living mentioned above, constitutes a public declaration of marriage, it is evident that the Burmese wedding presents us with a perplexing explanatory problem. Although the wedding validates the marriage by publicly announcing the couple's intention to live together as man and wife, and although the function is served with equal legal and moral force by these alternative means, the wedding is nevertheless a very important ceremony in the eyes of the Burmese. It is almost always performed in the case of a first marriage *(ngelin-ngemaya)*, and, even in the case of an elopement, a wedding is usually performed if and when the couple effects a reconciliation with their parents.[6] The only exception to this generalization consists of children of poor parents, who sometimes resort to elopement in order to spare their parents the expense of a wedding or the embarrassment of a small or non-existent dower.

Why, then, given the existence of alternative (and equally valid) means for effecting a marriage, should the Burmese view the wedding as such an important ceremony? Or, to put the question in its obverse form, why are they—and especially the parents of the couple—so strongly opposed to elopement *(hkou pyei)*? For the parents, and especially the girl's parents, elopement is a cause of such intense shame that they will often agree to their daughter's marriage, despite their disapproval of her intended husband, just so she will not elope.

One possible explanation, and this is the hypothesis I had initially entertained, is that the wedding is necessary to legitimize the offspring.

4. F. K. Lehman (personal communication) observes that, in reality, these expressions have a different meaning than that assigned to them by my informants, namely, "To give one's son or daughter as a husband or wife, and enjoy the results." In agreement with this interpretation, Theodore Stern (personal communication) adds that the high officials of the Burmese kingdom, known as *myousa* ("town eaters"), "were given a royal prebend for their enjoyment."

5. The Burmese emphasis on commensality as a crucial ingredient of marriage is found elsewhere in Asia. Thus, in Ceylon (Kandy) according to Yalman (1967:103), "a casual affair may turn into a more permanent relationship almost imperceptibly. The turning point is always the establishment of the cooking place: the relationship between a man and woman will hardly be worth mentioning unless a separate hearth has been set up."

6. This pattern is not unique to Burma in Southeast Asia. Common-law marriages are also valid, for example, in Thailand (Piker n.d., ch. 2:39), and there, too, the sequence of reconciliation and a subsequent wedding following an elopement is found *(ibid.:42)*.

Upon investigation, however, this turned out to be a false explanation. Not only are children of any valid marriage called by the same term, *thathami* (sons and daughters), but they all enjoy the identical legal, moral, and social status. Only when the identity of their *genitor* is unknown *(ahpei mapobu)* are the children stigmatizied, but in a common-law marriage the genitor is not only known, he is their legal *pater*. A few villagers, however, when pushed for an explanation—for they, too, were perplexed by the importance they themselves attached to the wedding—offered a qualified version of the legitimacy hypothesis. Although common-law marriages, they say, are valid *legally*, they personally do not accept them as valid. This being so, they would reject the children, including their own grandchildren, born from such marriages. This, however, was a distinctly minority view.

The great majority of the villagers offered two rather different reasons for the importance of the wedding. First, unlike the other ways of validating a marriage, the wedding, they claim, represents the only *unambiguous* means of announcing to the village, and especially to the headman and elders, that the couple intend to live together as man and wife. Second, the wedding is the only means of publicly declaring that the couple's parents have consented to their marriage. From these two unambiguous messages, the wedding produces a set of important consequences. First, since it unequivocally announces the fact that the couple are truly married, no one can contest the normal laws of inheritance by which, in the event of death, the property passes, first to the surviving spouse, and then to the children. In short, the wedding ensures the property rights of both sets of legitimate heirs. Second, the children can be assured of the physical care and financial support of their parents, for any dereliction on their part would be countered by the village elders. Third, in the event of divorce, the wife and children are protected against an irresponsible husband and father, for the elders can compel him to fulfill his economic obligations and to negotiate an acceptable property settlement. Finally, the wedding assures the girl of a dower—for only if there is a wedding is a dower negotiated—and this, as will be seen below, is of utmost importance for the bride and her parents.

Except for the argument concerning the dower, these essentially economic arguments for the importance of the wedding are not entirely convincing. Although the status of common-law marriages might be ambiguous in the (impersonal) city, it is hardly ambiguous in the village, where everyone knows everyone else, and where the rather simple question of whether a couple are living together as husband and wife is easily answered by the various criteria specified above. In short, in the village, at least, the economic protection of wife and children is as much assured by a common-law marriage as by one solemnized by a wedding. Moreover, even in the matter of the dower, there is no reason why it could not be negotiated and offered privately, without a public ceremony. To be sure, since it is negotiated by the parents, there obviously can be no dower in the case of an elopement which (by definition) occurs without parental knowledge or consent. In other common-law marriages, however, in which parents are aware and approve of the union, the dower can be easily arranged for.

If, then, the culturally defined functions of the wedding—the putative advantages accruing to the married couple and their children—are either achieved or achievable in a common-law marriage, perhaps the wedding has some other function which accounts for the importance the Burmese attach to it. And since it is the parents, rather than the newlyweds, who are most insistent upon a wedding, perhaps this function should be sought with respect to them. With this change in focus, let us begin by examining the parents' motives for performing the wedding, from which we might uncover the functions which it has for them. For the parents, I would suggest, the most important functions of the wedding relate to the all-important and ever-present Burmese motives of prestige-enhancement. I would further suggest that there are two prestige-related dimensions of the wedding, wealth and honor, and each will be treated separately.

In Burma (as in most cultures of South and Southeast Asia) prestige derived from wealth is directly proportional to the magnitude of (among other things) conspicuous display, including both conspicuous consumption and conspicuous waste; and there is little doubt that for the groom's parents, at least, the wedding provides an opportunity for both, because it is they who both finance the wedding and offer a publicly announced dower to the bride. The wedding, beginning with the first of these financial outlays, involves a significant display of wealth. Thus, the cost of thirty weddings (for which I have detailed information) in Yeigyi, a village whose annual average family income is K 1,000, ranged from K 100 to K 1,000. In short, the cost of the least expensive wedding was one-tenth of, and that of the most expensive was equal to, the annual income of the average village family.[7]

---

7. The magnitude of these expenditures, it must be noted, is not unique to Burma. The wedding is an occasion for conspicuous display in many societies, including those of South and Southeast Asia, and Indian weddings, for example, are often more lavish than Burmese. Summarizing a number and variety of studies, Mandelbaum (1970:115) notes that in India, weddings are, typically, a family's largest single expense. In a detailed study of a Mysore village, for example, it was shown that the poorest families expend three or four months' income on a wedding, while wealthy families expend as much as their total annual income.

Now what is impressive about these figures—and this relates directly to the issue of conspicuous display—is that the primary expense of the wedding has no relationship to the ceremony itself, but rather to the food and entertainment offered at the reception (*qehkan pwe*). Since wealth-derived prestige is a function of conspicuous display, the greater the number of guests, and hence the greater the expense of the reception, the greater the prestige value of the wedding. (But this is not the only display function of a large wedding; important, too, is the value of the wedding presents, of which the greater in number and the more expensive they are the greater the prestige for both sets of parents.)

In sum, to the extent that the motives of the parents, especially the groom's parents, to perform a wedding are related to economic display, it is not so much the ceremony itself, but the reception, which is important. Since, however, many families must go into heavy debt in order to perform a "proper" wedding, sometimes when prestige is balanced against indebtedness, a small wedding is performed. (In Rangoon high society, however, where K 10,000 is not an excessive cost for a wedding, a guest list of even three hundred is considered "small"!) But a small wedding presents other problems. First, it might lead to the suspicion that it is being held subsequent to an elopement, or that the parents do not fully approve of the marriage, both of which (if true) cause considerable loss of face. Second, since the Burmese are sensitive to being excluded from any celebration to which, by virtue of kinship or friendship, they think they ought to be included, a small guest list involves the not inconsiderable risk of causing unintended offense or slight. In addition, then, to missing an opportunity for enhancing their prestige, there are other reasons why the decision to hold a small wedding is a difficult one to make.

Sometimes a compromise is struck by inviting a large number of guests, while cutting costs by means of a less lavish wedding. This compromise, however, is usually unsuccessful because prestige is a function not only of the cost of the wedding, but also of its quality. If the food and entertainment are of only moderate quality, the parents' prestige is not enhanced, even if the guest list (and therefore the expense) is large. Moreover, in the case of inter-village marriages, a tacky wedding reflects adversely on the entire village. At one such wedding, the village headman apologized to me and other guests, saying, in an embarrassed tone, that the parents really did not know how to do things properly. He expressed his hope that we would return in a few weeks when a relative of his was sponsoring a Buddhist initiation. Then we would see how a ceremony should really be performed!

Turning now to a second prestige-related dimension of the wedding —honor—we might begin by noting that weddingless marriages are usually associated with elopement, a source of great shame for the families of both spouses because it constitutes a public declaration that their children did not give them even the courtesy of requesting their approval for the marriage. In a culture which places a high value on filial respect, this is a serious blow to their honor. If, in addition, the elopement was a consequence of parental disapproval of the child's intended spouse, the loss of face is even greater because the child's disobedience is an even stronger violation of the value of filial respect.

The girl's family—parents and brothers—suffer an additional and perhaps an even more grievous disgrace, for elopement implies a serious blemish on their daughter, one which reflects adversely on her honor, and hence on their own. Since many, though by no means all, elopements take place if the girl either has lost her virginity or is pregnant, it is generally presumed that any elopement is a consequence of one or both of these conditions. (Hence, elopement, in a typical Burmese circumlocution, is compared to the exchange of an unripe jackfruit, which has been beaten to look ripe, for a copper coin, which has been polished with mercury to look like silver.) Since, then, the loss of her virginity, not to mention pregnancy, is, perhaps, the greatest disgrace that can befall the family of an unwed girl—for it is they who are deemed responsible for her purity—the failure to perform a wedding, which might be taken as a public declaration of the one or the other, is a most serious threat to their honor. Non-virginity, of course, is susceptible to public concealment, but pregnancy is not. Hence, one of the explicit functions of the wedding (which, although stated jocularly, is intended seriously) is "to put the bride on show," that is, to demonstrate that the girl is not pregnant. Even so, urban gossips joke about "bouquet brides," who carry large flower bouquets to conceal their pregnancy.

Since the wedding is the occasion for the public announcement of the dower, and since the dower is a symbol of the girl's, and her family's, social status, the wedding has importance for the girl's family even beyond what has thus far been indicated. This, however, will be dealt with in a separate section.

It is apparent, then, that the wedding is more important for the girl's than the boy's family, and it is understandable that they (both her parents and her brothers) are especially distressed by, and react strongly to, an elopement. To be sure, the Burmese reaction is not as strong as it is in some other societies, such as Ceylon (Kandy), where an eloping couple is excommunicated (Yalman 1967:184), but it is strong enough. Thus, I know of one case in which the girl's brother refused to see her again and, when she died, he would not attend her funeral. Even more extreme is the case of the girl whose parents would not consent to her marriage because her intended husband was the son of a woman who had eloped more than twenty years before. (When, having no other alternative, their daughter eloped with this man, her parents severed all contact with her.)

Given these attitudes, and, moreover, given all the functions of the wedding, it is not surprisingly that, although their parents' honor is the most deeply affected, the girls' own disgrace is sufficiently strong that very few are willing to consider elopement even when there are compelling grounds for doing so. When Ma Shi and Kou Pyei, a native of Yeigyi, were planning their wedding, they encountered an important obstacle. Although they intended to live in Yeigyi, Ma Shi's village would not consent to their holding the wedding—village weddings are held in the home of the bride—unless her fiancé paid a "village entry fee" of K 250. Now it is standard practice for an in-migrant to pay such a fee for the privilege of settling in his adopted village. In this case, however, the fee was not only prohibitive, but since the couple were intending to live in Yeigyi, the insistence on any fee was absurd. (A smaller amount, to cover the rental of the communal utensils used in preparing the wedding feast, would have been entirely justified). Under the circumstances, her fiancé proposed that they get married without a wedding. Ma Shi refused, saying that however justified the provocation, she would be disgraced if they did not have a wedding. Although it was known that her parents approved of the match and had bargained for a valuable dower, gossip might still have it that she was not a virgin, and she refused to face that remaining consequence of an elopement.

Having described the several functions of the wedding, there remains to discuss one of its functions in greater detail, namely, the public announcement of the dower. The dower requires separate and more detailed treatment, not only because of its importance for understanding the wedding, but also because it raises a number of theoretical issues which are related, but not restricted, to the functions of the wedding.

The Dower

Cross-culturally viewed, we may distinguish four types of marriage payments: dowry, dower, groomwealth, and bridewealth. *Dowry* is often used to refer to property which, provided by his or her family, either spouse may bring to the marriage. In traditional European law, however, this term was often restricted to property provided by the family of, and brought to the marriage by, the bride (hence, the "bride's portion"), whereas property provided by the family of, and brought to the marriage by, the groom was referred to as *dower (Bouvier's Law Dictionary)*. By contrast with bridewealth, which will be examined below, dower and dowry share three attributes. First, the property can be viewed as the child's wedding present from his or her parents. Second, in those

societies which follow the rule of partible inheritance, it may further be
viewed as consisting—in whole or in part—of the child's pre-mortem
inheritance. Third, although brought to the marriage by only one of the
spouses, the property usually comprises, if only de facto, part of the
conjugal estate.

Often, however, one or more of these attributes does not apply. In
traditional English law, for example, the dower did not comprise part of
the conjugal estate; rather, it was set aside for the bride in the event that
she became a widow. *(Ibid.)* Although in this and similar cases, the dower
is brought to the marriage by the groom, in essence it becomes the
property of the bride. Similarly, although the dowry is brought to the
marriage by the bride, it is often offered to, and set aside for the use of,
the groom. Although for certain purposes it is important to distinguish
property which is brought to the marriage and which becomes part of the
conjugal estate from that which is controlled by only one of the spouses,
this distinction is not important for our present purposes. Hence, in our
usage, "dowry" will refer to property brought to the marriage by the
bride, "dower" to property brought by the groom, whether it becomes
part of the conjugal estate or is reserved for the other spouse.

Dower and dowry alike are to be distinguished from those forms of
marriage payments in which, rather than being brought to the marriage,
the property is offered to the family or lineage of one of the spouses. In
principle, this form comprises two types. In one, property is offered by
the family of the bride to the family or lineage of the groom; in the other,
it is offered by the family of the groom to the family or lineage of the
bride. So far as I can tell, however, only the latter type, known as
bridewealth, is found, whereas *groomwealth* (as we might term the former
type) seems to have no empirical instances. Hence, we need only be
concerned here with bridewealth. Although dower and bridewealth are
alike in that the groom's side are the property givers, they differ importantly because in the dower the property is brought to the marriage (and
usually becomes part of the conjugal estate of the newlyweds), while in
the bridewealth the property is offered to and becomes the possession of
the family or lineage of the bride. On this dimension, then, dower and
dowry, though polar opposites with respect to the identity of the property
givers, are distinguishable from bridewealth in that they bring property to
the marriage partners themselves.

Structure

The following generalizations summarize the situation concerning marriage payments in Burma. First, bridewealth is not practiced either in the
cities or in the villages. Second, dowry *(kyimyintho pyitsi)* is often

practiced in the villages, but it is an unimportant accompaniment of the dower. Dower *(tinthade pyitsi)* is an almost universal village practice and, moreover, it is an essential element in the marriage. Third, dowry is often practiced among the town and city elites, and when it is, it is an essential element in the marriage. Fourth, in pre-modern Burma, dower alone seems to have been practiced, or so at least it would appear from the older historical sources which go out of their way to contrast this Burmese custom with the European dowry (Sangermano 1893:165; Fytch 1878:70). It would seem, then, that the practice of the dower in contemporary village Burma represents the persistence of a traditional pattern, while the dowry (whether in the city or the village) is a relatively new institution. Let us now examine these generalizations.

As is true elsewhere in Asia, marriage payments in village Burma are not always unilateral. Indeed, in a detailed investigation of a sample of sixteen marriages in Yeigyi, nine—or almost 60 percent—included both dowry and dower, while the remainder included only dower. It is perhaps not inaccurate to say that a dowry is almost always offered if the bride's parents can afford one, but always it is offered in addition to, not as an alternative for, the dower. The relative unimportance of the dowry can easily be gauged by contrasting it with the dower on certain crucial dimensions. Thus, the dowry is voluntary, the dower mandatory; the value of the dowry is usually small, that of the dower substantial; the dowry is not an issue for negotiation (the bride's parents offer whatever they like), whereas the dower is negotiated (by the respective parents); the dowry is irrelevant to effecting the marriage, whereas the dower is necessary to effect the marriage. (If its value is not mutually agreed upon, the marriage is canceled.) In sum, the village dowry, unlike the dower, is perhaps best viewed as a wedding present *(letsaung)*, rather than a marriage payment.

The dower, as I have said, is a necessary instrument for effecting the marriage; negotiated by both sets of parents, the wedding cannot take place until they can agree on the amount. The property of the dower comprises a de facto part of the conjugal estate in that both spouses share in its usufruct. If, for example, it includes a house, the couple live in it together; if it includes paddy land, they both enjoy its income; if it includes oxen or bullocks or a cart, the husband uses them in his agricultural labor for their mutual benefit. Unlike other forms of prenuptially owned property which, in a *mutually agreed upon* divorce, reverts to their initial owners, the dower does not revert to the husband or his parents; nor, however, is it retained by the wife. Rather, it is divided in various proportions, depending on the circumstances, between the spouses. It might seem, then, that, like the dowry, the dower, too, is viewed as a wedding present to the couple, whose terms, however, have to be agreed to by the bride's parents in order for the wedding to take place. That this, however, is not the case is shown by the fact that if a man divorces his wife *without cause*, the wife retains the entire dower. In short, although the dower is de facto part of the conjugal estate, de jure it is the property of the wife, a legal right which, when it is most important for her, she can (and does) exercise.

How, then, do the negotiations concerning the dower take place, and what determines the amount? Actually, both sets of parents have a fairly accurate notion, even before their negotiations, of the amount to be ultimately agreed upon. Typically, the boy's parents make known their offer to a few respected village elders who, in turn, pass on this information to the parents of the girl. Typically, too, the value of the dower is expected (all things being equal) to comprise about 20 percent of the assets of the groom's parents. If the parents have other marriageable sons, the percentage is proportionately reduced, unless (as sometimes happens) the dower is construed as a kind of pre-mortem inheritance, and it is therefore understood that the groom will receive no additional property when his parents die.

It is not until the engagement that the two sets of parents, together with the headman and the village elders, enter into formal, face-to-face negotiations concerning the amount of the dower. If agreement is achieved, it can then be paid in two installments—half at the engagement and half at the wedding. If there is a disagreement, the headman and elders attempt to effect a compromise which, according to all informants, is always accepted, unless one set of parents, typically the girl's, is bent on sabotaging the marriage.

Although brief, this description of the village dower is perhaps adequate to pose the two theoretical questions with which this section is primarily concerned. The first, which arises from comparative perspective, is simply put: why, among the three forms of marriage payments delineated above, should the Burmese have traditionally ignored the two which are most frequently practiced (bridewealth and dowry), and have "chosen," instead, a form which seems to be very infrequently practiced?[8] That the Burmese should have "chosen" this least frequent

8. Indeed, even some of the reported cases of dower (which, however, are not always denoted by that term) are often not what they seem, for sometimes the dower is kept, either in whole or in part, by the bride's parents, as the following instances from China and the Middle East reveal. In West Town, for example, a rural market town in Western China, the boy's family gives a considerable sum of money to the girl's family, "supposedly to make up the girl's dowry." In fact, however, this marriage payment (which, in our terminology, would be denoted as "dower") is tantamount to bridewealth, for "only the generous family gives what is left over to the girl for her own use after marriage" (Hsu 1971:86). Again,

form of marriage payment is all the more perplexing in view of the fact that Burma's neighbors—the Central Thai (Sharp 1953:82) and the Indians (Karve 1968), as well as Burma's hill tribes, the Chin (Lehman 1963:100), Kachin (Leach 1964:149), and Shan (Milne and Cochrane 1910:76)—mostly practice bridewealth or dowry.[9]

The second theoretical question posed by the Burmese marriage payments is parochial rather than cross-cultural: why have the modern urban elites turned away from the traditional dower system and, instead, come to practice dowry as the preferred type of marriage payment? This question, like the first, can perhaps best be answered by identifying the motives for, and therefore the functions of, these different types of marriage payments for the Burmese actors.

Functions

We might begin our discussion by examining the reasons offered by Burmese villagers for practicing dower rather than dowry as a mandatory marriage payment. Not surprisingly, there are important differences of opinion among them. One group suggested that since it is the boy's parents who seek permission of the girl's parents for the marriage, her parents, having (as they say) the "upper hand," can insist upon a marriage payment for their daughter, whereas the boy's parents cannot make a parallel demand. This is not an entirely satisfactory answer for, of course, it merely pushes the question one step back, and none was able to explain why the girl's parents enjoy this advantage. If, indeed, the girl's parents have the upper hand, women would be expected to be especially valuable (as they are in bridewealth); but this in fact is not the case. Women are not, for example, in short supply in Burma—if anything, given a large

---

although Islam prescribes a dower (Levy 1962:113-115), it has developed, by a similar erosion of its intent, into bridewealth, the property being offered by the groom's father to the father of the bride. To be sure, the bride's father is supposed to use all or part of it on the outfitting of his daughter (Patai 1971:143), and in many cases (for example the Awlad Ali of the Egyptian Western Desert) he does in fact provide his daughter with a trousseau (Monsen 1970:225); but most often, as in Jordan (Antoun 1972:118-119), the father keeps the larger proportion.

9. Actually, the Indian case is rather more complicated than is usually suggested. Although it has become somewhat of an anthropological cliché to state that typically the dowry system obtains in North India, while bridewealth obtains in the South, many cases of "bridewealth" turn out, upon analysis, to be a form of indirect dower (not as Goody suggests, "indirect dowry"). Since, as Tambiah observes (Goody and Tambiah 1973:92), "bride-price as such is devalued" in India, some at least of the property received by her parents is transferred to the bride, especially in the form of jewelry. In India, then, in which bridewealth is sometimes transformed into dower, we see the reverse of what has happened in the Near East, in which, as noted in the previous footnote, dower is sometimes transformed into bridewealth.

celibate monkhood, the contrary is the case; and they are less important than men in the agricultural economy.

A second group of villagers explain the practice of dower by reference to four economic and domestic functions which it is intended to serve for the wife. First, the dower offers the wife a certain degree of economic security. Just as, before her marriage, the girl is supported by her father, so, during her marriage, it is expected that she will be supported by her husband—hopefully, at approximately the same level. If, however, the husband proves to be a poor provider, the wife can always fall back on her dower, if only as a temporary measure. (Consistent with this explanation, the value of the dower, it might be observed, tends to vary with the wealth of the girls' parents.) Second, and even more important, the dower provides the wife with economic protection in the form of (what might be termed) anticipatory alimony. For although, as we have seen, the property of the dower is held by the couple as community property, should the husband divorce or abandon the wife without cause, customary law prescribes that the wife retain the entire dower. This also accounts for what they designated as the dower's third function for the wife: that the husband must forfeit the dower serves as a constraint on a husband-initiated hasty or capricious divorce.[10] The dower's fourth function for the wife (indirect, to be sure) is to reduce the probability that her husband will take another wife, since the burden of a dower—which is now his, not his parents', obligation—allegedly diminishes his desire for polygyny.

These functions of the dower for the wife are both intended and recognized, and they constitute one (but, as we shall see, not the only) motive for the attempt of the girl's parents to maximize its value. Before examining the girl's parents' other motives, however, it is necessary to observe that the dower has economic functions for the husband as well as for the wife. Although these functions are not intended—that is, they do not comprise motives adduced by the villagers themselves for the practice of the dower—it is important that we recognize them and assess their possible relevance for the problem at hand.

I have already observed that although the content and value of the

---

10. In this connection, anthropologists will be reminded of the protracted debate between Schneider (1953), Gluckman (1953) and Leach (1953) concerning the possible function of bridewealth in contributing to marriage stability, the mooted thesis being that in bridewealth the wife's family restrains her from effecting a divorce since they must, then, return the property to the groom's family. In the Muslim Middle East, however, bridewealth serves as a constraint (as does the dower in Burma) on a husband-initiated divorce. Since only part of the bridewealth (perhaps as much as two-thirds) is paid at the time of the wedding, the remainder only if and when the husband divorces his wife, this deferred payment serves "both as a deterrent against divorce . . . and as a trust fund for the divorced wife to draw upon." (Patai 1971:143.)

dower are negotiated by the bride's parents, most of the property
—except for such personal effects as jewelry and clothing—forms, de
facto, a part of the conjugal estate. Since, then, the husband's eventual
inheritance is necessarily diminished by the size of the dower, the latter
might properly be viewed, as I have already indicated, as the husband's
pre-mortem inheritance. Coming into possession of this property when
he leaves his parental household, it might be viewed, specifically, as that
part of his inheritance which represents deferred payment for work
heretofore performed for his parents. (To be sure, he receives subsistence
for this work, but its economic value is less than the wages he might have
earned in the open market.) There can be no mistaking the economic
importance of his receiving the property at this time: having accumulated
no savings to purchase a home, cattle, land, and so on, this property
enables him to launch his marriage with some, at least, of these prerequi-
sites. In short, the dower provides the husband with capital at that period
in his life when he needs it most—when he enters into marriage and is
about to form a family.

    Although its economic functions for both spouses constitute a plausible
explanation for the practice of the dower, this explanation can be countered by three objections. With respect to the economic functions for the
wife, it might be asked, first, why Burmese women should enjoy protection against economic risks from which women in many other
societies—who, after all, are exposed to the same risks—are not protected. And even if it can be shown that Burmese women are particularly
vulnerable to these risks, it might be asked why dower rather than dowry,
is practiced when, in fact, dowry could serve this function equally well (as
we shall see). In short, even if the first objection were satisfactorily
answered, it would explain why *either* dowry *or* dower might be required,
but it would not explain the choice of dower *over* dowry. The same
problem—and this is the third objection to the economic explanation for
the dower—arises with respect to its function in providing the couple
with a conjugal estate, for this function, too, can be served by dowry. Let
us deal with these objections *seriatim*.

    With respect to the first objection it can be plausibly argued that
Burmese women require economic protection because there are at least
four ways in which they are particularly, if not uniquely, vulnerable.
First, many Burmese men have propensities for philandering and impro-
vidence, both of which constitute economic risks for the wife. Second,
divorce is extremely easy to obtain, so that legally (if not actually) there is
a high risk of divorce-induced economic insecurity. Third, this insecurity,
if actualized, has a high probability of becoming permanent since, given
the negative attitude towards marrying divorcées—Burmese men prefer

to marry virgins—the wife's chances of remarriage are not very good. Finally, since women are less important in the Burmese agricultural economy than men, the income of a divorcée is considerably less than that of a married woman. Given all these conditions, dower would seem to be an appropriate, if not required, form of marriage payment. And, indeed (with the possible exception of the first condition), these are precisely the conditions which obtain in the largest single culture area in which dower is practiced—the Muslim Middle East.

But this reply raises yet another objection: why is it that in Central Thailand (as well as in others of Burma's neighbors in Southeast Asia), in which the identical four conditions obtain, bridewealth is practiced rather than dower? Surely the Thai are no less concerned about protecting their women than the Burmese? An analysis of Thai "bridewealth," however, immediately dissolves this objection, for in every respect—not only in regard to its specific functions for the wife, but also with respect to its joint functions for the couple—Thai bridewealth is the functional equivalent of Burmese dower. Indeed, this underscores the point alluded to above concerning the semantic trap of the current terminology of marriage payments. For although the Thai marriage payment is offered to the bride's parents—hence, "bridewealth"—it works in exactly the same way as the Burmese dower. Let us see.

In the villages of Central Thailand, unlike the neo-local residence pattern in village Burma, the married couple set up permanent residence with the bride's parents (first in their house, and then, after the youngest daughter marries, in their compound) and they also acquire their agricultural necessities (land, farming equipment, and so on) from them. Hence, bridewealth, which is paid in cash, is explicitly intended to purchase for the couple residence rights in the house of the bride's parents and use-rights in their means of production. Moreover, since daughters alone share in the estate of their parents, it also ensures the couple's ultimate ownership of their share of the estate of the bride's parents. In short, bridewealth in Thailand explicitly and intentionally has the function of acquiring for the groom, and his descendants, substantial rights (first, of use, and then, of ownership) in the property of his wife's family (Piker n.d.:52)—an important function in a society in which daughters alone are their parent's heirs. If, however, the husband abandons or divorces his wife against her will, he loses his rights in this property, and she becomes its exclusive owner.

Thai bridewealth and Burmese dower are not, then, as different as these terms suggest. Unlike conventional bridewealth, in which the property receivers (the bride's family) remain in control of the property (which they may then use to forge new marriage alliances), the property of

Thai "bridewealth" is shared in the first instance with the property giver (the groom), and in the second instance with the bride. Hence, despite the fact that Thai bridewealth is offered to the parents of the bride, whereas Burmese dower is brought to the marriage, both have the same functions for the married couple: they both provide them with their domestic and agricultural economic requirements. In Burma this function is achieved directly (since the dower consists of property), while in Thailand, it is achieved indirectly (since bridewealth, which consists of cash, is exchanged for property). Moreover, both protect the wife from her special economic vulnerability, for in both the jointly owned property becomes exclusively the wife's should her husband abandon her.

Since Thai bridewealth is the functional equivalent (economically) of the Burmese dower, and given the requirement that the wife be protected against possible future economic loss, we may now perhaps identify the conditions that account for the "choice" between them —namely, variable residence and inheritance patterns. The Burmese are neo-local and practice brother-sister partible inheritance; the Thai are uxorilocal, and practice daughter-exclusive partible inheritance. Let us examine each of these conditions in turn.

When residence is uxorilocal, the bride's parents may demand compensation for the use of their capital, so that, unlike neo-local residence (in which their capital is not used), the marriage payment is offered to the bride's parents (in cash), rather than brought to the marriage (in property). By exchanging cash for property, the Thai husband, like his Burmese counterpart (who brings property directly to the marriage), acquires the requisites for an agricultural career. But if the permanent uxorilocal Thai husband must compensate his in-laws for the permanent use of their property, could it not be objected that the temporary uxorilocal Burmese husband—in Burma, the newlyweds live for a period, not exceeding three years, with the bride's parents—should compensate his in-laws for the same privilege? This, however, is not a valid objection because the Burmese husband does indeed compensate his in-laws, but—as is often the case in Africa—he does so by service rather than cash. Unlike Thailand, in which each couple in the household (or compound) forms a distinct economic unit, in Burma they comprise a common household economy so that the son-in-law (as was the case when he lived in his parental home) receives no payment for his agricultural labor. To the extent, then, that his temporary service to his in-laws more than compensates them for his (and his wife's) maintenance, it might be suggested that the (voluntary) dowry—which, as we have seen, is often practiced in village Burma—serves, among other purposes, to compensate the son-in-law for his loss.

With respect to inheritance patterns—the second postulated determinant of the choice between Burmese dower and Thai bridewealth—it need only be pointed out that when inheritance is daughter-exclusive (as it is in Thailand), the male's only opportunity for obtaining inherited property is to acquire a joint share in his wife's inheritance, and this is achieved by the bridewealth, which in effect constitutes a pre-mortem cash purchase from her parents. When, however, both sons and daughters share in the parental estate (as they do in Burma), the son automatically acquires his share of his parents' real property upon their death, and the dower which he brings to the marriage is his pre-mortem share of that inheritance. (That his sister is thereby deprived of a larger share of her post-mortem inheritance is compensated for in Burma by the custom of bequeathing the house to the daughter.)

In sum, Thai bridewealth does not refute the contention that Burmese dower is required to protect the wife against economic disabilities because, as functionally equivalent structural alternatives, the choice of one rather than the other seems to be governed by different residence and inheritance patterns.

Having countered this objection to the economic explanation of the Burmese dower, we must still attend to two other objections. Although its economic functions explain the necessity for some form of marriage payment, and one that will specifically comprise part of the conjugal estate—which, therefore, excludes the choice of bridewealth in the usual, not the Thai, sense—these functions do not explain the preference for dower over dowry since both can serve the same functions. That is, since the dowry forms part of the conjugal estate, it, too, satisfies the need of the couple for capital to launch their marriage. Moreover—and more important—if the wife requires a marriage payment as protection against economic insecurity, the dowry can serve the same function: should her husband abandon her, customary law could prescribe that, as in the case of the dower, the wife retains sole ownership of this part of the conjugal estate. (Indeed, since the wife brings the property to the marriage, there is even a stronger presumption in dowry than in dower that this should be done.) In short, although these economic requirements constitute a sufficient condition for the practice of some form of marriage payment (other than bridewealth), they do not constitute a necessary condition for the practice of dower. If so, the preference of dower over dowry in Burma must be sought in some other, non-economic, explanation.

Indeed, when viewed motivationally, the economic functions of the dower could explain the motives of only one of its principals—the bride (and even in her case, as we shall see, they are not her sole motives)—but it does not explain those of the other principals. Thus, the economic function of the dower for the husband, even if recognized, is not intended. (If it were, his family would not negotiate for a smaller dower than the bride's family demands. Moreover, this function was not mentioned by any Burmese informant.) For the bride's parents, who (of all the principals) are the most strongly motivated to negotiate for the most valuable dower possible, and who are certainly not indifferent to their daughter's economic welfare, the latter consideration is not their only, nor even necessarily their most important, motive. Finally, even the groom's parents who, as the property givers, sustain an economic loss, nevertheless have some interest in offering a reasonable dower. For all of the principals, then, we must look for non-economic interests in the dower, and these interests, as we shall see, involve honor, prestige, and status.

Beginning with the parents of the groom, it may be said that for them the prestige (goun) function of the dower is related to the Burmese emphasis on conspicuous display. Although the negotiations over the dower are conducted privately, its size and content are announced at the wedding, and it is as wealth display, therefore, that the dower confers prestige on the groom's parents. For them, however, its prestige value is limited. The size of the dower, it will be recalled, is expected to comprise about 20 percent of their assets. There is no incentive to offer more, since to the extent that prestige enhancement is achieved by a display of wealth, this display is more conspicuously achieved by the resources they lavish on the wedding. On the other hand, they usually do not wish to offer less because that might betoken penuriousness, or suggest that they are less affluent than they are (or than others believe they are). Hence, their motivation is to offer as much as, but no more than, is generally expected from persons of their economic means and social status. In short, unlike the case in China (Yang 1969:39-40) or India (Kapadia 1966:128-129), for example, in which the prestige value of the marriage payment is so important for the property givers that they often go into life-long debt to raise one of sufficient prestige-conferring value, the social status of the property givers in village Burma would be only mildly affected, if, by mutual agreement with the bride's side, the dower were eliminated from the marriage negotiations. That it is not eliminated is explained by the fact that it is the property receivers—the bride and, by extension, her family—for whom its prestige value is critical.

Although the prestige function of the dower is important for both the bride and her family, villagers disagree concerning for which of them it is the more important. For those who view its prestige value as being more important for the bride, a minority hold that since females (in accordance with traditional belief) are inferior to males, the dower is a means for *raising* the intrinsically low social status of the bride as a female. The majority, however, although subscribing to the belief in female inferiority, hold that the dower is a *measure* of the social status of the bride as a person, so that the higher the social value of the bride, the larger the economic value of the dower. This being so, the limiting case of a girl's worth is her inability to command any kind of dower. To marry without a dower would mean that the girl (as the Burmese say) has no value at all *(tanbou mashibu)*. In the Burmese context, to say that a girl "has no value at all" has a very specific meaning. According to Burmese marriage theory, marriage confers upon the husband exclusive rights to his wife's sexuality, and since her sexuality has important social value, it is for these rights that the wife (according to these villagers) can command something of value—the dower—in return. Since, however, the husband's rights are hardly exclusive if she has had sexual relations before marriage, the wife is not deemed worthy of a dower unless she is a virgin. Since it is her virginity, then, that is the irreducible basis for the girl's social value, for her to have "no value at all" means, minimally, that she is not a virgin, and to marry without a dower is tantamount to a public declaration that this is the case: why else would she relinquish the rights to her sexuality without demanding a comparable value in exchange?

Although most villagers agree with this interpretation, many contend that, nevertheless, it is not the girl but her family for whom the dower has the greater prestige value, for (so they argue) the social worth of the girl is a reflection, on three accounts, on that of her parents. First, her *ascribed* status is derived from the achieved status of her parents. Second, since her parents raised and trained her, they must also take credit or blame for her *achieved* qualities. Third, it is her parents and brothers who, by their surveillance, are responsible for her sexual probity. Since, therefore, it is her family's prestige which is most importantly at stake in the property that the girl can command in the marriage market, it is primarily in consideration of their own social status that they negotiate for as much property as possible. Hence, for their daughter to receive a dower of little value, let alone none at all, would constitute a serious threat to their social worth. This argument is entirely consistent with the above-mentioned normative expectation that the size of the dower be commensurate with the status and wealth of the girl's parents. If they are wealthy, the dower should reflect the prestige which the bride possesses as the daughter of a family of high economic status. Conversely, the daughter of a poor family need receive only a moderate dower, one which is commensurate with the modest economic status of her parents.[11]

11. In Central Thailand, the value of the bridewealth also varies with the wealth and prestige of the girl's family; the daughter of a landless peasant commands only one-fifth the amount of the daughter of a wealthy family (Piker n.d., ch. 2:53).

We may conclude, then, that the bride and her family alike have an important prestige stake in the dower. Which has the greater stake is less important for our present purposes than the fact that the girl's marriage exposes them both to considerable status vulnerability, and that it is the bride's side, therefore, rather than the groom's, for whom the marriage payment is important.

It would appear from this discussion that we have now identified the necessary and sufficient conditions for the choice of dower, rather than bridewealth or dowry, in village Burma. Although bridewealth could satisfactorily attend to the status vulnerability of the bride and her family, it is precluded as an appropriate form of marriage payment on two other accounts. First, since, in bridewealth, property is offered to and retained by the bride's family or lineage, this form of marriage payment could not attend either to the economic vulnerability of the wife or the requirements of the newlyweds for a conjugal estate. Second, since Burmese marriage does not transfer rights in the girl's productivity and reproductivity from the bride's to the groom's side—the usual grounds for the practice of bridewealth—the former have no grounds for demanding and the latter have none for offering bridewealth. In short, whereas in bridewealth the bride-receivers (the groom's family and lineage) offer property to the bride-givers in exchange for exclusive rights to their daughter's productivity and reproductivity, in the Burmese dower the bride-receiver (the husband) offers property to the bride in exchange for exclusive rights to her sexuality. Moreover, whereas in bridewealth, in which women are especially *valuable,* the bride-givers demand property (for themselves) as *compensation* for the loss of their daughter, in the Burmese dower, in which women are especially *vulnerable,* the bride-givers demand property (for their daughter) as *protection* against their daughter's possible loss.

Dowry, which has the converse strengths and weaknesses of bridewealth, is equally incapable of serving the functions served by dower. Although it could satisfy the economic requirements of the bride (and the conjugal pair) as satisfactorily as dower, dowry is an inappropriate form of marriage payment in village Burma because it does not attend to the critical status vulnerability of the bride and her family for which the dower is so important. If this is so, and if this indeed accounts for the choice of dower over dowry in *village* Burma, how can we explain the fact that in certain cases in *urban* Burma dowry, rather than dower, is the required form of marriage payment? With respect to the economic functions of marriage payments, can it be said that the wife is less vulnerable economically in the city? Or that the couple do not require working capital to launch their marriage? Even if both questions were to be answered in the affirmative—first, because the urban wife can always make a living as a petty trader or shopkeeper, small retail business being heavily, if not predominantly, in the hands of women; second, because the need of a rural couple for land and agricultural equipment is not operative in the city—these economic conditions do not account for the choice between dowry and dower, because, as we have seen, both can serve the same economic functions.

Since, then, it is the social vulnerability of the bride and her family that, as we have seen, explains the choice of dower in the village, can the historical shift to dowry in the city be explained by the fact that in the urban context they are not vulnerable? Is the girl's social value not important for her and her family's honor? Or, are they undisturbed that she offers her sexuality to her husband without receiving some consideration in return? Or, are they not interested in the validation of their social worth? The answers to these questions are unqualifiedly negative—urban motives with respect to these values are little different from those in the village. Rather, under certain conditions another motive may become of overriding importance, and it is this motive that accounts for the practice of the urban dowry. Let us see.

As already mentioned, the dowry is not a widely practiced urban institution. Rather, it is confined to the upper-middle and upper class elites, among whom (as has often been the case in the West) it is restricted to an infrequent form of marriage, which I shall call "complex hypergamy." Since moreover, there is no evidence that the dowry was practiced (among commoners) in pre-colonial Burma, its practice seems to be no older than the colonial period, which as we shall see made such marriages possible.

In pre-colonial Burma, the relationship between social and economic status, though not perfect, was strong; and since, in any event, village status differentials were (and are) small, village marriages must have taken place—as they do today—between spouses of more or less the same economic and social statuses. With the advent of British colonialism, however, status relationships became much more fluid, and some families began to exhibit an asymmetrical relationship between their social and economic statuses: some acquired high social prestige (*goun*), but little wealth, others great wealth (and the prestige associated with wealth), but little social prestige. The reasons for this development are well known. Because of the British-introduced educational system, sons of moderate income families were able to receive a university education and, thereby, to qualify for government service, which, because of the latter's relationship to power (*ana*) and authority (*awza*)—and the British!—became the ne plus ultra of social prestige. At the same time, the abolition of royal monopolies in trade and industry enabled families of moderate social status to acquire great wealth in the free market which, with the demise of the traditional sumptuary laws, could now, for the first time, be used for luxurious living. With both wealth and prestige becoming available or desirable values, these new economic and social elites (who, for obvious reasons, were confined to the towns and cities) could achieve both values by exchanging wealth for prestige. Using marriage as its medium, this exchange could be effected by a marriage between a groom of modest economic but high social status, on the one hand, and a bride from a family of high economic but low social status, on the other. (Hypogamy being disdained by the girls' families, such exchanges were restricted to hypergamy.) To effect such a marriage, the bride's family offered the groom the incentive of a large dowry.

It is in this type of marriage—complex hypergamy—that the dowry, as a required form of marriage payment, continues to be practiced in Burma (and in certain groups in South Asia) today. By providing their daughter with an enticing dowry, a nouveau riche merchant family, for example, can forge a marriage alliance with a son-in-law of high social status. If, in the colonial period, the ICS (Indian Civil Service) Officer, the cynosure of colonial society, was the favorite target of a girl's parents, today the graduate of a Western university, especially if he gives promise of a successful government career, is their choice. The functions of the dowry for all the principals in this form of marriage are obvious. The groom acquires wealth; the bride acquires a husband of high prestige, without, however—since the dowry accompanies her—suffering a decline in her standard of living; and the bride's parents acquire social prestige to add to their high economic prestige. (Needless to say, the enticement of a dowry is not an unknown basis for complex hypergamy in the West.)

The overriding consideration, then, that accounts for the willingness of the bride's side to suffer possible impugnment of their honor is their strong desire for prestige enhancement. Given this desire, there is a basic difference in the negotiating strength of the bride's family in complex hypergamy, as compared with marriages between status equals. Since, in complex hypergamy the bride-givers are eager to forge a prestige-enhancing affinal tie, it is they who approach the potential groom to offer the prospect of marriage with their daughter. Since, then, it is the groom who has the upper hand, the bride's parents can gratify their desire for prestige only by agreeing to gratify his desire for wealth. Although the groom has the upper hand in the negotiation of the marriage, it might be noted that the advantage passes to the bride once the marriage is contracted. For although this type of marriage enhances the *economic* position of the husband, by the same token it may often enhance the *political* position of the wife. Since it is she who has brought him his new-found affluence, she can exploit this fact, if it is necessary, to demean him. (He is, in the pejorative expression, a "bought husband.") Thus, in Burma, as in parts of Ceylon, the wife may use the dowry as "the prized verbal weapon to throw in the face of an unappreciative husband" (Ryan 1953:159).[12]

It will be noticed, then, that while structurally, dower and dowry are mirror images—in the former, men and property move together, in the latter, women and property move together—functionally, this is not at all the case. To be sure, in both instances the couple acquire a conjugal estate, but the other economic functions, as well as the prestige functions of these different types of marriage payments, are distributed rather differently. In dower, both sets of functions accrue to the bride's side; in dowry, they are split, the economic benefits accruing to the groom, the prestige benefits to the bride and her family. In addition to their differences in functions, dower and dowry work quite differently. In dower, in which the bride is the property receiver, the prestige motive of the bride and her family is to *validate* their social status. Hence, it is important for them that the content and value of the property be publicly announced. (Because the announcement takes place at the wedding, this explains in part why they attach such importance to this ceremony.) Since, therefore, the property of the dower is *displayed* for status, its value must be large enough to attract public attention. In dowry, however, in which the bride's side are property givers, their prestige motive is to *enhance* their social status; and since, in this case, property is *exchanged* for status, its value must be large enough to attract a socially desirable husband. (Hence, the wedding is important for them as a means for displaying their high-status groom *cum* son-in-law.) But it is precisely because of their prestige motive that (unlike the case in dower) the value of the dowry is not publicly announced—it is as if it does not even exist.

---

12. What might be termed the hypertrophy of complex hypergamy is found among the Kulin Brahmans of Bengal, among whom (unlike the case in urban Burma) this practice became uniform and all but mandatory. That is, the males refused to take a bride in the absence of an exorbitant dower, and poor girls were practically deprived of a spouse because, on the one hand, it became shameful to enter into a non-hypergamous marriage and, on the other, their fathers could not raise a sufficiently large dowry to attract a higher status groom. In some cases, this led to the practice of female infanticide among poor families. Moreover, the desire of the brides's family to marry their daughter to a husband of the highest possible status resulted in a dramatic increase in polygyny, with the additional consequence that some highly prestigious men acquired as many as fifty and even more wives (Risley, 1915: 165-171, 431-440).

The reasons are obvious. Its announcement would, in effect, constitute a public declaration that (a) being socially inferior to the groom, the bride's parents are buying his prestige; that (b) their daughter is unable to obtain a high-ranking husband on her merits alone, and that indeed she is "without value" for she has been offered to her husband as a free gift; and that (c) their son-in-law has married their daughter for wealth rather than for love. Indeed, in such a marriage, the bride's side is said to have "purchased a husband" *(lin wede)*, and the groom is referred to as a "bought husband." That their differential social status is well known anyway, and that, in any event, the value of the dowry always leaks out, are truisms. But then the Burmese are hardly the only people who are concerned with "face," or who engage in institutionalized "denial."

It might be suggested in passing that in Burma, in which there is no dowry in the case of simple hypergamy, the absence of a dower would not necessarily constitute a diminution in the honor of the bride's side since in this case, it could be argued, the girl is not "without value"—she is not a free gift—because the husband does indeed offer her a valuable resource (and one that is as valuable as property) in return for her sexuality —namely, prestige. Moreover, just as in a marriage between prestige equals, the dower is a measure of the bride's (and her family's) social worth, in simple hypergamy, the husband's prestige, so it might be argued, serves the same function. In complex hypergamy, however, this argument would convince no one, since in this case the husband's prestige is a measure not of the bride's family's worth, but of the purchasing power of their wealth.

From this analysis of the functions of Burmese dower and dowry, it may be concluded that marriage payments in Burma are based on a clear cost-benefit calculus. In complex hypergamy, in which marriage confers an *increment* in prestige on the bride's side, dowry is the required form of marriage payment because the groom can command wealth and the bride's family is motivated to part with it in *exchange* for social gain. In marriage between more-or-less social and economic equals, however, neither side has any incentive to part with property. That the dower nevertheless remains the required form of marriage payment derives from the fact that in the Burmese context (for all of the reasons discussed above), marriage may entail a *decrease* in both the social and economic status of the bride and her parents. Hence, the bride can command wealth and the groom's family is willing to part with it, because rather than providing her with a non-reciprocated economic gain, the dower serves as *protection* against social and economic loss. In short, in marriage between social and economic equals, in which the marriage itself is viewed by the bride as desirable, the possible social and economic risks of marriage make property necessary, and so the bride (and her family) demand a dower to make the marriage possible. In complex hypergamy, marriage in itself is not viewed by the groom as desirable, but marriage (for him) makes property possible, and so he demands a dowry to make the marriage desirable.

Part Four. Components of Marriage

8. Sexual Components of Marriage

Introduction

Some anthropologists have tended to view marriage and sex as relatively unrelated variables, so that many anthropological discussions of both the motives and functions of marriage stress such sociological themes as the consolidation of political power, the forging of social alliances, economic advantage and division of labor, legitimization of children, and so on—everything, in short, except sex. From these discussions, one would never know that, cross-culturally viewed, sexual behavior is a component of almost all marriages, that in most societies marriage is a necessary means for entering into sexual relations (for the female if not for the male), and that, consequently, sex is one of the important motivational bases for contracting a marriage. This is especially true in societies, such as Burma, in which premarital and extramarital sex are either prohibited, frowned upon, or difficult to achieve. If, then, a special chapter is devoted here to marriage and sex, it is not because the Burmese, unlike other peoples, are especially concerned with sex. Rather, it is because they, like most other peoples, view sex and marriage as intimately related, sex being one of the motives for, and an important ingredient of, marriage.

In this book, which is primarily concerned with family and kinship, there is yet another reason for discussing the sexual component of marriage. Kinship, as I have treated it here, includes, it will be recalled, three relatively independent dimensions: cultural conceptions of kinship and kinsmen, cultural norms governing their interaction, and individually acquired attitudes concerning kinsmen. To a great extent, sexual behavior and sexual attitudes are derived from and are a reflection of all three of these dimensions. The incest taboo, which was discussed in a previous chapter, is only one aspect of sexual behavior which is governed by kinship norms and attitudes. This chapter will deal, though by no means exclusively, with a number of others.

Importance of Sex
Sexual Desire

Most males in Yeigyi assert rather vigorously that of all drives the sex drive is the strongest and the most intense. As one man put it, men always talk about sex when they are together, and he had no doubt, he said, that women do the same. Another man said that, although he was married, he wanted to have intercourse with almost every female he met. The only defense against these desires, he claimed, is to willfully "control my mind." Another maintained that the sex drive is even stronger than the fear of hell, for although all Burmese know that adultery leads to hell, should their sexual feelings be aroused—and "they can be aroused by merely touching a woman"—they will succumb to the temptation. Still another man said that there is scriptural proof for the thesis that sex is the strongest desire. Thus, when Visākhā, the great female disciple of the Buddha, was asked if she ever forgets Him, she answered that He was always in her mind except when she was having sexual intercourse. Hence, he concluded, even for her sex was a regnant drive. Another villager, saying he wanted to become a godling in his next birth, explained his choice by observing that all sexual desire is completely satisfied in the heavenly abode. He, too, alluded to Visākhā who, he said, is now in heaven, where she has 500 males on her right side and 500 on her left, and she has intercourse with them all. For him, *that*—with, of course, the sex ratio reversed—was the quintessential image of paradise.

All the men admit that the intensity of the sex drive diminishes with age; as people grow older, other drives, first economic and then religious, become regnant. Nevertheless, regardless of age the interest in sex, they claim, is almost never extinguished, for "sex comes to an end only when a person can no longer carry even a handful of chaff."

To obtain a proper perspective on the Burmese view of the strength of the sex drive and the difficulty of controlling it, it is important to realize that their view is neither atypical nor extreme. Compare, for example, the views of a Greek pastoral group, the Sarakatsani, described by Campbell (1966:326).

Sensuality is a condition which constantly threatens to undermine this institution [the family] from within. It must, therefore, be disciplined by all the strength and will of each man and woman. . . . The Sarakatsanos accepts that sensuality is part of the human condition, but that he must struggle to contain and discipline it. . . . A man of God may win an individual and inward control over the condition of sensuality, but ordinary men need the help of kinsmen and the support of institutions in the unequal fight.

Although, given Burmese notions of sexual propriety, it was difficult to interview many women concerning sexual matters, it is probably safe to conclude that the women's sex drive is no less intense that the men's.

Indeed, the men believe, as we shall see below, that the women have stronger sexual desires than they, and there is some reason to assume that this is so—not, however, because of their stronger sexual drive, but because of sexual frustration. In any event, Burmese female informants (other than those of the highly repressed urban middle class) leave little doubt that sex is for them a strong drive, although (unlike the men) it is something which they rarely discuss since modesty forbids it. This is not the case, however, among university coeds, for whom sex—especially speculations about and curiosity concerning their experience on their wedding night—is a favorite topic of conversation. Nor are they backward in admitting to the importance of sex; indeed, some say that they could not live without it.

In any event, most Burmans, both male and female, are agreed that for women, no less than for men, sex is a strong drive, although it is one which a girl, so long as she is a virgin, can control. "If," however, "a girl has once tasted sex, she is worse [her sexual desire is stronger] than a boy." The same notion is expressed in the proverb, "Don't give beef to a fool." Like the fool and his beef, the villagers say, the virgin is content with her lot, but once she tastes sex, she wants more and more. This is reminiscent of the Sarakatsani whose unmarried women seldom go to the well alone and who, when they pass a man on the path, lower their eyes. This "tight prudential control, collectively exercised," is based on the assumption that, "If you put your hand in the fire, it gets burnt" (Campbell 1966:156).

If, then, it can be assumed that the sex drive is as important for females as for males, we can proceed to other measures of its importance. One such measure consists of the villagers' self-confessed low threshold for sexual temptation. Thus, when discussing the Japanese custom of mixed bathing (which the villagers observed during the Japanese occupation of Burma in World War II), some of the men commented on the impropriety of the custom, but others expressed astonishment at the self-control required by the Japanese males. As one put it, "If men are together with nude women, what happens to their penises?" They expressed similar astonishment at Western customs. Thus, some said that ballroom dancing could never occur in Burma, because it would inevitably lead to sex. "How can a man hold a woman in his arms without wanting to have intercourse with her. What could stop him?"

On this score, urban attitudes are little different from those found in the village. In Rangoon, many parents will not permit their daughters to attend dances on the grounds that the sexual temptations aroused by being held in a man's arms would be too strong to handle. Informants report many incidents of private dances being broken up by the stoning of the house by zealots who view such activities as sinful. In a similar vein, the Minister for Information of the military government announced after the coup that the new regime would not allow any newspaper photographs of women with exposed breasts, for they are "likely to arouse immoral passions in men." *(The Nation,* Rangoon, April 19, 1962.)

Their low threshold for sexual temptation also explains why a male and a female are prohibited from being alone together. It is assumed that any two persons of the opposite sex, not even excluding, it will be recalled, father and daughter, will be sexually tempted if they are alone. Indeed, that even moral people might succumb to incest temptations is advanced by some informants as still another indication of the strength of the sex drive, and to support this thesis one informant related the following folk tale. It seems that a certain king was presented with the riddle, "What is the most intense darkness?" and was challenged to find the answer within a week. As the week was drawing to a close, his daughter asked him why he seemed so troubled, and when he explained, she told him that if he would come to her bedroom at midnight he would find the answer. Complying with her suggestion, he discovered a nude woman in the dark room of his daughter, and, sexually aroused, he was about to have intercourse with her, when she identified herself as his daughter. In short, sex is the "most intense darkness" because, if the conditions are propitious, a man will sleep even with his daughter.

If a male and female in fact *are* seen together, especially at night, it is simply taken for granted that it is for the purpose of sex. Hence, even in Rangoon, proper women will not admit even their husband's friends into their house in his absence unless another woman is present, nor would a proper man expect to be invited in. Given these attitudes, it is understandable that the Burmese find it difficult to understand the self-restraint involved in the Western dating pattern. As one villager put it, if the Burmese, like the Americans, were to permit boys and girls to go on dates together, "every girl would soon be pregnant."

Another measure of the strength of their sex drive is the villagers' assumption that it takes Herculean strength to suffer the frustration of sexual privation. Buddhist monks are the most venerated persons in Burma, and their status is one to which most pious Buddhists aspire, but defer for a future rebirth, for the chastity incumbent on the monk is too severe. When laymen explain why they are not monks, their reason, almost invariably, is their inability to give up sex. Indeed, it is precisely because the monk is willing and able to suffer sexual deprivation that he is so highly revered by the laymen. Since, so the argument goes, the sex drive is so strong, the one who can withstand its frustration must possess, as a result of great merit acquired in many previous rebirths, special qualifications of mind and spirit (Spiro 1971:404-408).

The strength of their sex drive or, alternatively, their interest in sex, may be inferred from villagers' behavior, as well as from their self-reports and their expressed attitudes. Thus, for example, in view of the Buddhist prohibition of adultery, its incidence, as we shall see in a later section, is not low, and, moreover, half the divorces in Yeigyi are caused by sexual infidelity and sexual desertion.[1] Polygyny, too, is primarily instigated by sex, and its low incidence is due primarily to economic and moral constraints, and to the fear of public censure, rather than to lack of interest. The low incidence of polyandry and of female infidelity is similarly explained by the vigilance of their husbands and the women's fears of punitive social and physical sanctions.

A more obvious index of their interest in sex—more obvious because, being approved, it is near-universal—is found in the villagers' sexual banter which, in its sheer exuberance, is matched only by the sexual banter of the Burmese stage. Let us see.

Sexual Banter

Although explicit sexual discussions are prohibited in mixed company, sexual bantering is not only permitted but encouraged. So long as sexual remarks can be expressed by indirection, Burmese villagers, unlike some other traditional peoples, are not at all restrained in their references to sex in mixed company. This is true, as well, in the urban working class, but not in the middle and upper classes, who, at least publicly, are mid-Victorian in their attitudes, and claim that they expect to hear such things only from bazaar women and other "low types." In the village, however, sexual references, usually offered in a teasing or humorous vein, are frequent, and I view them as a reliable measure not only of the villagers' interest in sex, but of their free and non-puritanical attitude toward it.

The indirection in sexual allusions is made possible by the high potentiality of the Burmese language for the double entendre. This potentiality is developed to a fine art in the Burmese theater in which trenchant political criticism, interlarded with obscene sexual humor, comprise the standard fare of the virtuoso, slapstick comedian, who gets away with both when expressed in double entendre. The same technique is also used by ordinary villagers, who rarely resist an opportunity to exploit the sexual potential of a phrase or an expression while in sexually mixed work groups in the paddy fields. These groups engage in much banter and horseplay, for ordinary restraints are relaxed in this highly

1. In Java, too, the strong desire for extramarital sex is "a prime trigger" to divorce (Jay 1969:95).

informal atmosphere. The following are a random sample of the types of
sexual banter which I recorded among a variety of such groups.

A male tells of a woman who has just purchased a red skirt and red
jacket. Now, he said, she is *red* in her upper part and also in her *lower
part.* (Here, and in the other cases quoted below, the words with the
intentional double meaning are italicized.)

A male tells one of the females that if she would *send a sickle* to his
house after work, and powder her face, he would give her a beautiful
flower (a Burmese term for penis). She replied that if he did not give her
the *flower,* she would steal it from him.

One man asks another whether he had taught his wife to *put (htede* =
insert) the paddy plants in correct order before combining them in a
bundle, to which a third remarks that he has obviously not taught her to
put because they still have no children, and a fourth responds to the latter
remark by observing that the cluster *(qahpouk)* of paddy plants is too big
for a bundle. *(Qahpouk* refers to the female genitals as well as to a
"cluster").

A bride, working beside her husband, constantly criticizes him. Almost
invariably the young men tease her with the ambiguous phrase
mapyetba-ne, "don't be wide open."

As a man gets ready to return home his wife tells him not to forget to
hswa the sesamum plants when he returns, to which everyone laughs, for
hswa means "turn up"—hence, "arouse (sexual desire)."

Part of the group sings: "Now let us build a pagoda, Hey! Are there any
masons?" To which the others respond: "Here we are, but we are
letthama." (The latter is the term for carpenter, but it also means "one
who uses his hand," that is, a masturbator.)

A worker is talking to another about the efficient workers in the village,
when a young man shouts that his wife also is *good.* (This could mean
"good" in reaping or "good" in bed. There was no doubt, from their
shouts of "Ei! Ei! Hey! Hey!," how they took it.)

A young man comes and sits on the boundary of the field which is being
harvested. The foreman asks if he has permission to come to the field,
adding that his (the foreman's) permission is required. When the man
responded with a joking comment, the foreman told him not to belittle his
authority because, he said, he has *hnalounpyu,* at which all the workers
laughed. *(Hnalounpyu* refers to a double-barreled gun, but it literally
means "a pair of balls.")

A young man turns to a woman reaper and says his furrow is *wide,* while
hers is *narrow.* She laughingly disputes this, saying hers is wide and his is
narrow; this continues back and forth, five or six times, to the great glee of
the other workers.

During a work break a young woman asks a man to hand her her cup, identifying it by saying it has an *qakwe* (crack) in the middle. As he pretends to look for the cup, he asks whether *hers* has a crack in the middle, which leads to tremendous laughter.

It should be stressed, lest their attitude be misunderstood, that none of the above incidents is taken by the villagers as obscene; they are analogous, rather, to mildly off-color jokes in American society. Sexual obscenity is something else again. It is crude, the sexual references are direct and explicit, and it is almost always used as insult, invective, and aggression. (Interestingly, it is also believed to be a protection against evil spirits.) The following examples of obscenity, all from Yeigyi, are typical.

A seven-year-old girl is bathing at the well, when another, about the same age, tries to lower her bucket into the well before her. The former shouts, "I fuck you"—an invective, incidentally, which the men use against their oxen when working with them in the fields.

A field foreman, fed up with the bickering of two female workers, shouts: "Hey, the women with the long clitoris, shut up! I fuck your mother."

An old woman, complaining that no one in her house has fetched water for cooking, shouts: "The pricks (males) and cunts (females) in this house are useless. I have to look after all the pricks and cunts in this house, but no prick or cunt around here takes any responsibility. Instead of working, they keep their cunts wide open [all they do is copulate]."

The most hostile and insulting Burmese obscenities relate to oral sex, examples of which will be given in a later section. For the moment, then, these examples will suffice to indicate the distinction between sexual obscenity and sexual banter. For the villagers, the banter is good fun, and, occurring as it does in mixed company, I take it to be a valid measure of the non-puritanical attitude which they have toward sex. Sex is taken for granted as something to be enjoyed; villagers feel few constraints either in admitting that they are sexual creatures or in joking about sex in public. Sexual behavior, on the other hand, is strictly private, and (normatively at least) confined to husband and wife (which is why sex is an important part of, and a basic motive for, marriage).

Cultural Values Concerning Sex

It is paradoxical, at least on one level of analysis, that despite the importance which the Burmese attach to sexual satisfaction, and despite the freedom with which the villagers engage in sexual banter, Burmese cultural values are puritanical and restrictive. This paradox is not only interesting in itself—it constitutes yet another example of the well-documented thesis that personal desires and cultural values are frequently discordant—but it helps to explain important aspects of Burmese sexual behavior to be discussed below. Let us, then, examine some of these puritanical values.

In the first place, there is a strong cultural emphasis on modesty concerning the discussion of sexual matters, or the exposure of sexual organs, in mixed company. Although sex is a favorite topic of conversation in unisexual groups, and although sexual banter is permitted in certain contexts in sexually mixed groups, serious sexual discussion is prohibited in the presence of the opposite sex. When I wished to discuss sexual matters with village men, it was always necessary to make sure that women were out of earshot, and when, as in some cases, I discussed non-sexual matters with a panel of males and females, the latter always left when the discussion would take a sexual turn. (This prohibition does not apply, however, to pre-pubescent girls, who were allowed to come and go with impunity when I carried on interviews concerning sex with the men.) Needless to say, it was impossible to conduct interviews regarding sex with village women, except for those few who, in village terms, were highly liberated and (in one case) of dubious reputation. This was not the case with highly educated urban informants, who saw themselves as participants in a scientific research project. But in normal contexts, even they would no more engage in sexual conversation with men (including their husbands) than would the village women.

Modesty concerning bodily exposure is, if anything, even stronger. The Burmese, like almost all other peoples of Southeast Asia, consider it shameful to be seen nude, and one of the impressive feats of village women—one which I never ceased to admire—is their agility in changing into fresh clothing, after bathing at the village well, without exposing any part of their body. Even parents are prohibited from seeing their sons (above the age of twelve or thirteen) or their daughters (above the age of eight or nine) in the nude. Children, similarly, never see their parents nude, though there is no objection to their being present when their mother nurses a sibling, and the same prohibitions apply to adult siblings. These modesty patterns, as we shall see, are inculcated at an early age.

In addition to their emphasis on sexual modesty, Burmese values stress the baseness of sex. To be sure, these values do not entail the Pauline notion of sex as evil or sinful, for since each individual, according to Buddhism, is at a different stage en route to ultimate liberation from all passions (including the sexual), sex is as appropriate for the "worldling" who remains bound to worldly pleasures, as its extinction is appropriate for the saint who is liberated from them. Still, sex is nevertheless of the flesh, not of the spirit, and since the spirit represents a higher stage of karmic development than the flesh, the weaker the libido, the higher one's position on a scale of karmic progress.

This notion, of course, reflects the Buddhist conception of sex as a base thing. The Buddhist derogation of sex is emphasized throughout Scripture, it is basic to its soteriological message according to which the extinction of sexual desire is necessary for the attainment of nirvana, and it is intrinsic to its core institution of monasticism, a profoundly anti-sexual institution (Spiro 1971:295-300). It is implicit, too, in the origin myth (summarized in the previous chapter) according to which sex came into being as a result of the development of greed, anger, and lust in what had heretofore been sexless, celestial beings; as a consequence they lost their spiritual and occult powers, which rendered them terrestrial and incurred the wrath of the gods.

The Buddhist conception of sex is both symbolized by and expressed in the behavior of the celibate Buddhist monks, and the laymen's deep veneration for them is a measure of the Burmese dedication, at least on one level, to this conception. For despite the fact that they themselves prize sexual experience, the persons most venerated by the laymen are the monks, and, as we have seen, they are admired precisely because of their sexual renunciation. The same respect is tendered laymen who either reduce or suppress their sexual activity. Indeed, one of the important bases of the political charisma of U Nu, the last prime minister of Burma, derived from his public announcement that he had vowed to live with his wife as a sister.[2] Similarly, when my Burmese assistant, to take a less exalted example, informed a group of villagers that he (a man in his early fifties) had given up sex, his status was noticeably enhanced.

The same value system which applauds the inhibition, if not the extinction, of sexuality, places a negative value on its expression. Thus, just as men of ordinary sexuality are inferior to monks, so too, women (as we shall see) are inferior to men because (among other reasons) they are allegedly more concerned with sex. Similarly, men who are excessively interested in sex are viewed as "base," which is one of the reasons that villagers are constrained from taking a second wife. The same attitude toward excessively sensual women is even more derogatory. One of the more insulting invectives a woman may address to another woman is to accuse her of being oversexed. "You have a torn dirty cunt" (*saukpat pyet ma*), meaning that you copulate so much that your vagina is enlarged, and "your dirty cunt is inflamed" (*saukpat yaung ma*), meaning that your vagina itches for a man, are among the favorite expressions in this genre.

These negative values concerning sex are transmitted to children by their parents, both by what they say and by what they do not say, in the

2. Gandhi, it will be recalled, made the same announcement, with comparable political consequences (N. K. Bose, 1953: Ch. 18).

course of sexual training. This training begins early. If a parent sees an infant touching or playing with its genitals, he removes the infant's hand, perhaps slaps it lightly, and then covers the genitals with a cloth. As they grow older, children are verbally warned about masturbation, being told, for example, that it is a "nasty" thing to do, that it is "not good to look at," that "people will hate you," and that "you will have no friends." Typically, so parents say, children comply with their warnings, but if a child does in fact masturbate, they may spank him. These admonitions are delivered more strongly to boys than to girls, who, if they scratch their vagina, may be told to wash with soap and water, and, if they continue, may be given a spanking. Children's sexual behavior, whether homosexual or heterosexual, also meets with a spanking, either by parents (if seen in the home) or monks (if seen in the monastic school). In addition, children are warned that such behavior will be punished by rebirth in hell, by the loss of friends, by being hated by others, and so on. If this is not enough, they may also be warned that sex play leads to venereal disease, and boys may also be threatened with castration.

Values concerning sexual modesty, including both obscenity and bodily exposure, are also transmitted fairly early. Boys are expected to be fully clothed by the age of five, girls by the age of four, and they are scolded for any temporary lapses. A boy may be threatened with castration for exposing his penis in a monastery or a pagoda, or for urinating in the presence of others—he is taught to squat and to cover his penis with his hand—or for insulting a playmate by holding out his penis and saying he will copulate with the latter's mother. Children are scolded for using other obscenities, and, if they persist, they may be spanked. As is so frequently the case, parents are especially concerned for fear that they —the parents—will be blamed for the behavior of the children. It should be noted, finally, that by the time the children are twelve or thirteen, they are prohibited from playing together or from being alone together. The violation of this prohibition may also lead to spanking.

If sexual training is restrictive, sexual education is very limited. Although the Burmese are well aware of physiological paternity, parents say they are ashamed to discuss such matters with their children, and if the latter inquire about the origin of babies they are usually told that they drop from the sky and that a baby who likes a particular married couple enters the stomach of that woman. Nevertheless, most adults agree that children know the true facts by the age of eight or nine. If so, their knowledge is typically acquired from older children and by observing domestic animals.

Urban parents, even the highly educated, are also ashamed to discuss sexual matters with their children, but the latter's sources of information

are more various than those of their village counterparts. In wealthy
families, servants are an important source of information, as are novels
and movies. For girls, spinster aunts or grandmothers may also serve this
function, although their instruction is seldom direct or explicit. Still, they
do convey to them the notion that a wife has sexual "duties" to her
husband, and at the onset of menses they manage to inform them that
they are now capable of having a baby. Some girls, however, are raised in
almost total sexual ignorance. Thus, one woman, a highly educated and
successful professional woman, said she had not only received no sexual
instruction, but she had had no preparation for her first menstruation.
Frightened, she waited until the second day to inform her spinster aunt.
The latter told her that it was a normal thing, but she gave her no
explanation other than that she should not sleep with a man because she
might have a baby. Somehow, she divined—she does not know how—that
this did not merely mean that she should not lie next to a man, but that it
referred to sexual intercourse.

Although children receive no instruction from their parents concerning
sex, it is highly probable that most children learn about sexual behavior
from them in yet another way—by witnessing parental intercourse. In the
city, as well as the village, young children sleep with their parents—on a
mat in the village, in a bed in the city—sometimes until they are six or
seven. In the village, where the house usually consists of one room, they
continue to sleep in the same room until they are grown; in the city, they
may sleep in the parents' bedroom until they reach puberty. Most parents
wait until their children are asleep before having intercourse, but, as one
mother put it, "How do we really know whether they see or not?" And, in
fact, many parents admit that it is most probable that some of their
children have indeed seen them. In one case known to me, the six year
old "baby" of the family slept in one cot with his mother, while his father
slept in a separate cot. One morning, he ran to his grandmother to tell her
that his mother and father were "joined together."

Premarital Sex Prohibitions

Of all the values concerning sex, the most important, by far, and the
one implicit in the entire system of sex training, relates to premarital
virginity. Virginity, especially in girls, is almost as important in Burma as
it is in Near Eastern and Mediterranean cultures. Although the prohibition on premarital sex applies primarily to females, its effect on the
motivation for marriage is just as important for males, for given the female
sex prohibition, a young man (typically) must agree to marry a girl if he
wishes to have sexual relations with her. For the female, of course, the
prohibition is even more restrictive. Unless she marries, she is prohibited

from having sexual relations with anyone, whereas the male can visit a prostitute to satisfy his sexual needs, although village parents tell their sons that frequent visits to a prostitute may result in their penis being broken off. Some villagers have sex with prostitutes as their first sexual experience, others after they are married, but in either event their numbers are small. In the cities, however, according to doctors I interviewed, the number is much higher, for a young man must prove his manhood by having intercourse with a prostitute. (Hence, according to these same doctors, the incidence of syphillis is high.) For a villager to visit a prostitute requires a journey to the city—which is one of the reasons for the lower frequency—since there are no village prostitutes. Villagers claim that a prostitute would not survive in the village, regardless of the demands on her services, because she would be driven out, even though traditionally prostitution was sanctioned by the king, and prostitutes themselves were viewed as indispensable. Indeed, prostitutes were called the "country's eyes" and the "country's ornaments." (Personal communication, Daw Than Than Ohn.) The latter term is used even today to refer to prostitutes, as is the term "young goddess" (nathami).

In the cities, boys have still other opportunities for sexual experimentation. Unmarried women, past the usual age of marriage, often induct young boys into their first sexual experience. Alternatively, widows and divorcées, whose chances of remarriage are not very good, constitute another sexual outlet, as do the sexually frustrated mothers of the boys' friends. Since this information comes from selected urban informants, I do not, however, know the frequency, either absolute or relative, with which these experiences occur.

Girls, unlike boys, have no sexual outlet of any kind. For a girl, premarital sex, as we saw in the last chapter, is the worst possible stigma. Indeed, to as much as touch a man's hand, let alone to have intercourse with him, is improper for an unmarried girl, and it may seriously affect her reputation; it could "destroy her name" (name pyitte). It is little wonder, then, that a man who attempts to touch a girl may be charged in court, and, if found guilty, sentenced to prison.[3] Indeed, one such case occurred during my stay in Yeigyi. Nor is the city any more permissive in this regard. A Rangoon friend told me of a friend of his whose son briefly held the hand of a girl friend as they were walking home from work. Three days later the police arrested him, and, despite the efforts of a well known lawyer, he was tried, convicted, and sentenced to a year's imprisonment.

The same restrictive norms apply in the case of a married woman. To even touch the hand of another man's wife is tantamount to adultery.

3. The identical proscriptions are also found in Central Thailand (Piker n.d., ch. 2:38).

Indeed, this is merely one of five rather innocuous acts which, according to traditional values, either approximate or are tantamount to adultery when committed by a man with another man's wife. In addition to holding her hand, these include going to her house during her husband's absence, remaining with her in a secluded place, engaging her in conversation (if she is already suspected by her husband), and inviting her to his house during her husband's absence.

This seemingly punitive reaction is consistent with the admonition of the proverb, "A woman's most valuable possession is her modesty/A man's is his life" *(Meinma hma qashet/Yaukkya hma qathet)*, and if, to return to the unmarried girl, even the touching of her hand impugns her modesty, how much more is this the case if she should lose her virginity. In addition to moral considerations, however, there are important pragmatic grounds for a girl to remain a virgin, for if it is known that she is not a virgin, it is extremely difficult for her to find a husband. Non-virgins are called used, or defective, carts *(hle-gyou)*, and most men, viewing them as immoral, refuse to marry one. To discover that one's bride is not a virgin constitutes legitimate grounds for divorce (and most men, so they claim, would indeed divorce a non-virgin bride). I know of one man (an extreme case, to be sure) who, because his first wife had been known to be unfaithful, had the wedding invitations for his second marriage read: "the marriage of Mr. X to Miss Y, genuine virgin *[qapyousit]*." Thereby he accomplished two goals: he proclaimed that his second wife was superior to his first, and that he had therefore acquired a more valuable asset than his wife's lover had acquired.

In the past, at least, the husband's information concerning his bride's virginity was not left to chance. Older villagers say that, formerly, the husband's mother would come to the bridal chamber the morning after the wedding to inspect the white sheets for signs of blood. If there was none, the bride would have to explain this apparently damaging evidence.

If, after she marries, a girl is discovered not to have been a virgin, the prestige *(goun)* of her parents also suffers a serious blow, for it is their negligence that is blamed for her condition. Hence, parents do not respond to her condition lightly. During my stay in Yeigyi two such cases came to light. In one, the girl's father forced her to marry her lover, and he then sent them to live with his parents, saying he would not keep them in his own house. In the other, the father banished his daughter from his home, and, forced to move to another village, she found a home with an uncle.

If the loss of virginity is disgraceful for a girl, premarital pregnancy (which informants estimate as five percent of all pregnancies) is doubly so.

When the male responsible for her pregnancy is her sweetheart (her intended fiancé), the girl's parents normally insist on an immediate marriage, with or without an engagement or an elaborate wedding. Should the boy refuse to marry her, they will take the case to the headman. If, despite the headman's admonition, the boy still refuses, he must pay a heavy fine (the amount to be determined by the headman and village elders) to the girl's parents, who usually adopt and raise the child.

The stigma which normally attaches to an unwed mother is even more severe when the mother refuses to name the father. In the one case known to me personally, the girl's friends would have nothing more to do with her; and when, despite the request of the village elders, she still refused to name the father, she was banished from the village, for it is believed that the mere presence of a woman whose child has an unknown father will bring misfortune to the village.[4] In this case, the girl returned after the birth of her child, and was permitted to stay, but in most cases the girl would not want to return since the stigma is so great. Indeed, it is not uncommon for unwed mothers to commit suicide rather than face this social censure. Again, urban attitudes are little different from those found in the village, as the following case, typical of scores of similar anecdotes recounted by urban informants, reveals. A young man and his girl friend, having discovered that she was pregnant, decided to marry to protect her reputation. Despite their marriage, his parents (but not hers) refused to see them because of their resulting shame from her pregnancy, and subsequently the boy's grandmother suffered a heart attack.[5] It should be observed, however, that the stigmatization of the mother is only slightly shared by her child. Typically, he will be sent to the monastery when he is old enough, either because of his mother's poverty, or because of the need for male discipline. He may face some teasing from his playmates, who jeeringly refer to him as "a child who does not know his own father" (qahpei mapode hkalei), but this taunting disappears as he (and they) grow older. As an adult, his chances of finding a spouse are not seriously impaired by his illegitimate status.

Although the unwed girl's child is not stigmatized, her parents may be. Hence, it is understandable that they keep their nubile daughters under

4. Urban informants, with whom I discussed this case, suggested that the fear did not concern the child's unknown paternity, but rather the girl's promiscuity, for—they insisted—if she did not name the father it was because she *could* not, not because she *would* not.

5. Contrary to some views, it is not the case that the sinfulness of illegitimacy is a self-evident assumption of traditional society. In Europe, for example, it was not until the sixteenth century that bastardy was believed to be shameful. "Men took care of their bastards, were indeed often proud of them and in many cases brought them home to their wives or mothers to be brought up." (Pinchbeck and Hewitt 1969:201.)

the strictest surveillance. Indeed, boys and girls are separated as early as ten years old, and from that time a girl is not permitted to be alone with any male of her own age or older. Although this seems rather early, it should be remarked that for most girls the onset of menses typically occurs at the age of ten or eleven, and sometimes as early as eight or nine. An adolescent girl is not permitted to have a boy in her house unless her parents are present, and she is not let out at night unless accompanied by a chaperone. The fear is not only that she might be accosted by a male, but that her own impulses might lead her into temptation. The result of this surveillance is that most girls are not only virgins at marriage, but that their sole premarital experience consists of a fleeting touch of a male's hand, typically that of their future husband. Even in the cities, the vast majority of girls are virgins, for fear that the very boys who enjoy their favors might think them cheap and gossip about them with the other boys. Unlike village girls, however, urban girls, who have greater opportunity for contact with boys, usually have some sexual experience before marriage, including kissing and fondling. Overprotected daughters of wealthy families, on the other hand, may have almost no social contact with males other than the servants in their houses, and it sometimes happens that these are the men with whom they consequently fall in love, and subsequently run off with.

Boys, as we have seen, do not suffer from the same constraints as the girls since they are subject neither to the same taboos nor to the serious consequences of their violation. Nevertheless, although Burmese sexual morality clearly rests on a double standard, boys are not immune from parental pressures concerning sex. To be sure, the boy is not censured for not being a virgin at marriage, but promiscuity is viewed as a shameful thing, and to be known as one who "pursues enjoyment [sex]"—*qapyo qapa laikte*—can seriously impair a boy's chances of a good marriage. There are other reasons, too, why sex with a village girl is not to be undertaken lightly. Should the couple be discovered, the girl's elder brother, who keeps her under surveillance, will physically assault him. Moreover, if the girl should become pregnant, he may either have to marry her or pay a large fine. In short, for the boy, no less than the girl, premarital sex is, if for different reasons, a dangerous thing.

It is of interest to observe that parents not only make every effort to maintain their children's (especially their daughter's) virginity, but that custom requires that their virginity be lost in the parents' (preferably the girl's) home. It is there that the bridal chamber is set up, and there that the couple is expected to have their first marital experience.[6] Even urban

---

6. The bridal chamber must be prepared by a happily married couple. Widows, spinsters, and unhappily married couples are prohibited from performing this task.

and westernized couples spend the first night of their marriage in the bridal chamber. If they must leave because the husband has a job in another city, custom requires that they remain for at least three nights. Otherwise, they are expected to remain for at least a few months. By having her first sexual experience under the roof of her parents, it is as if the latter announce to the world that she has entered sexual life with their approval.

The Burmese concern with the virginity of their daughters stands in sharp contrast with the generally high status of women in Burmese society. As we shall see in the next chapter, Burmese women are among the most liberated in Asia, and until the relatively recent liberation of women in the West, they surely enjoyed a higher status and greater freedom than Western women. And yet the cultural emphasis on the protection of their virtue, though not as extreme as in Muslim culture, is yet much more consistent with the subjugated status of women in Islam than with their liberated status in the West. [7]

Before concluding this section, it is important to repeat an observation made in the last chapter: according to many, but not all, villagers, the sexual prohibitions discussed here are not premarital but rather pre-engagement. Once the engagement ceremony takes place, there is no serious objection, so these villagers claim, to a couple having sex relations, although it is preferred that they do not. In short, for these

---

7. In the Muslim Middle East, both premarital and extramarital sex on the part of the females is regarded with the utmost severity, and among the Bedouins a girl or woman who is guilty of either is put to death by her father or brothers (Patai 1971:121). This extreme measure is based, at least among the Bedouins of Egypt, on the conviction that the reputation of her lineage, as well as of the girl or woman herself, depends mainly on her willingness and ability to remain chaste and pure, for "the main contribution a woman makes to the honour of the lineage is through this passive role of preserving her chastity and purity" (Abou-Zeid 1966:253). Hence, even if she were raped, the girl would be put to death. In any event, the disgrace to the kinsmen is so great that they usually migrate to a region where they and their humiliation are unknown (ibid: 256).

Among most Mediterranean peoples, the situation is no different. Thus, for the Sarakatsani, a community of Greek pastoralists, virginity is not only mandatory for girls (and preferred for boys), but it is a quality that evokes a sense "almost of awe" (Campbell 1966:156). As among the Bedouin, an unmarried girl (or a married woman) discovered in a sexual affair is—or, at least, ought to be—killed by her father or brother (ibid: 170). For them, as for the Greek Cypriots (Persistiany 1966:182) and the Bedouins, a girl's purity is the responsibility of her parents and brothers so that her shame reflects directly on them.

In India (among the Hindus) virginity is so important that the moment their daughters enter puberty, they "become objects of great anxiety and care in the eyes of their parents" (Kapadia 1966:140). The strong emphasis on virginity is the basis, according to the same authority, for the acceleration of pre-puberty marriages among the Hindus.

In China, too, a girl is expected to remain a virgin until her marriage, but this norm does not seem to be as strongly held by the Chinese as by the Arabs or Hindus, and, if it is subsequently discovered that the bride had not been a virgin, no action will be taken against her, if only because of the damage to the family honor by the revelation of the fact (Hsu 1971:209).

villagers, it is not her unmarried state, but the risk to her future marriage chances, that is the barrier to a girl's sexual relations. Since the engagement ceremony is a formal, and public, declaration of the couple's *intention* to marry—this, it will be recalled, is its primary manifest function—it eliminates that risk, for the public declaration of intention to marry is tantamount to marriage. In short, it is not premarital intercourse, as such, but intercourse with a man other than her intended husband, that is shameful for the girl.

The engagement, moreover, removes the stigma not only from the loss of virginity, but also from a possible pregnancy. Although pregnancy is frowned upon even during the engagement, the major reasons for the stigma—an unidentified *genitor* or an unwilling *pater*—are removed. Should the girl become pregnant, the biological father is known to all, and since, typically, the couple will then marry, the child is assured of a social father. Moreover, in the unlikely event that her fiancé should refuse to marry her, the girl and her child are protected financially by the dower which, although normally not transferred until the wedding, is guaranteed by the agreement reached between the parents at the engagement. (Indeed, this is the case, as we have seen, even if the girl does not become pregnant: should the boy call off the marriage, the girl nevertheless receives the agreed-upon dower.) It should be noted, however, that urban informants unanimously and vigorously disagree with this view. For them, virginity is required until marriage; the engagement gives a couple no license to violate the taboo on premarital sex.[8]

To summarize, then, premarital (or pre-engagement) sexual behavior is severely regulated, especially for girls. Given these restrictions, it is impossible for a girl to satisfy her sexual needs outside of marriage without suffering serious consequences to her (and her family's) reputation and importantly jeopardizing her marriage chances. A boy, on the other hand, may satisfy his sexual needs by visiting a prostitute. Should he, however, have sexual relations with a non-prostitute, he too may suffer serious consequences: he may be forced into marrying a girl he does not love or into paying a heavy fine to her parents. Moreover, if he has sexual designs on a particular girl, and she insists on complying with the sexual prohibitions, the only way he can have sexual relations is to marry her. In short,

8. The village custom, however, is not at all unique to Burma. Until the Parliamentary Act of 1753, an engaged couple was permitted to have sexual relations in England, and despite this Act, "it seems improbable," comments Laslett (1971:142), "that so deep-seated a usage ever completely disappeared from the countryside." In any event, before this "usage" disappeared, it is assumed that brides "must normally have gone to their weddings in the early, and sometimes in the late, states of pregnancy" (*ibid.*)

for both sexes marriage, or the declaration of intent to marry, is typically the only way to achieve sexual gratification.

Sexual Behavior

Among the various forms of sexual behavior, only "normal" heterosexuality is found in the village. Other forms—homosexuality, various perversions, and rape—are either absent or highly infrequent. Nevertheless, before examining normal marital sex, we might briefly describe the attitudes toward these other forms and the frequency of their occurrence.

Manifest homosexuality seems to be entirely absent in the village, although other forms of unisexual intimacy—sometimes associated with latent homosexuality in the West—are frequent. Thus, one often sees two young men occupying the same mat with one lying against the other, or lying on the other's buttocks, or holding the other in his arms. Unisexual handholding, by both sexes, is also common among teenagers. Although rare or absent in the village, homosexuality is found to some extent, however, in the cities, as is male prostitution. In Mandalay, the haunts of homosexuals (*meinmasha*) are known to everyone, and they, as well as male transvestites (*gandu*), are viewed with a relatively tolerant attitude, although it is not unknown for boys to abuse and throw stones at them. Lesbians (*yaukkyasha*) are also found in the cities, and they, too, meet with the same relative toleration. The incidence of homosexuality and transvestitism seems to be especially high among male shamans, but otherwise it is my impression that their incidence, and that of lesbianism, is low.

If the older literature on Burma is credible, the infrequency of homosexuality in contemporary Burma represents an important historical change, for some of the older sources specifically mention the high incidence of homosexuality. Writing in the sixteenth century, Fitch describes a custom in which males insert little round balls in the penis (Pinkerton 1811:421-422). Some informants, he wrote, claimed that this custom was practiced to gratify the sexual desire of the women; but the real reason, he continued, was that "[the males] should not abuse the male sex; for in times past all those countries [Burma, Siam, and other countries of Southeast Asia] were so given to that villainy, that they were very scarce for people." Fitch also interpreted the female fashion (since given up) of wearing an unstitched sarong in a similar manner. The exposure of the women's thighs was intended to entice the men from their homosexual proclivities. Hamilton, an eighteenth-century traveler, alludes to this same female fashion, and attributes the same interpretation to his Burmese informants (1930:27-28).

It was first contrived by a certain Queen of that Country, who was grieved to see the men so addicted to sodomy, that they neglected the pretty ladies. She thought that by the sight of a pretty leg and plump thigh, the men might be allured from that abominable custom, and place their affections on proper objects, and according to the ingenious queen's conjecture, that dress of the *Lungee* (skirt) had its desired end, and now the name of sodomy is hardly known in that country.

Sangermano (1893:158-159) interprets male tattooing (of the upper thigh) in the same way. The exposure of the female thigh ("setting off the beauty of the women"), combined with the male tattoo (which "disfigur[ed] the men"), was calculated to help the women "regain the affections of their husbands."

Like homosexuality, perversions such as voyeurism and sexual exhibitionism are also infrequently found in the villages. During my stay in Yeigyi, I encountered one case of collective voyeurism and exhibitionism. As many as twenty young men would gather outside the house of a certain man, with his knowledge and consent, to witness his intercourse with his mistress. He would entertain them by asking her whether she enjoyed making love, whether she liked his technique, and so forth, so that they might hear her reply.

Although very rare, it is their fear that she might be raped (as well as seduced) that motivates some parents not to leave a teenage daughter alone at night. In the two-year period prior to my arrival in the village there were two cases of rape in Yeigyi. In one, a girl was raped by two boys from an adjacent village; in the other, a girl was raped by a village boy who, however, persuaded her to say she was seduced, with the agreement that he would marry her (which he did). In general, rapists are viewed throughout Burma as the lowest of criminals, and it is said that even in the jails they are shunned by robbers and murderers.

In general, then, village sexuality consists of normal, heterosexual behavior, typically with one's spouse. Since, however, certain physical types are preferred to others as sexual partners, it is relevant to summarize the physical characteristics which villagers look for in a spouse (or any other) sex partner. Burmese males, like many others, distinguish between a pretty and a sexually attractive woman, which is not to say that both attributes may not be found in the same woman. "Pretty" *(hlade)* is a term which is typically used to refer to a woman's face, while "attractive" *(yinde)*—literally, "graceful"—usually includes both face and figure. A sexually attractive woman may be referred to as "wife food" *(mayasa)*, and seeing her makes a male "hunger for a wife" *(mayahsa)*, for she makes "his penis erect" *(li ka)*.

Villagers are almost unanimous concerning the attributes of a sexually attractive female. They include long, narrow, and dark eyebrows; a long and narrow nose; long hair; good sized and firm breasts; narrow waist; sharp and shiny teeth; fleshy and soft fingers and toes; wide, firm and full buttocks; and light skin. They also agree that the first thing they look at in a woman is her buttocks. Long and slender legs are also preferred, but since Burmese women wear ankle-length sarongs, this criterion is typically inoperative. Although breasts are certainly erotic objects, and village men are attracted by them, they seem to be less important than they are to American men, or, for that matter, to Burmese urban men. Thus, the padded brassiere is both known and used among university coeds because, they claim, young men are attracted by large and well-shaped breasts, and more than one female informant in Rangoon commented bitterly—since Burmese, like most oriental, women are typically small-breasted—on men's preference for large breasts. Given the criteria of sexual attractiveness found among village men, many of them said that Indian women are more attractive (though not prettier) than Burmese women.

Women, who are somewhat vaguer in describing a sexually attractive man, do not distinguish between a man who is handsome and one who is attractive. In general, a man should not look "womanly" or "soft," but "manly," healthy, and vigorous. Tallness and slightly wavy hair—the Burmese men spend much time grooming their hair—are also important. But a man's grooming and his style are as important as his physical characteristics.

Turning now to sexual behavior, the first generalization we might make is that although the villagers (as we shall see) are fairly conventional in the scope of their sexual behavior, their restrictions are self-imposed, reflecting their own tastes, rather than consisting of cultural taboos. Indeed, except for the prohibition on anal intercourse, behavioral prohibitions are almost nonexistent. There are, however, *contextual* prohibitions, which relate to the time and place of sex. Thus, intercourse is prohibited when observing the Buddhist sabbath, any time after the fifth month of pregnancy, in the presence of one's parents, in the presence of the Buddha image, adjacent to the fetish of the house spirit, and during the period that the wife is nursing a child. In effect, the latter is a post-partum taboo. It is rarely observed, however, in the city where, indeed, intercourse may be even more frequent at this time because of the belief that a nursing mother is infertile.

A second generalization that might be made is that typically coitus is practiced for pleasure, not for babies, and if unwanted pregnancies occur, it is not because the Burmese do not know about the relationship between intercourse and pregnancy, but because birth control is unknown or not practiced. No villager with whom I spoke used, or knew how to use, any contraceptive device. A government nurse who has worked in village dispensaries said that Burmese herbal doctors sell "medicine" with alleged prophylactic powers to village women, but she did not know how many women actually use it or how effective it is. Village women do know about abortion, but it is rarely practiced because (so they claim) it is prohibited by Buddhism.

As might be expected, birth control methods are more widely known and practiced in the city, at least among the more educated population. Foam, diaphragms, and even birth control pills can be obtained from certain hospitals. In some cases, coitus interruptus is practiced. Condoms, too, are known and widely used, and some couples know about rhythm. Abortion is rarely practiced, not only because it is dangerous, but because it is illegal, and there is a chance that the performing midwife (unless bribed) might inform the police. (Since the military coup in 1962, all birth control devices have been declared illegal, and are obtainable only on the black market.)

Given that a newly married couple enters marriage with little knowledge concerning sex, and, in the case of the girl, even less experience, and given the restrictive and puritanical values concerning sex, it is not surprising that village sexual behavior is fairly conventional. Initiated by the husband—the average wife is sexually passive, rarely revealing her sexual desire to her husband—coitus is preceded by only a brief period of foreplay. Kissing, in the Western sense, is not practiced, and its equivalent practice—deep smelling and inhaling—is directed to the cheek and neck, not to the lips.[9] The man may fondle the woman's breasts, but only rarely (in the village at least) does he suck her nipples; men who do so are viewed as having much lust (*rāga*). The contrary is often the case, however, in the city, where some women complain (with some bitterness) that men think that the breasts are the only part of a woman's body that should be stimulated.

Cunnilingus and fellatio never occur, the very idea being viewed as physically disgusting. The former practice is viewed as especially loathsome, because of the men's view of the vagina as dirty and polluting, a view which we shall examine in some detail below. For the same reason, although mutual stimulation of the partner's genitals may be practiced, the man will not touch the vagina directly, but only from outside the skirt. Indeed, even during intercourse (which only occurs at night), neither partner removes his clothing completely. Hence, with few exceptions, the typical villager never sees a completely nude woman.

Intercourse is typically face to face, with the woman on her back. Its

9. Villagers distinguish the sexual "kissing" (*hsoude*) of adults, from the non-sexual "kissing" (*nande*) of, for example, parents and children.

frequency depends on how long the couple has been married. Immediately after marriage, the couple may have intercourse daily, even five or six times a day, tapering off to three or four times a month, or less, after they settle into their marriage. Although most men say that orgasm is found in both sexes, they claim that women seldom have one, and some are unaware of the existence of the female orgasm. (Hence, the literal meaning of the terms for orgasm, *pyothi* or *pyat hkwe thwabi*, are "to be soft" and "to have gone down," respectively). Unaware of, or attaching little significance to the female orgasm, the man is primarily concerned with his own, and since many men ejaculate rather rapidly, intercourse is usually a brief episode.

Sexual Frustration and Anxiety

From the above description of marital sex, it may be inferred that many women do not enjoy a satisfactory sex life. Entering marriage with little knowledge or experience concerning sex, they do not know what to expect from the sexual experience. Many of them have no knowledge of the female orgasm, and they submit to sex as a duty, rather than welcoming it as a source of pleasure. As one woman said, many women "endure" sex rather than enjoy it, and their husband's behavior does not help. As has been mentioned, many men have relatively fast ejaculations. Moreover, since many men are unaware of the female orgasm, they are insensitive to the sexual satisfaction of their wives, and they often do little to arouse them prior to intercourse. If a woman is not aroused, one woman observed, she will not be sexually satisfied, and since many husbands engage in only a brief period of foreplay, some women are penetrated before their vagina is properly lubricated. It is little wonder, then, that many wives are sexually unsatisfied, and that fully half of the divorces in Yeigyi are motivated by sexual frustration of the wife.

That the husband does little to arouse his wife, or to prolong the period of sex play, is attributed by the men to various factors. In the first place, since the entire family usually lives in a one-room house, the children (and sometimes older relatives) sleep in the same room as the parents, so that brevity and silence are required if privacy is to be achieved. Moreover, the typical village house has a bamboo floor, and sounds created by any strong movement are magnified, so that, again, privacy demands that action be constricted. Finally, sanitation conditions in the village are primitive, running water and latrines being far from the house, and in the absence of these facilities, there is little desire to continue with sexual activity following the first act of intercourse. For the man, for whom the vagina is a dirty thing even prior to intercourse, the latter factor is an especially important consideration.

But the woman's lack of satisfaction is related to other factors which are associated with their own behavior and circumstances. First, a proper Burmese woman, as we have seen, is not supposed to show that she wants to have sex. Since the wife seldom takes the initiative, the satisfaction of her sexual needs is dependent upon the initiative of the husband. Moreover, a proper woman is not supposed to show that she is sexually passionate. Hence, even sexually aroused women are often passive during intercourse, doing little to arouse their husbands, with the result, of course, that the latter do little to arouse them. Urban men, especially, complain about this, saying that their wives' passivity leaves them sexually dissatisfied.[10]

But if, in general, a proper wife, even when young, must show sexual modesty, a woman no longer young must be even more circumspect. A middle-aged woman—one whose children are sexually mature and are about to enter their own sexual lives—is supposed to be relatively asexual; sex is something she should neither think about nor care about. Still, this injunction is not institutionalized, as it is, for example, in China (Yunnan) where (since it is considered "disgraceful" for a woman to become pregnant after the birth of a grandchild), she and her husband sleep in separate rooms as early as the marriage of their sons, but no later than the birth of the grandchild. (Hsu 1971:109.) Nevertheless, in Burma, a spinster past thirty, or so, is looked down upon if she marries, and divorcées and widows face the same stigma. Again, however, the stigma is not nearly so strong as it is in China (Hsu 1971:103-104) or in India (Kapadia 1966:175-176), where the remarriage of a widow among Hindus is unheard of and where, since it is almost impossible for a woman to get a divorce, the remarriage of a divorcée does not arise. In Burma, remarriage can and does occur, but unless she marries a wealthy man—in which case her motive is viewed as security or prestige—the remarriage of a divorcée or a widow is considered to be highly unseemly because it indicates that the woman "cannot stay without a man." For the same reason, then, that it is unseemly for middle-aged widows and divorcées to remarry, middle-aged wives should also refrain from indicating sexual interest in or passion for their husbands.

10. A student of modern Ceylon suggests that there, too, many partners do not have a satisfactory sex life. It is doubtful, writes Wijesekera (1949:81), "whether the partners of a marriage derive the fullest satisfaction, mental or physical. This is a matter of serious doubt more so if it is remembered that the Sinhalese marry young and are not at all educated in sex matters. The subject of sex is taboo. Having little knowledge of sex the couple find themselves together in a strange relationship. Their feelings remain mixed with fear and happiness. The girl is frightened and goes through the night like a victim of sacrifice. And the man none the wiser resorts to brute force. The pain and fear lead to a nervous state in which love and innate bashfulness are at conflict. The first night is remembered by the majority who remain virgins up to that night."

A third basis for sexual dissatisfaction in some women, at least, relates to the marriage system, which prohibits the girl from taking the initiative in marriage. Since the girl's choice of a marriage partner is dependent upon the initiative of the boy, some girls marry husbands with whom they are not in love and for whom they feel no strong sexual attraction. Estimates vary, but sensitive informants say that 10 percent of the girls marry boys they do not love, and 15 percent marry their second choice. This, then, also contributes to some women's lack of sexual satisfaction. "If I don't love him [the husband]," the girls say, "his penis will be a nasty thing."

Withal, the most important cause of the women's unsatisfactory sex life, as we have seen, is related to the men's anxieties concerning sex and women. These anxieties are reflected in a variety of cultural beliefs and conceptions, according to which sex is not only base, but (as the men see it) it is also dirty and dangerous. This view, which is held even more strongly in other parts of Southeast Asia (see Hyman [n.d.:14] for Malaya), is expressed, in the first place, in the belief that the vagina is a dirty (*qanyit qakyei*) and polluting *(thana)* object, and therefore repulsive to both sight and touch. Hence, except for penile contact with the vagina during intercourse, it is otherwise avoided by men. Young boys are permitted to walk about nude—for the penis is a "golden flower"—but young girls must always wear a skirt, not only because of modesty, but because the vagina is repulsive to look at. During love-making, men neither look at the vagina, nor do they touch it with their hand, and—as we have seen—the very notion of cunnilingus is repulsive to them.

It is not surprising, then, that for males and females alike, accusations of cunnilingus are among the most hostile expressions in the Burmese repertory of invective, "dirty cunt licker" *(saukpatyet ma)* and "eater of cunt excrement" *(sauk hkyi thama)* being the favorites.[11] These invectives, as I have already noted, are entirely different from sexual banter, which is always humorous, and good fun, and in which the sexual allusions are indirect. These, on the contrary, are defined as obscenity, and are used only when angered or insulted, as the following examples, recorded in a mixed work group, indicate.

A reaper refuses to tie a bundle of sheaves for his female co-worker, and she tells him angrily to "eat my cunt shit."

---

11. Except in polite society, where it is never used, all bodily excretions, from whatever organ, are referred to as *hkyi*, excrement. Thus, nasal excretions, eye mucous, ear wax, vaginal secretion, and penile discharge, including semen, are all *hkyi*. Consistent, however, with the different cultural evaluations of the penis and vagina, semen is also referrred to by the polite term, *le-yei*, or the even politer, *qayei*, *hkyoyei*, *gweiyei*, or *thut-thwe*.

A group of young men tease a girl about having a certain sweetheart. Annoyed, she exclaims: "I wouldn't rub him with my cunt."

An elderly woman sees a neighbor take a piece of her jaggery. She tells him to "eat my cunt."[12]

An even stronger expression of aggression, one which is rarely used, is for a woman to publicly expose, or to even threaten to expose, her genitals. Typically, the hemline of the skirt falls to the ankles, and to lift it in anger, even to the knees, is a serious insult. An even graver offense, one which is intended and perceived as contemptuous and insulting, is for a woman to exclaim, "I'll raise my skirt as a flag." This verbal expression is obviously but a pale substitute for the traditional practice, reported by Brown (1915:135), in which an angry woman strips off her skirt, "slaps with her hand that which should be hidden, and hurls a rude invitation at her adversary."

Since it is polluting, any contact with the vagina or its discharges is dangerous. Intercourse, for example, may sometimes lead to impotence, and Buddhist meditation is sometimes recommended as a means of averting this, and other dangers of coitus. Of all the vaginal secretions, contact with menstrual blood is especially dangerous for a man, so that sexual intercourse is strictly avoided during the wife's menses, and many women refrain from visiting pagodas during their period. It must be remarked, however, that Burmese beliefs concerning menstruation are not nearly so severe as those found in such neighboring societies as India (Carstairs 1967:73) or Ceylon (Wijesekera 1949:78) where the woman must remain in seclusion during her period because anything she may touch is defiled.

The vagina is not only polluting—after intercourse, the pollution may be removed by bathing—but it can be a threat to the very source of a man's strength and power, his *hpoun*. Sometimes glossed as "glory," *hpoun* refers to a psycho-spiritual quality, an ineffable essence, which invests its possessor with superior moral, spiritual, and intellectual power. Possessed by men, but not by women, the loss of *hpoun* not only means a serious diminution in the above powers of a man, but his subordination to his wife and children within the family, and to other men outside it. The polluting quality of the vagina is such that if the lower part of a woman's body is higher than a man's head (the most sacred part of his body), his *hpoun* can be importantly diminished, if not destroyed. Hence it is that a woman may not stand over a man while he is sitting, nor may she be on the upper story of a house while he is downstairs. A modern coed said that she and her "progressive" girl friends get great fun from

12. It should be noted that, although the penis is a "golden flower," fellatio is as repulsive as cunnilingus, and fellatio accusations are also used as obscene invectives.

causing the boys (and some professors) discomfort by sitting on a high railing as the latter walk by them on their way to class.

But the threat from the vagina is so powerful that the same precautions apply to the woman's skirt, or any other article that is in contact with the vagina, as to the vagina itself. Thus, a man's *hpoun* is endangered merely by walking underneath a skirt hanging on a clothesline. More than that, care must be taken that men's and women's sarongs be laundered separately, and that they be segregated when they are hung in a closet or placed on a shelf.

In many cases, these beliefs are as strongly held by educated and sophisticated urbanites as by villagers. Even university coeds will not loosen and retuck their skirts when sitting beside a male because that too is a derogation of his *hpoun*. For the same reason, many women are careful not to leave their skirts on a chair, let alone at the head of the bed where they sleep with their husbands, or not to hang them higher than their husband's clothing, or not to hang a wet sarong in the bathroom or in the front of the house. When possible, male and female sarongs are even laundered in different tubs, and ironed with separate irons. In wealthy households males and females use different bathrooms or, when there is only one, they avoid using the same toilet and shower. Some urban informants suggested that this negative conception of the vagina explains why it is that so few Burmese obstetricians and gynecologists are male.

Although contact with the vagina, or with objects in contact with the vagina, is a threat to a man's *hpoun*, other forms of physical contact with women may also pose a threat. His *hpoun* is believed to reside in the man's right arm and shoulder, and it can be diminished merely by a woman's head resting on his right shoulder. Hence, a woman must never sleep on the man's right side, and, if possible, she should avoid walking, sitting, or eating on his right as well. Even a group of university coeds were shocked to see a photograph of one of their girl friends standing to the right of her boy friend. Informants recount a putative historical event in which a Burmese king gave his daughter to his traditional enemy, a Talaing (Mon) king, instructing her to place her head on his right shoulder. When the two kings went to war, the Talaing king was vanquished because he had lost his *hpoun*. Since, then, the woman may frequently, though inadvertently, rest on the man's shoulders during lovemaking, this is yet another reason that sex may be dangerous for the man.

But intercourse is believed to be dangerous for still another reason.[13] Following from traditional Hindu notions (which, the Burmese hold with

13. The dangers for a monk are much greater. Discovering that a monk had had intercourse with his erstwhile wife, the Buddha—in a text well known to monks—exclaimed:

a diminished intensity), it is believed that semen is the source of a male's strength, its absence in the female being the basis for her relative weakness. (See O'Flaherty [1973:261-279] for the scriptural and mythological sources of these Hindu beliefs, and Carstairs [1957:84] for their exemplification in village practice. Hence, intercourse leads to weakness in men because it results in the loss of semen. For some urban informants, this belief is an established "medical fact." If a man loses too much semen, he loses his strength because in discharging semen (*thut-twe*), he discharges blood (*thut* = coming out, *thwe* = blood). And since one drop of semen is the equivalent of one thousand drops of blood, the loss of strength is due to anemia. An eager groom is especially vulnerable, and one hears stories of young husbands being hospitalized after two or three days of excessive intercourse because of loss of strength brought on by semen loss.

The belief that semen loss can cause weakness in young men is supported by the observation that the drying up of semen accompanies the physical and intellectual degeneration of old age. Hence, old men often take "medicine" designed to replenish their supply of semen. Monks have power because, being celibate, their semen remains in the body. For the same reason, anyone who has traffic with supernaturals—a dangerous business at best—must control his sexuality, and exorcists especially reduce their sexual activity so as to have the power to confront the dangers inherent in their work. None of these beliefs, of course, is unique to Burma or Asia. They have all been found in the West as well. Take, for example, the following characterization of marital sex in seventeenth century France.

The dangers of conjugal life which I have been discussing are easily translated into explicitly sexual terms—and often were by more uninhibited seventeenth-century observers. The idea that marriage was somehow debilitating, that it made men softer, was based on the belief that sexual activity could be dangerous to the health and ought to be undertaken only at carefully spaced intervals. For this reason, Montaigne recommended late marriage and suggested that soldiers should follow a regime of celibacy. (Hunt 1970:74.)

But there is yet another basis for the male's sexual anxiety. Intercourse is not only *dangerous* for the men, but it may also be *threatening* to their

---

"It were better for you, foolish man, that your male organ should enter the mouth of a terrible and poisonous snake, than it should enter a woman. It were better for you, foolish man, that your male organ should enter the mouth of a black snake, than it should enter a woman. It were better for you, foolish man, that your male organ should enter a charcoal pit, burning, ablaze, afire, than it should enter a woman." (*The Book of the Discipline*, Pt. 1, p. 36.)

self-esteem as males. It makes demands on their virility which they may not be able to fulfill, and it raises a specter concerning their wives' fidelity. These threats, as we shall see, are associated with the putatively strong female libido. In Yeigyi many men view women as almost insatiable. Creatures of lust *(rāga)*, they are believed to have little sexual self-control. Whereas men are sexually satisfied after one or, at most, two acts of intercourse, women—so the men claim—require at least three, and even then they are not satisfied! "Women know only three things: eating, sleeping, and sex." Their strong libido is not only a matter of personal experience, but of "common observation." Thus, the men say, the wife of even a healthy, strong, and wealthy man will commit adultery, if she has the chance, even with a man of much lower prestige than her husband. This being so, how can there be any question about the intensity of the female sex drive?

The belief in the strong libido of women is expressed in and reinforced by a variety of literary sources, the locus classicus being the *Culla-Paduma Jātaka,* according to which a princess falls passionately in love with, and seduces, a man whose arms, legs, nose, and ears had been cut off. My Burmese assistant observed that men point to this one *Jātaka* tale as proof for the sexuality of women, while ignoring others that recount their loyalty, fidelity, and virtue. But of course this is a universal tendency: all peoples use their traditions selectively, in response to their own needs and perceptions. In any event, this particular *Jātaka* is a powerful charter for the male belief because it forms the basis for one of the best known classical dramas in Burma—*Paduma.*

Paduma's basic theme, reflecting the theme of the *Jātaka,* is the passionate nature of women (and, as we shall see, the infidelity of wives). Prince Paduma's friend, consoling him for the infidelity of his wife, observes: "It is the habit of women to fall in love with any man that they can see. They are ready to cling to any man as husband; they are attracted as by a magnet. Just as the ocean is ever receiving the great rivers and various streamlets, without turning away one, a woman is ready to welcome all men, whether they be old, or sick, or poor, or bad." (Htin Aung 1937:225.) And Paduma, himself, in the final speech of the play, says that the passion of women is so strong, "they will (even) kill their rightful husbands the moment they want a new lover. Their lust blinds them. . . . They receive all, just as a roaring fire receives all rubbish." *(Ibid.:231.)*

Woman's strong libido is a thesis by no means confined to *Paduma.* "There are five kinds of longing pertaining to women," exclaims King Wagaru's *Manu Dhammasattham:* "longing for dress, food, men, wealth, seeing." (Forschammer 1885:6.) *The Lokaniti* (Sein Tu 1962:355) makes the claim even more strongly:

> The appetite of women is twice that of men;
> The intelligence of women is four times that
>   of men;
> The diligence of women is six times that
>   of men;
> The sensuality of women is eight times that
>   of men.

As in so many other aspects of Burmese culture, it is important to note at least that almost identical views are found in most of South Asia, Southeast Asia, and the Middle East, among others. So far as India is concerned, it is not unlikely that the views expressed in *Paduma* were the prevailing Indian views of the period. Thus, according to the *Dharmásāstra*, "The sex urge in her [any woman] is so great that she will cohabit with any man she meets, irrespective of his age or appearance. If she be chaste, it is because she has not found a proper man, place, or opportunity." (Kapadia 1966:183.) Again, according to the same source, "Women do not care for beauty, nor is their attention fixed on age; they give themselves to the handsome as well as to the ugly, just for the fact that he is a man . . . (for) love of scandal and the lust of sex the Creator gave to women." (*Ibid.*:254.) Although literary sources like these exaggerate and distort, there is little doubt that the belief in the greater libidinality of women is widespread in India. Roy (1975) has most recently demonstrated this for Bengal.

The Arab view, it may be added, is little different. (Berger 1964:101.) Women, according to Arab belief, "are driven by inordinate sexuality. They are animalistic in their behavior." (Antoun 1968:691.) And this is not only because their lust is greater than men's, but because they are less able to control it. Hence, if their libido is to be controlled, it is necessary to subject them to infibulation, clitoridectomy, or social seclusion (Patai 1971:476-477).

In Southeast Asia, Javanese (Geertz 1961:130) and Malayan males certainly believe that the female libido is stronger than the male's. Indeed, many Malay divorces are initiated by men on the grounds that they cannot satisfy their wives' sexual expectations (Nash 1974:38).

In Burma, as well as in these other groups, the male belief in the strong female libido is most probably a myth. There are, to be sure, some overly sexed women in Burma, as there are anywhere else, but they are the true nymphomaniacs—known as *tanha kyide meinma*, "women with strong lust"—who are often turned to as mistresses, especially by men whose wives are frigid. The latter observation reminds us that there also are some overly repressed women in Burma, especially in the urban middle class, whose resultant puritanism is of the classic type. In general, however, Burmese women seem to have neither more nor less libido than any others. It is not unlikely that the claim of many men that they cannot satisfy their wives' sexual needs—a claim, it will be recalled, that is supported by the testimony of at least some women—is not a result of an excessively strong female libido, but of their own sexual behavior (most especially rapid ejaculation following brief foreplay). In short, what these men see as excessive libido in their wives is, more likely, sexual frustration. The same situation, perhaps intensified, is found in India (Roy 1975:Ch. 3) and China (Hsu 1971:247-253).

Hence, although their explanation may be invalid, those men who believe that they do not satisfy their wives' sexual needs are probably correct. This being the case, it is not unlikely that sexual intercourse poses a threat to their self-image as virile males. Although this threat may be defended against by the personal belief that (in the words of one informant) "it is only natural that a man be anxious about maintaining an erection," or by the cultural belief (implicit in the cultural notions concerning the vagina, semen, and *hpoun*) that intercourse is highly dangerous, such defenses would merely render the anxiety unconscious. Sexual anxiety is, of course, widespread in South and Southeast Asia,[14] and the concern with potency medicine is equally widespread. In Burma, this concern begins with the very inception of marriage when, after the wedding ceremony, the groom's friends feed him eggs and milk which, it is believed, "strengthen" his penis and increase his sex drive so that he can better satisfy his wife. All of this is consistent with the Rorschach finding (Steele n.d.) concerning the "lack of sexually potent phallic responses in the male protocols."

The men's anxiety concerning their ability to satisfy their wives exacerbates yet another anxiety, which concerns their wives' fidelity. Although men, as we shall see, are more adulterous than women, and although they, unlike women, may have multiple spouses, they believe that women are especially prone to infidelity. Villagers say that a man can never trust his wife outside of his eyesight, for at the first opportunity she will commit adultery.

Like their other beliefs concerning women, the men's belief in their wives' infidelity is found in a variety of cultures in Asia, the Middle East, and Europe. In Java, for example, husbands (and wives too) are so

14. Malay men may represent the extreme case in Southeast Asia (Hyman n.d.:37). Indeed, as Hyman's perceptive paper indicates, the Burmese conflicts concerning women and sex are, in all their aspects, relatively mild compared to those experienced by the Malays.

suspicious of their spouse's infidelity that it amounts to "an almost paranoid watchfulness." (Geertz 1961:133.) If anything, Arab men are even more anxious than the Javanese about their wives' fidelity (Berger 1964:104) which, no doubt, is one reason for *purdah*. The same anxiety, to turn to an entirely different time and place, is found in seventeenth-century France where, according to Hunt (1970:74), every husband was portrayed in satire as having "to face the danger of being betrayed by his wife." This ubiquitous concern is poignantly reflected in the words of Montaigne. "There is hardly one among us who does not fear more the shame which comes to him from the vices of his wife than from his own; who does not concern himself (astonishing charity) more with the conscience of his good wife than with his own morals; who would not prefer to be a thief and blasphemer and that his wife were murderer and heretic, than that she should be less chaste than her husband." (Hunt, 1970:74.)

As is the case in these latter cultures, in Burma, too, this belief is expressed in and supported by tradition. It is found in numerous tales and plays, and in some of the best known works of the classical theater, including, of course, *Paduma*.

> One is more certain of one's ability to drink up all the waters of the ocean, than of the faithfulness of one's wife (Htin Aung 1937:231).

A similar view is found in *The Lokaniti* (Sein Tu 1962:233):

> All rivers turn out to be winding;
> All Forests are full of kindling;
> All women, given a secluded place,
> end by sinning.

The Buddhist view of the wife's infidelity is exactly the same, as the following passage from a *Jātaka,* and attributed to the Buddha, indicates: "You couldn't be certain of a woman, even if you had her inside you and always walked about with her. No woman is ever faithful to one man alone" *(Andabhūta-Jātaka).*

If this picture of female sexual frustration and male sexual anxiety seems overdrawn, I hasten to observe that the quality of Burmese sexuality is little different from that in most other societies in which sex has been studied in detail (see Obeyesekere [1973] for Ceylon) rather than surveyed superficially. Freud's Vienna, as the comparative data alluded to throughout this section indicate, was not and is not the only cultural setting in which sex has posed problems. Since, sexual difficulties, of one kind or another, are widespread, most societies provide institutionalized means for dealing with them. Burma, of course, is no exception to this generalization, but since this aspect of the problem is not germane to our discussion of marriage, it will be dealt with elsewhere.

Extramarital Sex

Sexual anxiety and sexual frustration often lead to attempts to "prove" one's potency, or to achieve a more satisfactory sex life, by means of fresh or heterogeneous sexual partners and experiences. Adultery and (where it is permitted) polygamy are obvious expressions of such attempts. (Since, as we saw in the last chapter, "adultery" is a culturally variable concept, I shall use, instead, the descriptive, and morally neutral expression, "extramarital sex.") In this section, I wish to examine these hypotheses in the Burmese setting.

It has already been noted at the beginning of this chapter that men claim that sex is a regnant drive, that sexual temptation is omnipresent, and that if a man and a woman are together in private, the presumption is that their purpose is sexual. Even more important for our present discussion is the claim of many men that, after marriage, their sexual desire for other women may be stronger than that for their wives. This claim is reflected on the cultural level in a well-known and oft-repeated folk saying: "You may call a married man 'old,' but if he descends only three steps [from his house], he becomes a bachelor." That is to say, the moment a husband leaves his house, he is ready for a sexual adventure.

The men's assertion that the libidinal tie to the bride does not persist for long, or with much intensity, after marriage is consistent with a number of other findings. The frequency of sexual intercourse, as we have seen, drops off rather sharply after the early post-wedding period. Moreover, different terms of affection are used to describe the husband's (compassionate) feeling for his wife, on the one hand, and his (passionate) feeling for a sweetheart, fiancée, or mistress, on the other. Thus *hkyitte* is used to refer to love for wives, *kyaikte* for sexual attraction to others. There are some men, to be sure, who claim that in all cases the felt emotion is sexually based, but many say that the feeling for the wife is akin to that for the mother or sister, for whom the term *hkyitte* is also used.

These, moreover, are not the only lexical cues which point to the libidinal distinction between the (eroticized) non-wife and the (non-eroticized) wife. A spouse, like a parent or sibling, is properly characterized as an object of "loving kindness" *(myitta)* or of "longing attachment" *(thanyozin)*, but not, any more than the parent or sibling, as the object of "desire" *(tanha)*. As a technical term in Pali, the language of Buddhist Scripture, *tanha* is glossed as "clinging [to worldly things]," but as a Burmese loan word it has taken on a sexual connotation. Thus, to say of a person that he has *tanha*—literally, *tanha shide*, or "*tanha* exists [in him]"—is to characterize him as lustful, so that even if husband and wife love each other and enjoy a satisfactory love life, it would be considered crude and improper for either to say that he feels *tanha* for his spouse. With respect to other women, however, or to his wife before they are married, it is said that "he looks at her with *tanha*" or that "he feels *tanha* for her." All of these lexical distinctions, then, assimilate the wife to those close consanguineal kin (parents, siblings, and children) who, normatively at least, are non-erotic objects.

These disparate data suggest that sometime following marriage, love for wife loses much of its erotic component, that a once libidinal object has become in part delibidinized. Since Freud's early formulation, the dynamics by which this process occurs has been fairly well understood. "Where they love," Freud (1912:183) writes, "they do not desire and where they desire they cannot love. They seek objects which they do not need to love, in order to keep their sensuality away from the objects they love."[15] Consequently, females are (unconsciously) dichotomized into a pure, or asexual class (mother, sister, wife) and an impure, or sexual class (mistress, prostitute).

This dichotomy, it is important to note, is found in all of the major civilizations. In the West, its most famous cultural expression was found in the institution of courtly love, which was associated with the love of the Lady, on the one hand, and the adoration of the Virgin, on the other, with the wife being relegated to an unimportant, almost residual category (De Rougemont 1957:93-122). During this period and later, romantic love was considered possible only between lover and mistress, not between husband and wife, and it was not until the seventeenth century that "mature sexual satisfaction (was) considered possible in married as much as in illicit love." (Pinchbeck and Hewitt 1969:201.) The notion of the pure—and even the virginal!—wife is still found in pockets of Western civilization. It is said, for example, of contemporary Greek Cypriots, that "if it were possible to combine the concepts of virginity and motherhood the ideal married woman would be a married mother virginal in sensations and mind." (Peristiany 1966:182.) Similarly, among the Sarakatsani, Greek shepherds on the mainland, "even married women must remain virginal in thought and expression." (Campbell 1966:146.)

This bifurcation of the female into the pure (asexual) wife-mother and the impure (sexual) mistress-prostitute is also found in the Near East where, as Berger (1964:105) observes, romantic love and marriage "have thus far remained largely unconnected. In Arabic literature there is much

---

15. Ironically, Freud assumed that both the phenomenon and the process underlying it are peculiarly characteristic of modern man. It is the sexual (presumably, puritanical) ethic of modern, western civilization which, he believed, is responsible for this phenomenon. Since, however, this process is produced by sexual anxiety of a certain kind, and since the sexual ethic of modern civilization is not the only cause of this anxiety, it is not surprising that this phenomenon, as we shall see, is widespread.

courtship and romantic love but not between men and women who marry each other."

In South Asia, this bifurcation is not only as pronounced as in the previous culture areas, but it is there that it finds its strongest cultural expression (in religion and myth). Hindu culture, as Roy (1975:119) observes, "has not been able to accept sexual pleasure *(kam)* in conjugal as well as romantic love. . . . This conflict in attitude is reflected in the dichotomous image of two kinds of women—the mother (to be respected) and the mistress (to be desired sexually)," and the wife is classified with and assimilated to the goddess-mother figure. Indeed, in Bengal all eligible wives are classified terminologically as mother *(ma)*. [16] The identical process, as Obeyesekere (1973) has observed, occurs in sections of Ceylon, again at the levels both of culture and personality.

In East Asia, too, to take China as an example, romantic love and marriage are dissociated. The husband has sex with his wife in order to have children; for sexual pleasure, however, he turns to prostitutes and (if he can afford one) concubines. (Hsu 1971:104-106; Yang 1969:57). Although this dichotomy does not seem to be expressed in religious symbolism, it is expressed in other cultural forms. Thus, the romantic school of *Tz'u* poetry drew upon love affairs with prostitutes for "much of its motif" and traditional scholars wrote some of their best poetry in houses of prostitution (Yang 1969:57).

To summarize, then, the delibidinization of the wife is a widespread cultural phenomenon, one which is hardly restricted to Burma. This phenomenon, moreover, has important behavioral consequences. In its extreme form, it is expressed in the Don Juan character, who (in his Western manifestation) compulsively flees from mistress to mistress as each becomes delibidinized once she has become a sexual conquest, or who (in his Javanese and Malayan manifestation) pursues a relentless cycle of marriages and divorces. In a less extreme form, it may be expressed, as it is in Burma, in the less relentless form of extramarital sex. As in so many other matters, Burma falls between China and India in this regard. If, in China, romantic notions are systematically excluded from marriage, so that prostitutes and concubines are the primary, if not exclusive, means for sexual satisfaction (Yang 1969:54-57), and if, in India the "sexual desire [of a male] may remain unfulfilled all his life unless he has extra-marital 'affairs' with socially acceptable women such as prostitutes" (Roy 1975:121), in Burma, as we shall see, the situation is not at all that extreme; for although prostitutes and mistresses are important sexual

16. In India, moreover (or at least in Bengal), the same bifurcation occurs with respect to the male figure. For Bengali females, Śiva, the ascetic god, is the ideal husband image, while Krishna, the libertine god, is the ideal lover image (Roy 1972:182-183).

objects, they are an ancillary, rather than a central, means to sexual satisfaction.

Although a variety of conditions may produce the psychological need to dichotomize women into erotic and non-erotic objects, and, hence, to delibidinize the wife (relative to other women), it is not implausible to assume that in Burma, as in many other societies, this process is related to male sexual anxiety. Although our data are not sufficient to test the psychodynamic explanation for this anxiety which was suggested in the previous section, these data are at least consistent with that hypothesis. If this anxiety, as I argued above, explains the husband's rapid ejaculation, it might also explain the relative delibidinization of his wife. For if rapid ejaculation may be viewed as a means for coping with this anxiety by reducing the *duration* of the anxiety-producing experience, the delibidinization of the wife may be viewed as a defense against it because it reduces the *frequency* of the experience. If so, it is not a very efficient defense, for since the husband's sexual need persists, it is merely rechannelled onto other females; but since his anxiety remains, so does his need to "prove" his potency. On both accounts one would expect the delibidinization of the wife to be accompanied by a pervasive attraction for other women, and this, as we have seen, is indeed the case. It is this attraction, it may then be inferred, that leads to extramarital sex, the keeping of mistresses, and the taking of lesser wives.

The woman's interest in extramarital sex does not require such an elaborate psychodynamic explanation. Although the men's explanation for the women's extramarital impulses is misplaced, their assumption that many women have such impulses may be accepted as highly probable for a variety of reasons. First, given the woman's sexual dissatisfaction discussed in the previous section, the assumption is consistent with theoretical expectations. Second, there is the testimony of the less inhibited female informants who say that it is true. Third, there are the reports of successful seducers who claim that, given the proper circumstances, the seduction of a married woman is relatively easy. Fourth, there are the many cases—perhaps "reports" is the better word—of extramarital sex.

That both spouses evince a readiness for extramarital affairs is supported by the Thematic Apperception Test, which indicates that "both sexes have high romantic expectations and both sexes appear sexually impulsive so that relationships may be initiated or terminated through impulsive sexual liaisons. Failures in romantic expectations in one relationship and the resulting hostility may be 'acted out' by acquiring a new partner who at least for some period of time will fulfill the romantic ideal." (Steele n.d.)

Although it is impossible to obtain reliable quantitative data concerning extramarital sex, it is safe to say that it is more frequent among husbands than wives, and that it is more frequent in the city than in the village. Thus, for Rangoon, estimates of female infidelity (by female urban informants) range from 10 to 25 percent; male informants, on the other hand, claim that "most," or the "vast majority" of men, at one time or another, have had extramarital experiences. Unfortunately, village estimates are not comparable with those for the city because, when working in the villages, my concern was with "adultery" as the Burmese define this term, which, it will be recalled, is a more restricted category than "extramarital sex."

Turning, then, to these restricted data, estimates of village "adultery" were obtained in six villages from headmen and village elders. (Because adultery cases, if they are brought to court, are heard by these officials, it was assumed that they would be the most reliable informants concerning *known* cases of adultery.) In three villages, to which I came as a stranger, there were reported to be no known cases of adultery, while in the other three, in which I worked rather extensively, the reports were different. In one, my question evoked only the qualitative estimate, "many." In a second, the estimates were 10 percent for women and 25 for men. "Where ever there is a village," the elders of this village (quoting a folk-saying) observed, "there you will find adultery." In Yeigyi, the third village, the estimates were 5 percent for women and 10 for men. I personally, however, knew of five cases of adultery which occurred during my research in Yeigyi, including one in which the husband was having an affair with the wife of his best friend, while his own wife, in turn, was having an affair with another man.

These data raise at least four questions. First, in the case of husbands, why is there less "adultery"—extramarital sex with married women—than other kinds of extramarital sex? (This question applies only to husbands for, it will be recalled, any form of extramarital sex is "adultery" for a wife.) Second, why is the incidence of infidelity lower among females than males? Third, why is its incidence lower in the villages than the cities? Finally, why is there a wide discrepancy between the desire for, and the incidence of, extramarital sex, especially among women? These questions can be answered *seriatim*.

That males practice extramarital sex less frequently with married, than unmarried, women is hardly surprising, given the Burmese values concerning "adultery" and the punitive consequences (both natural and supernatural) associated with it. To seduce another man's wife is viewed as a highly immoral act which, if discovered, causes the adulterer much shame, stigmatizing both him and his family. In addition, the seducer, as we have seen, is liable to both criminal and civil damages, including imprisonment and the payment of a fine to the cuckolded husband. Moreover, although a husband's infidelity is not considered to be "adultery," it is nevertheless grounds for divorce. To be sure, the wife is reluctant to sue for divorce, and she can usually be talked out of it because a lawsuit makes her husband's infidelity public, and this is a source of great shame for her. Nevertheless, should she press her charges, she can not only obtain a divorce, but her husband must forfeit the dower, as well as other kinds of property that are ordinarily divided upon partition. Finally, there is the fear of karmic retribution, for, as we have seen, the Buddhist punishment for adultery is twofold: rebirth as a homosexual, followed by rebirth in hell.[17]

Unlike the seduction of a married woman, seduction of an unmarried woman is not considered to be shameful for a married man, and although it, too, is immoral and subject to punishment, neither the one nor the other is sufficiently serious to serve as an important deterrent. To be sure, the seduction of a virgin, especially one from a good family, is extremely immoral and dangerous; her male relatives will take physical revenge and the law will claim damages. Typically, therefore, sex with an unmarried woman is sought either with a widow or divorcée, or with a girl from a depressed social class concerning whom there is little social opprobrium or punitive recourse. In Yeigyi, for example, the favorite objects of extramarital sex are either seasonal farm workers or Mandalay prostitutes. In the city, too, the unmarried women are usually prostitutes, and among the wealthy, servant girls may serve this function.

Although there is little danger or opprobrium attached to a husband's infidelity with an unmarried woman, a distinction must be made between casual extramarital sex and the keeping of a mistress. Casual sex, whether it be with a prostitute or a non-prostitute, is rarely censured, and if anything it is taken for granted, even by the wife. She might object if he visits prostitutes regularly, but even then her objection is not so much moral or emotional as financial. As in China (Yang 1969:57) her objection is to his squandering of the family income. The keeping of a mistress,

---

17. Although Scripture does not specify the karmic consequence of adultery, the belief that it is punished in hell is based, according to village informants, on a well-known folk tale which, in addition, has been popularized in a song composed by the famous Burmese actor, Shwe Maung Tin Maung. It seems that each of the four sons of a rich man seduced a married woman, and then were consequently reborn in hell, where they were immersed over their heads in a boiling cauldron. Periodically, each would emerge from the cauldron long enough to utter the first syllable to the first word of a sentence before falling back into the boiling water. The first syllable, respectively, uttered by each—the entire word, not to mention the rest of the sentence, was never completed—was *du, tha, na, thaw;* hence the title of Shwe Maung Tin Maung's song—*Duthanathaw.* It is from this tale that it is known that the karmic punishment for adultery is rebirth in hell.

however, is another matter, and although the wife's objections may not be based on moral grounds, they are nevertheless serious. A mistress (*qapyou maya,* "unmarried wife;" or even *mayange,* "lesser wife") is a threat to the wife in at least four ways. First, she is expensive. Moreover, she takes the husband away from the home, for, unlike the Chinese concubine who is taken into the home, the Burmese mistress is rigidly segregated from the family. Again, since her husband prefers to be with his mistress, the wife loses face. Finally, the mistress is a potential lesser wife (of which more below). In short, the wife's opposition to her husband's having an affair is based essentially on pragmatic, not moral, grounds.

So far as the community is concerned, an affair evokes censure only if it becomes public. This is especially the case with respect to those men who are notorious for their frequent and public infidelities. Such censorious attitudes are more frequently held by women than by men, for whom the gay seducer—"[he who] pursues and is hungry for women" (*meinma laik hsade*)—is often an ambivalent object, publicly censured but (more often than not) secretly envied by his fellows. Moreover, as an indication both of wealth and sexual attractiveness, his many affairs may actually enhance his prestige (*goun*). Nevertheless, although secretly envied, such a man—who, unlike his counterpart in China, cannot use the need for children as a convenient and acceptable rationalization for his behavior (Hsu 1971:104-106)—is publicly condemned by males as well as females. Indeed his public condemnation is so strong that, until recently, he could not even be portrayed in fiction. As Hla Pe (1965:182) has observed, "A novel in which the hero has a mistress in every village and town he visits was not allowed to be seen in most of the 'drawing rooms' of that [the 1920s] period."

Of the two kinds of extramarital sex, the keeping of a mistress is the less frequent because, among other reasons, few men can afford the expense. According to informants, a large percentage of those who can afford a mistress do in fact have one—and this, as Sangermano (1893:164) reports, was true in the nineteenth century as well—but their absolute number, given this economic constraint, is small. For this reason, as well as for others discussed below, the mistress is an almost exclusively urban phenomenon.

For the wife (for whom all extramarital relations are adulterous), infidelity entails the same karmic consequence as it does for the husband, but the social consequence is even more serious. Women, as we have seen, are expected above all to maintain their reputation (*qathayei*) as virtuous and modest wives, and the smallest challenge to their virtue —the touch of a man's hand, a conversation in a private place, the very hint of flirtatiousness—is enough to cause the "loss of reputation" (*qathayei hpyette*) or the "destruction of her [good] name" (*name hpyette*). For a woman adultery is an unthinkably disgraceful act, one which stigmatizes her and disgraces her children. Nothing, including her husband's infidelity or his sexual indifference, can condone her infidelity; unlike the Chinese wife, she may properly seek (and receive) a divorce if either of these conditions disturb her, but she may not commit adultery. If stigmatization is not a sufficient deterrent, the woman has also to consider that if she is discovered, her lover's wife (if he is married) may work sorcery on her, her husband will almost certainly divorce her (leaving her penniless), and he may also—as numerous newspaper reports testify—beat and even kill her. Although these are serious enough, the traditional punishment for an adulteress was even more serious. After shaving her hair—a symbol of her stigmatized state—the husband was permitted to sell her into slavery (Hamilton 1930:28).

Given this set of values and negative sanctions relating to adultery, the fact that its incidence, though low, is even as high as it is, is a measure of the strength of the desire; and this in itself, I would suggest, adds additional credence to the explanation for adultery suggested above. That its incidence (and that of infidelity in general) is less in the village than in the city, can be accounted for (as the villagers themselves suggest) in at least four ways. First, the chances of discovery—and, hence, of punishment—in a large and anonymous urban setting are much smaller than in the village, where it is all but impossible for anything to be kept private. Second, villagers have a more sincere commitment to traditional Buddhist values and are more sensitive to the requirements of Buddhist sexual morality. Third, having more strongly cathected the Buddhist cosmology, villagers are more strongly motivated by the predictable karmic consequences of violating Buddhist morality. Finally, the villagers are typically too poor to afford the expense.

These urban-rural differences aside, it should now be obvious that if a married man wishes to have an extramarital affair, he is best advised to choose an unmarried mistress. This choice, however, may create still another set of problems, for unlike a married mistress, who is supported by her husband, one unmarried expects to be supported by her lover. Even more serious, she may insist that the latter take her as a "lesser wife" as the price for continuing the affair, which brings us to the subject of the next section, polygyny.

Polygyny

Polygyny is a legally permitted practice in Burma—as it is in China, but not in India—and it is accepted, if not approved, by Buddhism. Moreover, unlike some other societies in which polygyny may be based on economic and political motives, its motivation in Burma is almost entirely romantic (including sex and affection). Before proceeding, however, it is necessary to define some terms.

Although colloquially even a mistress may be called a "lesser wife" (*mayange*), technically this term is reserved for a woman, other than his first, or senior, wife (*mayagi*), with whom a man is not only having sex, but with whom he lives and eats under a common roof. These three activities, it will be recalled, constitute the criteria for marriage. Typically, as I have already suggested, a lesser wife begins her relationship as a mistress, and it is only when she threatens to terminate the relationship that the man, usually reluctantly, agrees to elevate her status to that of wife. At her insistence, they may even have a wedding, though this is uncommon. The lesser wife not only lives with the man as his wife —though not under the same roof with the senior wife—but she and her children have stipulated rights in the man's estate. Moreover, the husband introduces her in public as his "wife" (never as his "lesser wife" which, as we shall see, would be degrading). The lesser wife (*mayange*) is to be distinguished, in turn, from the co-wife (*maya pyaing*), the latter being the equal of the first wife in almost every sense, most especially in that she and her children have equal inheritance rights with the senior wife and the latter's children.

Both in villages and in the city it is rare for the two wives to live in the same household. "A woman," according to the oft-quoted proverb, "will share a piece of cake with another woman, but she will not share a man with her." Hence today, as in the past, a polygynous male typically lives in his official residence with his senior wife, while his lesser or co-wife resides in a separate household. (This is also the case in Java [Geertz 161:132] and the Kandy region of Ceylon [Yalman 1967:112-113], as well as in certain tribal groups in Burma [Lehman 1970:122].) Indeed, the co-wife usually lives in a separate city, not merely in separate household. Actually, polygynous households are more frequent in the village than in the city, where they almost exclusively consist of cases of sororal polygyny. (Such cases are found even in the highest social strata: both the former Commissioner of Police and the secretary to the National Planning Commission maintained such a household.) Since the village is small, and the joint wives would necessarily interact with each other anyway, the importance of separate households for maintaining domestic tranquility is less obvious. Moreover, the village polygynist is usually less capable of supporting two separate households.

When they live in separate households, the husband not only divides his time between his wives, but he usually segregates them socially as well. His social life with his senior wife includes the circle of friends acquired during their marriage, a circle into which his lesser wife does not intrude. With her, he has an entirely different social circle. Moreover, it is his senior wife who, if he is a government official or a business or professional man, serves as his official hostess and who accompanies him to official parties and receptions. (This is one of the reasons that lesser wives have often been called "concubines" by Westerners.)

Despite its legality, the incidence of polygyny in Burma (as in China) is small, a generalization which seems to hold for all periods in Burmese history for which we have information. Indeed, Forbes' (1878:64) description of nineteenth-century Burma—"except among officials and the wealthy [polygyny] is seldom practiced. In ordinary life a man with more than one wife is talked of as not being a very respectable person"—applies without change to contemporary Burma. And if Conti is correct—"This people," he wrote, "take only one wife" (Forbes: *ibid.*)—it applied to the fifteenth century as well.[18] My own survey in Upper Burma yielded similar results. Thus, in Yeigyi, there is only one man who currently has two wives—he took his second after his first became ill, and now both live in the same house—although there were three other cases in the past. Data from ten other villages are similar to those from Yeigyi. In six, there were no cases of polygyny, although in three of the six there had been at least one polygynous marriage in the past (including one in which the wives lived in the same house). In three of the ten there was one case of polygyny each (and in one, the wives lived in the same house), and in one there were three cases.

This negligible incidence of polygyny in these Upper Burma villages not only holds for villages in Lower Burma (Pfanner [1963:135] reports no polygyny in the village he studied), Central Thailand (Piker [n.d., ch. 2:40] reports only one case in the region he studied), and Java (Geertz [1961:131] reports a rate of 2 percent for the subdistrict in which she worked), but it holds for urban Burma as well, although villagers assume as a matter of course that in the city, any wealthy man, including foreigners, will have at least two wives. When friends from Yeigyi saw me at a pagoda festival with my wife and two other women, one Indian and

18. Since few men, whatever their value system, can afford multiple wives, it is safe to assume that historical reports that convey a contrary impression—thus, Conder (quoting Hough) refers to polygyny as "abound[ing] in this country" (Conder 1826:89); and Bell (1852:84) writes that the Burmese would take as many as "three or four wives in the course of a month"—could only have been referring, their hyperbole aside, to government officials, the nobility, and the court. Indeed, royalty practiced prescriptive polygyny, for, in addition to a very large harem, the king had to have four queens, one for each of the cardinal directions. As for government officials, even older informants today report that in the past officials kept wives in different parts of the district they served, a practice which (so they say) only gradually died out as a result of British influence.

one American, they took it for granted that the latter were my lesser wives, and they never quite believed me when I said they were only friends. The fact is, however, that the incidence of urban polygyny is probably not much higher than it is in the village. Although, unlike the village, I have no survey data for the city, the same urban informants who acknowledged the very widespread practice of extramarital sex said that probably no more than 5 percent of urban males, if that, have multiple wives.

It should also be noted that very few polygynists have more than two wives. In my ten village survey, I discovered only two cases of a husband with three wives (and in both cases they all lived in one household). Such cases are somewhat more frequent in the city—but they are usually confined to the wealthy—and the number of wives varies. The upper limit, in my research at least, is thirty-three, the husband being a very wealthy Muslim timber merchant. Other well-known cases are far less dramatic. In Mandalay, one of the leading Buddhists of the city, and a well-known physician, had four known wives. In Rangoon, a well-known financier, and the founder of numerous monasteries, had "countless" wives (and over fifty children). In the same city, a Vice Chancellor of Rangoon University, whose senior wife was European, had five lesser wives before he was dismissed from his post for marrying a sixth.

The infrequency of polygyny, especially in comparison to the frequency (at least in the city) of extramarital sex, is a challenging finding, one which is best explained by the stigma which attaches both to the husband and to the lesser wife. The lesser wife is always considered inferior to the senior wife. Often she is viewed as no better than a prostitute, not only because she is viewed as having broken up a home, but because, usually much younger and of a lower social class than her husband, she is viewed as having married him only for his money. Even when mitigating circumstances (as when the first wife is a permanent invalid, or has given birth only to girls) constitute morally justifiable grounds for taking a second wife, the stigma still remains to some extent.

The stigma attaching to the man is just as great, but even harder to sustain, for he is stigmatized by his friends and family, persons who are of little importance to the lesser wife, but who, for him, constitute his most important reference group. The reason for his stigma is two-fold: first, for having committed an immoral act, second, for his indiscretion in permitting his first wife to know of his second marriage. Normally, even those who are aware of the marriage pretend that it does not exist, and, following the well known admonition, "As for knowing, let [them] know, [but] don't let them see" *(thida thisei mamyin)*, the husband does not advertise it. Those few who violate this precaution usually do so at the insistence of the second wife, or because of the prestige which they derive from it. In Burma, as in Java (Geertz 1961:131), to afford more than one wife is a sign of wealth; it is also, moreover, a sign of virility as well as a measure of the man's attractiveness to women. Although, on these accounts, the polygynist is at least an object of ambivalence for his fellows, if not of secret envy and admiration, they will condemn him for his thoughtlessness concerning his first wife and his children. In the first place, he causes her humiliation because his second marriage announces, as it were, that she does not satisfy him sexually, and working-class women, especially, have been known to murder husbands and second wives as a result. If his lack of sexual satisfaction is then interpreted as a function of his own immoderate sex drive, his children are also humiliated by the fact that their father is a man of excessive sex *(tanha)* or lust *(rāga)*. Indeed, I have known sons who have cursed, and even struck, their fathers after becoming aware of their polygyny. The father's fear of the son after taking a lesser wife is a folk theme. Daughters, too, often leave, or threaten to leave, home when their father takes a lesser wife.

In addition to humiliating his wife and children, the polygynist causes them financial loss, the second basis for his thoughtlessness. In supporting a second wife (and her children) the husband necessarily deprives his first wife and her children of additional income. More important, they forfeit part of their inheritance to the second wife, for since 1948, when the inheritance rule was liberalized, both wives have equal rights to the husband's estate. Even before 1948, however, when the first wife was the sole heir, the law stipulated that the second wife and the children of the first wife divided the estate upon the latter's death. For both reasons, the stigma attached to a wealthy polygynist is less than that to a man of ordinary means.

A final reason for the infrequency of polygyny, both in village and city alike, is the husband's fear of being harmed by his first wife, for women, as we shall see in the next chapter, can acquire magical power to dominate or harm their husbands. The husband's fear of this power is a very important deterrent to the taking of a second wife.

If polygyny is only rarely employed by men as a means for dealing with their sexual tensions, polyandry is even less frequently used by women. It is universally abhorred, and almost nonexistent. Urban informants tell of isolated cases of a young student, or a younger distant relative, who, living in the home of a married couple, becomes the wife's lover (with or without the knowledge of the husband). But, of course, he is a lover, not a husband. They also tell of cases of poor women who, with the approval of their husbands, take wealthy lovers to improve their economic position. In these cases, too, the second male is a lover and not a husband. Indeed, the only genuine case of polyandry I discovered in my investigations occurred in a village close to Yeigyi. This being a unique, as well as an especially interesting, case, it is worthwhile examining it more closely.

The first husband of the polyandrous wife had been a monk, who had left the order to marry her. Owning no land, and having few agricultural skills, he eked out a living as a hired hand. From the very beginning, he was henpecked by his wife, and humiliated by her sharp tongue and—a rare thing in Burma!—her physical beatings. About fifteen years later, the wife took a second husband ten years her junior and of not inconsiderable wealth; she married him, so the villagers claimed, for money and sex. Whatever her motives, the marriage led to a great outrage, and the woman was forced to move (with her second husband) to another village. Sometime later her first husband became ill, and her relatives, who refused to care for him (his relatives lived in another part of the country), requested that she return to the village. Viewing her as a prostitute, the villagers objected to her return, but they had no legal basis for excluding her.

From the moment she returned, she and her two husbands were completely ostracized. When, a few years later, her first husband died and her second husband contracted an insidious skin disease, the working of karmic punishment was seen by everyone. A few months before I arrived in this village, the woman, whose children were now in their teens, pleaded with the headman and elders to permit her to join the mutual aid society (from which she had heretofore been excluded) so that she might perform the Buddhist initiation rite for her son. Although persuaded by her religious motives, they only reluctantly agreed to lift the ban.

Why, then, is polygyny a legal and recognized form of marriage, while polyandry is illegal, punishable by ostracism and banishment? The Burmese have few (if any) satisfactory answers to this difference in attitude. Some informants explain the difference by invoking the proverb, "If a tree is good, ten thousand birds can take shelter in it" *(thitpin kaungyin/hnget tathaung na hlaingthi)*; that is, since the man is the breadwinner, he can marry as many women as he can support, while the woman, who is economically dependent on the man, cannot have more than one husband. This is obviously no answer, not only because many women are breadwinners and can indeed support more than one husband, but because the opposition to polyandry is emotionally and morally, rather than practically, based.

Other informants relate Burmese attitudes toward polyandry to the belief (and the legal principle) that the husband "owns" his wife's sexuality. On this premise the prohibition of polyandry rests on the same grounds as the prohibition of female adultery or premarital sex, namely, the husband's exclusive rights to his wife's sex.

For many Burmese, especially villagers, there is no need to explain the difference in attitude between polygyny and polyandry. It is "only natural" that (together with the other differences between men and women) men, but not women, should have the right to multiple spouses. For a woman to have two husbands is tantamount to prostitution. "Beyond that," as one villager put it, "there is nothing more to say about it!"

But, of course, there *is* more to say about it, for although polyandry, unlike polygyny, has a very restricted cross-cultural distribution, its most important provenance is the area to the north (the Himalayas) and south (Ceylon) of Burma. Moreover, Ceylon, like Burma, is a *Theravāda* Buddhist society, with a rice economy, a bilateral kinship system, nuclear family households, stringent premarital sex taboos, inheritance through both males and females, belief in male superiority, and so on. In short, except for caste, Ceylon is a society whose primary cultural and structural features are very similar to Burma's. Nevertheless, polyandry (especially adelphic polyandry) was an accepted and a legal Sinhalese practice in the past (Cordiner 1807:164; Haeckel 1883:237), and, despite the fact that it subsequently became illegal, it is still practiced with impunity (Ryan 1953:151; Tambiah 1966; Yalman 1967:108-112). To be sure, polyandry is rare in Ceylon, as it is wherever it is found, but is is not as rare as polygyny.[19] Although this is a perplexing problem, like the Burmese themselves, I have no answer for it.

19. In light of the Burmese data, Leach's explanation for Sinhalese polyandry is untenable. "Polyandry exists in Ceylon," Leach argues (1955:185), "because, in a society where both men and women inherit property, polyandrous arrangements serve, both in theory and practice, to reduce the potential hostility between sibling brothers." Even for Ceylon this argument is weak—it leaves unexplained the vast majority of marriages that are not polyandrous—and in the light of the Burmese data it is weakened further, for in Burma, which has the same inheritance system as Ceylon, polyandry is not only virtually absent, but is abhorred. Tambiah (1966:296) explains Sinhalese polyandry as an attempt to combine resources (especially land) where neither husband has sufficient resources to support a family independently. Since, however, many villagers are embarrassed to talk about polyandry, and since in some cases, at least, the wife takes the initiative by sexual advances toward the future second husband, it is doubtful that this is the only basis for its practice.

9. Interpersonal Components of Marriage

To understand the relationship between husband and wife, it is first necessary to understand the relationship between the sexes in general. Since, however, this relationship is both influenced by and expressed in cultural values and norms, it is necessary to consider not only the relative structural positions of the sexes in Burmese society, but also the cultural ideology of the male-female relationship. Following that we shall treat the cultural norms which are expected to govern the relationship between the spouses, and, finally, we shall describe the actual relationship of husband and wife. This actual relationship, as we shall see, represents a complex compromise of the inconsistencies that obtain among various cultural, structural, and personality variables.

Structural Equality of Males and Females

Burmese women are not only among the freest in Asia, but until the relatively recent emancipation of women in the West, they enjoyed much greater freedom and equality with men than did western women. Today, as we shall see, they control not only the family economy but most retail trade as well—village hawkers, and the proprietors of the stalls and shops in town and city bazaars, are preponderantly women. Women are well represented, too, in large business enterprises. Moreover, except for engineering, women are liberally represented in the professions. In the villages, women participate in the productive phases of the agricultural economy, and they receive the same wages as men for the same work (even though, according to men and women alike, men accomplish more because of their greater strength).

Legally, women are the equals of men. The family estate is divided equally between sons and daughters, women own property in their own name, and after marriage husband and wife own all property jointly.

Moreover, girls, as we have seen, enter freely into marriage and wives have the same right as husbands to initiate divorce. Indeed, in some respects, as we have seen, women are men's superiors in domestic matters, for it is the bride, not the groom, who receives a marriage payment, and it is the girl's hand, not the boy's, that is sought in marriage.

Politically, too, women enjoy high status, if not equality. In modern Burma, women have the right to vote, and they have been members of parliament, ambassadors to foreign countries, and members of international delegations. Even in traditional Burma, daughters (in the absence of sons) could succeed to the hereditary headmanship. On the other hand, only one woman has served in the cabinet, none has been prime minister, and none has served as an officer in the civil administration, the real sinews of government. The Burmese point out that it would be most difficult for men to offer a woman the formal symbols of deference that the office requires.

Finally, women enjoy social equality with men. Such customs as the veil, purdah, child betrothal, foot binding, widow immolation—these, and all the other disabilities suffered by the women of India, on the one side of Burma, and of China, on the other, have always been absent from Burma. Men and women, observed an early commentator, "are suffered to have as free intercourse with each other as the rules of European society admit" (Symes 1800:328). And Symes was not the only early observer to comment on the freedom and social equality of the Burmese women. Forbes (1878:56) remarks that the "exclusion of females" is practiced "among no class in Burma," and that women "of the highest rank have the same freedom of action as the ladies of Europe." Similarly, Hough (1826:88), describing an even earlier period, comments:

The female branches of the family are not recluses here, neither are they reserved or shy in their manners: they form a constituent part of domestic and public society. . . . The wife of a judge or governor is often seen at his side, assisting in the decision of cases; and the wives of viceroys and other high officers are often permitted to hold their own courts, and decide independently on petitions presented to them. Women of all ranks enjoy a high degree of freedom, appear abroad unveiled whenever they choose, ornamented according to the taste and fashion of the country, and add zest to public scenes of amusement by their presence and gaity.

Although the Burmese female is especially privileged, it should be noted that the Burmese pattern of sexual equality is only slightly less pronounced throughout the rest of Southeast Asia. In Thailand, to take but one example:

The social position of the Thai peasant woman is powerful: she has long had a voice in village governmental affairs; she often represents her household at village meetings when her husband cannot attend; she almost always does the buying and selling in the local markets. (It is so unusual for a Thai male to do this that it elicits comment if he does.) Through their marketing activities Thai farm women produce a sizeable portion of the family cash income, and they not only handle the household money, but usually act as the family treasurer and hold the purse strings (de Young 1955:24).

Male Ambivalence to Females

The Ideology of Male Superiority

Despite the remarkable extent of sexual equality in Burmese society —remarkable not only by contrast with the status of women in Asia, the Middle East and traditional Europe, but also with significant segments of the contemporary West—it is nevertheless a basic premise of Burmese culture that men are *inherently* superior to women. This belief, of course, is widely distributed in human cultures, for despite certain contemporary views which view sexism as a peculiarly Western phenomenon, the belief in male superiority is much more strongly held (and practiced) in the great civilizations, for example, of China (Hsu 1971), India (Kapadia 1966), and the Middle East (Patai 1971) than in the West. The reasons offered, of course, vary from culture to culture, but even in this regard the similarities are rather striking.

In Burma, the primary reason offered for male superiority is the belief that men possess that innate, inborn quality, known as *hpoun*, that was alluded to in the previous chapter. Usually glossed as "glory," *hpoun*, it will be recalled, is a psycho-spiritual quality, an ineffable essence, which invests its possessor with superior moral, spiritual, and intellectual attributes. Since, except for Withaka, the famous female disciple of the Buddha, no female has ever possessed *hpoun*, and since every male has *hpoun*, males are both nobler *(myatte)* and higher *(myinte)* than women. It is for this reason, villagers say, that when spouses are walking together, even if a man is physically shorter than his wife, he will seem to be taller than she. As a measure of their conviction concerning the truth of male superiority, villagers are not unwilling to accept its *reductio ad absurdum*, expressed in the proverb "A woman is not as noble as a male dog" *(meinmaka hkwei di lauk mamyatbu)*. This is, of course, a hyperbole but it does convey the intended sentiment—that the masculine is much superior to the feminine—much as the *yin-yang* distinction does in China.

The belief in the spiritual superiority of males, it must be emphasized, is not restricted to males.[1] On the contrary, it is held, or at least asserted, as

1. Nor, of course, is it restricted to Burma. In a modern publication summarizing the traditional Muslim conception, the author writes that "the physical and animal side in

strongly by females as by males. Indeed, it was from a woman that I first
heard the proverb about the superiority of male dogs to human females,
and the most sophisticated woman in the village became openly hostile
when I suggested that she, of course, did not believe in it. To be sure,
sophisticated, urban women characterize this proverb as "old
fashioned"—"no one," they claim, "says this anymore"—but inquiry
revealed that it is not *that* old fashioned. Even university coeds continue
to say it, and (if my informants are correct) they also believe it, although if
a male student taunted them with it, they would "slipper" him. But even
the urban women who reject the proverb agree that *spiritually* (though
not in the other ways to be discussed below) males are superior to
females. This includes Mi Mi Khaing, one of the most sophisticated and
westernized women in Burma.

> For us (women) it is no less than a glorious truth to recall that the greatest
> concentration, clear thought, and enlightenment was attained by the Buddha as a
> man who had discarded his family ties ruthlessly. So, there is no doubt in our
> minds. Spiritually, a man is higher than a woman.
>   This is not just an abstract idea belonging to religious philosophy. Conviction of
> it enter(s) our very bones.. . .
>   It is irrelevant who wields the bigger stick or brings home a richer basket. The
> important question is who wears the crown. And that mark of glory rests upon the
> man's head. And the whole of society is as sure about this as he is himself. As to
> what the wife thinks, there is hardly a Burmese woman who doesn't feel this deep
> inside her, brag though she might about every other ability of hers. (Mi Mi
> Khaing, "The Burmese Woman," in *The Nation*, Rangoon, June 4, 1961.)

Sharing the belief in male superiority, all women recite, as part of their
Buddhist devotions, the following conventional prayer: "Before attaining
nirvana, I pray that I may be reborn as a male in a future existence." This
is an ancient prayer, found in the inscriptions of Pagan. "And I wish to be
freed from this state of a woman, and when in future existences I pass
through abodes of men and spirits, I wish to be born a man endowed with
virtue, understanding, truth, and faith" (Pe Maung Tin 1961:418). Similarly, when asked what they aspired to in their next rebirth, the great
majority of village women, after responding with the conventional "nirvana," say they wished to become a male (preferably a wealthy male!). To
be sure, it is not only because of their spiritual superiority that women
wish to be reborn as men. As the women see it, men lead more pleasant
lives because women suffer the pains *(dukkha)* of menstruation, preg-

---

woman is stronger than in man," and "the spiritual and angelic is stronger in man than in
woman" (quoted in Patai 1971:472).

nancy, and childbirth, they function as servants to their husbands, and they assume most of the domestic responsibilities.[2]

The belief in the spiritual superiority of males is symbolically projected onto inanimate objects. Thus, the eastern side of the house is the noble side, and therefore it is the side on which the men sit (and on which the Buddha shrine is kept). The western side is the ignoble side; it is the side on which the women sit, and where childbirth, an ignoble act, takes place. (Childbirth is ignoble because the accompanying blood and after-birth, and the womb from which they issue, are all ignoble.) The invidious, sex-linked symbolism of the house is carried even further. If the house has two rooms, the eastern (male) room is made of long (superior) planks, the western (female) room of short (inferior) planks.

Although the spiritual superiority of males is based on their *hpoun*, its proof, according to the Burmese, is found in a number of Buddhist beliefs and practices. Only a male has the Buddhist initiation ceremony (*shinbyu*), only a male can become a monk (which leads to a vicious circle: the male's innate superiority enables him to become a monk, which in turn increases his already pronounced superiority to the female),[3] only a male can become a saint (*arahant*), and most important, only a male can become a Buddha. (It is not true, however, as some Western writers have claimed, that males alone can attain nirvana.) Hence it is that in all Buddhist ceremonies, males sit in front, and females sit behind them. Even in school assemblies, all the boys, regardless of age, sit in front of the girls who may be much older. Similarly, in all formal religious celebrations, men eat after the monks are fed, and only then do the women eat.

Male superiority in the religious sphere seems to reflect the belief that the male is a sacred being relative to the female. Hence, the wife pays homage to her husband in the same manner in which she pays homage to the "Five [traditional] objects of worship"—the Buddha, the Law, the monastic order, parents, and teachers—namely, by prostrating herself before him. Given this contrast between "noble" males and "ignoble" females, it is no accident that, whereas the Buddhist monkhood, the

2. Compare the Sinhalese proverb: "Women are born to three miseries, 1st., to quit the place of their birth, 2nd., to bear the pains of child-birth, 3rd., to be under subjection to their husbands" (Pieris 1953:223).

3. Still, given this contrast, there is one curious, even anomalous, practice in Buddhism. The boy's initiation into the Buddhist novitiate (*shinbyu*), the most sacred of Buddhist ceremonies, is always accompanied by a girl's ear-boring (*natwin*), a non-Buddhist, entirely secular, ceremony. Nevertheless, the two are not only conjoined, but (the villagers say) without an ear-boring, one cannot hold a *shinbyu*. In short, the boy's most sacred ceremony is dependent upon the availability of a girl.

noblest of all callings, is restricted to males, (non-Buddhist) shamans, practitioners of an ignoble role, are overwhelmingly female (with the few exceptions believed to be homosexual).

Man's spiritual superiority finds expression in non-religious customs as well. Because of man's *hpoun*, he can have as many weddings as he has marriages, but not so a woman. Should she marry a second time, she may not have a wedding. It is man's superiority, then, that explains the proverb, "Woman has only one *mingala* [a wedding is termed *mingala saun*], but for a man *mingala* never ends."

In the village, at least, there are other reasons, as well, for the superiority of men. We have already seen that the male sex organ is a "golden flower," while the female's is filthy and even polluting. Indeed, it might be speculated that the over-valuation of the penis is the ultimate root of the male feeling of superiority, and that, since the women themselves agree with the negative evaluation of the vagina this is the ultimate basis for the women's acquiescence in the belief in female inferiority.

Again, men, so they themselves claim, are more intelligent than women. This explains, according to village men, why many more females than males believe so firmly in witches, spirits, shamanism, and the like. A columnist for the important Burmese daily *Bahosi* shares this village view. Blaming women for the success of certain occult leaders, whom he views as charlatans—they have become wealthy, he claims, because of the "gullibility" of women—he comments, "A woman is a woman after all. However developed she may be mentally, she cannot escape the snare of deception."

The intellectual inferiority of women is summed up, according to villagers, in a proverb: "If a woman had no nose, she would eat excrement." Their inferiority, moreover, is biologically rooted, and hence inescapable. Intelligence is determined by, among other things, the length of the intestines, and while the male intestine (according to tradition) is 32 yards, the female's is only 28. Interestingly, the Burmese have never drawn the same conclusion as the Arabs who, on the basis of their belief in the intellectual inferiority of women (Patai 1971:476-477), concluded that it would be useless to give them any formal education. Even in the villages, many Burmese women receive (and have always received) formal schooling, and although their literacy rate is lower than that of men, it is nevertheless high for a peasant society.

Although agreeing to their spiritual superiority, many women deny the intellectual superiority of males. Thus, for example, some women say that the greater length of the male intestines gives men more courage, not more wisdom, than women, and it is their greater courage that renders them less susceptible to supernatural beliefs. Other women, however, agree with the belief in male intellectual superiority, and they too adduce the female vulnerabilty to supernatural beliefs as evidence.

It is because of their greater intelligence that, according to the villagers, males alone are headmen and village elders (although in the past women, in the absence of a male heir, could succeed to the hereditary headmanship), and that they alone voice their opinions at village meetings. Similarly, when men discuss religion or politics, often late into the night, women remain at home because, being less intelligent than men, their knowledge in these matters is limited and their opinion unimportant.

Women are also believed to be socially inferior to men because in the village, at least, women possess no social status in their own right, their status being dependent upon that of their father (when they are single) or their husband (when they are married). In this regard, women are like children: "Women and children," as one villager put it, "have no separate *goun.*" The secular concept, *goun,* which might be glossed as "prestige," is the secular counterpart of the spiritual notion of *hpoun.* In the secular order, people are ranked on a scale of prestige, their rank being determined by a combination of family background, education, influence, and wealth. It is in this ranking system that a woman is believed to have no identity separate from that of her father or husband. In support of this thesis, villagers point to the convention in which the wife of a high-status person—a teacher, for example, or a government official—is referred to as "the teacher's wife" *(hsaya gado)* or "the officer's wife" *(min gado),* which, of course, is similar to the German usage of, for example, "Frau Professor."

Men are also believed to be morally superior to women, for if, on the one hand, the cultural ideology attributes to women a deficit in spiritual and intellectual qualities, on the other hand, it confers upon them an excess of the baser instincts, especially greed and sex. So far as greed is concerned, I can do no better than quote again from the *Bahosi* columnist. "Women are never satisfied with their gold and silver ornaments however valuable they may be. Although they may be worth hundreds of thousands of kyats, they still want more. This is the nature of women: they are full of greed." As for sex, all men agree (as we have seen in the last chapter) that women have a much stronger libido than men. Given the Burmese view of sex as something base, the latter belief—especially because it subsumes the belief that women are prone to adultery—is an important basis for their conception of the moral inferiority of women.

What is seemingly anomalous about the Burmese ideology of the inferiority of women—an anomaly that does not apply to the same ideology in India or the Middle East, where it is consistent with the inferior social status of women—is that this ideology is found in a society in which, as we have seen, women are the structural and jural equals of men. This apparent anomaly, moreover, is compounded by the additional inconsistency between the ideology of male superiority and the men's fears of and anxiety concerning women. For despite this ideology, the men are not entirely confident that they are in fact superior. On the contrary, many feel threatened by women, so much so that, psychodynamically viewed, the wide acceptance of this ideology may best be viewed as a defense against this threat.

Male Fear of Women

Although putatively superior to and more intelligent than women, men nevertheless believe that they must be on constant guard against them because they are untrustworthy. As one villager put it: "Women are less intelligent than men, but they have greater intelligence in knowing how to swindle people." Because of this view, men must always be careful in their dealings with women. This attitude is reflected in and reinforced by various cultural traditions. Women, according to the well-known proverb, are one of the "Four things [together with thieves, rulers and boughs of trees] that cannot be trusted." They are also one of "Three crooked things" of another proverb: "Brahmins are crooked, rivers are crooked, and women are crooked." The pervasive belief in the evil of women, a belief which, not surprisingly, is found with equal conviction in Hindu culture,[4] is expressed in an even more extreme form in *The Lokaniti* (1962:279). "Fire, water, women, serpents, and royal kinsmen; these should be approached with great circumspection; for they may take life in an instant."

If the secular tradition were not sufficient, the belief in the dishonesty of women is supported by the sacred tradition of Buddhism. The following quotations from the *Jātaka*, and attributed to the Buddha Himself, are representative of the Buddhist attitude:

> 'Tis nature's law that rivers wind;
> Trees grow of wood by law of kind;
> And, given opportunity,
> All women work iniquity. *(Andabhūta-Jātaka)*

---

4. "Woman," according to the *Maitreyani Samhita*, "is on a par with dice and drink, a major social evil, the spirit of untruth, the genius of darkness." (Quoted in Singh 1967:74-75.) These sentiments are echoed, and carried further, by Manu, the great Indian lawgiver. "Woman is as foul as falsehood itself. When creating them, the lord of creatures alloted to women a love of their beds, of their seat and ornaments; impure thoughts, wrath, dishonesty, malice and bad conduct." *(Ibid:75.)*

> A sex composed of wickedness and guile,
> Unknowable, uncertain as the path,
> Of fishes in the water—womankind
> Hold truth for falsehood, falsehood for the truth!
> (*Ibid.*)

> It is impossible to keep guard over a woman;
> no guard can keep a woman in the right path.
> (*Rādha-Jātaka*)

These proverbs, folk-sayings, and scriptural passages, it must be stressed, are not arcane lore. They are alluded to by parents and taught in school (in both village and city). Moreover, they are used and quoted, whenever appropriate, in the context of everyday life, and when not quoted, then they are referred to. Thus, if a man is thought to be crooked, he might be compared to a woman. Hence, at a village meeting, when a man stressed that his words could be trusted, he said he was "not like a female who talks behind people's backs." Again, when describing a factional conflict in the village, a man said that "the other side [the opposing faction] always engaged in intrigue—just like widows and females."

It is tedious, but necessary, to observe that identical sentiments are found among even the most Westernized urbanites. Men say, for example, that women are dangerous because untrustworthy. University coeds report that when a girl drops a boy, his typical comment to her, as well as his friends, is: "You are dangerous and dishonest, not to be trusted." When women wish to insult a man, they say that he has "a woman's tongue," that is, his words are not to be trusted. Or, when angry with a girl friend for letting them down, coeds often say, "Oh well, you know she's a female." (So what can you expect?) Of a boy they might say, "He's like a girl—very crooked." And, when such a boy is seen approaching, the provocative comment is, "Look out, the woman is coming! the woman is coming!"

The untrustworthiness of women is especially evident (and especially threatening) with respect to their putative inclination to marital infidelity. Since this, however, has been discussed in the previous chapter, there is no need to repeat that discussion here.

Women are dangerous not only because untrustworthy, but because, as we have already seen, they threaten, even unwittingly, the very basis for men's superiority—their *hpoun*. A man's *hpoun*, it will be recalled, can be diminished, if not destroyed, if a woman's head rests on his right shoulder, or if she sleeps, walks, sits, or eats on the right side, or especially if the lower part of her body or her skirt is higher than he. The latter threat, it will be recalled, relates to the dangerous character of the vagina and the womb. This attribute of the female genitalia account for the especially dangerous quality of a post-partum woman. Thus, for the first forty-nine days following the birth of a child, its father does not visit his wife and child without first removing the talisman *(lethpwe)* that all men wear around their necks, for the contamination from the mother would destroy its efficacy and he would thereby lose his *hpoun.*

Women are not only an unwitting source of danger to a man's *hpoun,* without which he can be easily vanquished, but in other ways as well. If, for example, a woman washes her hair while a relative is traveling, he will have an accident. Their "power" can even have an adverse effect on nature. Thus, during the famous pagoda festival in Kyaukse, a normally dry river bed always flows—miraculously!—with sufficient water to meet the needs of the pilgrims and their oxen. If, however, a woman should step across the stream, the water will dry up. Since so much of her power and danger are related to her sexual organs, it is understandable that a pregnant and menstrual (like a post-partum) woman is especially dangerous. Thus, if a pregnant woman should touch medicine, it loses its potency (conversely, she herself is invulnerable to dangerous forces, the poison of a snake, for example); and if she uses a knife to pare her nails, someone might be injured. If a menstrual woman plants a tree, it will not grow. Moreover, it is not only unwittingly that women exercise dangerous and evil power. Although witches are both male and female, the latter are the more prevalent, the more powerful, and hence the more feared.

Although these general remarks on the harmful power of women do not relate directly to their relationship with men, they are nevertheless relevant to the final, and most important, fear which men have of women, namely, their desire to dominate men. It is their power which makes their desire for domination so threatening. If, then, women constitute an *unwitting* threat to men's *hpoun,* they constitute a *witting* threat to (as the men see it) their inherent right of domination. This threat stems from the perception of woman as temptress and as sorceress.

Woman as temptress is a ubiquitous theme among Burmese men. In the last chapter it was observed that men find it difficult to avoid the temptation of an attractive woman. The difficulty is increased by the deliberate attempt of some women at least to attract them. Hence, if men commit adultery or take a lesser wife, the opprobrium, in the first instance, usually falls on the woman, for the man is believed to be a kind of passive agent who has succumbed to the wiles of a seductive woman. The Burmese attitude in this regard is similar to, though not as extreme as, the Greek (the Sarakatsani). For them, "woman has a natural predisposition to [sexual] evil. Her powers of sexual attraction are of a supernatural order. Even unconsciously she may lure a man to disaster without a glance or gesture" (Campbell 1966:156). In the Burmese view, however, women may use their sexual wiles not merely to attract men, but also (and this is much more threatening) to dominate them.

Male fear of domination by women is of course found in many societies. The Burmese fear is little different, for example, from that expressed by the seventeenth-century Spanish priest, Father Joseph Haro, whose views, according to Pitt-Rivers (1966:68), are still expressive of the "traditional way of thinking" in Andalusia. Women, he wrote, "have naturally the ambition to attain command and liberty, and they wish to invert the order of nature, attempting (even though it may involve the greatest cruelties) to dominate men." In traditional Europe, just as in Burma, this fear has led men to view marriage as threatening. The "real trouble with marriage," Hunt (1970:73-74) observes in the case of seventeenth-century France, consisted in the fact that it "subject(ed) men to their wives. . . . It was held that women used craft and deception to gain the upper hand over their husbands while ostensibly they continued to go through all the conventional rituals of submission."

Again, in traditional Europe, just as in Burma, the most cunning craft employed by women for this end is believed to be sexual. In traditional Europe, "it is through their sex [so men believe] that women acquire power over men" (Pitt-Rivers 1966:68), and it is by their sexual "wiles" that women, according to Burmese tradition, attempt to subjugate men. Thus, the *Dhammathat* list forty such "wiles"—a list, it might be noted, which is a relatively small number compared to the sixty-four of which the Sinhalese women are accused.[5] These wiles include the following:

(1) Stretching the body and arms, at sight of a man while standing near him, as a sign, whether pre-concerted or not, that he is thought of favourably by her and with a view of engaging affections; (2) letting something fall as if accidentally, and

5. In general, the similarities between the traditional Burmese and Sinhalese attitudes are remarkable, as the following description indicates: "Generally women [in Ceylon] have always been considered to be inferior to men in all respects and full of wiles and wickedness. No doubt there were exceptions to this, and at times they are depicted as of exemplary character as mothers and wives. . .but in general all were grouped together as a constant source of trouble in this world and as wicked by nature. 'The women deceive the men, therefore they are a delusion. They cannot be relied upon, they are like a mirage. They are a mine of danger, sorrow and illness. They are like snares laid by Māra to capture passionate men, like a cave where dwell she-bears, like a door of the cave of Māra. If a man were to place any confidence in a woman who is such, he is ignoble.' (Sdhlk: 363). They are never satisfied with the number of men they have.. . .Their thirst for sensual pleasure, ornament, and decoration can never be satiated (*ibid*. 437). They are counsellors to birth in purgatory (*ibid*. 764, 40). They are the cause of all ills, and embrace men for their own gains, just as the creepers [use] the trees for their own support (*ibid*. 600). They are always looked upon as full of wiles, *māyam*, which are said to be 64 in number. The *KSil* describes women thus: They are a festival to the five senses, whirlpools in the ocean of life, a tap-root of the creeper of craving, a door open to purgatory (v. 87). It is the universal nature of women, says the *Pjv*, to see the beauty of other women and wish that they were as beautiful; to see the heroic deeds of a man and wish he were her husband; to see the caresses of another's child and wish the child were hers (Pjv 280) (Ariyapala 1956:301-302).

picking it up in such a manner as to show off her figure to the best advantage; (3) exhibiting studied elegance and gracefulness in dress and movements; (4) pretending to be modest by covering the exposed parts of her body, or (5) by leaning against another; (6) trampling one foot by the other; (7) writing on the ground; (8) lifting up another's child or her own, or (9) making others lift him; (10) kissing him, or (11) making others kiss him; (12) playing with him, or (13) making others play with him; (14) embracing him, or (15) making others embrace him; (16) eating anything with him, or (17) making him eat something given by her; (18) giving him something such as flowers, fruits, etc.; (19) asking for the return of the thing given; (20) mimicking the child's movements: (21) speaking in praise or in disparagement of a man; (22) letting a man know her wishes in an overt, or (23) a covert manner, by signs such as dancing, singing, playing on musical instruments, weeping, moving about or dressing; (24) laughing boisterously to convey some secret meaning; (25) ogling at a man; (26) shaking the waist, or (27) some concealed part of the body; (28) exposing the thighs as if by accident; (29) pretending to cover them again; (30) exposing the breasts; (31) the armpit, or (32) the navel; (33) winking; (34) raising the eyebrows; (35) biting the lips; (36) protruding the tongue; (37) allowing her dress to slip off partly as if by accident; (38) re-arranging the dress; (39) loosening hair already tied in a knot, and (40) tying loose hair into a knot. [Maung Maung 1963:11-12]

These wiles, the *Dhammathat* quaintly concludes, "are for all good men to be wary of."

The fear of these wiles is compounded by the fact that in some instances the female who employs them may not be a woman, but a form of spirit known as *ouktazaun*. Indeed, the belief in *ouktazaun*, female spirits who guard buried treasure to be used at the coming of the future Buddha, may be said to represent the quintessence of the dangerous temptress. Lonely for human contacts, an *ouktazaun* may attempt to escape her solitary fate by assuming the guise of a beautiful, human maiden, and enticing a man into falling in love with her. Should he, succumbing to her blandishments, have sexual intercourse with her, he will die, and will then have to join her in guarding the treasure. There are known cases—I myself observed one such case—of men falling in love with *ouktazaun*, and having to be saved from their clutches by the most powerful of exorcistic rites (Spiro 1967:174-194).

If a woman is unsuccessful in dominating a man by means of her wiles, she may then turn to witchcraft, sorcery, or other forms of malevolent magic to accomplish this end. To be sure, not all women are believed willing to employ such evil techniques, but their numbers are sufficiently large that even highly educated men, let alone village farmers, have no doubt about the danger. As one Rangoon lawyer said to me, the data are so compelling that "we have to accept them as facts." A Rangoon businessman, now the head of a large firm in Bangkok, became visibly agitated when I queried him about this matter. "There is no doubt about it," he said, "for the fact is that [Burmese] women can be *very* wicked," though not as wicked as Thai women, who attempt to subjugate not one, but many men.

The magical techniques employed by women to dominate men are many and varied, and most of them are obtained from a male sorcerer (*aulan hsaya*). I shall mention only the most important ones. The sorcerer may give the woman a "medicated" white candle, which she lights and offers to certain evil spirits (*nat*) together with raw beef, liquor, or fried chicken (depending on which spirit she propitiates). Alternatively, the sorcerer provides her with an *in*, a kabbalistic inscription, inscribed with her husband's name, which she wraps in a piece of cloth cut from the skirt she wears during her menstrual period, and places inside the man's pillow. The most powerful techniques consist of love potions. Known as *hsei hkatte*, these potions, also obtained from male sorcerers, are mixed in the man's food. One consists of a concoction of menstrual blood and water which is filtered through a sieve, and the congealed globs of blood are placed in the man's food. Another consists of a bit of betel nut, which the woman places in her vagina—preferably, but not necessarily, during her menstrual period—until it is saturated with vaginal or menstrual secretions, which she then grinds up and offers to the man together with his regular betel. (This potion is known as *taik hlaung kunthi*—the nut that is stored in the brick building.)

The latter techniques are exceedingly powerful, enabling the woman to acquire complete control over a man, "as if he had been drugged." Hence, he is known as "the man living under the influence of 'medicine' " (*yaukkya hseinu neide*). Skeptical Burmese women in Bangkok told me that while living in Rangoon, they had believed that these potions were confined to the villages, and especially the Shan states. After arriving in Bangkok, and observing many high-status men (though married to beautiful wives) taking up with unattractive, lower-class Thai women, they themselves began to believe in the reality of the potions—how else could one account for this anomaly? (One woman, however, reported that a "study" of these cases had revealed that the success of the Thai women was not due to these potions, but to "the arts of love.")

These, then, are some of the fears and anxieties which men entertain toward women. When we add the sexual fears and anxieties which were discussed in the previous chapter, it is obvious that the ideology of male superiority is only one among a complex of attitudes that males hold concerning women. Indeed, given these fears and anxieties, it would be more accurate to state that the attitude of Burmese men toward women is one of ambivalence and conflict. On the one hand, men are attracted by women as sexual objects; on the other hand, they view women's sexuality as a threat and a snare. On the one hand, they view themselves as innately superior to women; on the other, they permit women to enjoy almost complete social and legal equality and, in some respects, economic superiority. On the one hand, as we shall see, men are dependent upon women, permitting their wives to assume the dominant role in the management of the family affairs; on the other, they not only view women as stupid and untrustworthy, but they fear their domination.

Many of these themes emerge from the projective tests which provide independent confirmation for some of these conclusions. In his analysis of the Rorschach protocols, Steele (n.d.) observes that the men are "especially anxious" about mothers or females, and that this anxiety is "free-floating," or "not subject to analysis" by the subject. In his TAT analysis, Steele (n.d.) observes that men and women alike tell stories in which the men have little control over women, unless the relationship is between father and daughter, "and even here the control is tenuous;" that women "appear more self-confident than men;" and that their greater self-confidence seems to be related to a "seductive sexual manipulation of the men and [to the women's] capacity to leave the relationship without facing effective reprisals or sanctions."

The men's ambivalence toward women—they view them as nurturant and desirable, but also as a danger and a threat; they want to be loved and cared for by them, but they fear them—is expressed at the cultural level, as Gorer has brilliantly observed, in the ogre-princess theme of the Burmese drama. Sometimes, the cannibalistic ogress turns into a kindly and self-sacrificing woman, who, instead of devouring her prey, falls in love with him, and sometimes a woman is mistaken for an ogress and (unjustly) put to death. "An analysis of these plays shows, I think convincingly, that . . . the ogress is one aspect of the princess, the princess a disguise of the ogress" (Gorer 1943:45). And this is more than a dramatic convention. Off the stage it is not uncommon for a young man to say of a girl, "She is beautiful, but I don't dare go near her, she's an ogress."

Whenever we find such a curious mixture of conflicting emotional elements, we can be sure that we are witness to a complex set of psychodynamic forces.[6] In this case, I would argue that the internalization

6. Although I am not concerned here with the ontogenesis of this conflict, it might be observed that it begins rather early. Burmese children, as we have already seen, are deeply attached to their mothers, the most important—and the dominant—figure of their lives. And, then, with the beginning of school, there comes a "twist," as Gorer calls it, in the boy's life. Having grown up at home "under petticoat government," he is taught in a monastery school that "men really are more important, that a woman is an inferior being, that spiritual perfection can only be achieved by a male" (Gorer 1943:31). Gorer, incidentally, sees this as a nuclear experience for the Burmese male, one "which makes Burmese character so paradoxical and Burmese behavior so unpredictable" (ibid.)

of the cultural belief in the superiority of the male constitutes a defense whose function is to protect the men against their fear of the women's threat to their dominance. But this is a fragile defense because, as we have seen, men not only fear being ensnared by women, but they also fear that their *hpoun* is jeopardized by the very presence of women. However these conflicting elements be interpreted, it is against this background that we can better understand the relationship between the spouses, the focal concern of this chapter.

Cultural Norms Concerning the Ideal Spouse

Since males are superior to females, it is proper, according to Burmese cultural norms, that the husband should be dominant over the wife. Although the rationale may differ, male dominance in marriage is the prevalent ideology in most peasant societies (Michaelson and Goldschmidt 1971). The Burmese ideology is rather moderate compared, for example, to India or China. Although the Burmese husband may be known as "the lord who lives in the head of the house" *(qein qu nat)*, he is neither revered as a god, nor is he worshipped by his wife, as is the case in India.

The wife's duties to the husband, as described in one *Dhammathat*, a compendium of Burmese customary law, include the following: "Rising from bed before the husband rises; retiring to bed after he has done so; taking his instructions for her day's work; carrying out his behests according to his wishes; speaking to him in a pleasant and affectionate way; and providing against the inclemencies of the weather for the husband's comfort" (quoted from the Manugye *Dhammathat*, in Maung Maung 1963:50).

The husband also has duties or (as they are called) "good qualities." As described in the Kaingza *Dhammathat*, they include: "Striving to acquire wealth; providing the wife with a good house; maintaining the wife, children, and slaves with tender watchfulness; looking after the cattle with care; supporting those of the relatives who are poor" (quoted in *Ibid*:51). It goes on to say that if the wife does not respect a husband who shows these qualities, she shall be "criminally punished," and that if he does not show these qualities she may "abuse him with impunity" *(ibid.)*.

These traditional duties of the husband are still taught in the schools —they are known as the *lin wut ngaba*—and mothers transmit them to their daughters as their expected rights when entering marriage.

In addition to enumerating the virtues of both spouses, the *Dhammathat* also enumerate the vices of the wife—but not, significantly, of the husband. Thus, there are five "improprieties" of which a wife may be guilty, and for which she may be "gently chastized" with a beating

(Maung Maung 1963:13). Although Maung Maung, a jurist, claims that both the improprieties and the punishment "have become obsolete," he may be right so far as the law is concerned, but in fact both are still practiced, at least in the villages. What, then, are the "improprieties" of the wife?

With regard to food, when she takes her meals before her husband does so; or when she indulges often in her husband's absence in eating rich food; or when she gets up late in the morning and the first thing she does is eat; or when she eats stealthily the greater portion of any food obtained and leaves only a little of it for her husband; with regard to behavior toward men, when her conduct toward all men she comes across is as free as toward her husband; with regard to dress if she puts on inappropriate dresses when she attends feasts, or stays at home, or goes on a journey, or attends to her duties as a wife and as a mother; with regard to looking when she looks at a man with eyes as restless as those of a crow; or when she is in the habit of looking at men when they are dressing or undressing, or when they are bathing [Maung Maung 1963:12-13].

Forschammer, quoting another (King Wagaru's) *Dhammathat*, refers to six kinds of "evil practices" in wives: drinking intoxicating liquor, "gadding about" the entrance to the house, habitual visiting of others, causing her husband to become angry, neglecting her domestic duties, having a lover (Forschammer 1885:6). These, too, are still taught by mothers to daughters.

It should be obvious by now that most of the attributes of the ideal wife reflect the ideology of male superiority, as well as the male anxieties concerning women described in the last section. If wives behaved in the manner prescribed in the *Dhammathat*, husbands would be the dominant spouse, wives would serve them submissively, and the men's anxieties concerning the dangers posed by women would remain latent at most.

This conclusion holds as well for the attributes of the ideal spouse found in contemporary village Burma. Indeed, the similarities between the two formulations, the traditional and the contemporary, constitute an impressive index of the conservatism of Burmese culture with respect to the domestic domain. Let us see.

As part of a larger study of family relations, twenty-one married villagers (eleven males and ten females) were asked to describe the qualities which constitute a "good husband" and a "good wife," and to specify their duties to each other. Since males and females gave almost identical responses, and since there was almost complete overlap between the "qualities" of a good spouse and his "duties," both results can be summarized in one table (Table 18). The items included in the table comprise the most frequent responses; those occurring only two or three times were not included.

Although Table 18 speaks for itself, it may be well to clarify certain potential problems. It will be noticed, first, that villagers list sexual

TABLE 18. *Typical Characteristics and Duties of the Ideal Village Spouse*
    (N = 21)

Ideal Husband (including husband's duties to wife)	Ideal Wife (including wife's duties to husband)
1. good provider	1. efficient performance of domestic duties, especially cooking, cleaning house, washing clothes
2. hard and dedicated worker	
3. leads a "simple life" — refrains from drinking, gambling, womanizing, squandering of savings	2. industrious, not given to idleness
	3. remains at home; does not "roam about" the village
	4. goodnatured, unquarrelsome
4. goodnatured, easy tempered	5. efficient manager of family finances
5. worldly wise	6. concerned with pleasing husband; respects and obeys him
6. does not physically mistreat wife	7. sexual fidelity

fidelity as an attribute of the ideal wife, but not of the ideal husband. The
reason for this disparity is that periodic sexual lapses on the part of the
male are, as we have seen, neither unexpected nor threatening to the wife
unless they involve the squandering of family savings, whereas any sexual
lapse on the wife's part is not only a most serious moral breach, but is
highly threatening to her husband. This is why a good wife, as the table
indicates, does not "roam about" the village: roaming can lead to all kinds
of troubles—spreading of gossip, quarrels, not attending to household
chores—but above all to sexual infidelity.

Unlike infidelity, hard and efficient labor is listed as an important
attribute, perhaps the most important, of both spouses. The ideal spouse
works hard and saves the meager family income—so as to maintain its
standard of living, keep it solvent, and accumulate savings for meritorious
Buddhist ceremonies. There is one important difference, however, between the expectations of the husband and those of the wife. The wife is
concerned that the husband not only work hard, but that he refrain from
squandering his earnings (and his wife's) on wine, women, and gambling,
a concern which she shares with her Thai cousin.[7] The ideal wife, on the
other hand, is not only a hard worker, but her work is expected to serve

7. "For the Thai woman," writes Piker (n.d., ch. 2:48), "the reliability of the husband as a
provider is a paramount concern. In practice, it is the worry that he won't be—that he either
won't work well or, what is feared even more, that he will squander family resources by
profligacy—that carried most saliency, and constitutes one of the major sources of anxiety
concerning anticipated marriage on the part of the young women."

her husband and to satisfy *his* needs. Over and over again it was urged that the husband's welfare be the wife's main concern. In stressing this theme, villagers employed the same expression that is used in the *Dhammathat:* the ideal wife arises before her husband and retires only after he has gone to bed. What is particularly singled out, however, is her role as provider of food. The wife should have her husband's meals prepared whenever he arises and as soon as he returns from work. It is expected that he receive the first and the best portion of whatever food is in the pot. Even if he is not at home when the meal is served, the first portion must be set aside for him for his return.

This stress on the wife's nurturance is especially relevant to certain of the men's anxieties concerning women, and it is consistent with the generally symbolic importance of food in Burmese marriage. Commensality, it will be recalled, is the basic symbol of marriage; in the absence of a wedding, the sharing of a common hearth is ipso facto the evidence for a common-law marriage. A man who wishes to get married is said to "hunger for a wife," and even the man who pursues extramarital adventures is known as "one who chases and eats" women. Food, then, is a pivotal symbol in Burma, as it is elsewhere,[8] in the system of reciprocity that obtains between the spouses—the husband provides it, the wife cooks it. It is hardly accidental, then, that in serious marital quarrels, a wife's punitive response is to stop cooking for/or eating with her husband, and that, as a sign of reconciliation, she invites him to join her in a meal. But, if Gorer's (1943:28) speculation (based on the ogre-princess theme in Burmese drama) that "the dominating fear of the Burmese [men] is that the kind and desirable woman will suddenly turn into a cannibalistic ogress" is correct, it might then be suggested that the emphasis on the wife as provider of cooked food, and on the shared hearth as the symbol of marriage, has an even "deeper" meaning. In such a context this emphasis might serve as a persistent defense against this fearful fantasy, a defense in which the frightening "cannibalistic ogress" of fantasy is turned into the "kind and desirable woman" of reality: instead of being an eater of men, the woman becomes a nurturant feeder of men.

The ideal wife not only serves her husband, but (to return to Table 18) she also respects and obeys him. The asymmetry of this norm—wives are expected to obey husbands, but not the reverse—is defended on the

8. In Ceylon (Kandy), for example, "the provision and cooking of food [are] at the top of the list of reciprocal obligations. As far as the Kandyans are concerned, food is the most fundamental element in the relations between husbands and wives." Moreover, "cooking for a man and eating the food he has provided in the same household signifies the marital relationship" (Yalman 1967:108).

grounds of male superiority. In view of this superiority, it is only proper (according to husbands and wives alike) that the husband should be the dominant, and the wife the submissive, partner. As the *Kaingza Dhammathat* puts it: "The husband is the lord and master of his wife even though she be the daughter of a king. The man who is governed by his wife is sure to be ruined" (Gaung 1905:64). Indeed, the men believe this so strongly that they (but not the women!) believe that wife-beating is justified if the wife violates this expectation. If, then, as Table 18 indicates, a characteristic of the ideal husband (but not of the ideal wife) is that he does not beat his spouse, it is precisely because many husbands sanction, and some practice, wife-beating as a means of keeping their wives submissive and under their control. In this they are in agreement with the *Dhammathat* which, it will be recalled, specify beating as an appropriate punishment for five "improprieties" of the wife.

In view of the men's ambivalence toward women, and their distrust of them, it is little wonder that husbands are concerned about their ability to control their wives, so that respect and obedience are held to be important attributes of the ideal wife. Indeed, although the wives in the sample also agree that they should respect and obey their husbands, it seems not altogether wrong to suggest that the males' conception of the ideal wife—submissive, obedient, respectful, self-sacrificing, and so on —reflects their anxiety about women in general and their ability to control their wives in particular. Their need to be dominant is sufficiently strong that some urban men, for example, prefer to marry village girls on the grounds that such marriages will guarantee their dominance. University coeds report that male students often say to them, "You can be proud now, but after marriage, you will work for me. After I get you, I will dominate you." Although many men refuse to beat their wives in order to attain this end, even they say that the husband should not show her too much affection. They are supported in this belief by two well-known proverbs:

> Don't show affection to your wife, lest she take
> advantage of you.

> A woman is like an ox; one should not display
> affection to either of them.

Dominance and Reciprocity in the Husband-Wife Relationship
Dominance

The *formal* relationship between husband and wife exhibits all the patterns of deference and respect required by the cultural norm of male dominance. In the house, it is the husband who sits on the auspicious side of the room; in public, it is the wife who carries the packages or bundles when she and her husband are traveling together; and anywhere the wife works hard for her husband, prepares his food on time, satisfies his requests, and obeys his orders. A wife, moreover, will never shout at her husband, nor will she ever contradict him in public.[9] The husband, in short, seems clearly to be the dominant spouse.

It is a truism, however, that formal dominance, manifested essentially in ritualized expressions of deference, is not in itself a measure of actual dominance. Sometimes, as the following case reveals, there may be a discrepancy between them. Ma Nain is probably the most articulate woman in the village, and one of the few who, in the course of numerous interviews, consistently expressed independent and autonomous judgments. Hence, it came as no surprise to discover that this young woman exercises the greatest control over her husband. Although, to take (what is in Burmese terms) the most extreme example, she has been involved in a number of extramarital affairs, her husband has always turned the other way (and the other cheek). Nevertheless, and despite the fact that all the villagers agree that she is the dominant partner in her marriage, were a stranger to observe her public behavior, he could only conclude that she was, instead, the submissive partner. When guests visit their home or when Ma Nain and her husband visit outside of their home, she rarely speaks, unless she is spoken to directly, whereas her husband often speaks and offers his opinion. Moreover, he tells her—the contrary never happens—to fetch his glasses, prepare tea for the guests, bring him his tobacco, and so on; and invariably she obeys with a quiet smile and with the usual signs of respect and deference. To cap it all, it was Ma Nain who, as reported above, became angry at my suggestion that she, surely, did not believe in the superiority of male dogs to human females.

Albeit an extreme case, Ma Nain's is by no means an isolated one, either in contemporary or historical Burma. Western observers, both early and late, have frequently commented on the dominance of the wife in Burmese marriage. Forbes (1878:56), for example, states that "the women rule the roost," and Fielding Hall (1913:239), well known for his sentimentalized portrayal of the Burmese, characterizes the wife as "the

9. These, of course, are typical Asian patterns. In Ceylon (Low Country) for example: "It is the wife who follows, on the lane and in eating. She will never sit in the presence of her husband and his friends. He sleeps on a bed, she on the mat. She gives him obeisance which he accepts as a due. Her manner and voice tone is submissive (except in quarrels). The symbolism of the association, and the apparent content, is indistinguishable from that of a master-servant relationship." (Ryan 1953:158.)

predominant partner."[10] More recently, Nash (1965:253-54), based on his anthropological study in Upper Burma, writes: "In theory and in public the husband is supposedly dominant, but this dominance is so tenuous, so indefinite, and ambiguous that its social visibility is virtually nil." Finally, in my own observation of Yeigyi families for over a year, it was my impression that wives are the dominant partners in many, perhaps the majority, of the marriages that I know best.

All of these impressions, of course, are subject to judgmental error, and as a check on my own errors, three "objective" techniques were employed. First, the self-judgments of twenty-two (randomly selected) couples concerning dominance in their own marriage was compared with that in other marriages. With respect to their own marriage, both spouses almost invariably—twenty out of twenty-two—named the husband as the dominant one. But when these same respondents were asked to identify the dominant spouse in other marriages, they most frequently—sixteen of the twenty-two—named the wife. It is probably fair to conclude that their self-judgments reflect the cultural ideology of male superiority and the cultural norm of husband dominance, while their judgments of others more accurately reflect the actual relationship.

Still, this technique has obvious flaws which I hoped to overcome by a second technique. I selected a panel of four men—women were deliberately excluded—who were known to me as very knowledgable about village and especially domestic affairs (the headman, two village elders, and the local native doctor), and asked them to jointly conduct a case-by-case examination of thirty-nine marriages. They concluded that the husband is the dominant spouse in seventeen marriages, the wife in sixteen, and six are ambiguous.

As a check on these findings for Yeigyi, interviews were conducted with elders of two other villages. In both it was stated flatly that the wife is the dominant partner in a "majority" of marriages.

These three techniques, of course, have flaws, but given that the findings of all three are consistent with each other as well as with my own

10. A British civil servant, and a sincere believer in the White Man's Burden, Fielding Hall, advocated the end of female dominance in the aid of Burmese progress and modernization. His comments on the status of Burmese women (1913:239-240), quaint to modern ears, and quintessentially Victorian, are yet not entirely devoid of worth. "It is inevitable that she [the Burmese woman] should retire.. . .She attracts by her freedom, her industry, her independence. So all men praise her. They take her for the strength of the nation. Yet she is perhaps a symptom and a cause of its weakness.. . .Woman's influence is good provided it does not go too far. Yet it has done so here.. . .Therefore the peculiar charm that all travelers see in the women of Burma is bound to fade. They have had their day. They have contributed to make the nation what it is, gay, insouciant, feminine. They have brought

judgments, it is probably safe to conclude that there is a marked discrepancy between the cultural norm of the husband dominance, on the one hand, and the actual dominance structure in marriage, on the other.

"Dominance," of course, is an ambiguous word, and in this context it may also be misleading. It is most often used with the meaning of overt command and submission, as in a master-slave, parent-child, or employer-employee relationship. According to this meaning, the husband is the dominant partner in Burmese marriage. But "dominance" is used in yet another manner to refer to control, to the ability of ego to influence alter in such a manner that ego's, rather than alter's, will is carried out. Often, of course, both aspects of dominance are exercised by one and the same person in a dyad, but sometimes they are separate, so that the ostensibly superordinate person is in fact subject to the will, and hence under the control, of the other. It is in the control sense of dominance that it can be said that the wife is dominant in a majority of Burmese marriages. Her control may be expressed in the kinds of clothes the husband wears, the type of food he eats, the friends he brings to the house, where and how often he spends his time away from the house, and so on, not to mention his bending to the wife's will with respect to her own desires. Her control in such matters may be achieved because of the passive role of the husband (a function of male dependency to be discussed below), her own active role (including nagging, complaining, and the refusal of sex), and the husband's anxiety concerning her possible use of magical power.

There is still another matter, however, in which the wife is dominant, and there is reason to believe that the three techniques employed to measure dominance underestimated the proportion of wife-dominant marriages because this measure was ignored by the respondents. Thus, a pattern in which the wife literally holds the purse-strings—in which the husband turns his earnings over to the wife, and must even ask her for spending money, which she may or may not give him—would probably be viewed by most students of family life as an important measure of wife dominance; and in village Burma, as almost everywhere else in Southeast Asia, the above pattern is almost universal.[11] Typically, it is found in urban households as well. Nevertheless, no one in our various samples took this as a measure of "dominance." For them, it is only natural that, as

religion to the pitch it reached. But the world is a man's world, and now that Burma has come out of the nursery it must learn to be a man.. . .Burma has been the converse of India in this matter. In India all women except the very poorest are idle, dependent, secluded. In Burma all are active, independent, open. They are the two extremes, and both are bad."

11. This pattern is pronounced, for example, in Muslim Java (Geertz 1961:123), Buddhist Thailand (Mentzer 1972:96), and Cambodia (Steinberg 1959:79).

the proverb has it, "[the husband's responsibility is to ensure that] water flows, [the wife's responsiblity is like an] earth bank [to] contain it" (*side yei/hsede gazin*). Surely, however, the scientist must exercise some independent judgment in these matters, and if he decides—as I do—that such control is an important measure of dominance, then the proportion of wife-dominant marriages is obviously much higher than villagers are prepared to recognize.

There is, of course, an important methodological issue involved here, the issue of (what has come to be called) emic versus etic definitions. In this case the fallacies entailed in accepting an emic definition of domestic dominance are obvious. First, it would preclude the possiblity of establishing any cross-cultural (or cross-species) definition of "dominance," for if control over consumption is not a measure of dominance, what other measures could possibly be agreed upon? Second, it would ignore the obvious fact that in a society, such as Burma, whose ideology stresses male dominance, any seeming contradiction to this ideology must be ignored, or rejected as a means of reducing dissonance. Third, it would place the student of Burma in the theoretically absurd position of classifying as "wife-dominant" only those marriages characterized by husband-beating (one hears of isolated cases), flagrant infidelity (here too there are isolated cases), or persistent assaults on the husband's esteem, for these alone are the marriages which all Burmese agree are *mayaga nainde*, wife-dominated. This is the term which everyone uses to refer to the marriage, for example, of Maung Kyi Yin. And how could it be denied? His parents opposed his wife and yet he married her. She insults them by speaking in vulgar and obscene language, and—what is worse—by rubbing her vagina in their presence (an egregious insult), while taunting them with their inability to move their son to divorce her. Although a typical husband would have divorced her for such outrageous behavior, Maung Kyi Yin will not leave his wife. This is real wife-dominance, caused (so the villagers say) by his wife's use of a love potion. Since a commitment to emic definitions would constrain us to identify as "wife-dominated" only such *mayaga nainde* marriages, such a definition would obviously be methodologically absurd.

Although different scholars may adopt different methodological stances in regard to this question, the facts of the case are clear. The husband may be the object of deference and respect, he may walk in front of his wife and sit in front of her in religious ceremonies, he may speak in the highest councils of village government while she merely listens (or, more frequently, remains at home), he may even beat her (one-third of the men in our sample reported having beaten their wives at least once), but it is the wife who assumes the responsibility for maintaining the family and retains control over its financial affairs. This may explain, in part, why many commentators on Burmese women have noted (in the words of one of them) "a sense of responsiblity and something of the hardness which we are accustomed to look for in men" (G. Brown 1925:34).

To be sure, the willingness to accept responsibility is a double-edged sword, and it need not necessarily be taken as a measure of dominance. The Burmese, agreeing that in domestic matters the wife is much more responsible than the husband, and conceding that to that extent she is dominant in the family, nevertheless contend that such dominance is of little significance because it pertains to "worldly" matters (*loki*) only, while in the things that really count—that is, in spiritual matters (*lokouttara*)—it is the husband who is dominant. Indeed, the women themselves view their extra responsibility as extra drudgery—it must be remembered that women not only run the household, but they are also active in some of the back-breaking chores of the agricultural economy, such as transplanting and harvesting—and one of the reasons they wish to be reborn male is to escape the extra burdens of the female role.

But these considerations are not entirely relevant to the problem under consideration. However unimportant the wife may be in "spiritual" matters, her holding of the purse strings is a measure both of her control of her husband and of his dependency on the wife. In assuming responsibility for the financial welfare of the family, the wife controls her husband within the family. Outside the family, in the domains of symbolic power, such as religion and village politics, the men control the women, for it is they who manipulate the symbols and control the tokens of power. But in the domain of real power, in the family and household, the men are manipulated and controlled by women (after marriage, by their wives and, before marriage, by their mothers).

The obverse of the wife's control of the husband is the husband's dependence on the wife. If, for example, the wife controls the family finances, it is because the husband, as Table 18 indicates, wants her to do so; he wants a wife whom he can depend upon to assume this responsibility. And in assuming it, the wife is consciously aware of her control and of his dependency. Thus, the very women who refused to view their financial control as an index of dominance explained that men are economically irresponsible—something like children—who, were it not for the restraining influence of their wives, would squander the family income on women, gambling, drink, and other such pleasures. As they see it, therefore, it is necessary for the wife to control the purse strings. Some go even further and say they accept this responsibility out of compassion for their husbands. If, they say, the wife permitted her husband to squander his money, he would have to work all the harder to support his family, and the wife wishes to spare him this added burden. It is hardly necessary to comment on either the condecension inherent in these statements or on the perception of the husband's dependency implicit in them, both of which, it might be added, are found throughout Southeast Asia.[12]

This dominance-dependency pattern is not restricted to village marriages. Some, but not all, urban informants agree that it is the typical pattern in city marriages as well. Those urban informants who disagree with the notion that the wife is the dominant partner agree that although the wife holds the purse strings, it is the husband who makes the major decisions in the marriage. Nevertheless, even they—and these are female informants—observe that the wife subtly structures the context of decision making so that the husband makes the decision she wants him to make, while yet permitting him to believe that the decision is really his.

The latter qualification is extremely important, for the husband, whether rural or urban, is content to remain dependent on his wife so long as the facade of male dominance is retained. The shrew is not only a source of humiliation for her husband, but she, in turn, is an object of social censure, and the wife is careful that her dominance remain subtle. In some cases, of course, this is not necessary. Some husbands are personally weak, and even put up with wives who beat them. Others, urban husbands who are "bought" with high dowries, are structurally weak, and submit even to humiliating wives. Typically, however, the husband will not put up with a wife who, even in subtler ways, threatens his claim to dominance. Thus, a friend in Mandalay divorced his wife simply because she was making more money than he, and refused to comply with his request that she give up her business. He divorced her, he said, on two accounts. First, it is offensive to a man's dignity that a wife should make more money than her husband. Second, the husband "must be the master, and obeyed at all times." His wife's superior income challenged his superiority, and her refusal to retire threatened his right of dominance.

Short of such blatant expressions of dominance, however, the husband is quite content that he be controlled by his wife so long as his own dependency needs can thereby be satisfied. Indeed, to the extent that casual relationships can ever be discovered in such matters, it is not unlikely that the dominance of the wife is explicable in terms of the males'

12. In Java, for example, men themselves "express the belief that they are incapable of handling money carefully, whereas women are supposed to have thrift and foresight" (Geertz 1961:123), and the attitude of the Javanese woman to her putatively financially incompetent and irresponsible husband is, if anything, even more condescending than that of the Burmese. (Jay 1969:92).

anxiety concerning, and their emotional dependence upon, women. Having already discussed the former dimension, I might say a few words about the latter.

As the more sophisticated urban women see it, the husband expects the wife to be the synthetic embodiment of mother, sister, and friend. As friend, she is the one from whom he seeks advice concerning daily problems. As sister, she is expected to be submissive and to execute his will. As mother, she is expected to be nurturant, thus permitting him to be dependent. The wife, as mother symbol, is not of course a uniquely Burmese phenomenon. According to psychoanalytic theory, at least, many of the attitudes of the husband to the wife—indeed, the very choice of a wife—may be modeled after the relationship of the son to the mother. The latter relationship is often paradigmatic for his relationship with his wife, and is the basis for the (unconscious) symbolic equation, wife=mother. Not surprisingly, the dependency element in this equation is almost everywhere an important one, and this is no less true in Burma.

As we have seen in a previous chapter, daughters usually become the favorites of their fathers after early childhood; sons of their mothers. The son is pampered and "spoiled" not only by his mother, but by other female kinsmen—elder sisters, grandmothers, parents' sisters, and so on. Hence, his attachment to the mother and mother surrogates, and his dependency on them, is often very strong, and it is not unusual for a boy to go into a tantrum of frustration and rage when they disappear. As they become teenagers, the relationship between parents and children is reversed: the girl becomes closer to the mother, the boy to the father. But the father-son (unlike the mother-daughter) relationship is not an intimate one, and it does not begin to satisfy the strong dependency needs which had been both acquired and satisfied in the boy's relationship with his mother (and mother surrogates). It is understandable, then, that the husband—as the above-mentioned informants stressed—attempts to satisfy his frustrated dependency needs in his marriage, that in his relationship with his wife, he seeks to recapitulate his early relationship with his mother. What, on one level, then, is seen as the husband's domination *by* the wife, may be seen, on another level, as his dependency *on* the wife. And it is on this level, I would suggest, that the previously noted importance of commensality as the symbol of marriage and of the wife as the symbol of nourishment takes on additional meaning. To nourish is to nurture, and it is the nurturant person who satisfies the need for dependency.

It should be remarked in conclusion that the pattern we have been delineating in this discussion—formal deference of the wife to the husband (based on an ideology of male superiority) combined with the husband's control by and dependence on the wife—is hardly unique to Burma. The same inconsistency between ideology and practice, between culture and social structure, is widespread in Southeast Asia, and elsewhere. To take but one example, in Java, whose Islamic religion supports an extreme patriarchal ideology, it is the wife again who is the dominant spouse. As Geertz (1961:46) points out: "The wife makes most of the decisions; she controls all the family finances, and although she gives her husband formal deference and consults with him on major matters, it is usually she who is dominant. Strong-willed men may have a relationship of equal partnership with their wives, but families actually dominated by the man are exceedingly rare." Jay, likewise, paints a picture of dominant wives (1969:124) and of "henpecked" husbands (ibid., 87) in Java.

It is perhaps worthwhile to remark in passing that in this regard, Southeast Asia offers a dramatic contrast to South and East Asia. Whereas in Southeast Asia, the ideology of male superiority, in Buddhist and Muslim cultures alike, marks a strong contrast with the actuality of wife dominance, in South and East Asia this ideology, which is found in Buddhist Ceylon, Hindu India, and Confucianist China, is consistent with the actuality of husband dominance. (See Ryan [1953:157-158] for Ceylon, Mandelbaum [1970:74-79, 85-87] for India, Hsu [1971:ch. 4; and Yang 1969:ch. 2-4] for China.) The differences in the actual position of the wife between these culture areas is consistent with another structural difference between them. Thus, when (despite their neo-local preference) joint families are formed in Southeast Asia, they consist predominantly of parents and married daughters. In South Asia and China, on the other hand, they consist of parents and married sons.

Suppressed as wife, the South Asian woman emerges triumphant, however, in other roles. Nowhere in Southeast Asia is the mother elevated, as she is in India and Ceylon, "to a realm of near-worship by beholden and adoring males'. (Ryan: ibid.), let alone to the realm of actual divinity, which she attains in the famous mother goddesses of India, and to a lesser extent, of Ceylon (Obeyesekere n.d., ch. 4). In this regard, China, despite the late transformation of Kwanyin into a female deity, is more like Southeast Asia (and, for that matter, the Middle East).

Although, to return to Burma, the exploration of the contradictions and inconsistencies, between the cultural and structural dimensions of the relationship between the sexes would be a fascinating subject in itself, it would take us too far afield. It need only be observed that, psychodynamically viewed, the Oedipal situation described in Chapter Five, the sexual picture portrayed in Chapter Eight, and the seemingly paradoxical pattern of wife dominance delineated here, are threads woven from the same social fabric.

Reciprocity

In general, it is probably safe to say that spouses are close to, but not intimate with, each other, a conclusion which emerges from both behavioral observation and personal interviews. Husbands and wives alike say that they almost never turn to each other for consolation or assistance in times of emotional difficulty or stress. (But, then, they also point out that they seldom turn to anyone else either.) Nor do they usually discuss their intimate thoughts and desires with their spouses. (But again, they point out that they rarely discuss them with anyone else.) In short, it is fair to say that the spouse is only slightly more important in the villager's emotional life than are other persons. To be sure, spouses are much more intimate in village Burma than in many parts of Asia—such as in India (Roy:1972) or China (Yang: ch.6), where the affectionate needs of the wife are painfully frustrated by their emotionally indifferent and unaffectionate husbands, or in Java, where the relationship between the spouses is "shallow" and "fragile" (Jay 1969:127).

In Burma, unlike these other societies, such sentiments as love and affection are certainly found in the marital relationship. Indeed, Burmese, like English, has many, if ambiguous, terms to designate these emotions, and different villagers (referring to them variously by such Burmese and Pali terms as *myitta, tanha, thamudaya, thanazaya,* and *thanyozin*) designate these sentimental ties as the bases for their continuing marriage. Some of these terms are more expressive of sexual and romantic attachments, while others connote attachments of sympathy, affection, and common ties. In short, although love and affection often comprise important emotional components of the marriage relationship, they are not often manifested in psychological intimacy or the sharing of emotional burdens, anymore than they are in most societies of the world outside the modern West.

Absent, too, from the typical Burmese village marriage is a great deal of reciprocity—not, however, because of the character of the marital bond, but because the sexual division of labor is much less rigid than in many other peasant societies. Thus, except for ploughing and harvesting, women may participate in almost every aspect of the village agricultural economy, and, conversely, men may participate without any cultural impediments in such domestic chores as cooking or laundering.

Because of this fluidity in the division of labor, there is more sharing than reciprocity in village marriage. When queried about their shared activities, almost all spouses single out two activities for special mention: work in the paddy fields and orchards, and pagoda worship and pilgrimage. Obviously, they do many other things together as well, but these are the two activities which (from their point of view) uniquely characterize the activities of spouses. Work is not only a shared economic activity of the spouses, it is also the occasion for conversation between them. Their conversations, however, are restricted in scope, relating primarily to financial and economic matters; apart from these, most spouses say, they have little to talk about to each other. It is not surprising, then, that the husbands in our sample (and many of the wives) said they prefer to spend their leisure time conversing with (same-sex) friends rather than remaining at home with their spouse.

In short, except for those couples in the West who have been influenced by the ideology of the "companionate marriage," the quality of marriage in village Burma, so far as intimacy and sharing are concerned, is pretty much as it is in most other parts of the world.[13] Since, unlike some modern Americans, the Burmese do not expect that this one institution will satisfy all their needs, they are perfectly content with their marriage system as it is. Marriage for them remains a most important institution, and divorce is relatively infrequent. Despite its infrequency, we must nevertheless examine Burmese divorce, not only because of its intrinsic interest, but for the light it may shed on the sources of strain and tension in marriage.

Tension and Divorce

Unlike the situation in traditional India and China, where divorce is all but impossible for the wife, in Burma (as elsewhere in Southeast Asia) divorce is rather easy to achieve by either spouse. As I have already indicated, this is another measure of the legal equality of Burmese women. In India, women were not granted the right of divorce until 1955, and even then the stigma is so great that few take advantage of the new law (Kapadia 1966:183ff). In China, too, there were no grounds on which a woman could obtain a divorce until 1930, and again few women take advantage of the new law. Arab countries are even more conservative, for to this day Muslim women do not have the right to initiate a divorce (Patai 1971:105-107). Their husbands, on the other hand, may obtain a divorce simply by reciting, "I divorce you," three times in the presence of two witnesses.

In Burma, either spouse can initiate a divorce on the following grounds: desertion (one year in the case of the wife, three in the case of a husband),

---

13. Compare, for example, the following description of the Sinhalese (Kandyan) marriage (Yalman 1967:108): "These various obligations aside, husband and wife have little to do with each other. They sleep separately; they eat separately; they work separately; and when they have time to spare, they associate with persons of their own sex. It is unbecoming for a man to be seen in the company of women too frequently. Their lives are separate and tend to converge in formalized channels."

cruelty (both physical and mental), and adultery. Whether these conditions rarely obtain, or whether there are other reasons, our data indicate a
low incidence of divorce for village Burma.[14] Thus, a survey of six villages
revealed ten cases of divorce in one, five cases in two, two cases in one,
and no cases in one. The infrequency of divorce in Upper Burma is
replicated in Lower Burma, where Pfanner (1962:136) reports that for the
village of Mayin only 2 percent of the females (fourteen years or older) and
none of the males were divorced or separated. This relative stability of
village marriage,[15] which according to urban informants is found in the
cities as well, contrasts sharply with the marital instability found in other
Southeast Asian societies, where the divorce rates range from high to very
high. Thus, in Java, nearly half of all marriages end in divorce (Geertz
1961:69). In Malaya, the divorce rate is equally high—30 to 50 percent in
the Kelantan (Nash n.d:36), and 50 percent in Jelebu (Swift 1965:119).
For Central Thailand the data are contradictory, but in general, the rate is
high. Whereas Piker (personal communication) reports a "very low divorce rate" for the villages he surveyed, Phillips (1965:26) reports that 20
percent of the marriages he studied had dissolved within a four-month
period, and Mentzer (1972:77) writes that 25 percent of known marriages
in his village ended in divorce. In South Asia, the divorce rate approaches
the Burmese. In Ceylon (Kandy), for example, it is only 10 percent
(Yalman 1967:186).

The stability of Burmese marriage does not mean that couples are
always happy or that they do not have quarrels. On the contrary, quarrels
occur not infrequently, and sometimes with marked intensity. In Yeigyi,
for example, the frequency of self-reported "serious" quarrels ranges (in
our sample) from once a day to once or twice a year, the mean being once
a month. By a "serious" quarrel, I mean one in which one or both of the
spouses manifests one or more of the following attendant consequences:
social withdrawal for as many as four or five days, physical withdrawal of
the husband from the house for as many days (this would be unthinkable
for a wife, unless she were intent on divorce), refusal to talk to each other,
refusal to eat together, and refusal of the wife to cook for the husband.

14. Since Sangermano is otherwise a most reliable reporter, it is difficult to account for
the high divorce rate he reports for the eighteenth century. "Nothing is here more common
than divorces, caused primarily, perhaps, by the speedy loss of beauty by the women. While
young they are winning and gay: but after their first child-bearing, they become so changed
and deformed that they can scarcely be recognized for the same." (Sangermano 1893:164.)
My own observations differ from his not only in respect to frequency of divorce, but also in
respect to the loss of female attractiveness following childbirth.

15. There are some exceptions. For Yadaw, a village in upper Burma, Nash (1965:253)
reports six divorced men and seventeen divorced women in a population of six hundred
persons.

(The latter, of course, is especially serious because of the symbolic importance of food discussed above.)

Although quarrels are instigated by a variety of provocations, typically they are initiated when one spouse violates the other's expectations concerning the characteristics of the ideal spouse (enumerated in the previous section). Thus, husbands report that they become angry or quarrel when their wives do not cook well, are poor housekeepers, give some suspicion of infidelity, are spendthrifts, act like busybodies, and are indolent in their work. Wives report that they are angry or quarrel when their husbands drink or gamble (thereby squandering the family income), stay away from home overnight, and are indolent in work.

It is these same provocations that lead one or both spouses to request the village headman for a divorce. The headman in each of six villages surveyed reported that at least two requests come to them each year. Most of them, however, do not end in divorce, for typically it is not quarreling, so much as real or alleged injuries, that eventuate in divorce. Thus of the thirteen divorces tracked down in Yeigyi—ten contemporary, and three remembered from the past—six resulted from adultery or desertion for another partner, three by the husband and three by the wife; two resulted from greater conern for parent than for spouse; and one each resulted non-support by the husband, his attempting to bring a second wife into their house, his not taking care of his sick wife, and his public humiliation by his wife. (In one, I neglected to ascertain the grounds.)[16]

A few observations may be made about these divorces. First, wives initiate divorce proceedings much more frequently than husbands: eight of the thirteen divorces reported were initiated by wives. This generalization also holds for the six other villages I investigated, and it was reported for nineteenth-century Burma as well (Fielding Hall 1903:215). Since women, as we have seen, are the more sexually discontented, this finding is consistent with a second finding that almost half the divorces in Yeigyi were initiated because of infidelity, or desertion on sexual grounds. The second most frequent cause of divorce is conflict between loyalty to

16. Again, comparisons with other societies in Southeast Asia are instructive. Unlike the relatively serious Burmese provocations, Thai divorces may result from rather trivial causes: a husband decides to work for a particular person, a wife disagrees with her husband over the person from whom she should buy lottery tickets, a husband and wife disagree about the number of monks to be invited to officiate at a religious ceremony, and so on (Phillips 1965:26). In Java, however, we encounter some of the serious provocations found in Burma, such as sexual infidelity or economic irresponsibility, as well as the more trivial ones found in Thailand, such as simple dislike (Geertz 1961:139-142). In Malaya, an important cause of divorce—one not reported in these other societies—is the husband's feeling that he cannot satisfy his wife's demanding sexual expectations (Nash 1974:38).

spouse and loyalty to parent—a conflict I have commented on more than once—and its resolution in favor of the parent. This conflict, which Nash (1965:252) also discovered to be "one of the chief reasons" for divorce in the Burmese villages he studied, is an important cause of divorce in Java as well (Geertz 1961:141). Because this conflict is often a source of tension even when it does not lead to divorce, I shall briefly summarize these two cases. In one, the husband divorced his wife because she did not attend sufficiently to his sick father with whom they were living. "If she really loved me, she should also have loved my father; if she does not love my father, she does not love me." In the second case a woman abandoned, and eventually divorced, her husband because she wanted to live with her aging mother in Yeigyi, while her husband, fearful of the insurgents in the area, insisted on living in Mandalay.

We may now return to the problem which has been implicit from the very beginning of this section. Given that divorce is relatively easy to obtain, and given that quarreling and dissension are not unknown in Burmese marriage, why is it that the divorce rate is so low, especially in comparison with other societies in Southeast Asia? Tentatively, I would suggest six answers: freedom to choose a spouse, property considerations, the restraining influence of village officials, concern for "face," social disapproval, and the difficulty (especially in the case of the wife) of remarriage.

An important difference between Burma, with its low divorce rate, and Malaya and Java, which have high divorce rates, is that in Burma marriage is based on free choice, while in Malaya and Java marriage is arranged. Marriage with an unloved spouse in a society (such as Java or Malaya) where sexual problems are serious, and divorce (for the male) easy to obtain, would seem to constitute one royal road to a high divorce rate. Thus, if even in Yeigyi (where marriage is based on choice), as many as half of the divorces are sex-related, it is not surprising that in Java (where marriages are arranged) the most frequent basis for divorce is infidelity (Geertz 1961:139). From South Asia, the Sinhalese (Kandyan) case presents no challenge to this explanation, because although Ceylon combines a low divorce rate (compared to Java) with arranged marriage, infidelity is both frequent and accepted (Yalman 1967:187). Thailand, however, with its combination of freedom of marital choice and a high divorce rate, does seem to present a challenge, one which brings me to the second explanation for the low Burmese rate.

The low rate of divorce in Burma does not, it will be remembered, reflect an absence of marital tensions or a disinclination for divorce. Since at least two petitions for divorce come to the Yeigyi headman each year, if each petition were granted, the divorce rate in Yeigyi would approximate the high rate found elsewhere in Southeast Asia. That it does not is attributable in part to the restraining influence of the village headman and elders. (In the city, a similar influence is exerted by a senior or respected member of the family, a *lugyi*.) Almost without exception they attempt to dissuade the divorce petitioner from his intention, and their attempts are usually successful—as the discrepancy between the incidence of divorce and of petition for divorce indicates. The following remarks, though made by village elders of the last century, accurately describe the role of contemporary headman and elders.

> If we were to grant divorces every time a woman came and demanded it, we should be doing nothing else all day long. If a husband comes home to find dinner not cooked, and speaks angrily, his wife will rush to us in tears for a divorce. If he speaks to another woman and smiles, if he does not give his wife a new dress, if he be fond of going out in the evening, all these are reasons for a breathless demand for a divorce. The wives get cross and run to us and cry, 'My husband has been angry with me. Never will I live with him again. Give me a divorce.' Or, 'See my clothes, how old they are. I cannot buy a new dress. I will have a divorce.' And we say, 'Yes, yes; it is very sad. Of course, you must have a divorce; but we cannot give you one to-night. Go away, and come again in three days or in four days when we have more time.' And they go away, *thakin*, and they do not return. Next day it is all forgotten [Fielding Hall 1903:215].

Today, as I have said, this same procedure is followed. When a person requests the headman for a divorce, the latter tells him to think it over for a week or two, by which time—so the headmen report—the petitioner usually decides to discontinue the divorce proceedings. As one headman put it: "By this time [after about two weeks] the original reason for the request is forgotten and they remain married."

A third restraining influence on the frequency of divorce is exerted by its economic consequences, and, more particularly, by customary law regulating the disposition of property at partition. This influence can best be approached by examining the difference between what might be termed "formal" and "informal" divorce in Burma. Formal divorce (known as *lin-maya kwa gin*) is initiated by a complaint to the village headman and is validated by a formal decree issued by the village elders following a public hearing. Informal divorce (termed *lin-maya kwe-gin*) is effected by the mutual consent of the spouses without these official procedings, and is recognized as legally valid after a three-year separation (though there are cases in which one or both spouses marry almost immediately after their separation). In the city, formal divorce is obtained in court, and informal divorce is announced in the newspapers (since, unlike the village case) word of mouth is not sufficient to broadcast the termination of the marriage). Of the thirteen divorces in Yeigyi, five were formal and eight informal, and a systematic comparison revealed no differences with respect to such variables as age at marriage (they range from sixteen to thirty), duration of marriage (they range from six months to seventeen years), age at divorce (they range from seventeen to forty-two), nativity (they include natives and non-natives of Yeigyi), type of marriage (all had a formal marriage), or number of children (they range from zero to five). Rather, the crucial differences between formal and informal divorce has to do with property arrangements (including the economic value of the dower) and the disposition of the children. An examination of these differences will bring us to the third one, the economic constraint on divorce, but first let us examine these differences.

If both spouses agree to the divorce, and if they also agree on the partition of the property and the disposition of the children, divorce is consistently "informal." If, on the other hand, the spouses are in disagreement over the divorce, or if, though agreeing, they disagree over the property settlement or the disposition of the children, then, consistently, one of them brings the case to the village elders for formal adjudication. The elders then render a judgment within the following constraints set by customary law. [17]

If the husband initiates the divorce with cause (cruelty, desertion, adultery), he retains the community property, the dower is returned to him, and (in the case of adultery) he retains the children if he wants them. (For all other conditions of divorce, the wife, with certain exceptions noted elsewhere, retains the children.) If the husband initiates the divorce without cause, the community property is divided equally, but the property the wife had brought to the marriage is retained by her, as is the dower. [18] If the wife initiates the divorce with cause, the community property is divided equally, but her personal property as well as the dower is retained by her. If she initiates the divorce without cause, the property arrangements are as those when the husband initiates the divorce without cause. [19]

Given these principles governing property settlement, we can now understand, first, the conditions for formal versus informal divorce, and, second, the economic constraints on divorce. Where property is at stake,

17. Javanese customary law is very similar to the Burmese in these matters (Geertz 1961:50).

18. According to customary law, a married couple have both personal and community property. Both the dowry and the dower, as well as other gifts that either might receive at the wedding, are personal property, *de jure* (they are known as *kanwin pyissi*), although *de facto* they are community property. Property owned by either spouse prior to the marriage (*payin*) remains pesonal. Property acquired after marriage, through inheritance, gift, or labor (*lethetpwa*), may be either personal or community, depending on the decision of the couple. Property jointly purchased by the couple subsequent to their marriage (*hnapazoun*) is, of course, community property.

19. The following early account of the manner in which property is distributed at partition is one I neither observed nor heard about. The husband and wife·"respectively light two candles, and shutting up their hut, sit down and wait quietly until they are burned up. The one whose candle burns out first, gets up at once and leaves the house (and forever), taking

neither spouse wishes to initiate, or even agree to, a divorce unless he believes that he can convince the elders (or the court) that he has cause. Thus, for example, if a wife can prove mistreatment, if a husband can prove adultery, or if either can prove desertion, then (other things being equal), there is no hesitation about bringing formal charges to the village elders, for in such cases the plaintiff acquires the bulk of the property. For exactly the same reason, however, the defendant in such cases will not only deny any culpability, but, even if he desires the divorce, he will try to convince the elders that he opposes it, for if he succeeds, he can retain most of the property. The following case is a dramatic illustration of these various complications.

Kou Khin Maung, a native of Yeigyi, married Ma Thein Khin, a resident of another village, when he was nineteen and she was seventeen. Her father was a landless peasant, while his, a farmer of means, gave Ma Thein Khin a dower consisting of a pair of bullocks and a cart (valued at K 1000), a pair of gold studs (valued at K400), and a wrist watch (whose value I did not determine). When I first met Kou Khin Maung, he and his wife were separated. According to him she had left after a series of quarrels, and although he had invited her to return, she refused. Their quarrels, he explained, were occasioned by his disapproval of her sending part of his hard-earned income to her parents. Still, it was she, he insisted, not he, who wanted a divorce.

Most villagers told a different story. Kou Khin Maung, according to them, was not a very good husband; he not only quarreled with his wife, but when angered he would beat her. Shortly after leaving him, Ma Thein Khin had become ill and he had refused to take care of her, sending her instead to her native village to be cared for by her mother. When she returned to him, he not only refused to take care of her, but, despite her lingering illness, insisted that she cook his meals. When she refused, he ordered her from the house, and she returned to her mother (her father had already died). Shortly after, Kou Khin Maung's relatives asked her to return, but Ma Thein Khin said she never wanted to see his face again, to which Kou Khin Maung replied that he would never again initiate a reconciliation. Nevertheless, he subsequently wrote her a letter, saying he would welcome her return. Some months later, Ma Thein Khin's mother asked the village elders to grand her daughter a divorce, and a formal hearing was held shortly after I arrived in Yeigyi.

The chairman of the village elders opened the hearing by asking Ma Thein Khin whether she would change her mind and return to her husband. She said she could not do so because he had treated her cruelly

nothing but the clothes he or she may have on at the time; all else then becomes the property of the other party." (Vincent 1882:27-28.)

and had driven her from the house, and that if he really wanted her back he would not have waited for so many months to call her. The elders said that if she returned to her husband, they would instruct him, as well as his relatives, never to mistreat her again, and if he violated their instructions, they would then take action against him.

When Kou Khin Maung testified, he denied that he had mistreated his wife or that he had driven her from the house; she had, he claimed, left voluntarily. When an elder asked him whether he had requested his wife to return because he really loved her, or because he wanted others to believe that he loved her, Kou Khin Maung replied it was because he loved her; if she would accompany him, he said, he would take her to his house that very evening. Then, said the elder, he must promise not to abuse her; else, what assurance would she have that he would not mistreat her again? To this Kou Khin Maung said he could not make such a promise because any couple may quarrel from time to time. Nevertheless, he said, he wanted her to return.

But why, another elder asked him, did he not want a divorce? Was it because he loved her, or because he did not want to lose his property? It was, Kou Khin Maung replied, because he loved her. If so, retorted the elder, why should he not promise not to abuse her? If he loved her, surely he would be willing to make such a promise? To this Kou Khin Maung demurred: since quarrels are inevitable, he might indeed beat her, and (having violated his promise) he would then be liable to punitive action.

The elders then announced that since they could not decide a case in which husband and wife could not agree, they would postpone the hearing until the following night when the headman, who was away from the village, would return.

When the hearings resumed the following night (without the headman, who was still absent), a spokesman for Kou Khin Maung said that if his wife still wanted the divorce, he would agree to it, and he would pay her K 300 and permit her to retain the wedding ring. The spokesman for his wife said she would accept these terms, and the elders agreed to the conditions. The dispatch with which this public agreement was reached suggested to me that it had been preceded by a private deal, as indeed, I subsequently discovered, it had been. Representatives of each spouse had gone to the girl's uncle, and he had convinced them that a settlement of K 300 (about one-third of the dower) was fair to both sides.

What, then, was involved in this complex maneuvering? The answer, of course, is property. If Kou Khin Maung could have convinced the elders that his wife had left him without cause and of her own accord, she would then have forfeited her right to any property. If, on the contrary, his wife could have proved that he had ordered her to leave, Kou Khin Maung would have had to forfeit the entire dower (as a young couple, they had acquired no additional property), and he was prepared to do almost anything, including the commission of perjury, to avoid this. Hence the proposed settlement was acceptable to him because if his wife had taken him to court, as she had threatened to do, she would have obtained the divorce (which, of course, he wanted too), and if the court were to have believed her charges, she could have retained the entire dower, and he would have had to sustain the court costs as well. The proposed settlement was acceptable to his wife who, fed up with him, was willing to accept a divorce even without a satisfactory property settlement, especially since—as I later discovered—she had already agreed to marry another man, and did not need the dower.

This case, then, not only illustrates the conditions under which a formal divorce is sought, but it indicates the third reason for the relatively low incidence of divorce, namely, the risk of suffering property loss. If a large dower and other kinds of property are at stake, both spouses hesitate to bring a divorce action, especially without cause. The wife hesitates because, unless she expects to remarry, she may be left without any means of support. The husband hesitates because he may lose not only the joint property of the marriage, but the dower as well. Hence, if he is in love with another woman, it is to his advantage to keep her as a mistress, or even to take her as a "lesser wife," rather than divorce his first wife. These constraints do not operate elsewhere in Southeast Asia, where the divorce rate is high, because, as in Java, there is no dower, and except for property acquired subsequent to their marriage, each spouse retains exclusive possession of the property he brought to the marriage.

Since the Burmese urban elites do not practice dower, the economic constraint on divorce, especially among the wealthy, is somewhat different. For the wife, enjoying a comfortable life, divorce usually means a considerable decline in her standard of living. To be sure, if she initiates divorce with cause, or if her husband divorces her without cause, he is legally obliged to provide her with a maintenance allowance, as well as a penalty. The latter, known as *koubou*, "the price of the body," is viewed as compensation for his having destroyed her virginity and, hence, diminished her acceptability to other men. (The *koubou*, then, can be viewed as the functional alternative to the village dower.) Nevertheless, the husband may refuse to comply with the court order, and it is not only difficult for her to bring him once again into court, but equally important, she is usually unwilling to face the shame.

Indeed, the shame in taking him to court in the first place is a fourth constraint on a wife-initiated divorce in the city. This is especially the case if the grounds for seeking the divorce are adultery, for the wife then has to publicly testify to her husband's infidelity, which causes her to lose face. The same considerations of face hold to an even greater extent in the case of a husband whose wife has commited adultery. Unless her adultery is flagrant, and therefore already public, the shame of publicly testifying that he had been cuckolded, serves as a powerful constraint on the husband initiating a divorce.

The reverse considerations apply to the adulterous spouse who, even if in love with mistress or lover, is reluctant to seek a divorce. The adulterous husband is reluctant because he does not wish to suffer important property losses, not to mention the stigma of having broken up a family. Hence, he prefers to continue his affair or to elevate his mistress to the status of a lesser wife, rather than seek a divorce. For the adulterous wife, however, the latter option is not available. Nevertheless, even if her lover is willing to marry her, so that there is no economic incentive to remain with her husband, she is unwilling, except in the case of true infatuation, to suffer the stigma of breaking up a family.

The mention of stigma points, of course, to the final reason for the low incidence of divorce. For despite the ease with which it can be obtained, divorce is viewed as a shameful thing, especially for the wife to initiate, and more especially if she has children. A mother who would intentionally break up a home is stigmatized. This is not the case with respect to the husband, however, which is one of the reasons that although there are two terms for a divorcée *(tahkulat* and *talinkwa)*, there is not even one for a divorcé. Hence a man may perform a wedding if he remarries, but a woman is prohibited from doing so.

In some cases the stigma is viewed as very great indeed. The following urban example, though hardly typical, indicates how strong the feeling can become. In this case, the son of a woman who had divorced her husband in order to marry her lover was rejected—thirty years later!—as a son-in-law by parents of the girl he wished to marry. When the girl later eloped with the boy, her parents disowned her, and to this day they have rebuffed her attempts at reconciliation. Thus, not only had the mother's stigma remained even after a lapse of thirty years, but her son was tarnished with the same brush.

One consequence of this stigma is the difficulty a divorcée has in obtaining a husband. Thus, while 50 percent of the divorcés in Yeigyi have remarried, not one of the divorcées has obtained a husband. To be sure, prejudice against divorcées is not the only reason. Many men, as we have seen, prefer to marry a virgin. In addition, some divorcées themselves refrain from remarriage because it is considered unseemly for a middle-aged woman to marry since this indicates that she is still interested in sex. In part, however, the difficulty of remarriage reflects the disapproval with which men and women alike view a divorcée, especially if she had had children. This is not to say that the attitude to a divorcé is neutral. "Good" families, especially, disapprove of, though they do not prohibit, the marriage of a daughter to a divorced husband.

A second consequence of stigma, especially for the wife, is found in the fact that in all ten cases of divorce in Yeigyi, one of the spouses left the village, and in seven of the ten it was the wife who left. I am told that the same pattern is found in the city where it is the wife, especially if she hopes to remarry, who moves to a new neighborhood.

References Cited

Antoun, Richard T.
    1972   *Arab Village*. Bloomington, Indiana University Press.
Ariyapala, M. B.
    1956   *Society in Medieval Ceylon*. Colombo, K.V.G. de Silva.
Ba Aung, U
    1914   "Why Burma is Sparsely Populated." *Journal of Burma Research Society*, 4:224-225.
Bell, Henry G.
    1852   *An Account of the Burman Empire*. Calcutta.
Berger, Morroe
    1964   *The Arab World Today*. Garden City, N.Y., Doubleday.
Berlin, Brent, Dennis E. Breedlove, and Peter H. Raven
    1968   "Covert Categories and Folk Taxonomies," *American Anthropologist*, 70:290-299.
The Book of the Discipline, Vol. 1
    1949   Translated by I.B. Horner. London, Luzac.
Bose, Nirmal Kumar
    1953   *My Days with Gandhi*. Calcutta, Nishana.
Brown, G. Grant
    1915   "Burmese Modesty." *Man*, 15:134-136.
    1925   *Burma as I Saw It*. New York, A. Stokes.
Burling, Robbins
    1964   "Cognition and Componential Analysis: God's Truth or Hocus-Pocus." *American Anthropologist*, 66:20-28.
    1969   "Linguistics and Ethnographic Description." *American Anthropologist*, 71:817-827.
    1970   "American Kinship Terms Once More." *Southwestern Journal of Anthropology*, 26:15-24.
Campbell, J. K.
    1966   "Honour and the Devil." In J. G. Peristiany (ed.), *Honor and Shame*, Chicago, University of Chicago Press.

Carstairs, G. Morris
    1967   *The Twice Born*. Bloomington, Indiana University Press.

Condor, Josiah
    1826   *A Popular Description of Birmah, Siam, etc.: Geographical, Historical and Topographical*. London, J. Duncan.

Cordiner, James
    1807   *Description of Ceylon*. London, Longman, Hurst, Rees, Orme and Brown.

Davis, J.
    1969   "Honor and Politics in Pisticci." *Proceedings of the Royal Anthropological Institute*.

Evans-Pritchard, E. E.
    1929   "The Study of Kinship in Primitive Societies." *Man* 29: 190-194.
    1932   "The Nature of Kinship Extensions." *Man*, 32:12-15.

Evers, Hans-Dieter
    1969   "Models of Social Systems: Loosely and Tightly Structured." In Hans-Dieter Evers (ed.), *Loosely Structured Social Systems: Thailand in Comparative Perspective*. New Haven, Cultural Report Series No. 17, Yale University, Southeast Asia Studies.

Ferrars, Max and Bertha
    1900   *Burma*. London, Sampson Low, Marston.

Fitch, Ralph
    1811   *The Voyage of Mr. Ralph Fitch, Merchant of London, to Ormuz and So. to Goa in the East Indies, 1583 to 1591*. London, Longman, Hurst and Rees.

Fei, Hsiao-tung
    1939   *Peasant Life in China*. London, G. Routledge & Sons.

Fielding Hall, H.
    1903   *The Soul of a People*. London, Macmillan & Co.
    1913   *A People At School*, London, Macmillan & Co.

Forbes, C. J. F. S.
    1878   *British Burma and Its People*. London, John Murray, 1878.

Forschammer, Emmanuel
    1885   *An Essay of the Sources and Development of Burmese Law*. Rangoon, Government Printing, 1885.

Fortes, Meyer
    1958   "Introduction." In Jack Goody, *The Developmental Cycle in Domestic Groups*. Cambridge, Cambridge University Press.

Fox, Robin
    1967   *Kinship and Marriage*. Harmondsworth, Penguin Books.

Frake, Charles O.
    1962   "The Ethnographic Study of Cognitive Systems." *Anthropology and Human Behavior*, Washington, D.C., Anthropological Society of Washington.

Freud, Sigmund
    1912   "On the Universal Tendency to Debasement in the Sphere of

Love," *The Standard Edition of the Complete Psychological Works of Sigmund Freud,* Vol. 11, London, Hogart Press.

Furnival, John Sydenham
1911   "Matriarchal Vestiges in Burma." *Journal of the Burma Research Society,* 1:15-30.
1948   *Colonial Policy and Practice: A Comparative Study of Burma and the Netherlands Indies.* New York, New York University Press.

Fytche, Albert
1878   *Burma, Past and Present with Personal Reminiscences of the Country.* 2 vols. London, Routledge & Kegan Paul, Ltd.

Gaung, U
1905   *A Digest of the Burmese Buddhist Law Concerning Inheritance and Marriage,* Vol. 2. Rangoon, Government Printing.

Geertz, Hildred
1961   *The Javanese Family.* Glencoe, The Free Press.

Gluckman, Max
1953   "Bridewealth and the Stability of Marriage." *Man.* 53: 141-143.

Goldschmidt, Walter, and Evalyn J. Kunkel
1971   "The Structure of the Peasant Family." *American Anthropologist,* 73: 1058-1076.

Goodenough, Ward
1970   *Description and Comparison in Cultural Anthropology.* Chicago, Aldine.

Goody, Jack, and S. J. Tambiah
1973   *Bridewealth and Dowry.* Cambridge Papers in Social Anthropology 7. Cambridge, Cambridge University Press.

Gorer, Geoffery
1943   "Burmese Personality." New York, Institute for Intercultural Relations (mimeograph).

Government of India
1892   *Census of India.* 1891, Vol. IX (Burma Report). Rangoon, Government Printing.
1912   *Census of India.* 1911, Vol. XII, Part 1 (Burma Report). Rangoon, Government Printing.

Government of the Union of Burma
1960-61 *Report on the Survey of Rural Household Expenditures.*

Haeckel, E.
1883   *A Visit to Ceylon.* London, Kegan Paul.

Hamilton, Alexander
1930   *A New Account of the East Indies.* 2 vols. London, Argonaut Press.

Hickey, Gerald Cannon
1964   *Village in Vietnam.* New Haven, Yale University Press.

Hla Pe
1965   "Burmese." In Arthur T. Hatto (ed.), *Eros.* The Hague, Mouton.

Hsu, Francis L. K.
1963   *Clan, Caste and Club.* New York, Van Nostrand, Reinhold.

1971   *Under the Ancestors' Shadow*. Stanford, California, Stanford University Press.

Htin Aung
1937   *Burmese Drama*. London, Oxford University Press.
1954   *Burmese Folk Tales*. London, Oxford University Press.

Hunt, David
1970   *Parents and Children in History: The Psychology of Family Life in Early Modern France*. New York, Basic Books.

Hyman, Gerald
n.d.   *Freud, Sex, and the Malays (ms.)*.

The Jātaka.
1957   E. B. Cowell (ed.), London, Luzac & Co.

Jay, Robert R.
1969   *Javanese Villagers*. Cambridge, The MIT Press.

Judson's Burmese-English Dictionary.
1953   Rangoon, Baptist Board of Publications.

Kapadia, K. M.
1966   *Marriage and Family in India*. London, Oxford University Press.

Karve, Irawati
1968   *Kinship Organization in India*. New York, Asia Publishing House.

Khuri, Fuad I.
1970   "Parallel Cousin Marriage Reconsidered: A Middle Eastern Practice that Nullifies the Effects of Marriage on the Intensity of Family Relationships," *Man* 5: 597-618.

Kolender, Pauline M.
1968   Region, Caste, and Family Structure: A Comparative Study of the Indian Joint Family, in Milton Singer and Bernard S. Cohn (eds.), *Structure and Change in Indian Society*. Viking Fund Publications in Anthropology, No. 47, New York.

Lahiri, Sisir Chandra
1957   *Principles of Modern Burmese Buddhist Law*. Calcutta, Eastern Law House.

Laslett, Peter
1971   *The World We Have Lost*. London, Scribners.

Leach, Edmund R.
1953   "Bridewealth and the Stability of Marriage." *Man*, 53:179-180.
1955   "Polyandry, Inheritance and the Definition of Marriage." *Man*, 54:182-186.
1964   *Political Systems of Highland Burma*. London, G. Bell & Sons.

LeBar, Frank M. *et al.*
1964   *Ethnic Groups of Mainland Southeast Asia*. New Haven, Human Relations Area Files Press.

Lehman, F. K.
1963   *The Structure of Chin Society*. Urbana, University of Illinois Press.
1970   "On Chin and Kachin Marriage Regulations," *Man* 5:118-125.

1970a   "Some Diachronic Rules of Burmese Phonology," *Occasional Papers of the Wolfenden Society on Tibeto-Burman Linguistics, II.*

Levy, Reuben
     1962   *The Social Structure of Islam.* Cambridge, Cambridge University Press.

The Lokaniti.
     1962   Translated by U Sein Tu. Mandalay, Mandalay University Research Council Publication No. 9.

Mair, Lucy
     1971   *Marriage.* Harmondsworth, Penguin Books.

Malcom, Howard
     1839   *Travels in Southeastern Asia.* 2 Vols. Boston, Gould, Kendall & Lincoln.

Mandelbaum, David G.
     1970   *Society in India.* Berkeley, University of California Press.

Maung Maung
     1963   *Law and Custom in Burma and the Burmese Family.* The Hague, Martinus Nijhoff.

Mentzer, E. Hollis
     1972   *Affective Dimensions of Thai Peasant Personality.* Unpublished Ph.D. Thesis, University of Washington.

Michaelson, Evelyn, and Walter Goldschmidt
     1971   "Female Roles and Male Dominance Among Peasants." *Southwestern Journal of Anthropology,* 27:330-352.

Milne, Mary (Mrs. Leslie Milne)
     1910   *Shans at Home.* London, Murray.
     1924   *The Home of an Eastern Clan.* Oxford, Oxford University Press.

Mi Mi Khaing
     1961   "The Burmese Woman." *The Nation,* Rangoon, June 4, 1961.

Mohsen, Safia K.
     1970   "Aspects of the Legal Status of Women Among Awlad'Ali." In Louise E. Sweet (ed.), *Peoples and Cultures of the Middle East,* Vol. 1, New York, The Natural History Press.

Murdock, George Peter
     1949   *Social Structure.* New York, Macmillan.
     1960   "Cognatic Forms of Social Organization." In George Peter Murdock (ed.), *Social Structure in Southeast Asia,* New York, Viking Fund Publications in Anthropology.

Myint Thein
     1970   *Burmese Folk Songs.* Oxford, The Asoka Society.

Nash, Manning
     1965   *The Golden Road to Modernity.* New York, Wiley.
     1974   Peasant Citizens: *Politics, Religion, and Modernization in Kelantan, Malaysia.* Ohio University Center for International Studies. Southeast Asia Series No. 31, Athens, Ohio.

Nash, June, and Manning Nash
 1963 "Marriage, Family and Population Growth in Upper Burma."
  Southwestern Journal of Anthropology, 19:251-66.
Obeyesekere, Gananath
 n.d. *The Goddess of Patini: Virgin, Wife, and Mother* (ms.).
O'Flaherty, Wendy Doniger
 1973 *Asceticism and Eroticism in the Mythology of Śiva*. London, Oxford
  University Press.
Patai, Raphael
 1971 *Society, Culture, and Change in the Middle East*. Philadelphia,
  University of Pennsylvania Press.
Pe Maung Tin
 1961 "Women in the Inscriptions in Pagan." *50th Anniversary Publica-
  tion*, Burma Research Society.
Pfanner, David E., and Jasper Ingersoll
 1962 "Theravada Buddhism and Village Economic Behavior." *Journal of
  Asian Studies*, 21:341-61.
Phillips, Herbert P.
 1965 *Thai Peasant Personality*. Berkeley, University of California Press.
Pieris, Ralph
 1953 "The Brodie Papers on Sinhalese Folk Religion." *University of
  Ceylon Review*, 11:110-128.
Piker, Steven
 n.d. *A Peasant Community in Changing Thailand* (ms.).
Pinchbeck, Ivy, and Margaret Hewitt
 1969 *Children in English Society. Volume I: From Tudor Times to the
  Eighteenth Century*. London, Routledge & Kegan Paul.
Pinkerton, John
 1811 *A General Collection of the Best and Most Interesting Voyages and
  Travels in all Parts of the World*. Vol. 8. London, Longman, Hurst
  and Rees.
Pitt-Rivers, Julian
 1966 "Honor and Social Status." In J. M. Peristiany (ed.), *Honor and
  Shame*, Chicago, University of Chicago Press.
Queen, Stuart A., and Robert W. Habenstein
 1967 *The Family in Various Cultures*. Philadelphia, J. B. Lippincott.
Risley, Herbert
 1969 *The People of India*. (second edition), Delhi, Oriental Book Reprint
  Corporation.
Romney, A. Kimball, and Roy G. D'Andrade
 1964 "Cognitive Aspects of English Kin Terms." *American Anthropologist*, 66:146-170.
de Rougemont, Denis
 1957 *Love in the Western World*. Garden City, N.Y., Doubleday.
Roy, Manisha
 1975 *Bengali Women*. Chicago, University of Chicago Press.
 n.d. *Bengali Women as Respect Objects* (ms.).

Ryan, Bryce F.
    1953   "The Sinhalese Family System." *The Eastern Anthropologist,*
              6:143-163.
Ryan, Bryce F., and Murray A. Straus
    1954   "The Integration of Sinhalese Society." *Research Studies of the State*
              College of Washington, 22:179-227.
Sangermano, Vicentius
    1893   *The Burmese Empire a Hundred Years Ago.* Westminster, A. Const-
              able.
Sapir, Edward
    1916   "Terms of Relationship and Levirate." *American Anthropologist,*
              18:327-337.
Scheffler, Harold W., and Floyd G. Lounsbury
    1971   *A Study of Structural Semantics: The Sirionó Kinship System.*
              Englewood Cliffs, N.J., Prentice-Hall.
Schneider, David M.
    1953   "A Note on Bridewealth and the Stability of Marriage." *Man,*
              53:55-57.
    1968   *American Kinship: A Cultural Account.* Englewood Cliffs, N.J.,
              Prentice-Hall.
Sharp, Lauriston
    1953   *Siamese Rice Village.* Bangkok, Cornell Research Center.
Singh, Khushwant
    1967   *The Sikhs Today.* New Delhi, Orient Longmans.
Spiro, Melford E.
    1966   "Buddhism and Economic Saving in Burma." *American An-*
              thropologist, 68:1163-1173.
    1967   *Burmese Supernaturalism.* Englewood Cliffs., N.J., Prentice-Hall.
    1968   "Politics and Factionalism in Upper Burma." In Marc Swartz (ed.),
              Local Level Politics, Chicago, Aldine.
    1969   "The Psychological Functions of Witchcraft." In William Caudill and
              Tsung Yi Lin (eds.), *Mental Health in Asia and in the Pacific,*
              Honolulu, East-West Center Press.
    1971   *Buddhism and Society: A Great Tradition and Its Burmese Vicis-*
              situdes. New York, Harper & Row.
Steele, James
    n.d.   A Preliminary Analysis of the Burmese Rorschachs (ms.)
    n.d.   Burmese TAT Analysis: Preliminary Findings (ms.)
Steinberg, David J.
    1959   *Cambodia.* New Haven, HRAF Press.
Swift, M. G.
    1965   *Malay Peasant Society in Jelebu.* New York, Humanities Press.
Symes, Michael
    1800   *An Account of an Embassy to the Kingdom of Ava.* London, Printed
              for J. Sebrett.
Tambiah, S. J.
    1966   Polyandry in Ceylon—with special reference to the Leggala Region.

In Christoph von Furer-Haimendorf (ed.), *Caste and Kin in Nepal, India and Ceylon*, pp. 264-358. Bombay, Asia Publishing House.

1970   *Buddhism and the Spirit Cults in Northeast Thailand*. Cambridge, Cambridge University Press.

Trant, T. A.

1827   *Two Years in Ava from May 1824 to May 1826, by an Officer on the Staff of the Quarter Master General's Department*. London, John Murray, Publishers, Ltd.

Sein Tu

1964   "The Psychodynamics of Burmese Personality." *Journal of the Burma Research Society*, 47:263-286.

Tyler, Stephen A.

1969   *Cognitive Anthropology*. New York, Holt, Rinehart & Winston.

Vincent, Frank

1882   *The Land of the White Elephant*. New York, Harper.

Wallace, Anthony F. C.

1965   "The Problem of the Psychological Validity of Componential Analysis." *American Anthropologist*, 67:229-248.

Wallace, Anthony F. C., and John Atkins

1960   "The Meaning of Kinship Terms." *American Anthropologist*, 62:58-80.

Westermark, Edward

1922   *The History of Human Marriage*. New York, Allerton Book Co.

Wijeskera, N. D.

1949   *The People of Ceylon*. Colombo, M. D. Gunasena.

Wolf, Eric R.

1966   *Peasants*. Englewood Cliffs, N.J., Prentice-Hall.

Yalman, Nur

1967   *Under the Bo Tree*. Berkeley, University of California Press.

Yang, C. K.

1969   *Chinese Communist Society: The Family and the Village*. Cambridge, The MIT Press.

Shway Yoe (Sir James George Scott)

1896   *The Burman: His Life and Notions*. London, Macmillan & Co.

Young, Michael and Peter Willmott

1965   *Family and Kinship in East London*. Harmondsworth, Penguin Books.

Index

Abortion, 232

Adolescents, chaperones for, 226. *See also* Boys; Girls

Adultery: acts tantamount to, 223-224; concept of, 151-152; as grounds for divorce, 248, 286, 290; incidence of, 216, 247; male fear of, 241; resulting in hell, 213; stigma and punishment for, 248-250. *See also* Infidelity

Affines: consanguineal kin compared to, 49-52; "core affines," 68-69, 94-95; cultural norms of, 94-96; defined, 94; and neo-local residence, 114-115; step-parent, 96; tensions among, 95, 123-126

Age: in kinship terminology, 54-55, 134-135; for marriage, 147-148; respect patterns for, 166; of spouse, 157

Aged parents, 136-137

Agriculture: attitudes of cultivators, 40-41; work shared with spouse, 284; in Yeigyi, 29-31, 33-34

Alimony, 197

Arab countries, 125; divorce in, 285; women in, 240, 242. *See also* Muslim culture

Arranged marriages, 153

Asia, Southeast, 283, 288

Astrology, and marriage, 157, 180-181, 182

Aunt: classification and terms for, 168-175; education of niece by, 222; marriage with nephew, 158; and uncle dyad, 88

Authority in the household, 117, 135, 137; in truncated stem family households, 138-139

Autonomy: vs. economic advantage, 139; via marriage, 150; and parent-child tensions, 116-117

Bachelors, 108, 147

Basketmakers: marriage of, 148, 155-156; occupation of, 27-29 *passim*

Bequests: of houses, 78; of land, 77. *See also* Inheritance

Biological ties: of kinship, 44-49, 57; of mother-child bond, 83-84, 89. *See also* Consanguines

Birth control, 231-232

Blood, and kinship ties, 44-45

Boys: during initiation of marriage, 179-180; promiscuity of, 226, 228; separated from girls, 226; sexual outlets for, 223

Bridal chamber: in bride's parents' home, 226-227; stoning of, 184-186

Bride: age of, 154, 157; pregnant, 191; prestige value of dower, 202-203; status vulnerability of, 203-204, 205; "without value," 208. *See also* Dower; Dowry

Bridewealth, 162, 195, 196; defined, 193; as inappropriate marriage payment, 204; in Thailand, 199-200

Brother(s): erotic overtones with sister, 130-132, 133; as guardian of sister's virginity, 132; marriage of younger sister, 133; rivalry and conflicts between, 127-129; role of, 86-87

Brother-in-law: tensions, 160-161; usage of term *yaukhpa*, 133-34

Brother-sister exchange, 159-161

Buddhism: basic tenets of, 39-40; initiation ceremony in, 90-91; male spiritual superiority in, 260; objects of worship, 75, 261; precepts, 151; sex in, 219-220; shrine in house, 105. *See also* Karma

Burmese language, 216